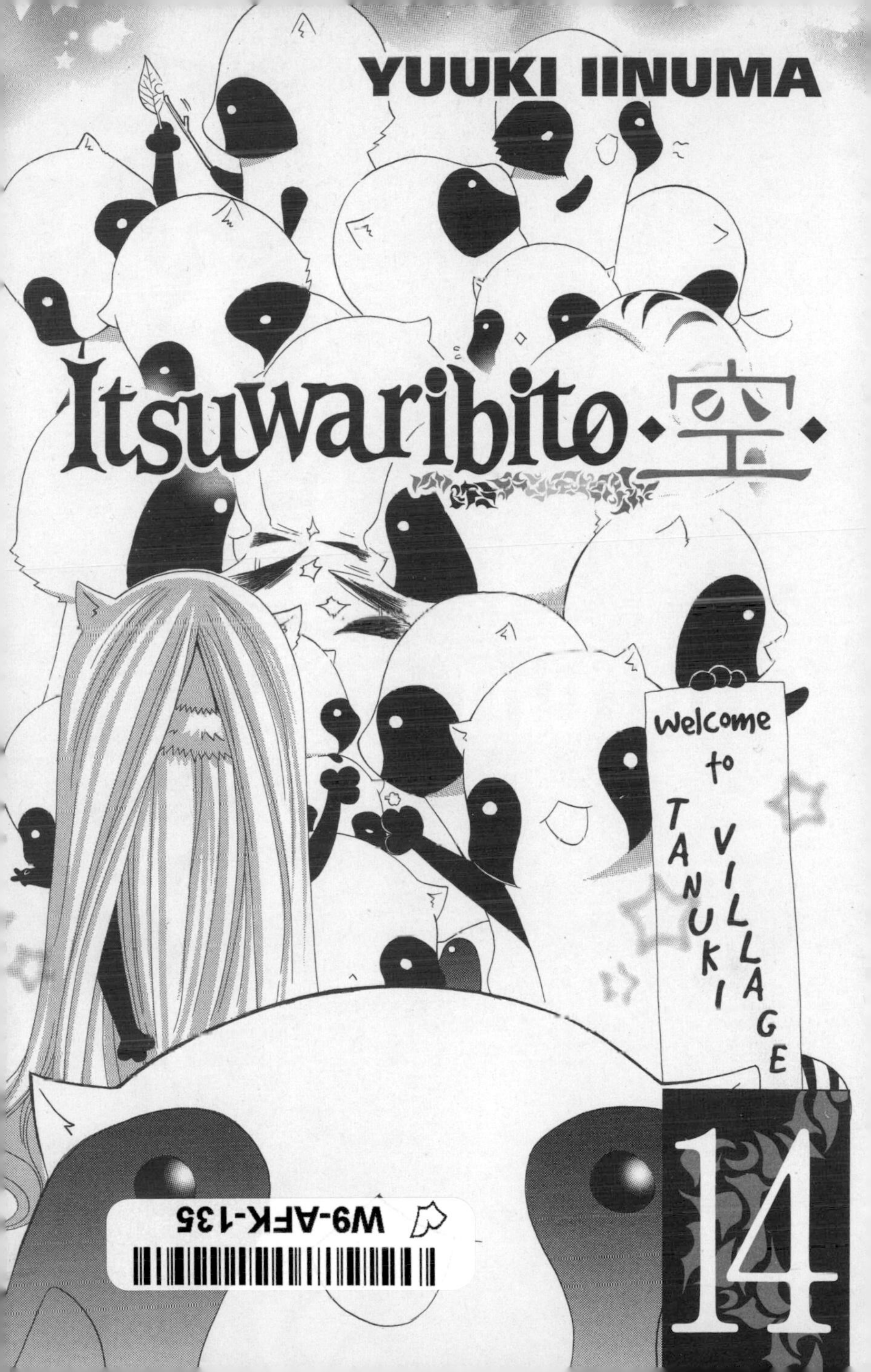
YUUKI IINUMA
Itsuwaribito・空・
Welcome to TANUKI VILLAGE
14

Contents

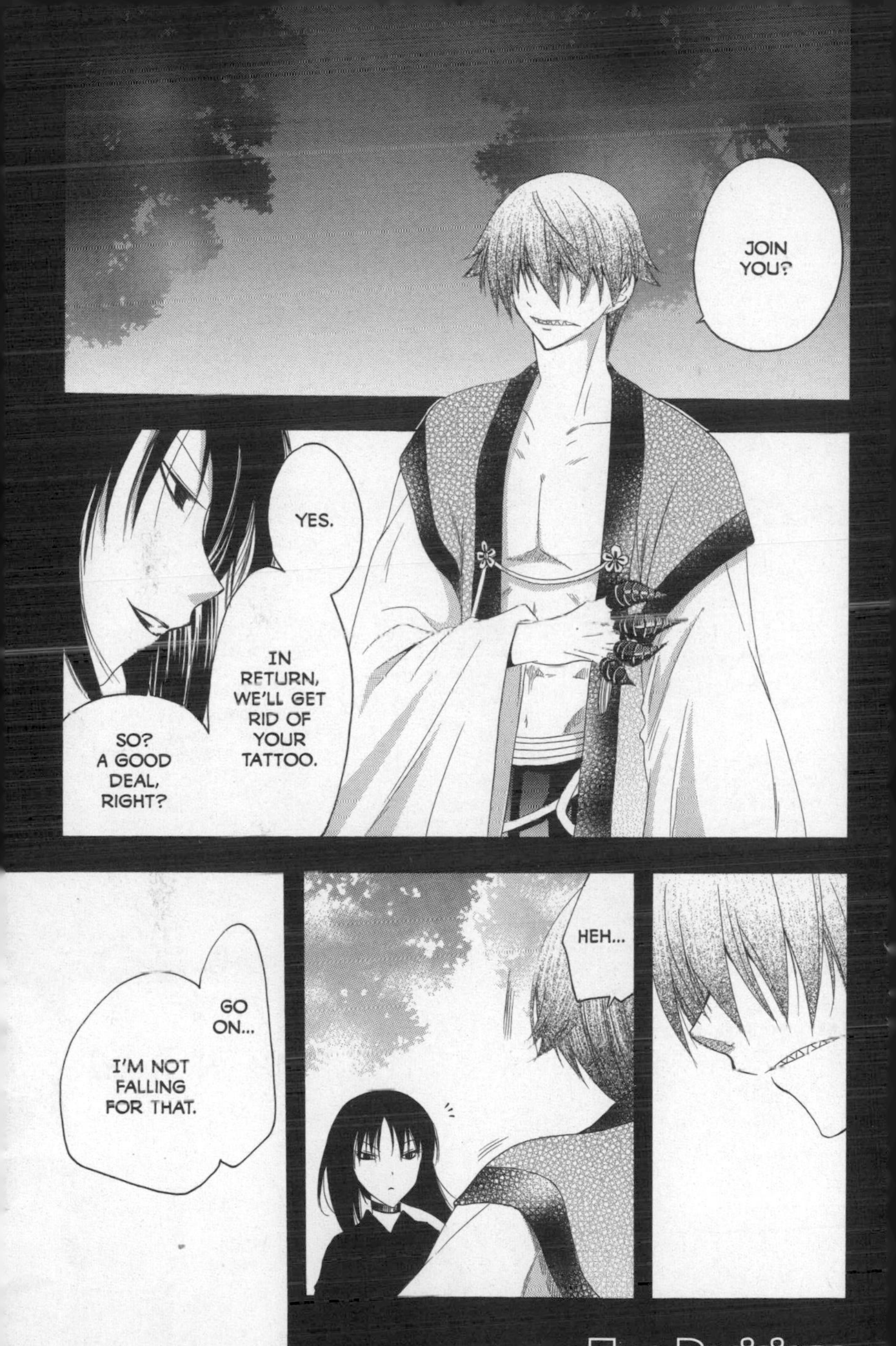
JOIN YOU?
YES.
IN RETURN, WE'LL GET RID OF YOUR TATTOO.
SO? A GOOD DEAL, RIGHT?
HEH...
GO ON...
I'M NOT FALLING FOR THAT.

Chapter 128 Two Decisions

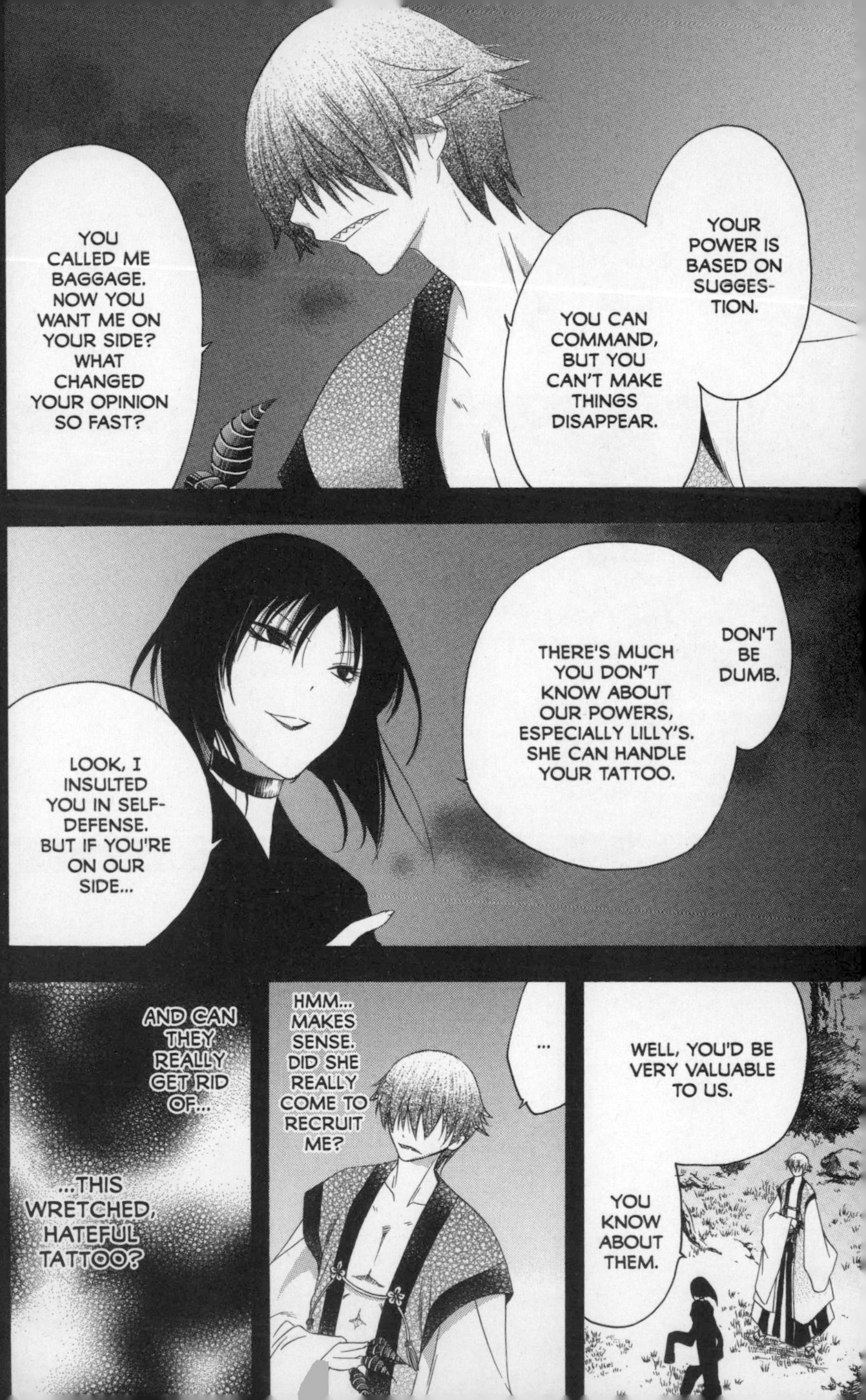
YOUR POWER IS BASED ON SUGGES-TION.
YOU CAN COMMAND, BUT YOU CAN'T MAKE THINGS DISAPPEAR.
YOU CALLED ME BAGGAGE. NOW YOU WANT ME ON YOUR SIDE? WHAT CHANGED YOUR OPINION SO FAST?
DON'T BE DUMB.
THERE'S MUCH YOU DON'T KNOW ABOUT OUR POWERS, ESPECIALLY LILLY'S. SHE CAN HANDLE YOUR TATTOO.
LOOK, I INSULTED YOU IN SELF-DEFENSE. BUT IF YOU'RE ON OUR SIDE...
WELL, YOU'D BE VERY VALUABLE TO US.
YOU KNOW ABOUT THEM.
...
HMM... MAKES SENSE. DID SHE REALLY COME TO RECRUIT ME?
AND CAN THEY REALLY GET RID OF...
...THIS WRETCHED, HATEFUL TATTOO?

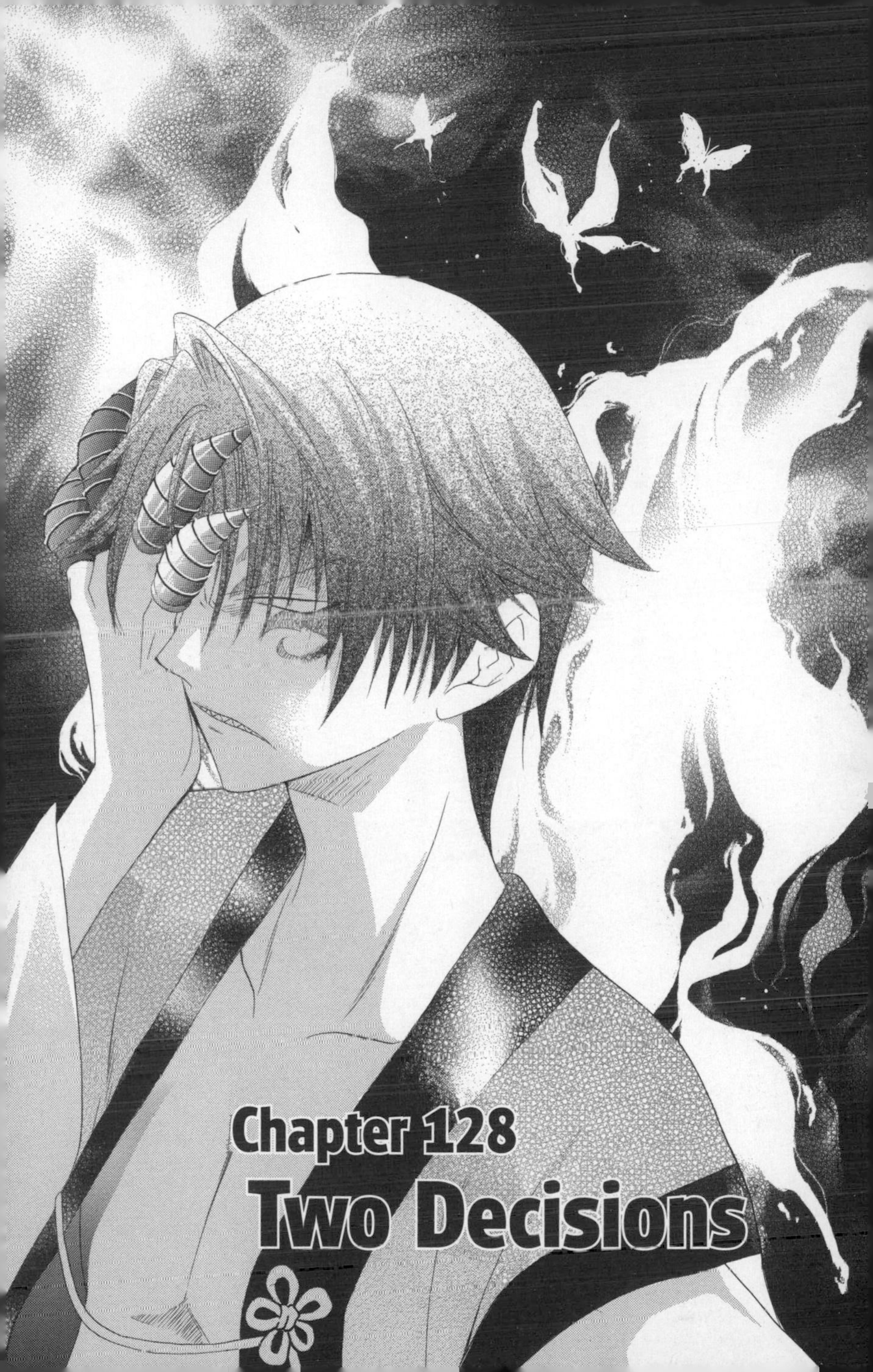
Chapter 128
Two Decisions

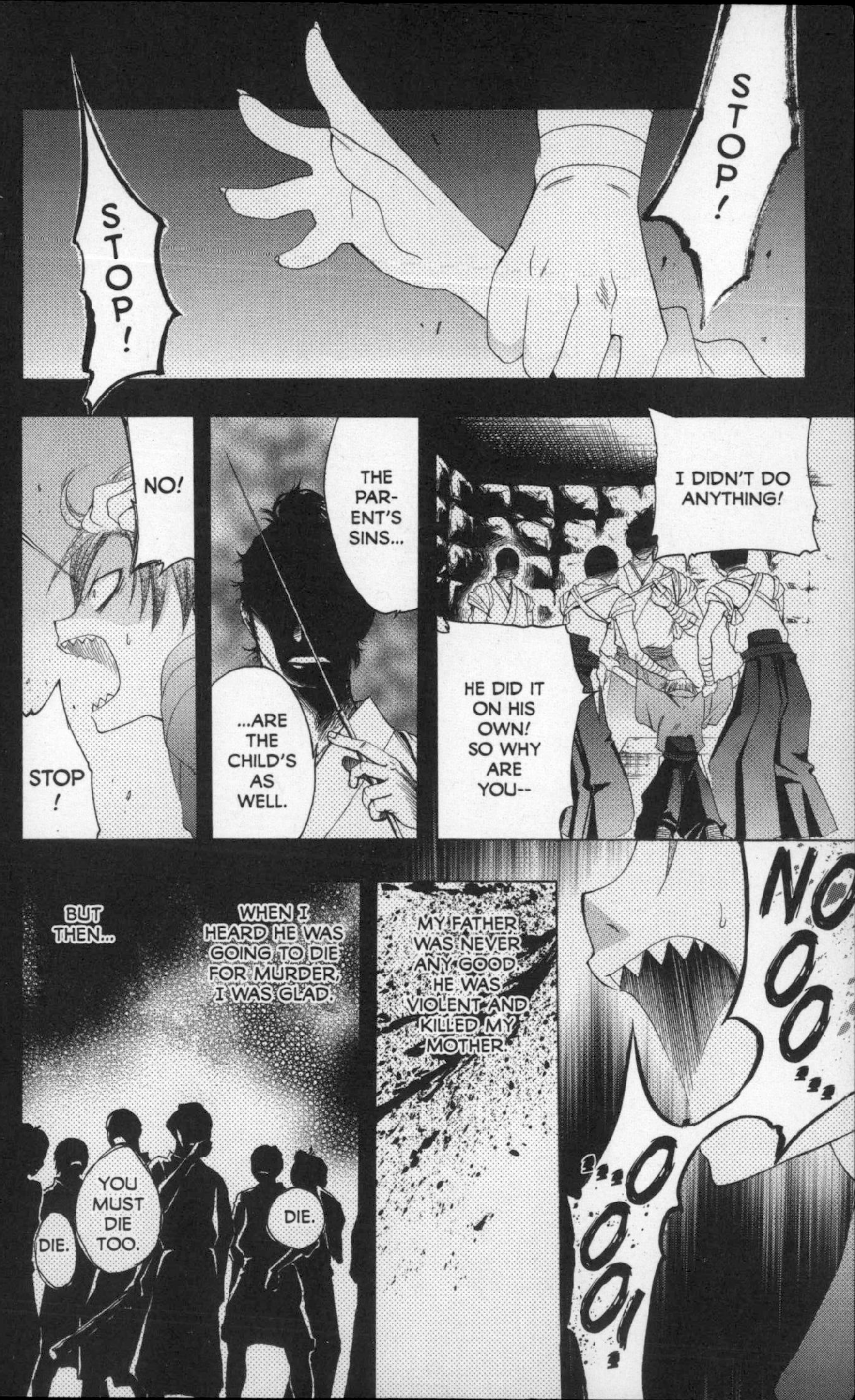
STOP!
STOP!
I DIDN'T DO ANYTHING!
HE DID IT ON HIS OWN! SO WHY ARE YOU--
THE PAR-ENT'S SINS...
...ARE THE CHILD'S AS WELL.
NO!
STOP!
NOOOO...OOO!
MY FATHER WAS NEVER ANY GOOD. HE WAS VIOLENT AND KILLED MY MOTHER.
WHEN I HEARD HE WAS GOING TO DIE FOR MURDER, I WAS GLAD.
BUT THEN...
DIE.
YOU MUST DIE TOO.
DIE.

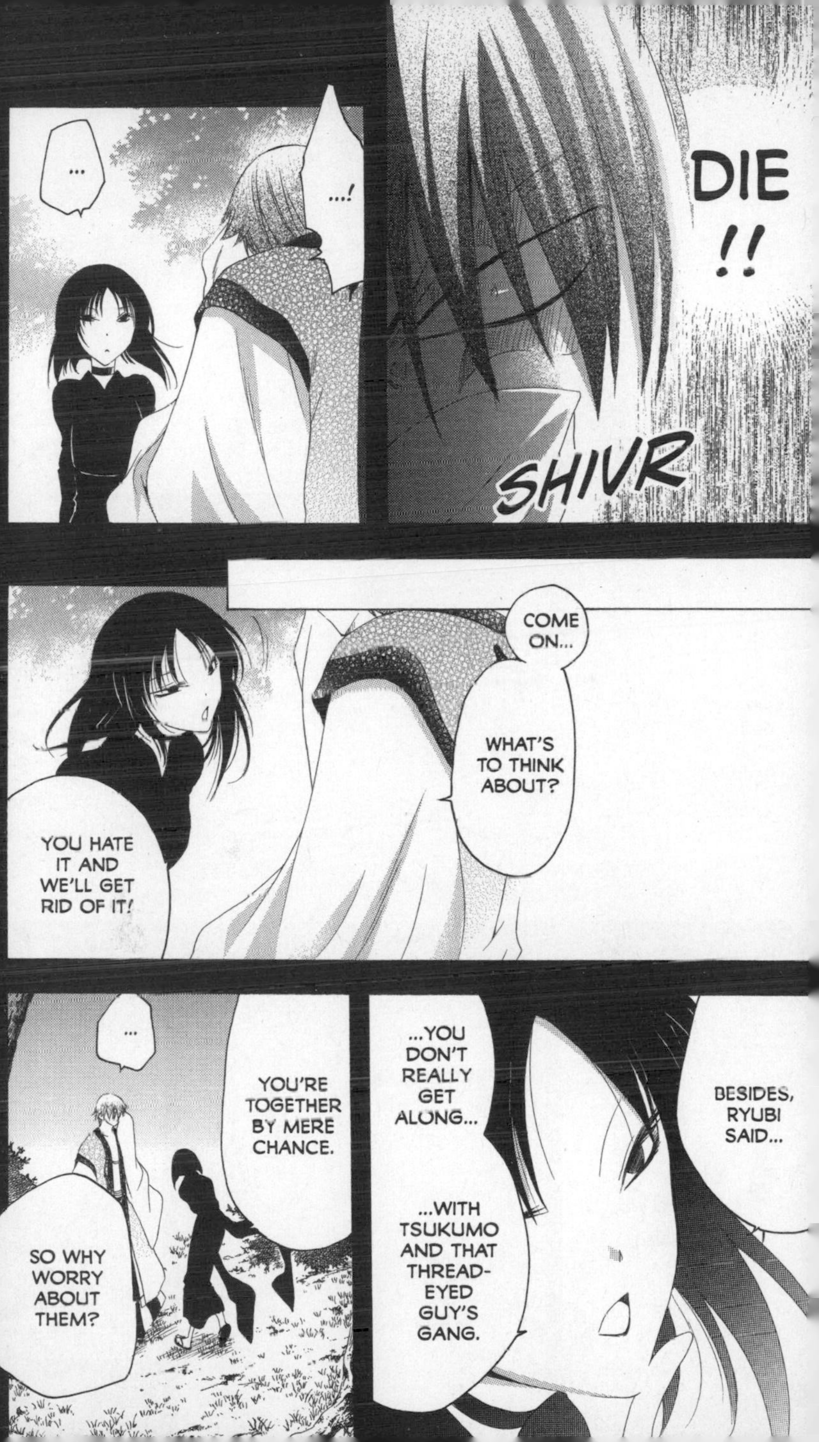
DIE !!
SHIVR
...!
...
COME ON...
WHAT'S TO THINK ABOUT?
YOU HATE IT AND WE'LL GET RID OF IT!
BESIDES, RYUBI SAID...
...YOU DON'T REALLY GET ALONG...
...WITH TSUKUMO AND THAT THREAD-EYED GUY'S GANG.
YOU'RE TOGETHER BY MERE CHANCE.
...
SO WHY WORRY ABOUT THEM?

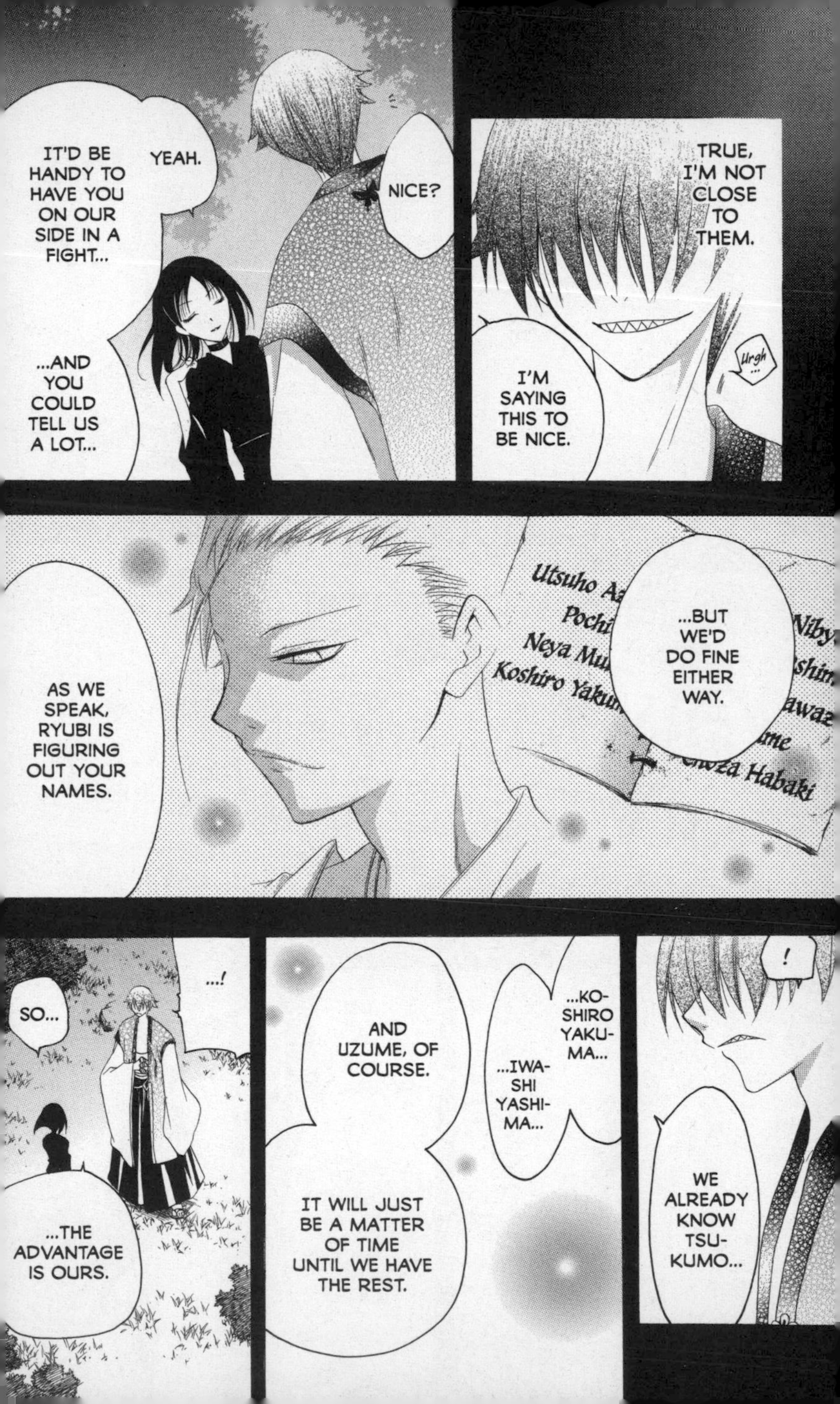
TRUE, I'M NOT CLOSE TO THEM.
Urgh...
I'M SAYING THIS TO BE NICE.
NICE?
YEAH.
IT'D BE HANDY TO HAVE YOU ON OUR SIDE IN A FIGHT...
...AND YOU COULD TELL US A LOT...
...BUT WE'D DO FINE EITHER WAY.
AS WE SPEAK, RYUBI IS FIGURING OUT YOUR NAMES.
!
WE ALREADY KNOW TSU-KUMO...
...KO-SHIRO YAKU-MA...
...IWA-SHI YASHI-MA...
AND UZUME, OF COURSE.
IT WILL JUST BE A MATTER OF TIME UNTIL WE HAVE THE REST.
...!
SO...
...THE ADVANTAGE IS OURS.

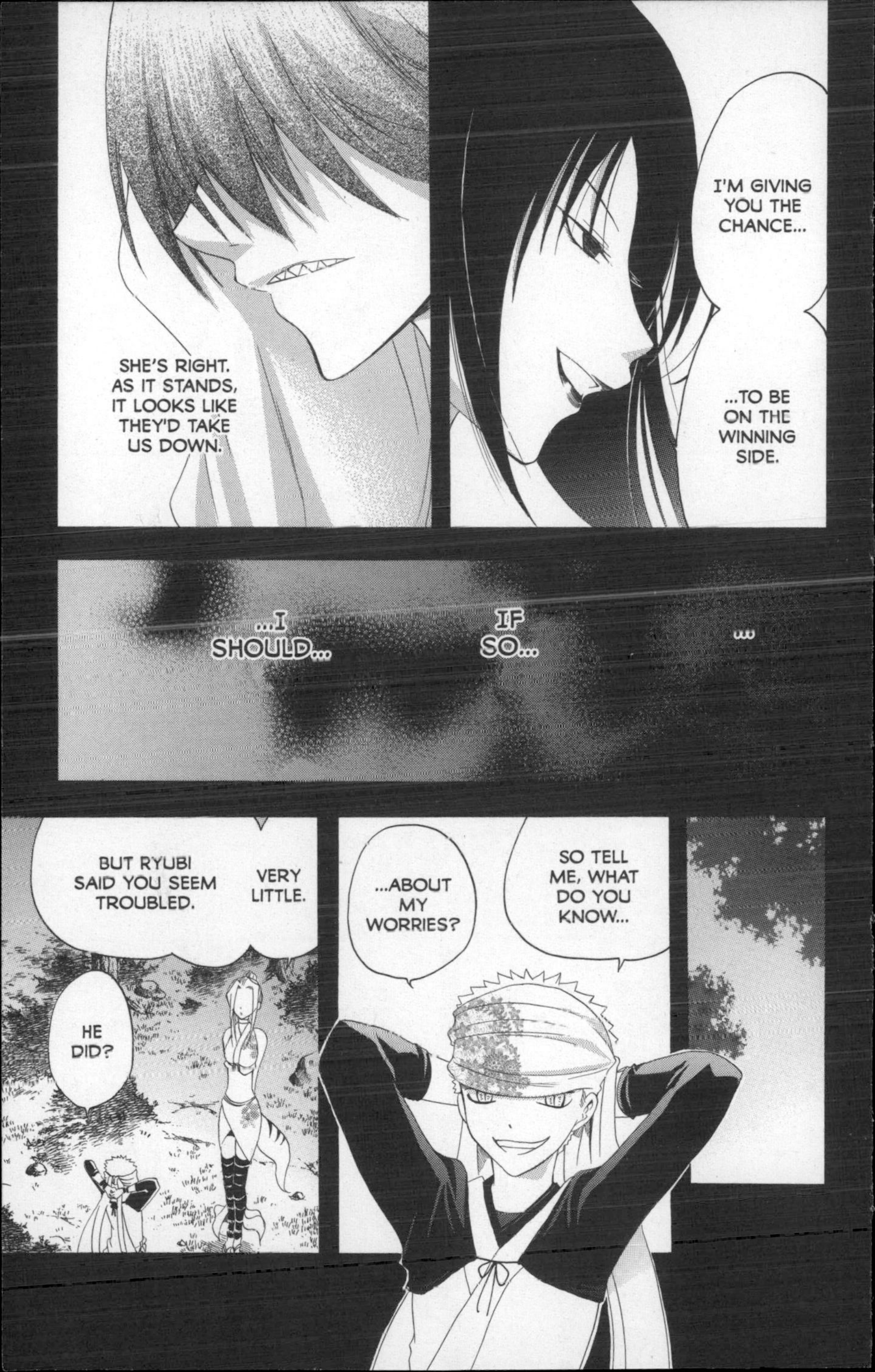
I'M GIVING YOU THE CHANCE...
...TO BE ON THE WINNING SIDE.
SHE'S RIGHT. AS IT STANDS, IT LOOKS LIKE THEY'D TAKE US DOWN.
...
IF SO...
...I SHOULD...
SO TELL ME, WHAT DO YOU KNOW...
...ABOUT MY WORRIES?
VERY LITTLE.
BUT RYUBI SAID YOU SEEM TROUBLED.
HE DID?

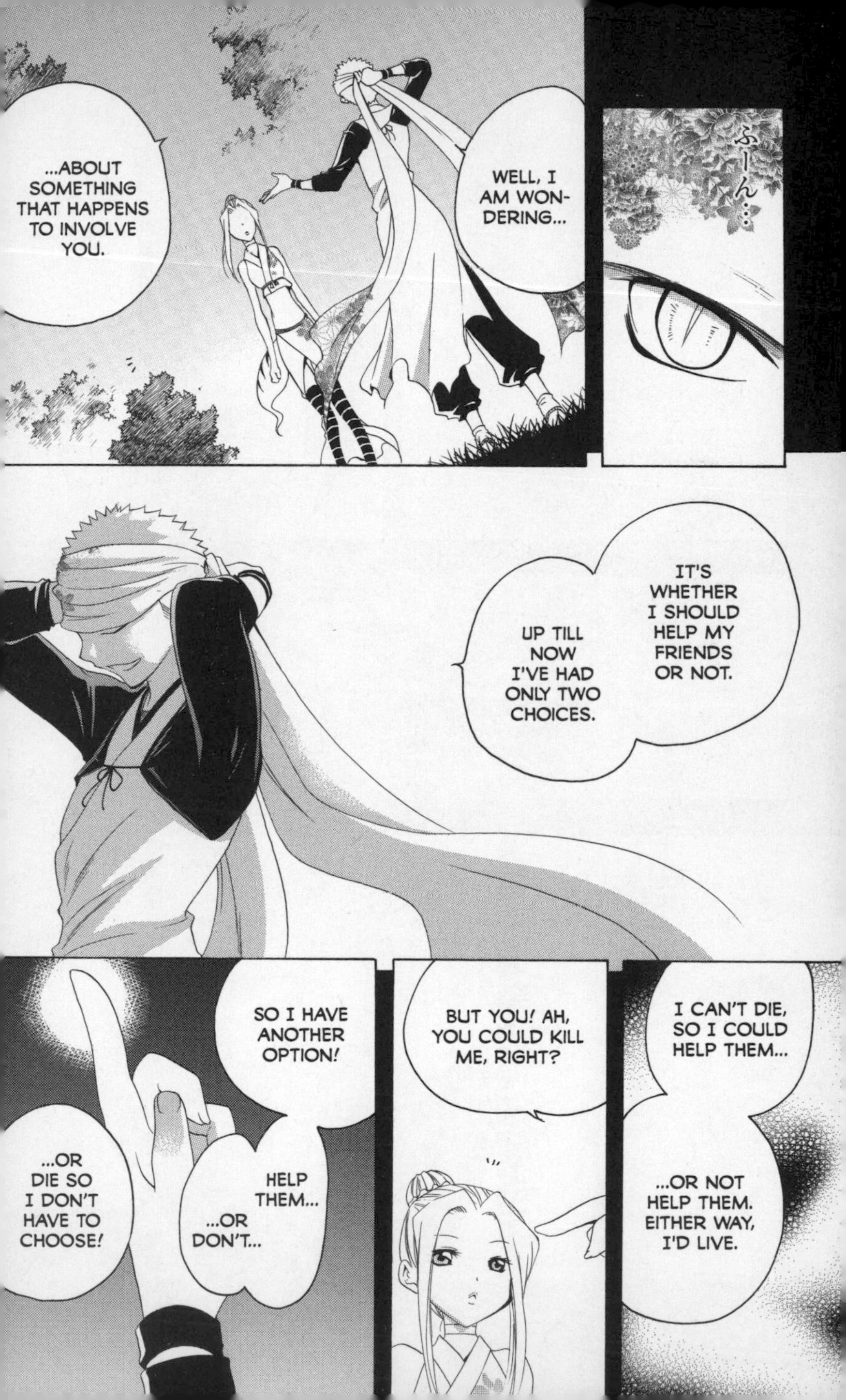
ふーん…
WELL, I AM WON-DERING...
...ABOUT SOMETHING THAT HAPPENS TO INVOLVE YOU.
IT'S WHETHER I SHOULD HELP MY FRIENDS OR NOT.
UP TILL NOW I'VE HAD ONLY TWO CHOICES.
I CAN'T DIE, SO I COULD HELP THEM...
...OR NOT HELP THEM. EITHER WAY, I'D LIVE.
BUT YOU! AH, YOU COULD KILL ME, RIGHT?
SO I HAVE ANOTHER OPTION!
HELP THEM...
...OR DON'T...
...OR DIE SO I DON'T HAVE TO CHOOSE!

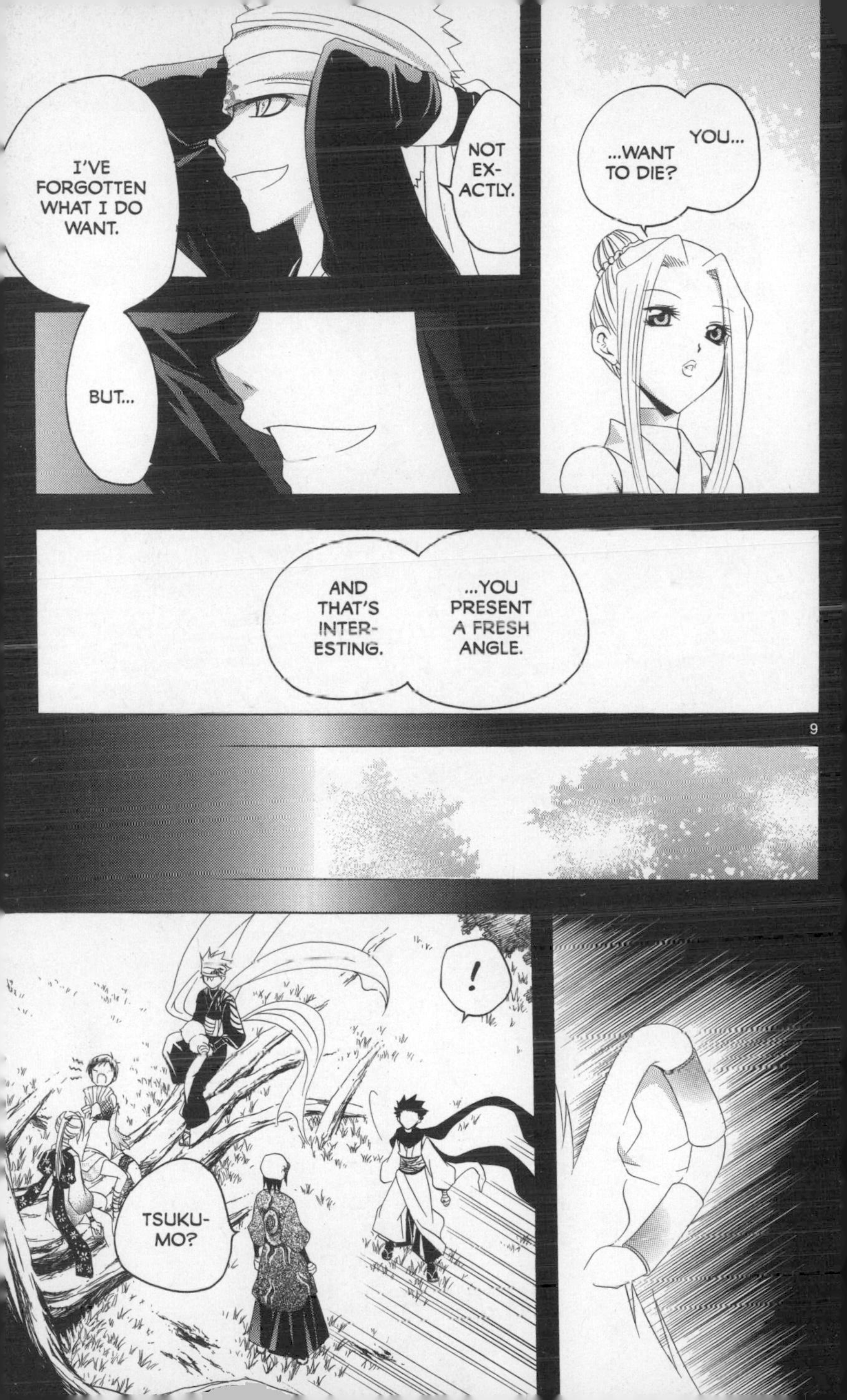
YOU... ...WANT TO DIE?
NOT EX-ACTLY.
I'VE FORGOTTEN WHAT I DO WANT.
BUT...
...YOU PRESENT A FRESH ANGLE.
AND THAT'S INTER-ESTING.
!
TSUKU-MO?

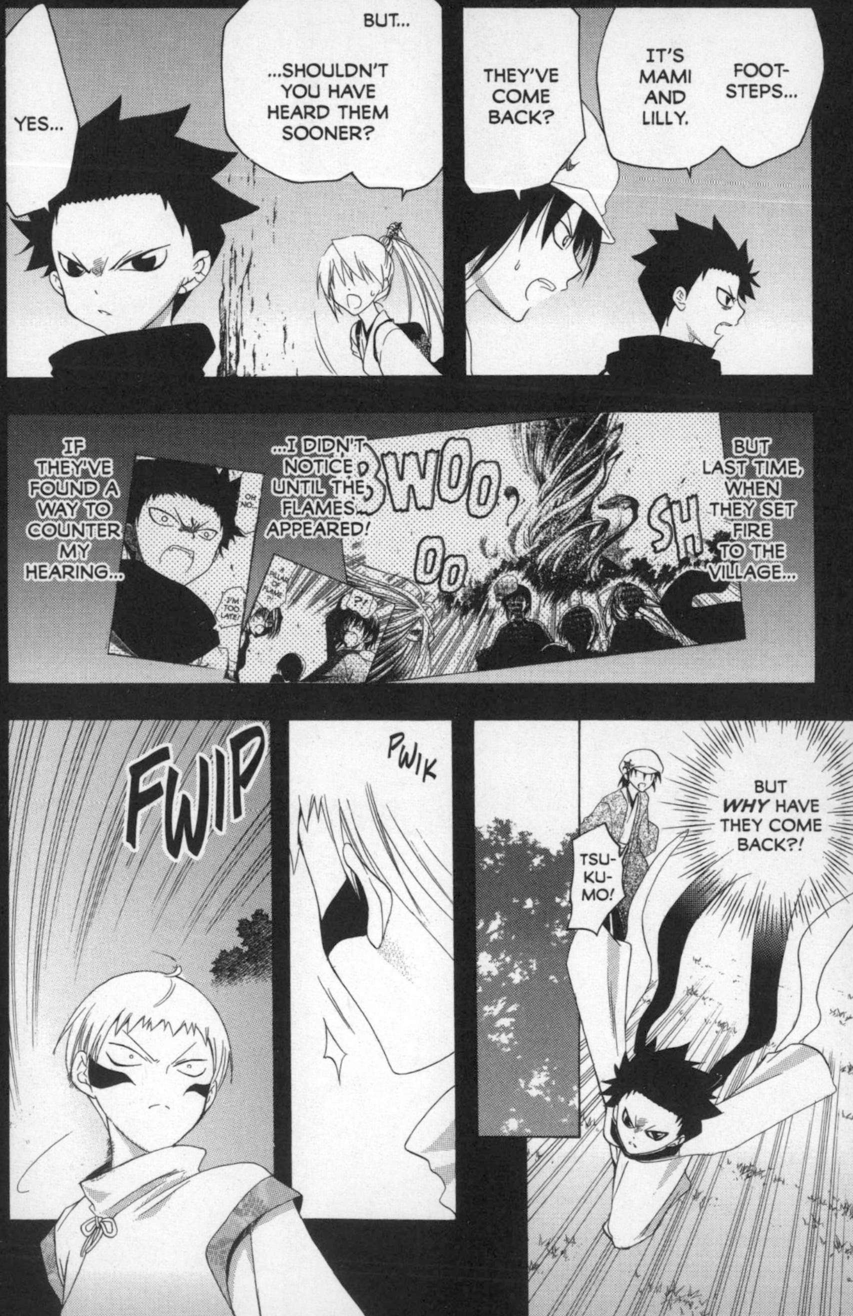
FOOT-STEPS...
IT'S MAMI AND LILLY.
THEY'VE COME BACK?
BUT...
...SHOULDN'T YOU HAVE HEARD THEM SOONER?
YES...
BUT LAST TIME, WHEN THEY SET FIRE TO THE VILLAGE...
BWOO, OOSH
...I DIDN'T NOTICE UNTIL THE FLAMES APPEARED!
OH NO...
A PILLAR OF FLAME?!
?!
I'M TOO LATE!
IF THEY'VE FOUND A WAY TO COUNTER MY HEARING...
BUT WHY HAVE THEY COME BACK?!
TSU-KU-MO!
PWIK
FWIP

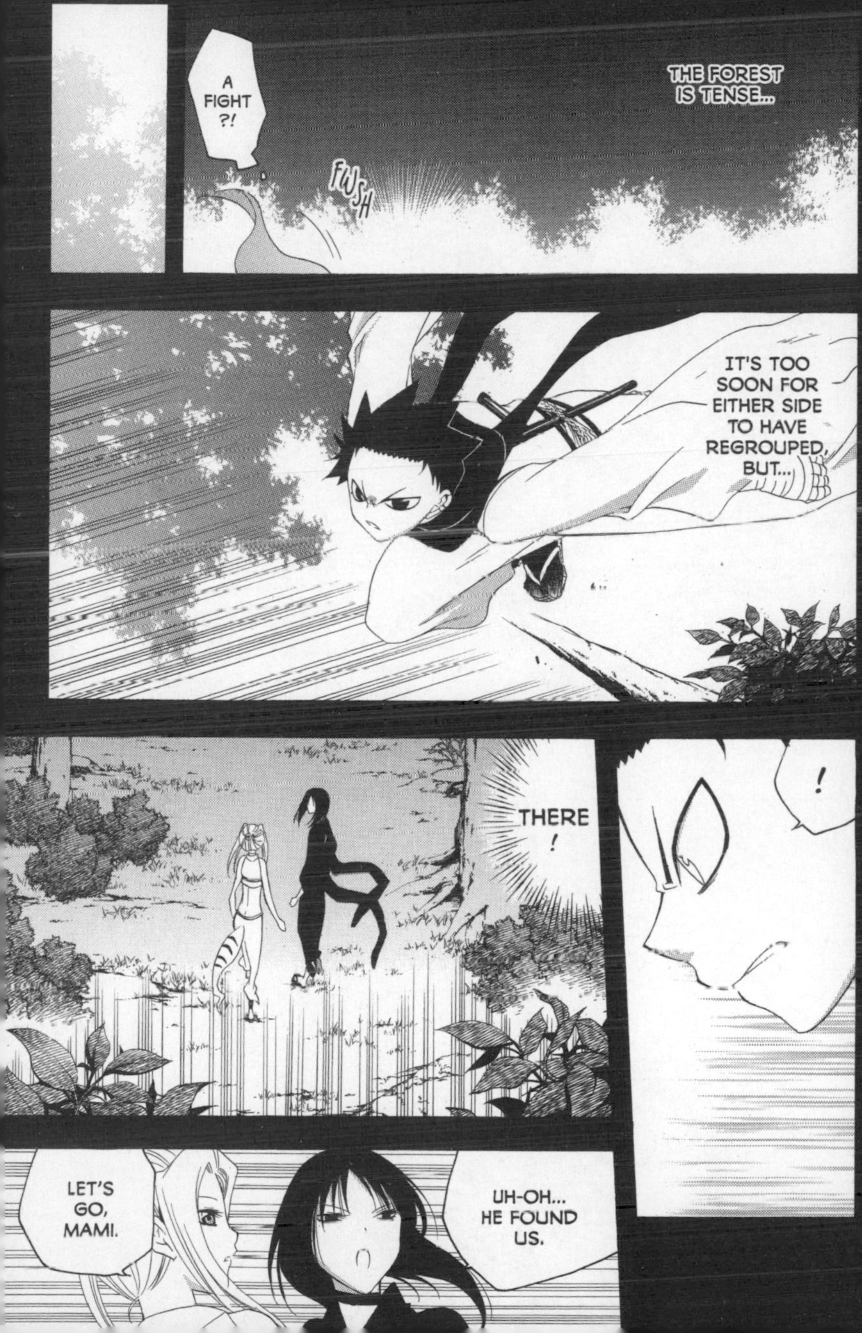
THE FOREST IS TENSE...
A FIGHT ?!
FWSH
IT'S TOO SOON FOR EITHER SIDE TO HAVE REGROUPED, BUT...
!
THERE !
UH-OH... HE FOUND US.
LET'S GO, MAMI.

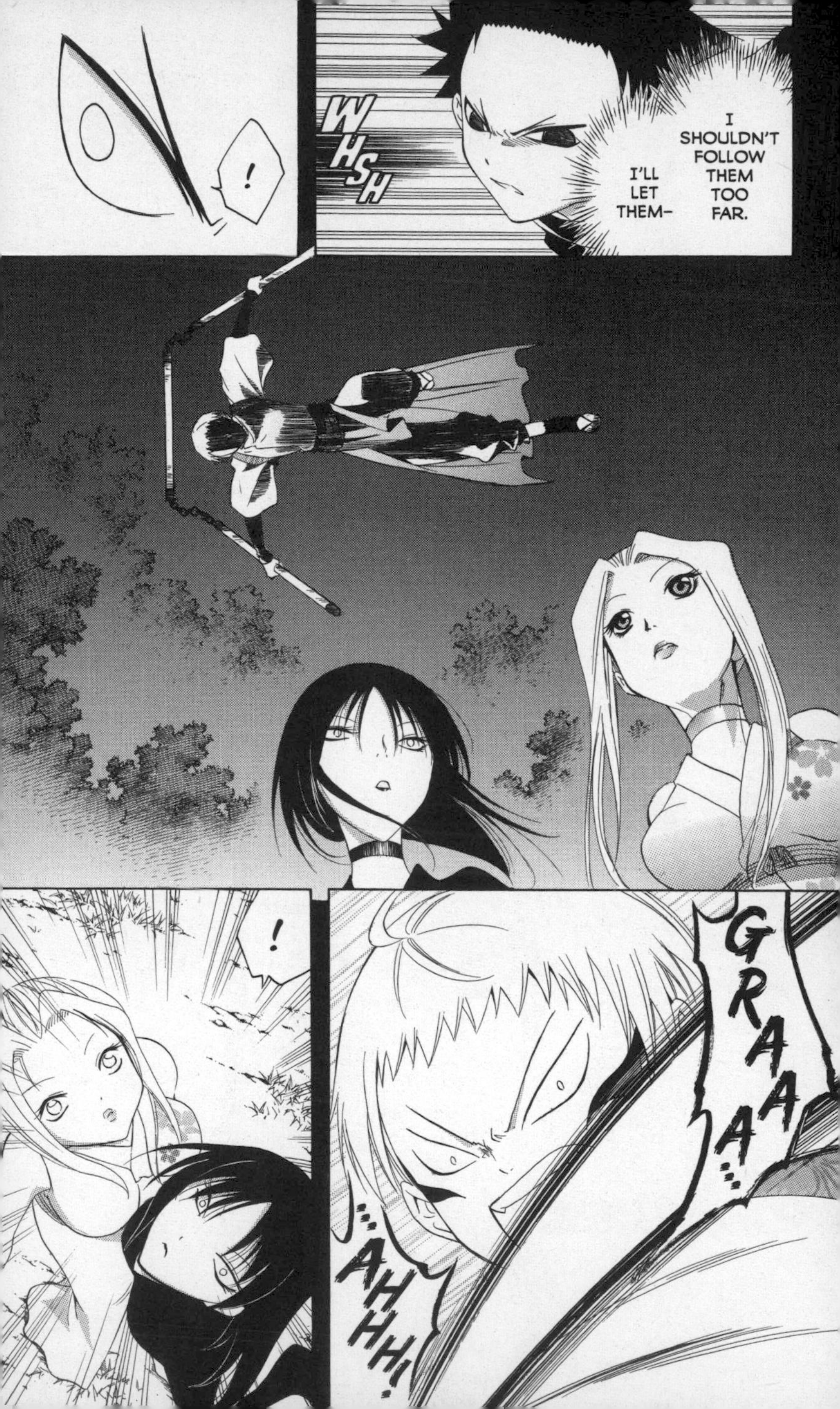
I SHOULDN'T FOLLOW THEM TOO FAR.
I'LL LET THEM–
WHSH
!
GRAAAA...
...AHHH!
!

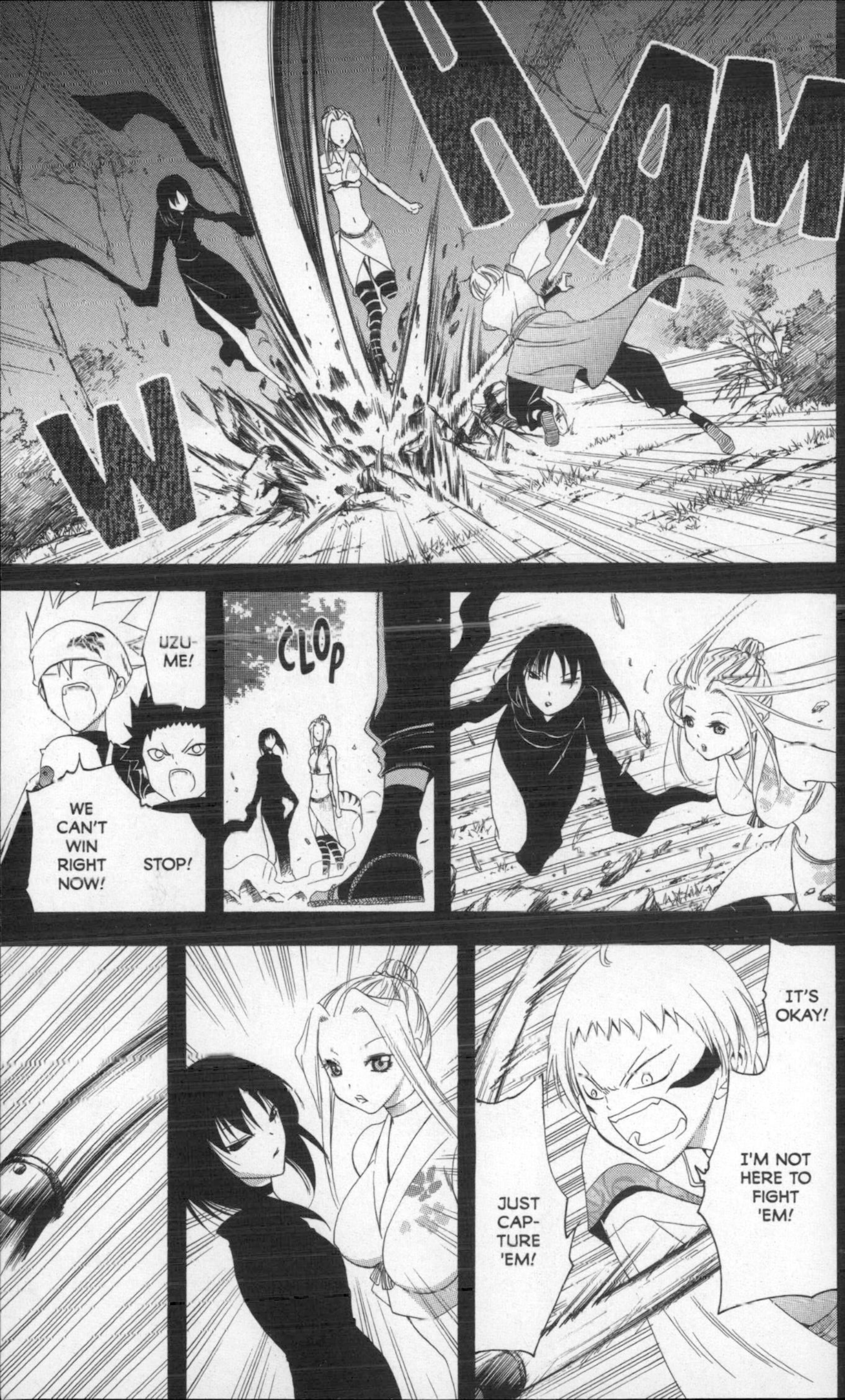
WHAM
CLOP
UZU-
ME!
STOP!
WE
CAN'T
WIN
RIGHT
NOW!
IT'S
OKAY!
I'M NOT
HERE TO
FIGHT
'EM!
JUST
CAP-
TURE
'EM!

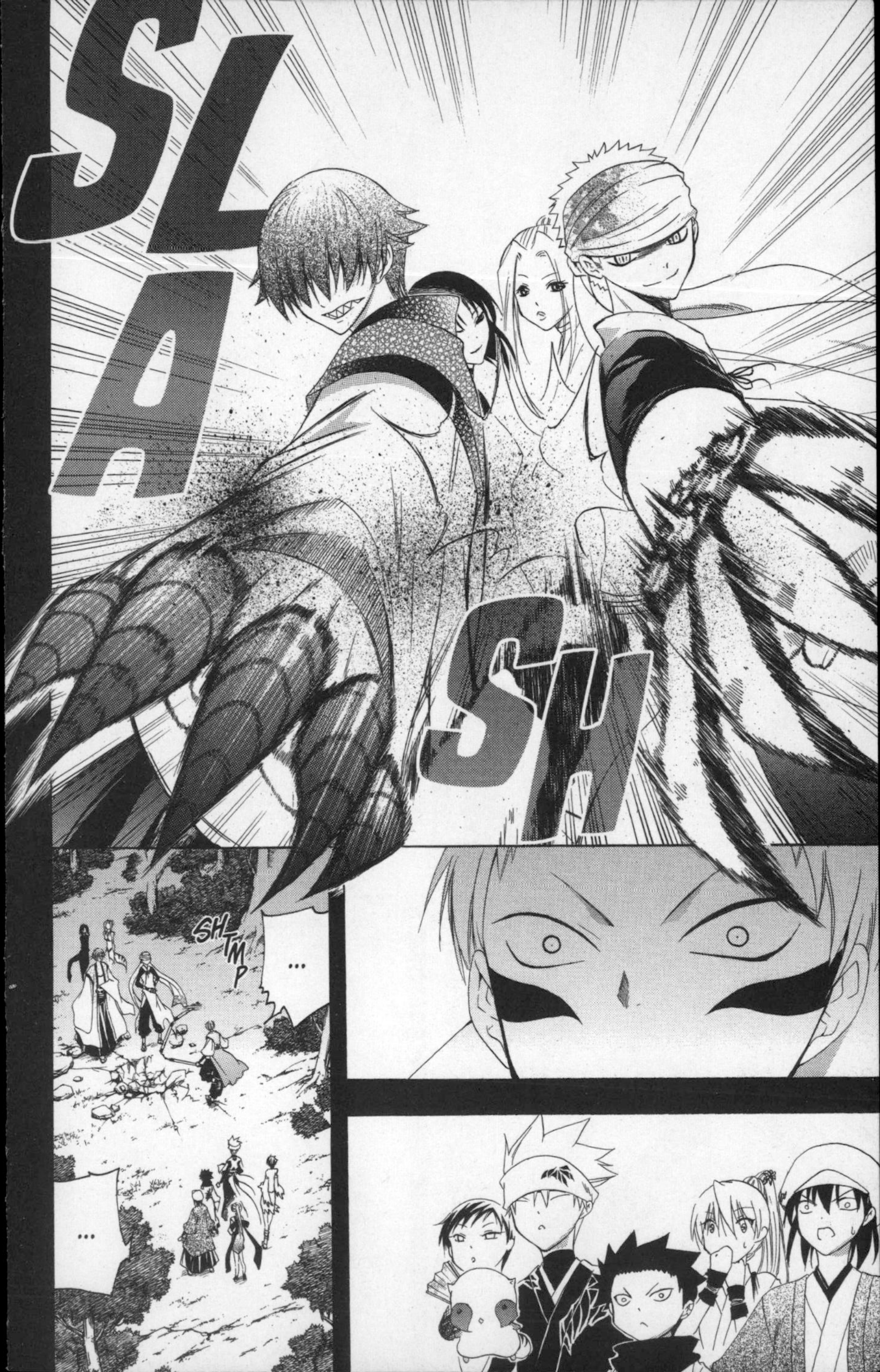
SLASH
SHTMP
...
...

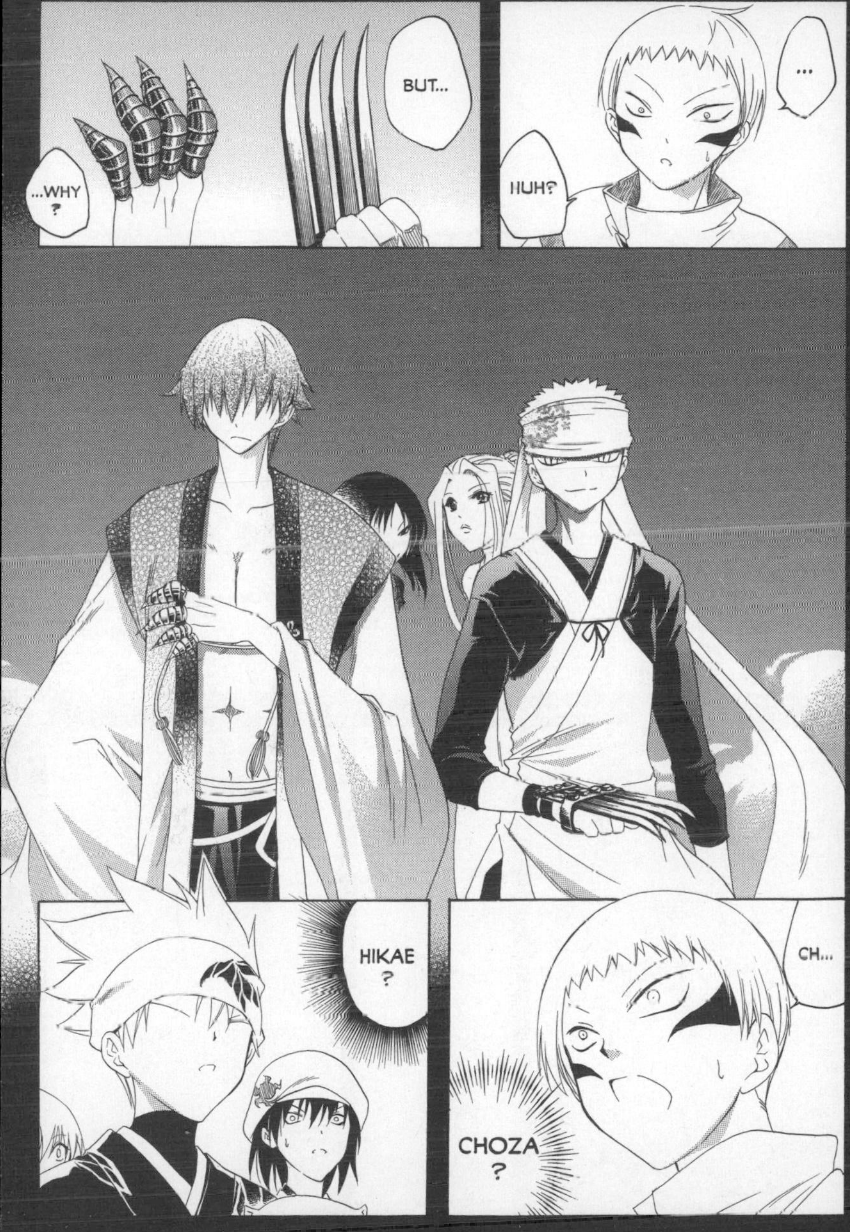
...
HUH?
BUT...
...WHY ?
CH...
CHOZA ?
HIKAE ?

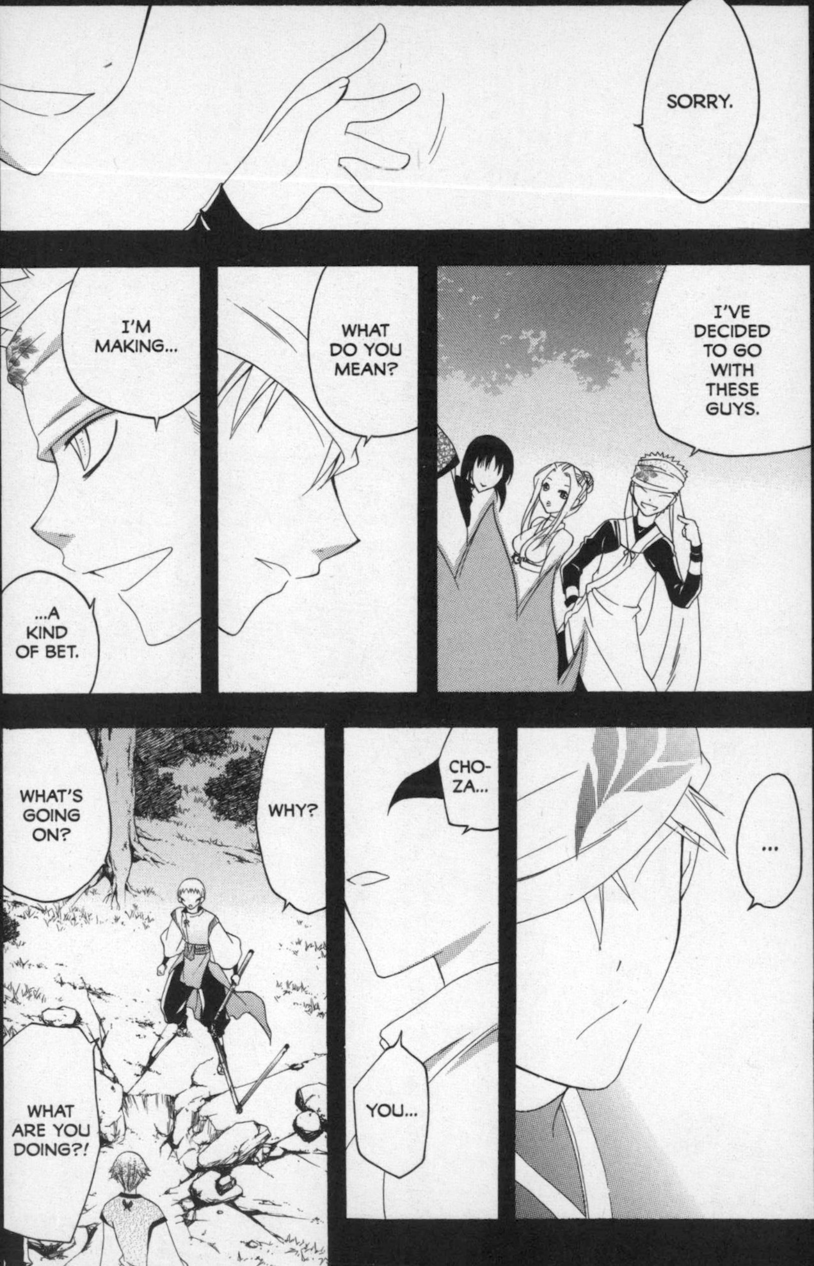
SORRY.
I'VE DECIDED TO GO WITH THESE GUYS.
WHAT DO YOU MEAN?
I'M MAKING...
...A KIND OF BET.
...
CHO-ZA...
YOU...
WHY?
WHAT'S GOING ON?
WHAT ARE YOU DOING?!

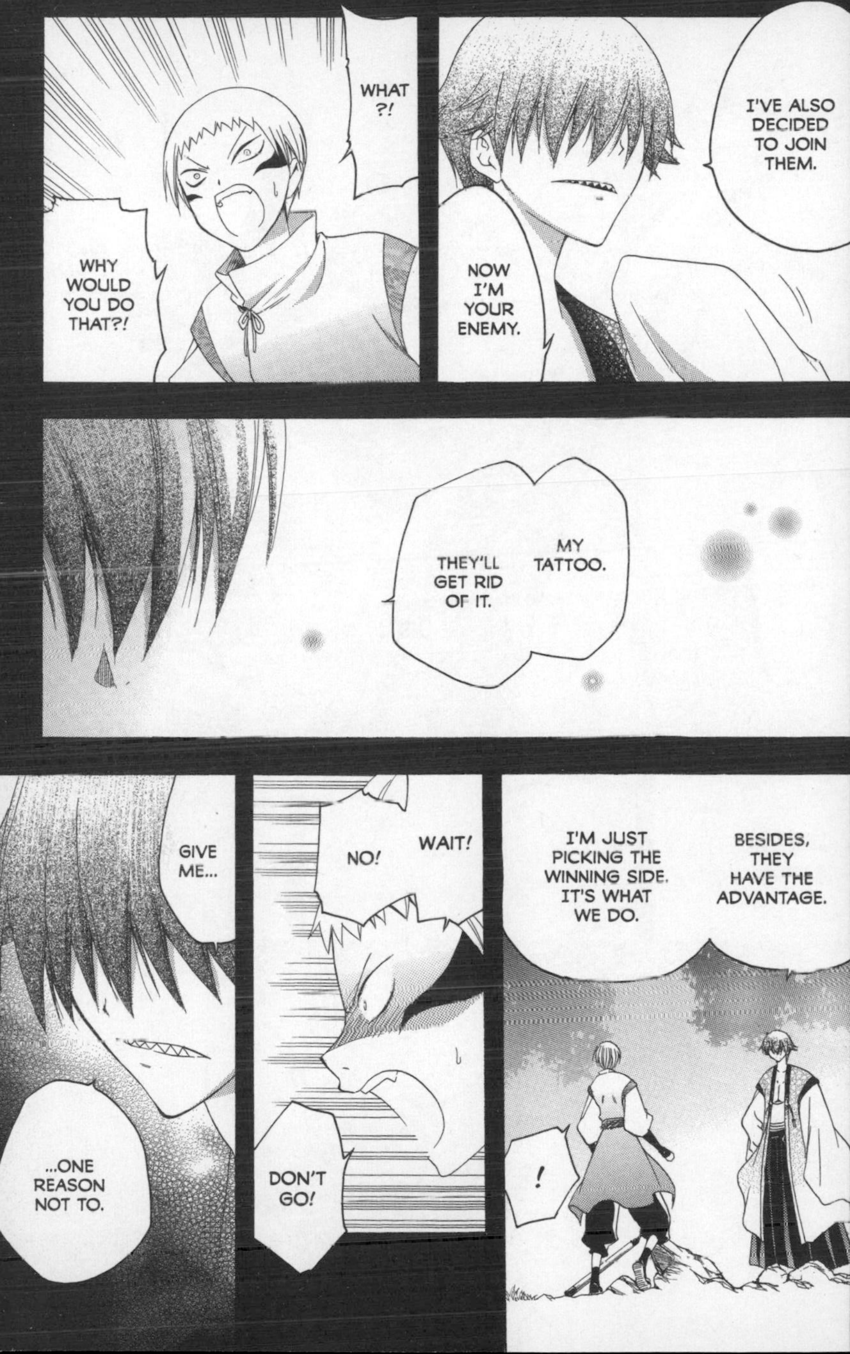
I'VE ALSO DECIDED TO JOIN THEM.
NOW I'M YOUR ENEMY.
WHAT ?!
WHY WOULD YOU DO THAT?!
MY TATTOO.
THEY'LL GET RID OF IT.
BESIDES, THEY HAVE THE ADVANTAGE.
I'M JUST PICKING THE WINNING SIDE. IT'S WHAT WE DO.
!
WAIT!
NO!
DON'T GO!
GIVE ME...
...ONE REASON NOT TO.

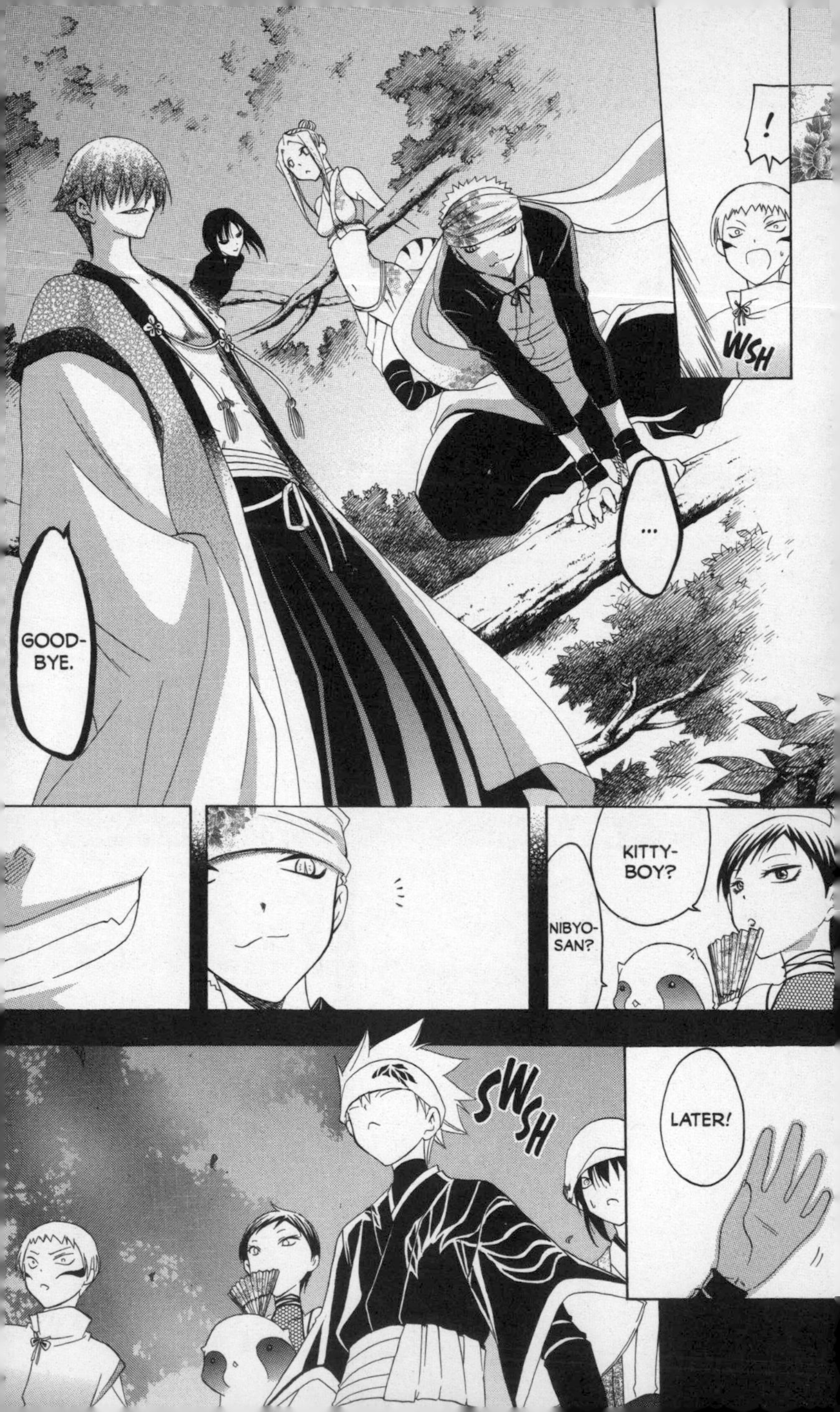
!
WSH
...
GOOD-BYE.
KITTY-BOY?
NIBYO-SAN?
LATER!
SWSH

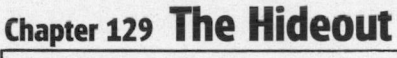

Chapter 129 The Hideout

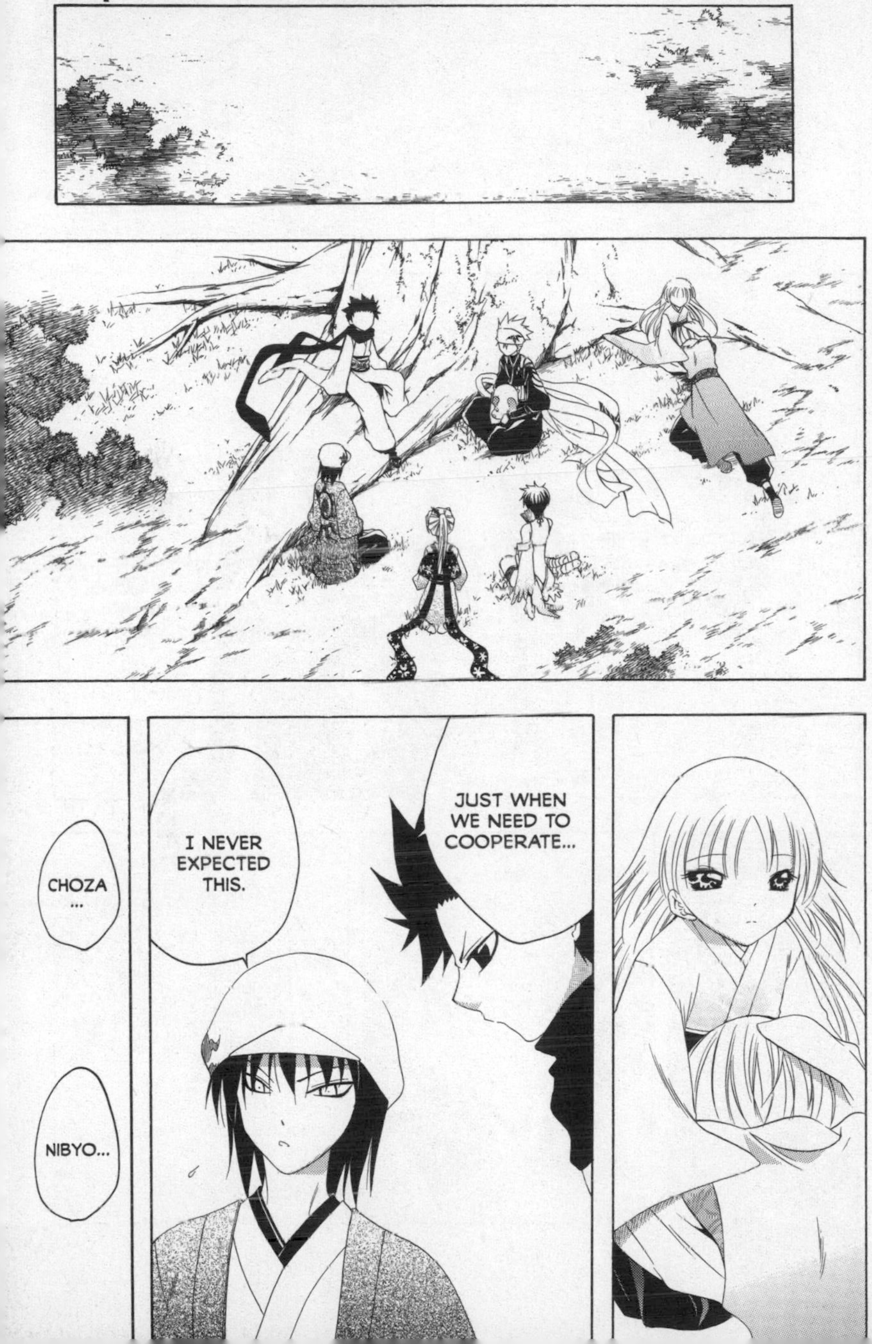
JUST WHEN WE NEED TO COOPERATE...
I NEVER EXPECTED THIS.
CHOZA ...
NIBYO...

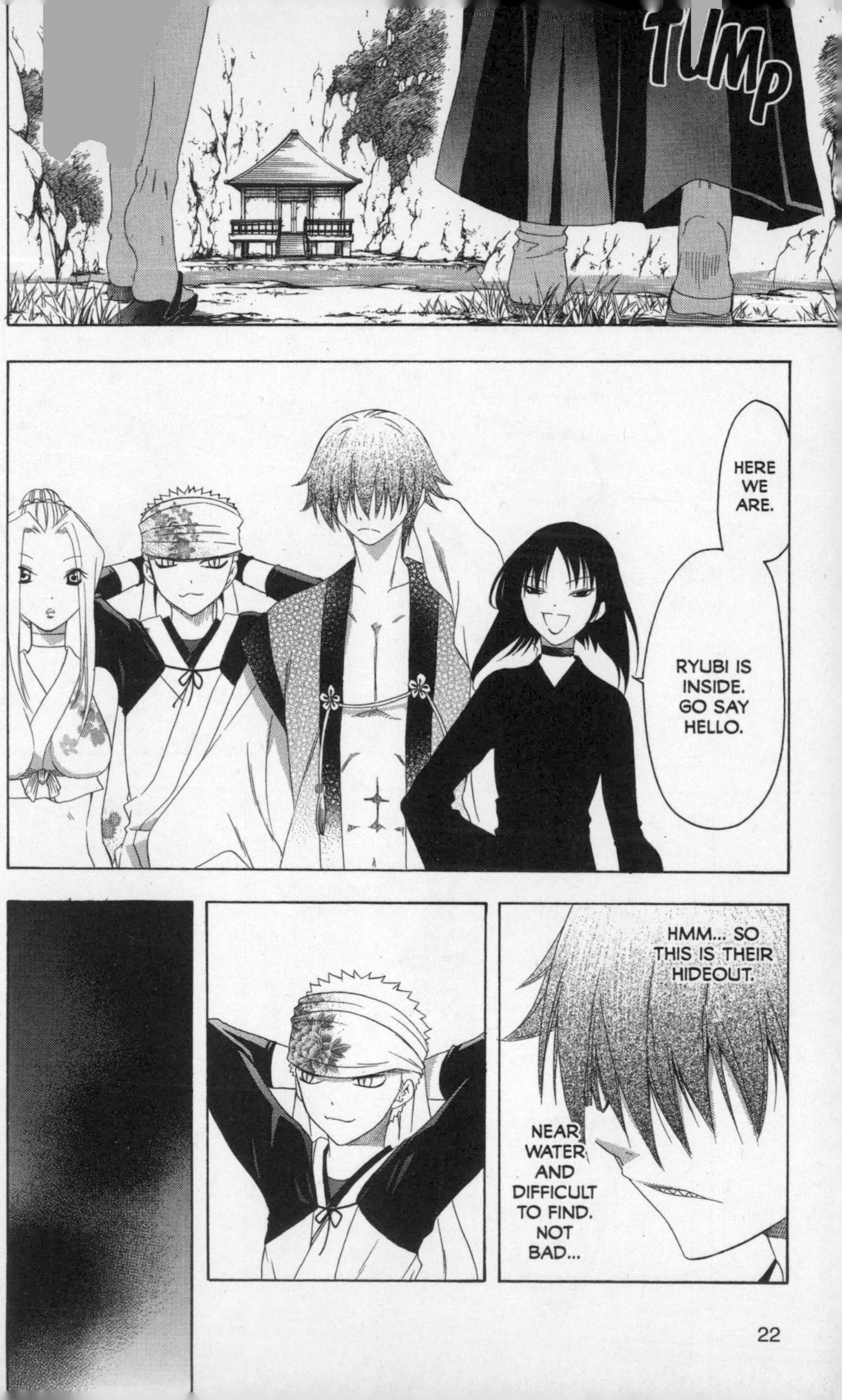
TUMP
HERE WE ARE.
RYUBI IS INSIDE. GO SAY HELLO.
HMM... SO THIS IS THEIR HIDEOUT.
NEAR WATER AND DIFFICULT TO FIND. NOT BAD...

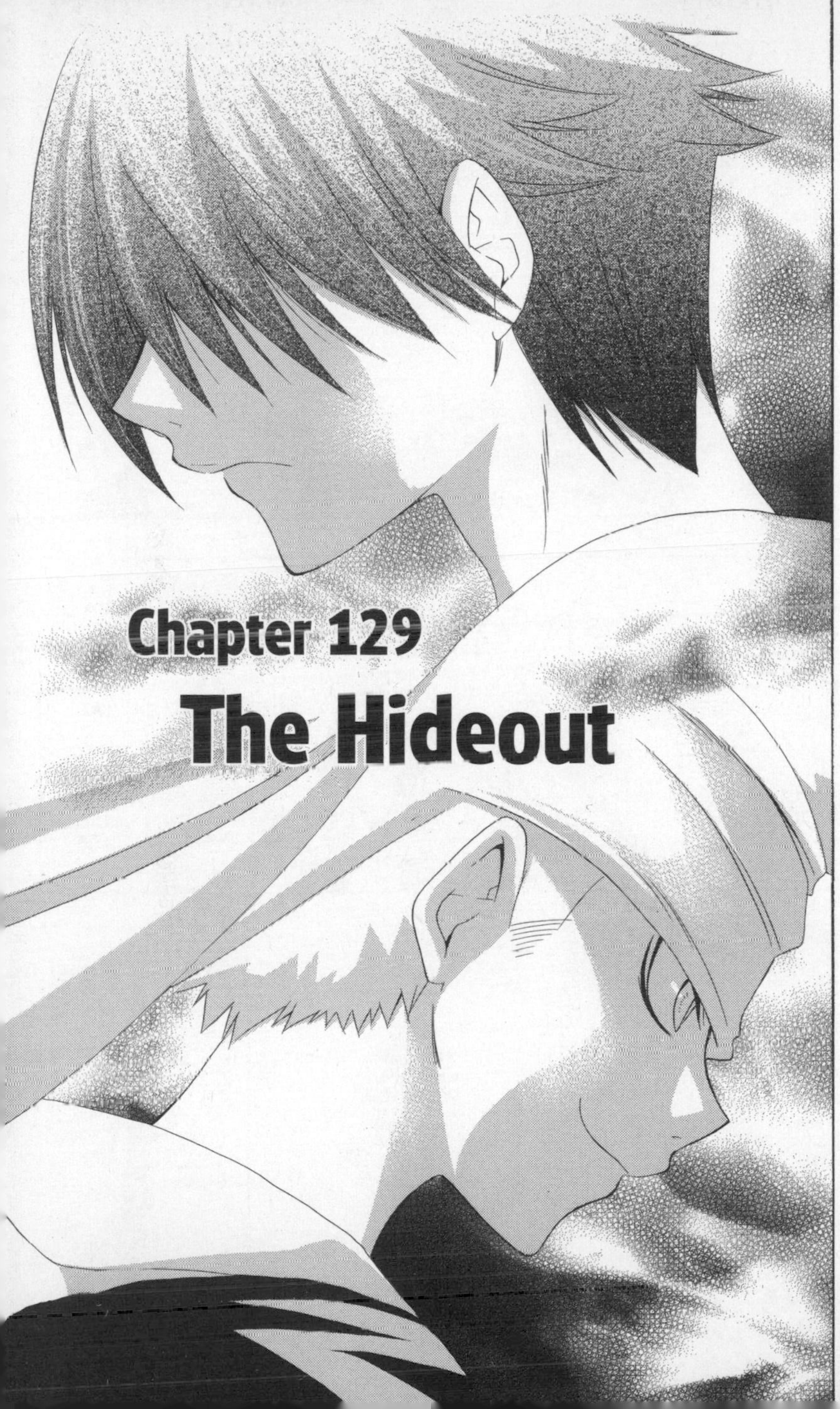
Chapter 129
The Hideout

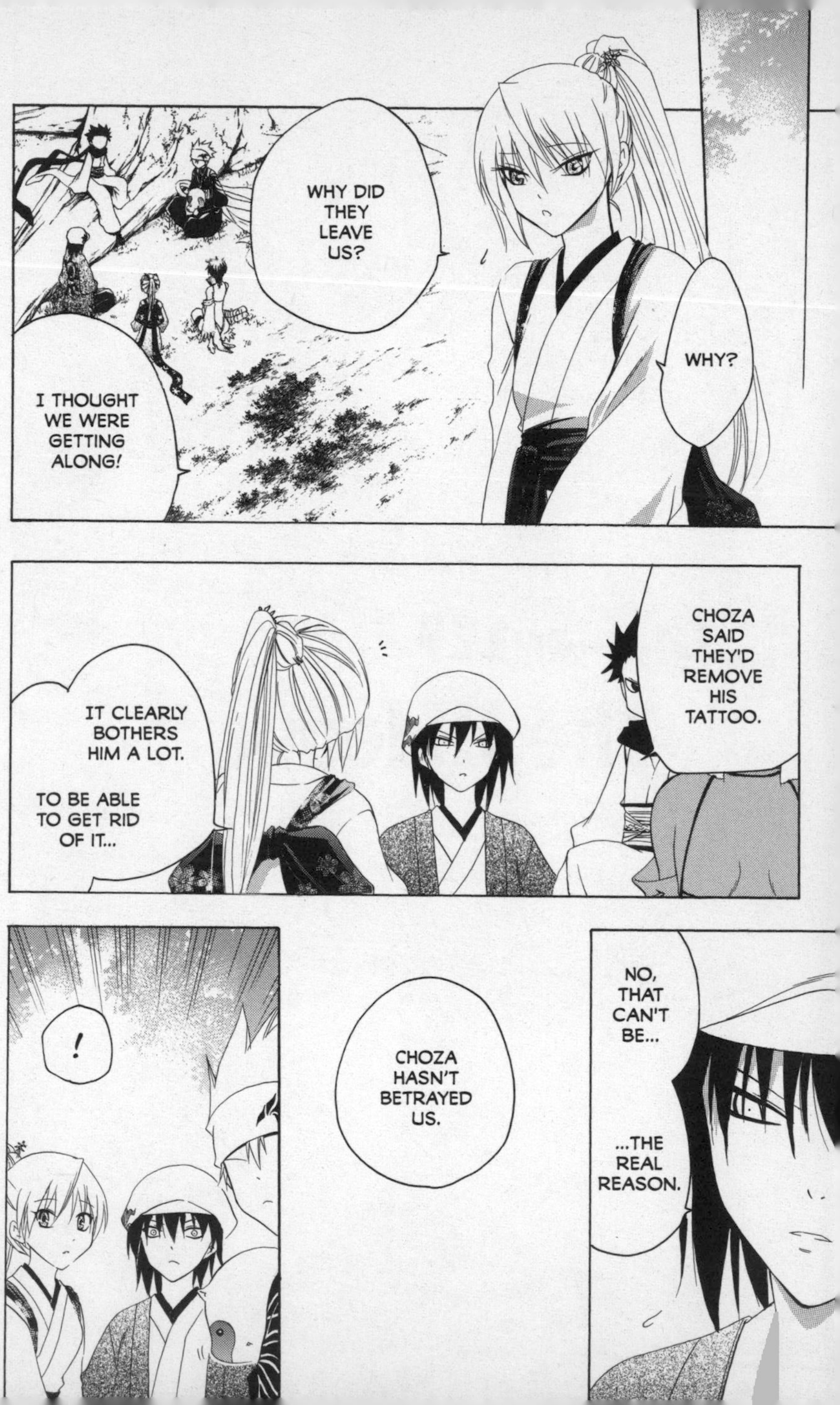
WHY?
WHY DID THEY LEAVE US?
I THOUGHT WE WERE GETTING ALONG!
CHOZA SAID THEY'D REMOVE HIS TATTOO.
IT CLEARLY BOTHERS HIM A LOT.
TO BE ABLE TO GET RID OF IT...
NO, THAT CAN'T BE...
...THE REAL REASON.
CHOZA HASN'T BETRAYED US.
!

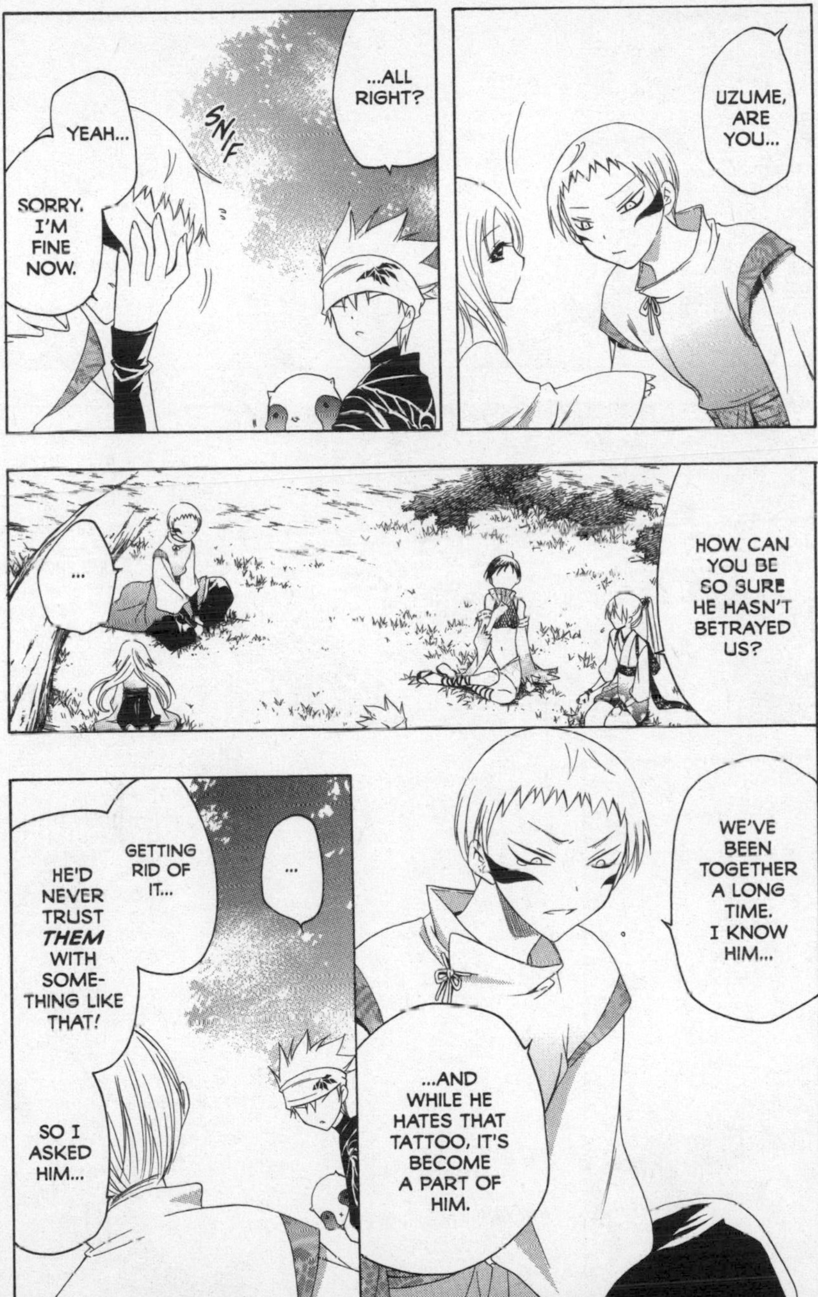
UZUME, ARE YOU...
...ALL RIGHT?
SNIF
YEAH...
SORRY. I'M FINE NOW.
HOW CAN YOU BE SO SURE HE HASN'T BETRAYED US?
...
WE'VE BEEN TOGETHER A LONG TIME. I KNOW HIM...
...AND WHILE HE HATES THAT TATTOO, IT'S BECOME A PART OF HIM.
...
HE'D NEVER TRUST *THEM* WITH SOME-THING LIKE THAT!
GETTING RID OF IT...
SO I ASKED HIM...

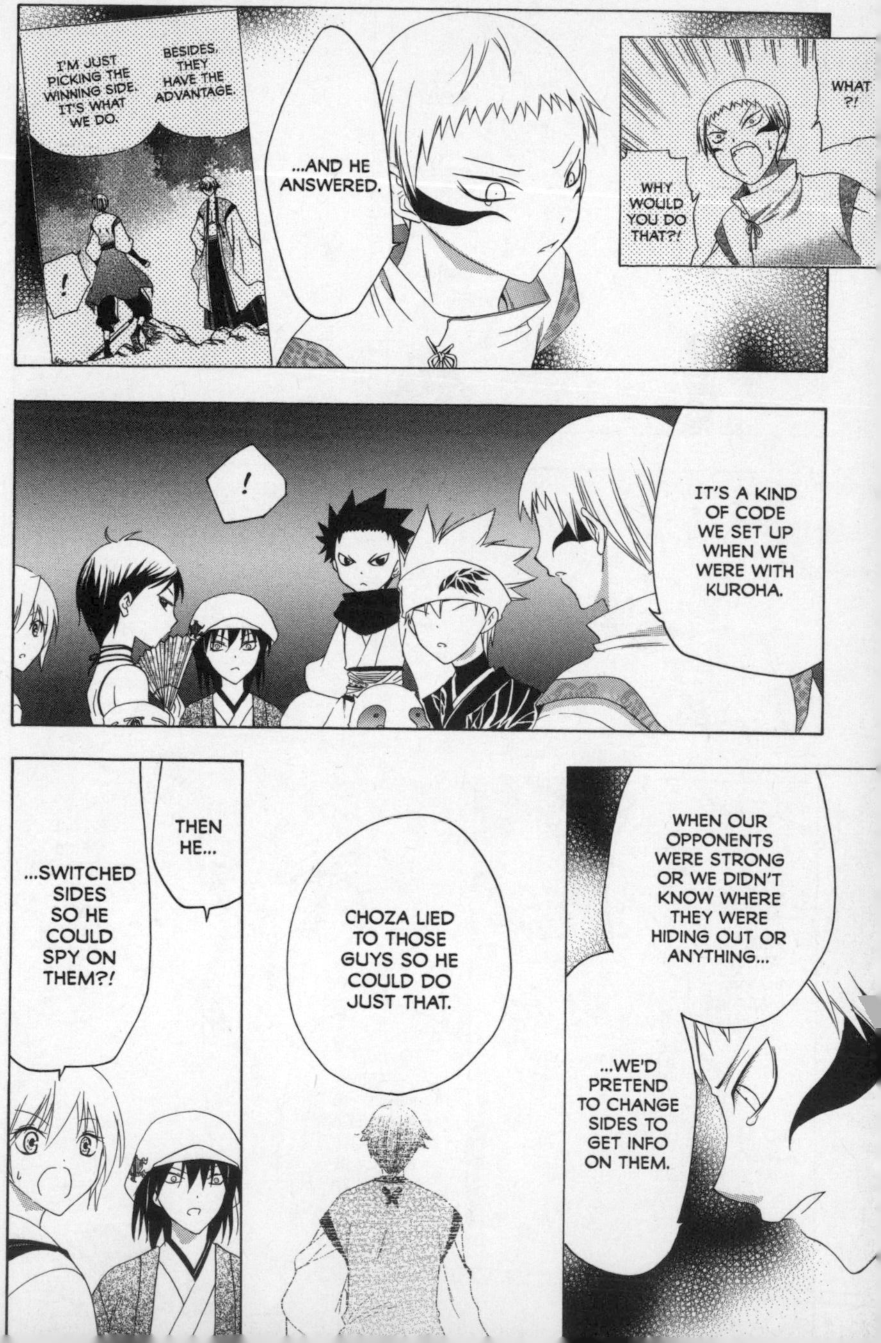
WHAT ?!
WHY WOULD YOU DO THAT?!
...AND HE ANSWERED.
BESIDES, THEY HAVE THE ADVANTAGE.
I'M JUST PICKING THE WINNING SIDE. IT'S WHAT WE DO.
!
IT'S A KIND OF CODE WE SET UP WHEN WE WERE WITH KUROHA.
!
WHEN OUR OPPONENTS WERE STRONG OR WE DIDN'T KNOW WHERE THEY WERE HIDING OUT OR ANYTHING...
...WE'D PRETEND TO CHANGE SIDES TO GET INFO ON THEM.
CHOZA LIED TO THOSE GUYS SO HE COULD DO JUST THAT.
THEN HE...
...SWITCHED SIDES SO HE COULD SPY ON THEM?!

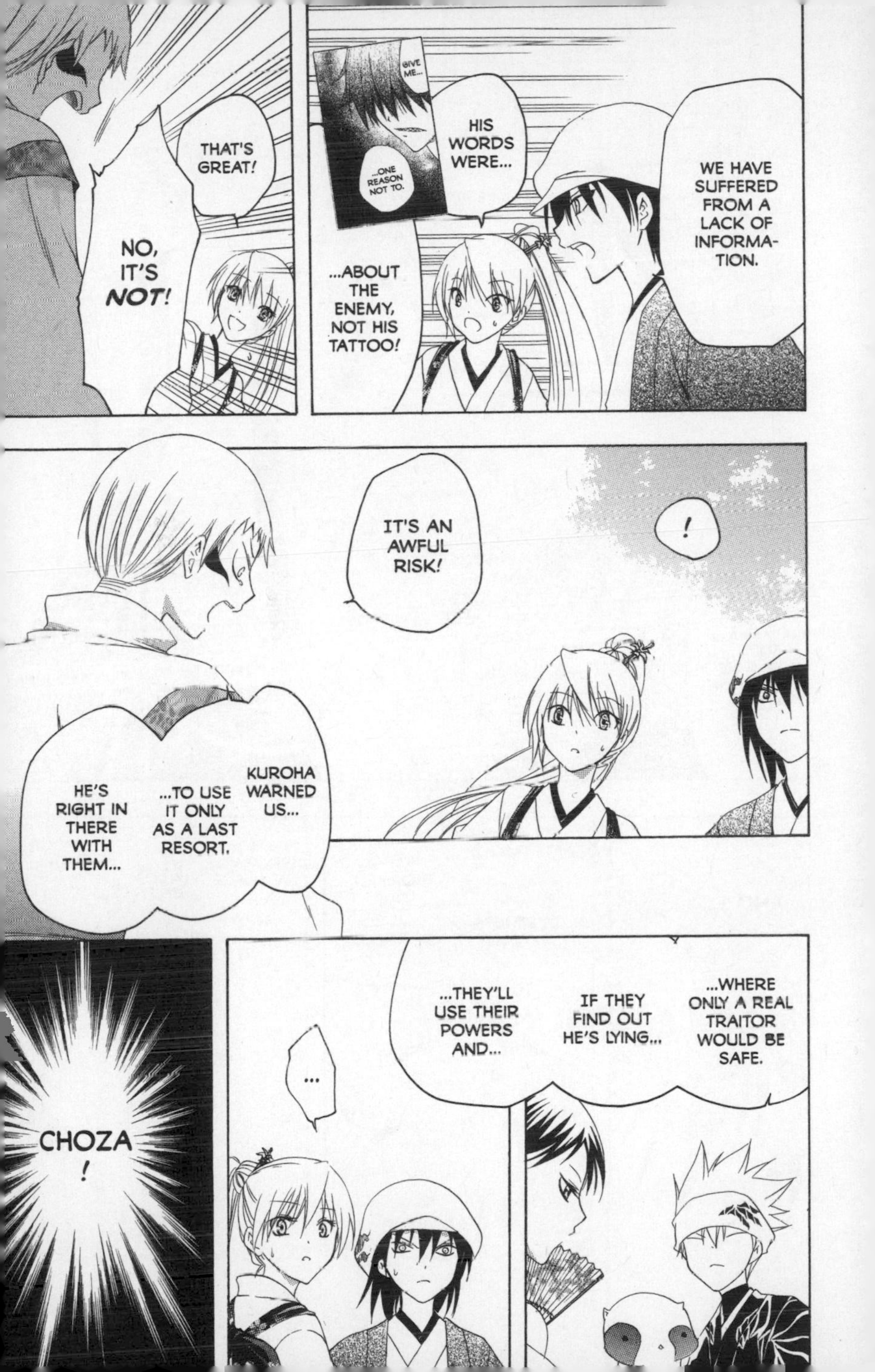
WE HAVE SUFFERED FROM A LACK OF INFORMA-TION.
HIS WORDS WERE...
GIVE ME...
...ONE REASON NOT TO.
...ABOUT THE ENEMY, NOT HIS TATTOO!
THAT'S GREAT!
NO, IT'S *NOT*!
!
IT'S AN AWFUL RISK!
KUROHA WARNED US...
...TO USE IT ONLY AS A LAST RESORT.
HE'S RIGHT IN THERE WITH THEM...
...WHERE ONLY A REAL TRAITOR WOULD BE SAFE.
IF THEY FIND OUT HE'S LYING...
...THEY'LL USE THEIR POWERS AND...
...
CHOZA!

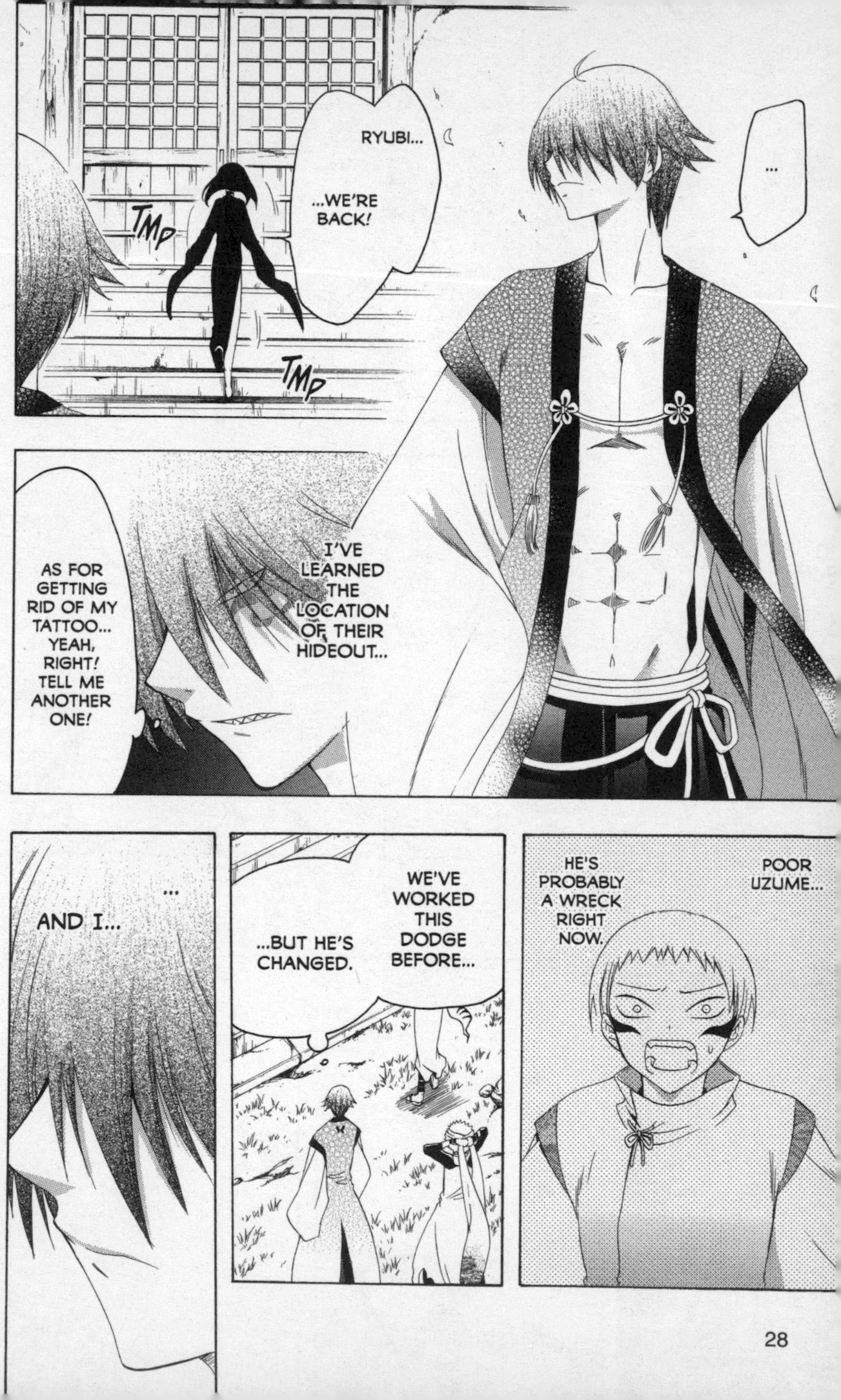
...
RYUBI...
...WE'RE BACK!
TMP
TMP
I'VE LEARNED THE LOCATION OF THEIR HIDEOUT...
AS FOR GETTING RID OF MY TATTOO... YEAH, RIGHT! TELL ME ANOTHER ONE!
POOR UZUME...
HE'S PROBABLY A WRECK RIGHT NOW.
WE'VE WORKED THIS DODGE BEFORE...
...BUT HE'S CHANGED.
...
AND I...

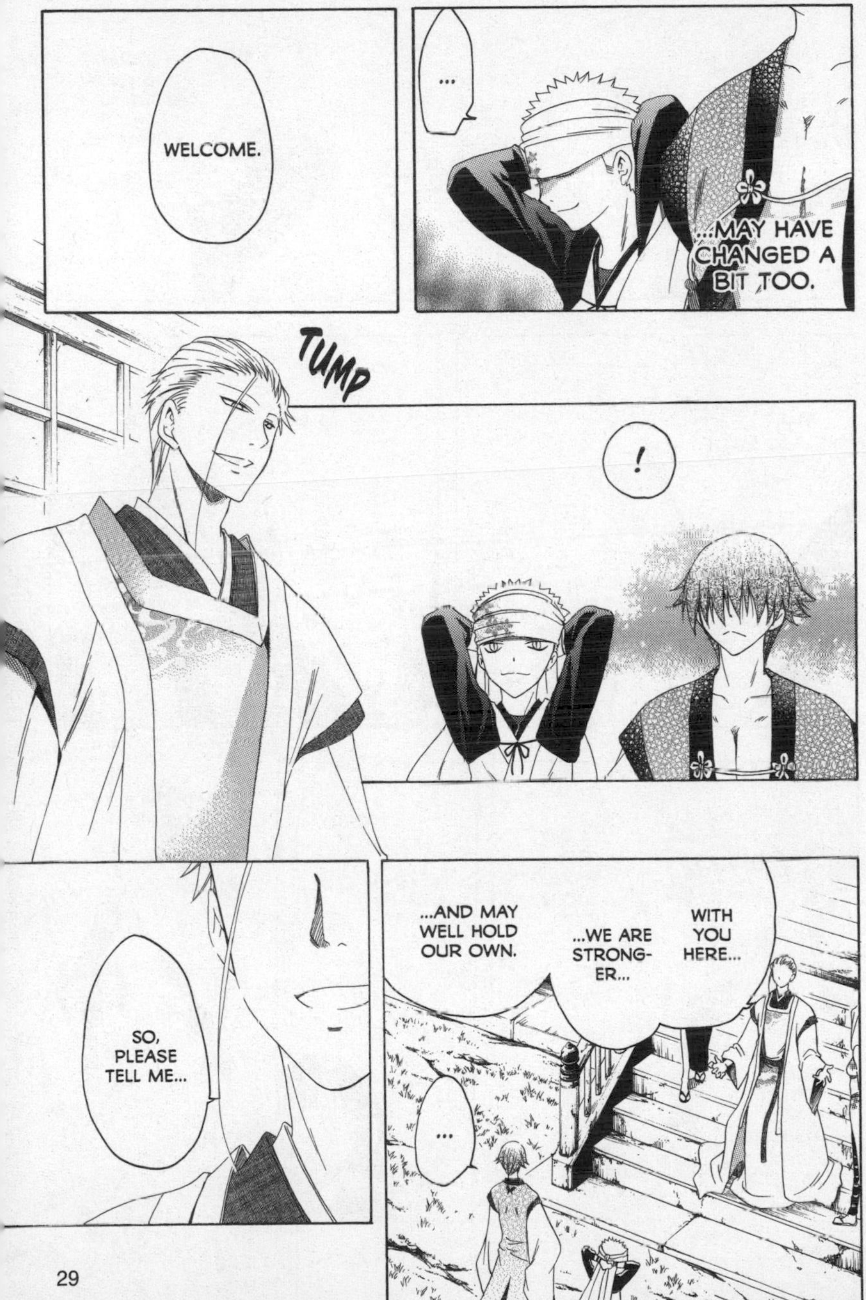
...
...MAY HAVE CHANGED A BIT TOO.
WELCOME.
TUMP
!
WITH YOU HERE...
...WE ARE STRONGER...
...AND MAY WELL HOLD OUR OWN.
...
SO, PLEASE TELL ME...

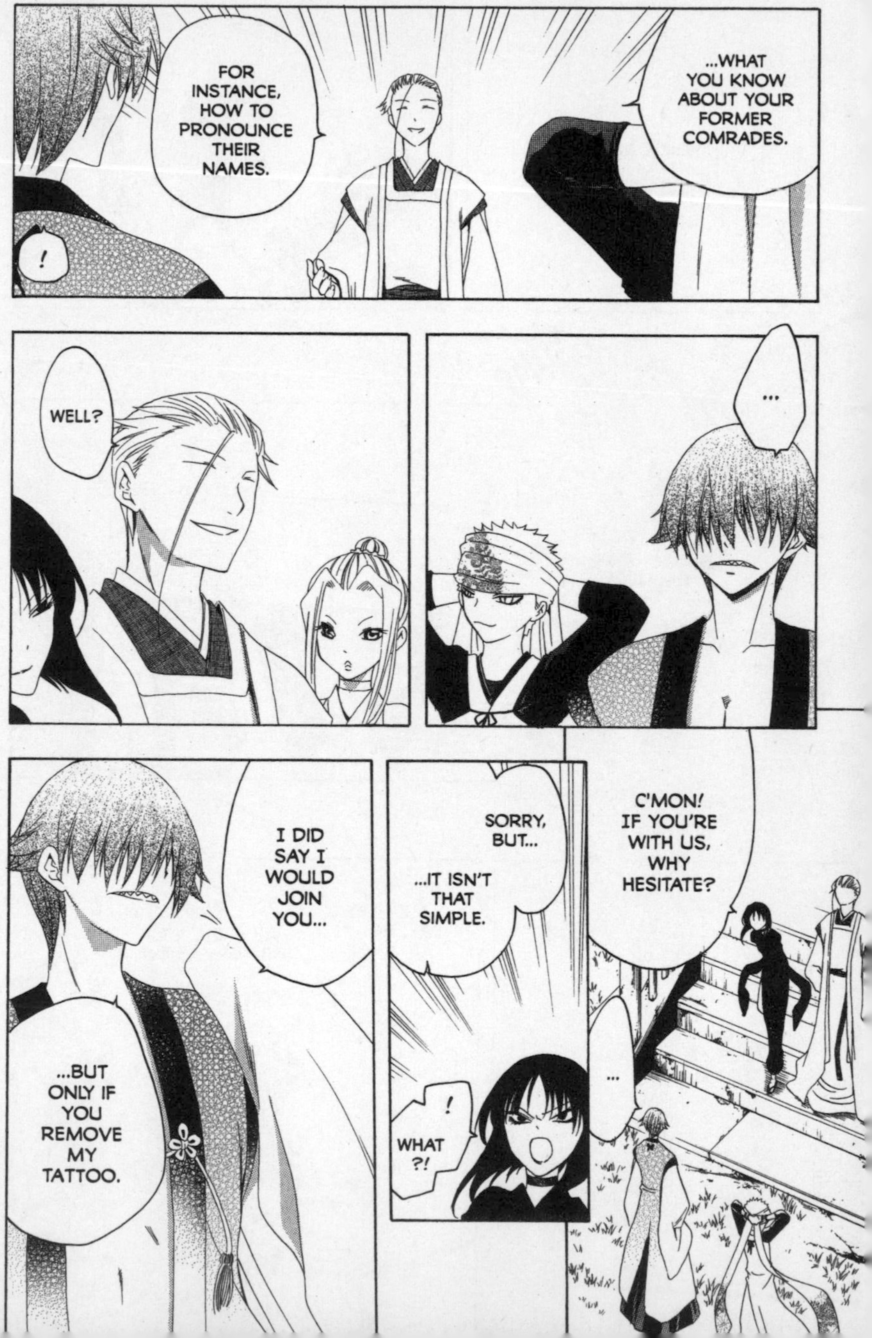
...WHAT YOU KNOW ABOUT YOUR FORMER COMRADES.
FOR INSTANCE, HOW TO PRONOUNCE THEIR NAMES.
!
...
WELL?
C'MON! IF YOU'RE WITH US, WHY HESITATE?
...
SORRY, BUT...
...IT ISN'T THAT SIMPLE.
!
WHAT ?!
I DID SAY I WOULD JOIN YOU...
...BUT ONLY IF YOU REMOVE MY TATTOO.

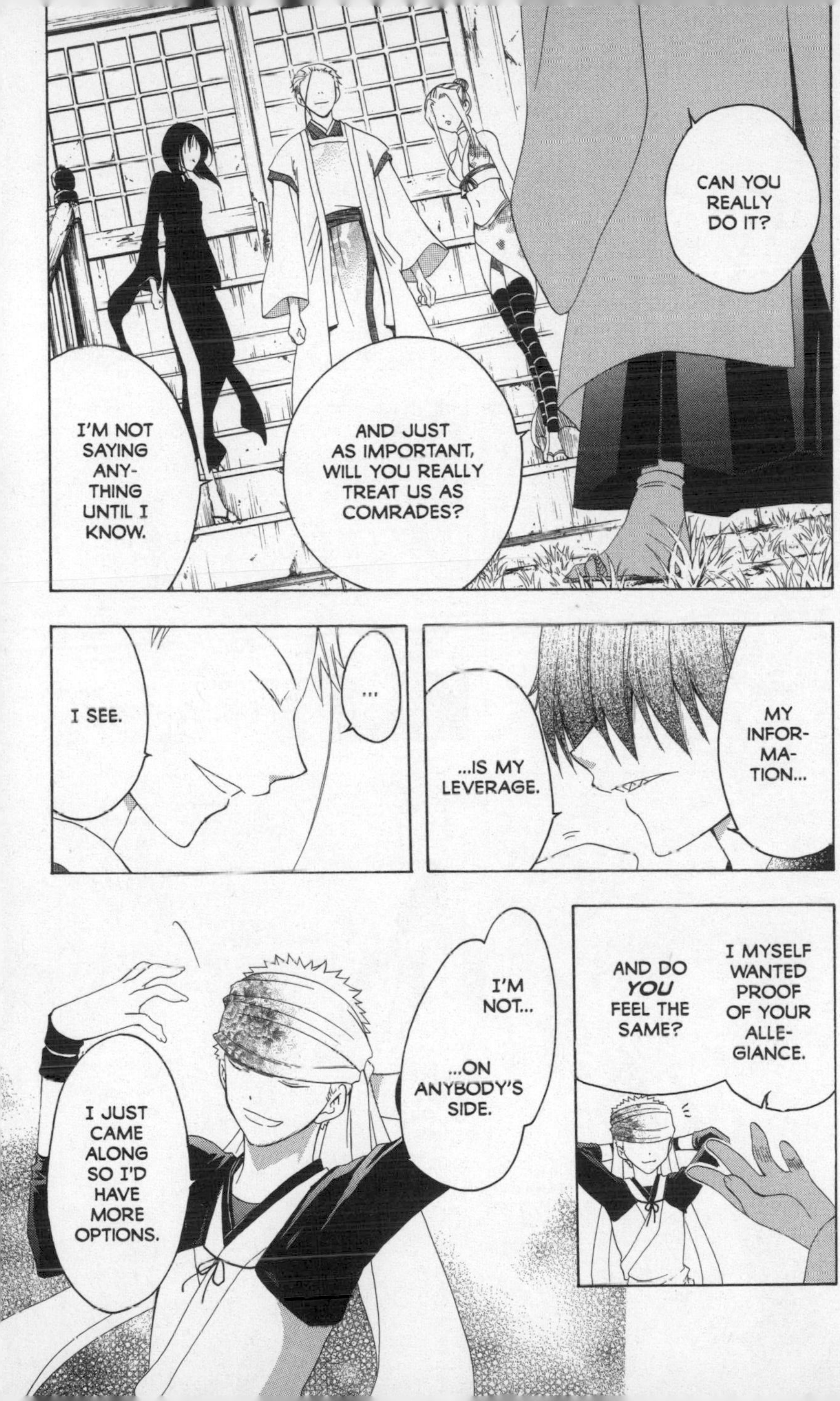
CAN YOU REALLY DO IT?
AND JUST AS IMPORTANT, WILL YOU REALLY TREAT US AS COMRADES?
I'M NOT SAYING ANY-THING UNTIL I KNOW.
MY INFOR-MA-TION...
...IS MY LEVERAGE.
...
I SEE.
I MYSELF WANTED PROOF OF YOUR ALLE-GIANCE.
AND DO *YOU* FEEL THE SAME?
I'M NOT...
...ON ANYBODY'S SIDE.
I JUST CAME ALONG SO I'D HAVE MORE OPTIONS.

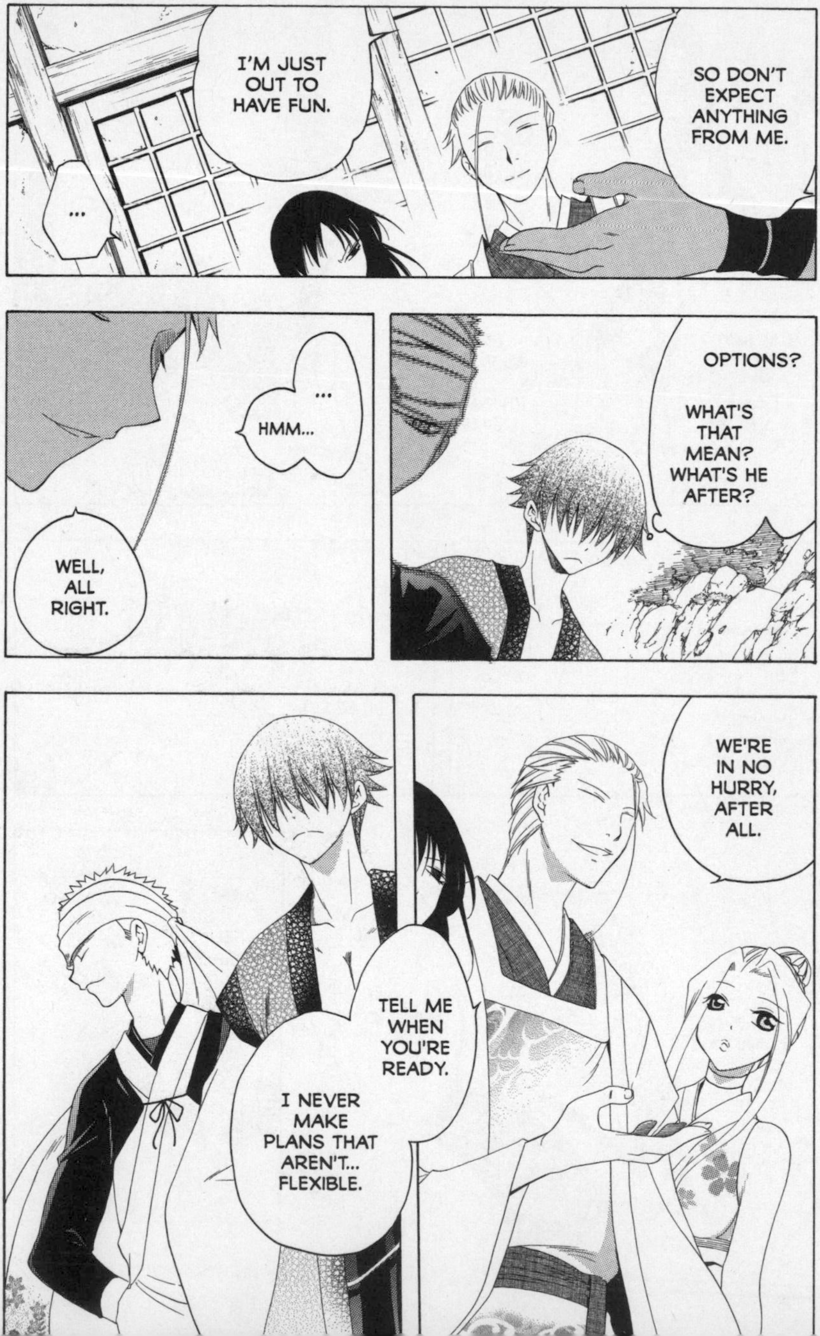
SO DON'T EXPECT ANYTHING FROM ME.
I'M JUST OUT TO HAVE FUN.
...
OPTIONS?
WHAT'S THAT MEAN? WHAT'S HE AFTER?
... HMM...
WELL, ALL RIGHT.
WE'RE IN NO HURRY, AFTER ALL.
TELL ME WHEN YOU'RE READY.
I NEVER MAKE PLANS THAT AREN'T... FLEXIBLE.

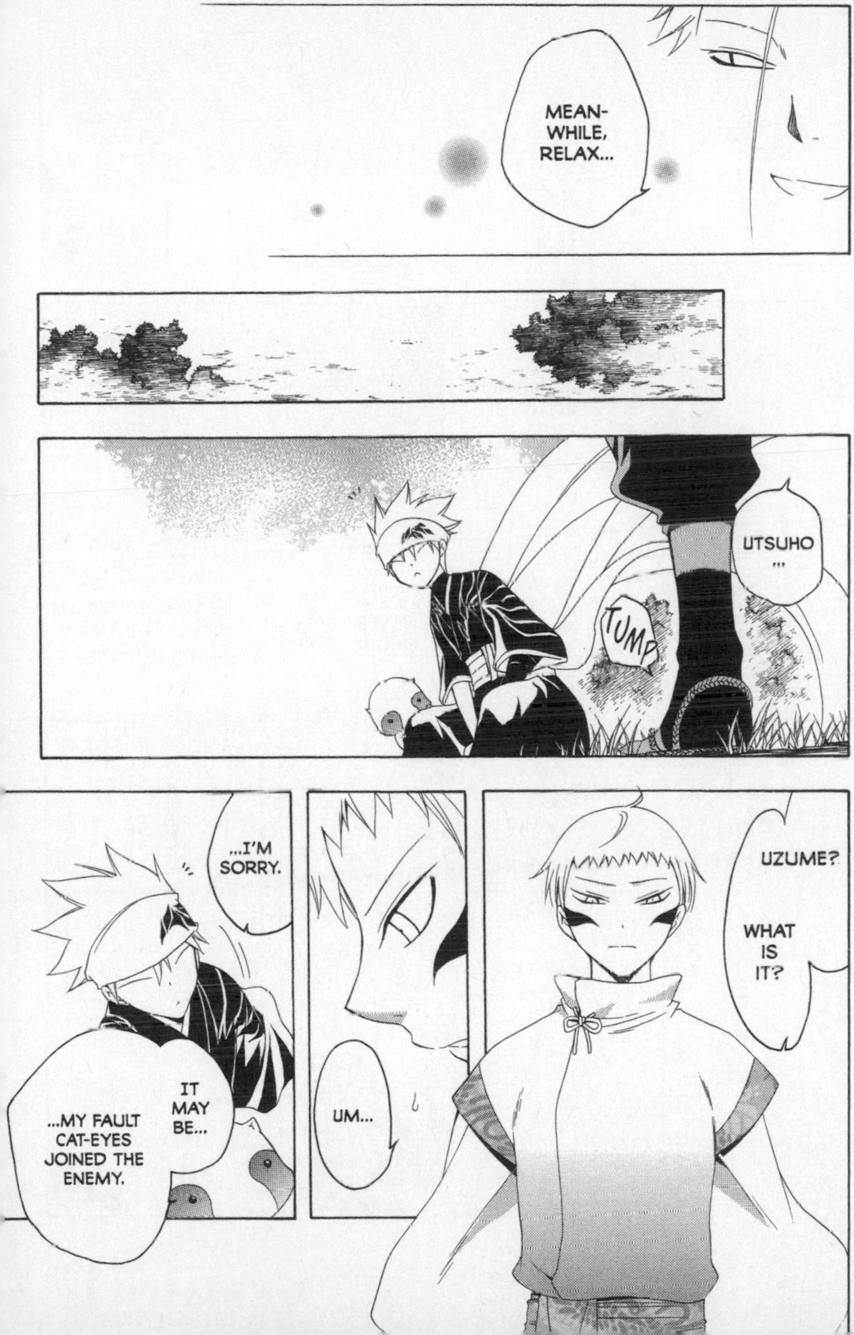
MEAN-WHILE, RELAX...
UTSUHO ...
TUMP
UZUME? WHAT IS IT?
UM...
...I'M SORRY.
IT MAY BE...
...MY FAULT CAT-EYES JOINED THE ENEMY.

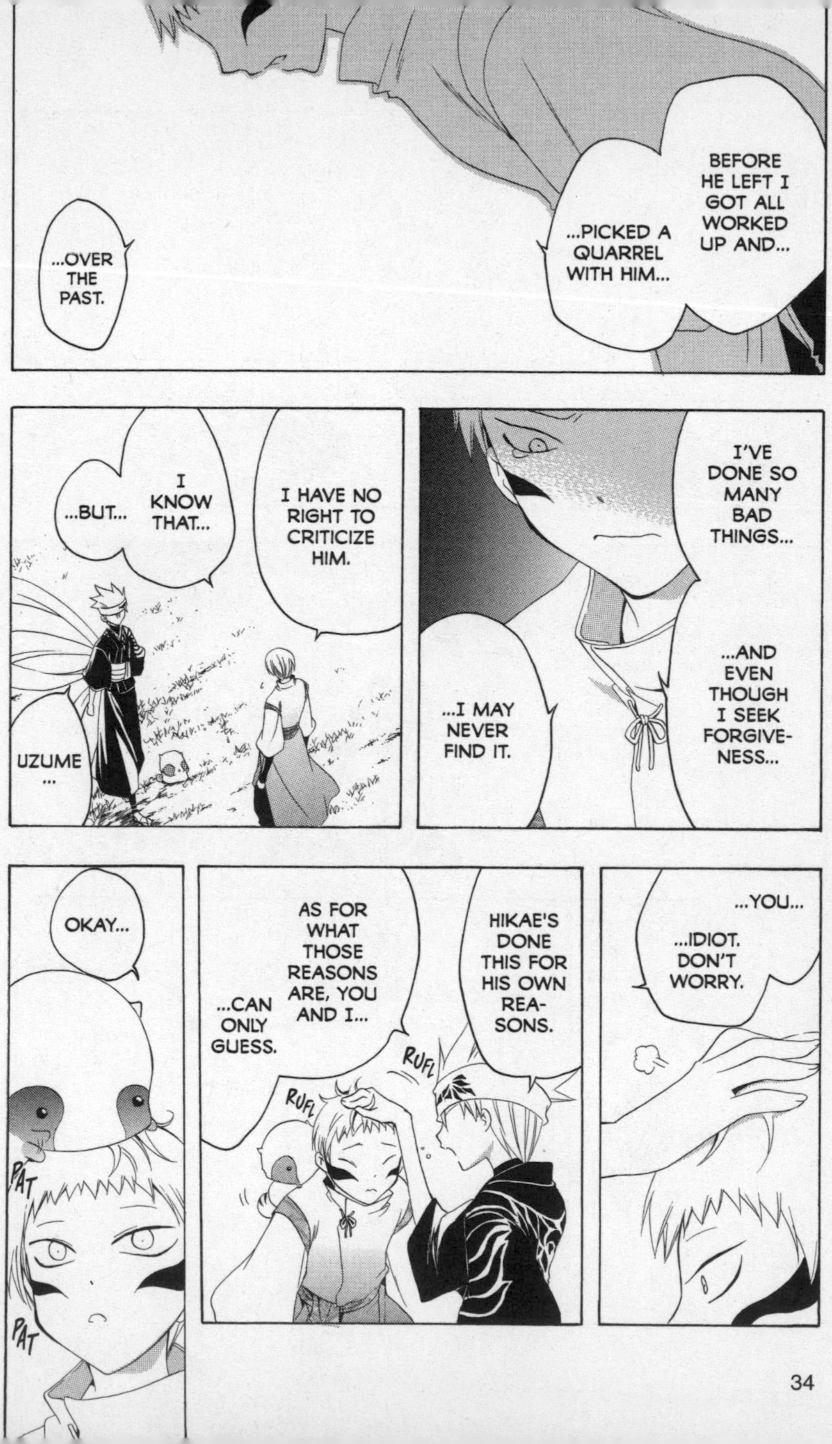
BEFORE HE LEFT I GOT ALL WORKED UP AND...
...PICKED A QUARREL WITH HIM...
...OVER THE PAST.
I'VE DONE SO MANY BAD THINGS...
...AND EVEN THOUGH I SEEK FORGIVE-NESS...
...I MAY NEVER FIND IT.
I HAVE NO RIGHT TO CRITICIZE HIM.
I KNOW THAT...
...BUT...
UZUME ...
...YOU...
...IDIOT. DON'T WORRY.
HIKAE'S DONE THIS FOR HIS OWN REA-SONS.
RUFL
RUFL
AS FOR WHAT THOSE REASONS ARE, YOU AND I...
...CAN ONLY GUESS.
OKAY...
PAT
PAT

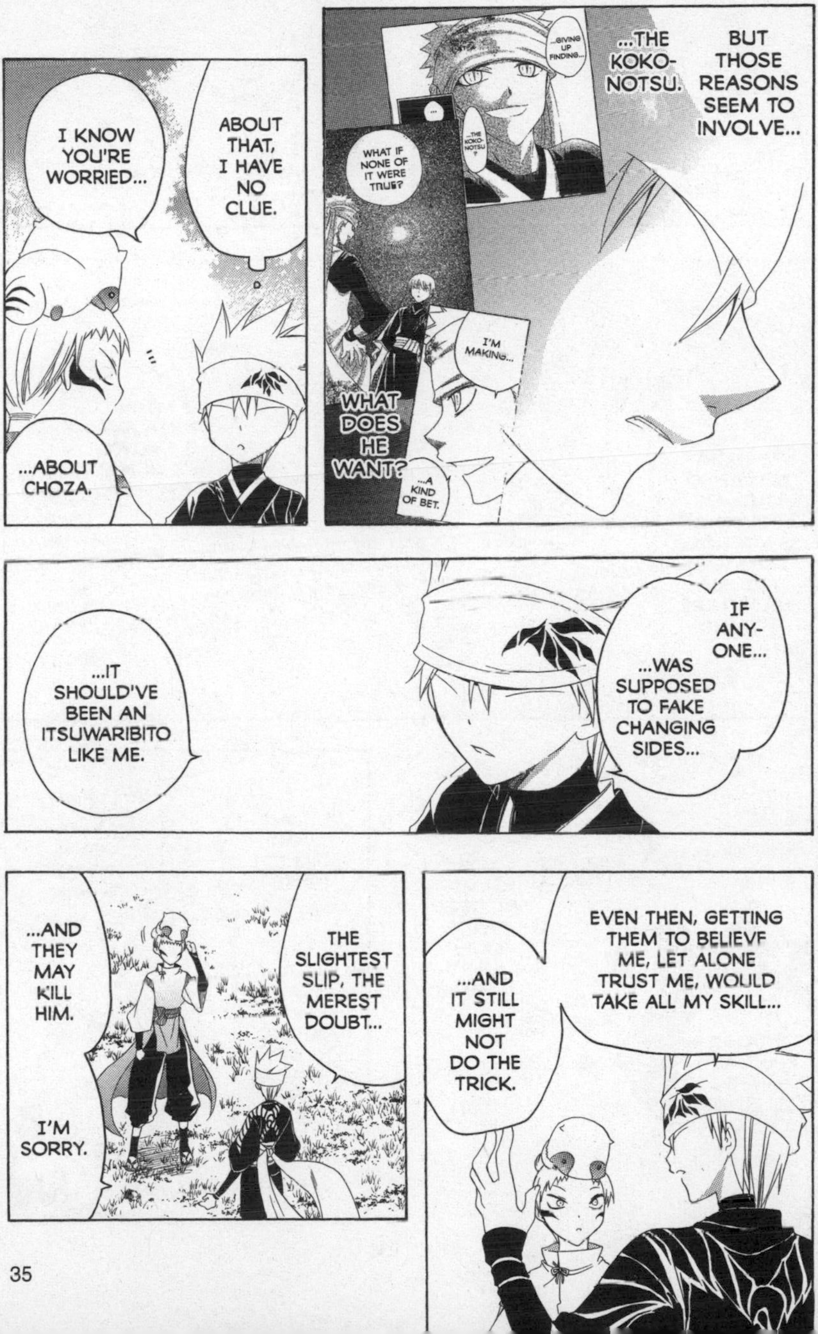
BUT THOSE REASONS SEEM TO INVOLVE...
...THE KOKO-NOTSU.
...GIVING UP FINDING...
...
...THE KOKO-NOTSU?
WHAT IF NONE OF IT WERE TRUE?
I'M MAKING...
WHAT DOES HE WANT?
...A KIND OF BET.
ABOUT THAT, I HAVE NO CLUE.
I KNOW YOU'RE WORRIED...
...ABOUT CHOZA.
IF ANY-ONE...
...WAS SUPPOSED TO FAKE CHANGING SIDES...
...IT SHOULD'VE BEEN AN ITSUWARIBITO LIKE ME.
EVEN THEN, GETTING THEM TO BELIEVF ME, LET ALONE TRUST ME, WOULD TAKE ALL MY SKILL...
...AND IT STILL MIGHT NOT DO THE TRICK.
THE SLIGHTEST SLIP, THE MEREST DOUBT...
...AND THEY MAY KILL HIM.
I'M SORRY.

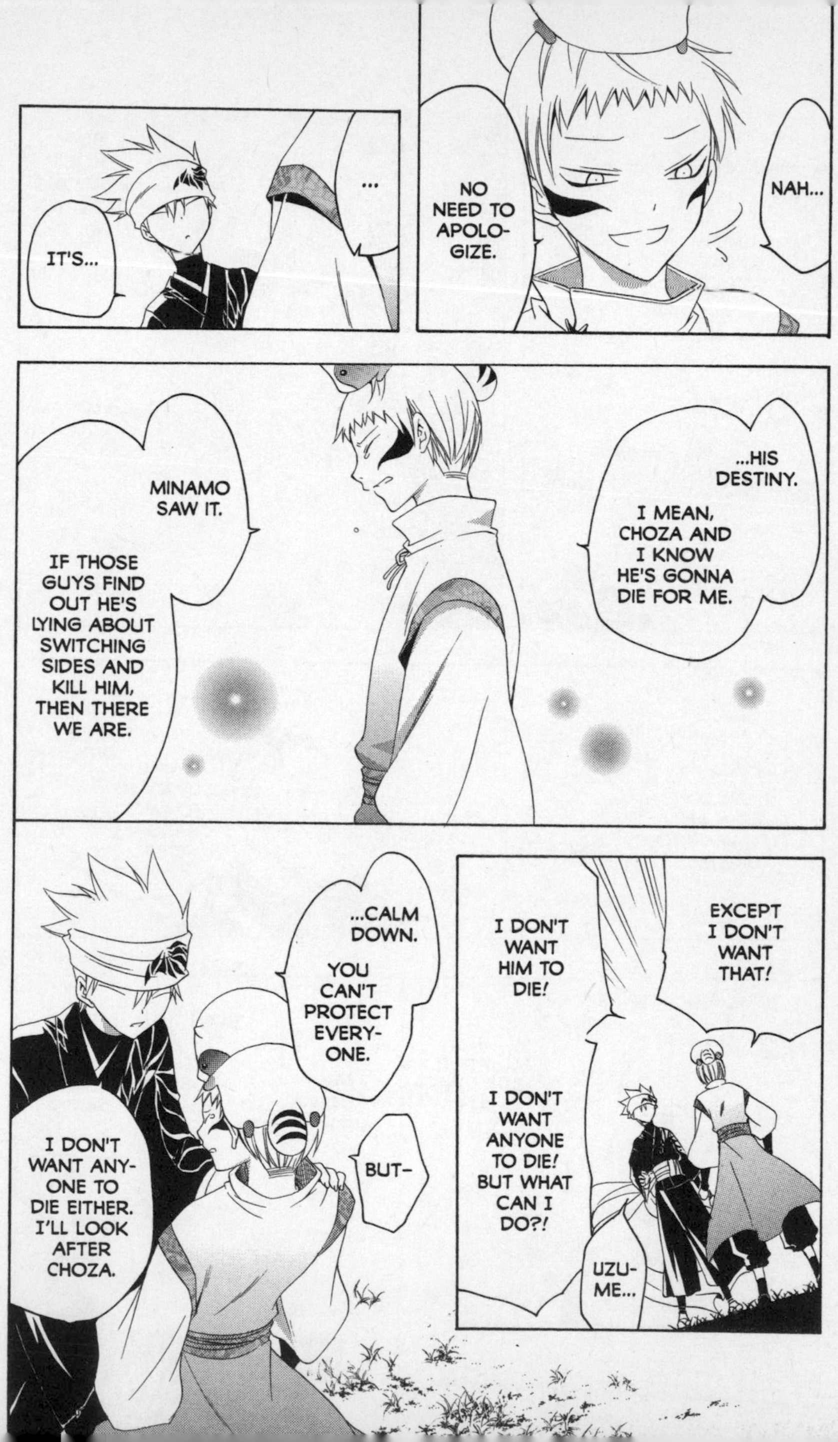
NAH...
NO NEED TO APOLOGIZE.
...
IT'S...
...HIS DESTINY.
I MEAN, CHOZA AND I KNOW HE'S GONNA DIE FOR ME.
MINAMO SAW IT.
IF THOSE GUYS FIND OUT HE'S LYING ABOUT SWITCHING SIDES AND KILL HIM, THEN THERE WE ARE.
EXCEPT I DON'T WANT THAT!
I DON'T WANT HIM TO DIE!
I DON'T WANT ANYONE TO DIE! BUT WHAT CAN I DO?!
UZU-ME...
...CALM DOWN.
YOU CAN'T PROTECT EVERY-ONE.
BUT-
I DON'T WANT ANY-ONE TO DIE EITHER. I'LL LOOK AFTER CHOZA.

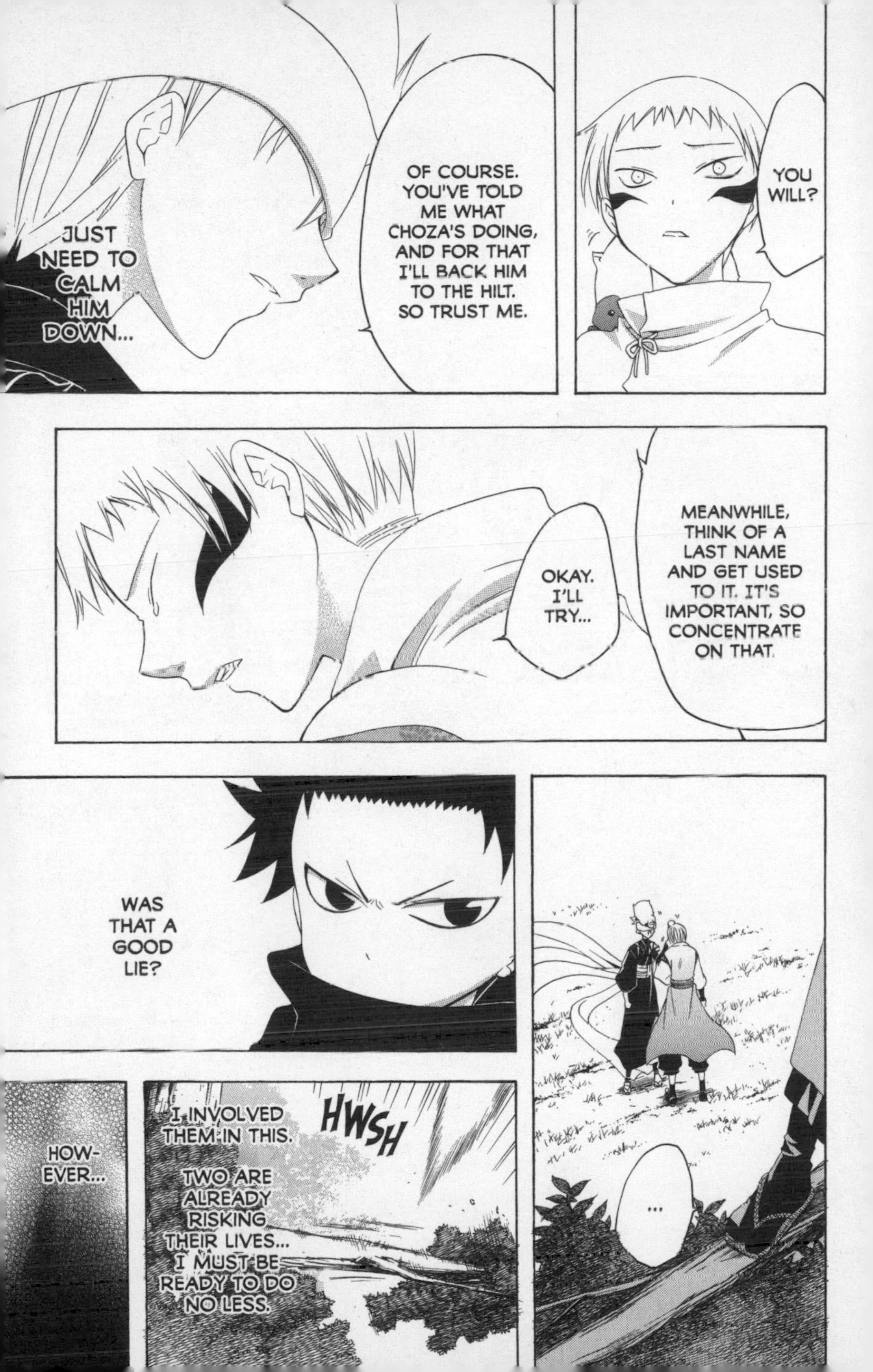
YOU WILL?
OF COURSE. YOU'VE TOLD ME WHAT CHOZA'S DOING, AND FOR THAT I'LL BACK HIM TO THE HILT. SO TRUST ME.
JUST NEED TO CALM HIM DOWN...
MEANWHILE, THINK OF A LAST NAME AND GET USED TO IT. IT'S IMPORTANT, SO CONCENTRATE ON THAT.
OKAY. I'LL TRY...
...
WAS THAT A GOOD LIE?
I INVOLVED THEM IN THIS.
HWSH
TWO ARE ALREADY RISKING THEIR LIVES... I MUST BE READY TO DO NO LESS.
HOW-EVER...

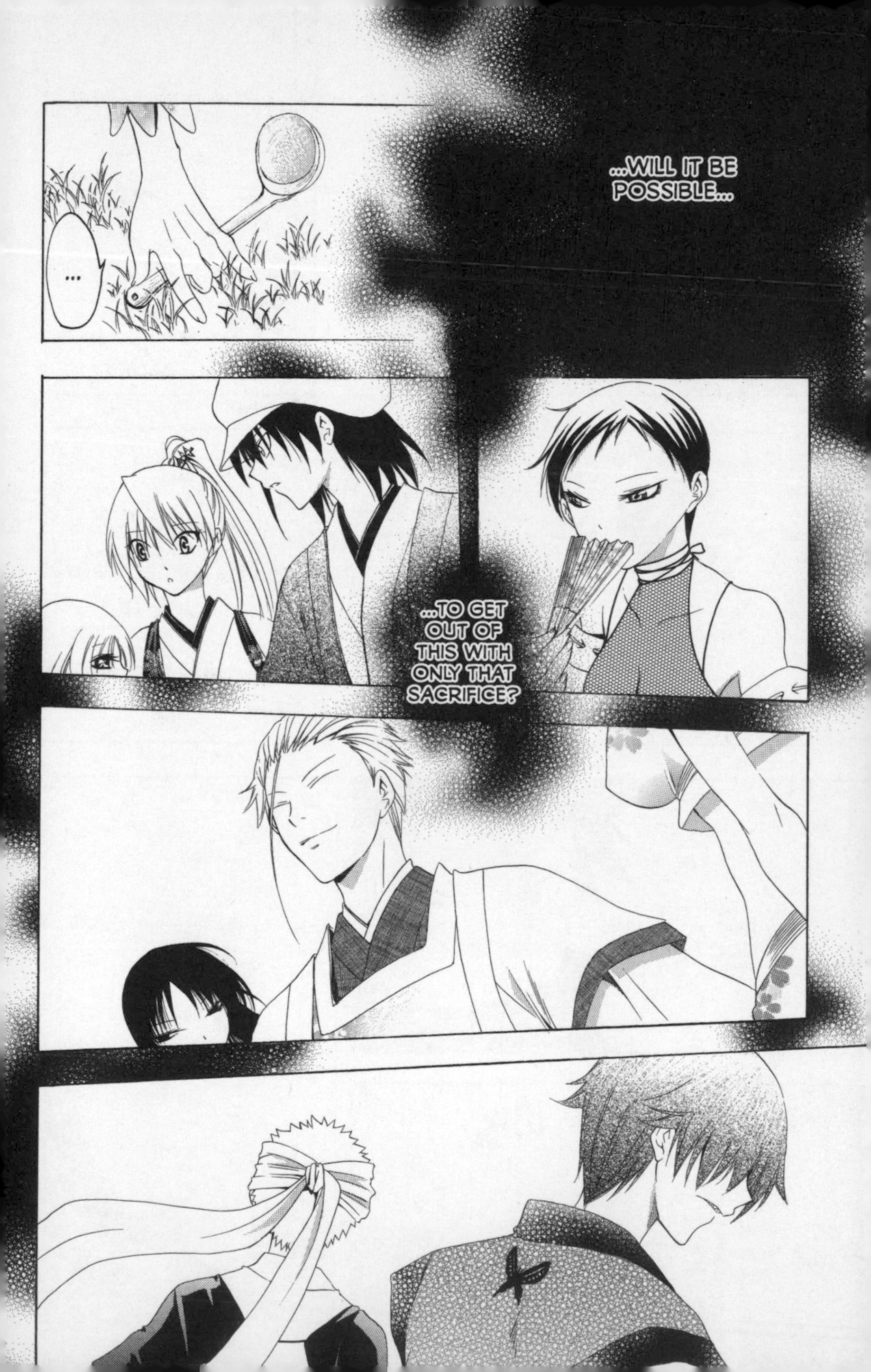
...WILL IT BE POSSIBLE...
...
...TO GET OUT OF THIS WITH ONLY THAT SACRIFICE?

Chapter 130 Shopping

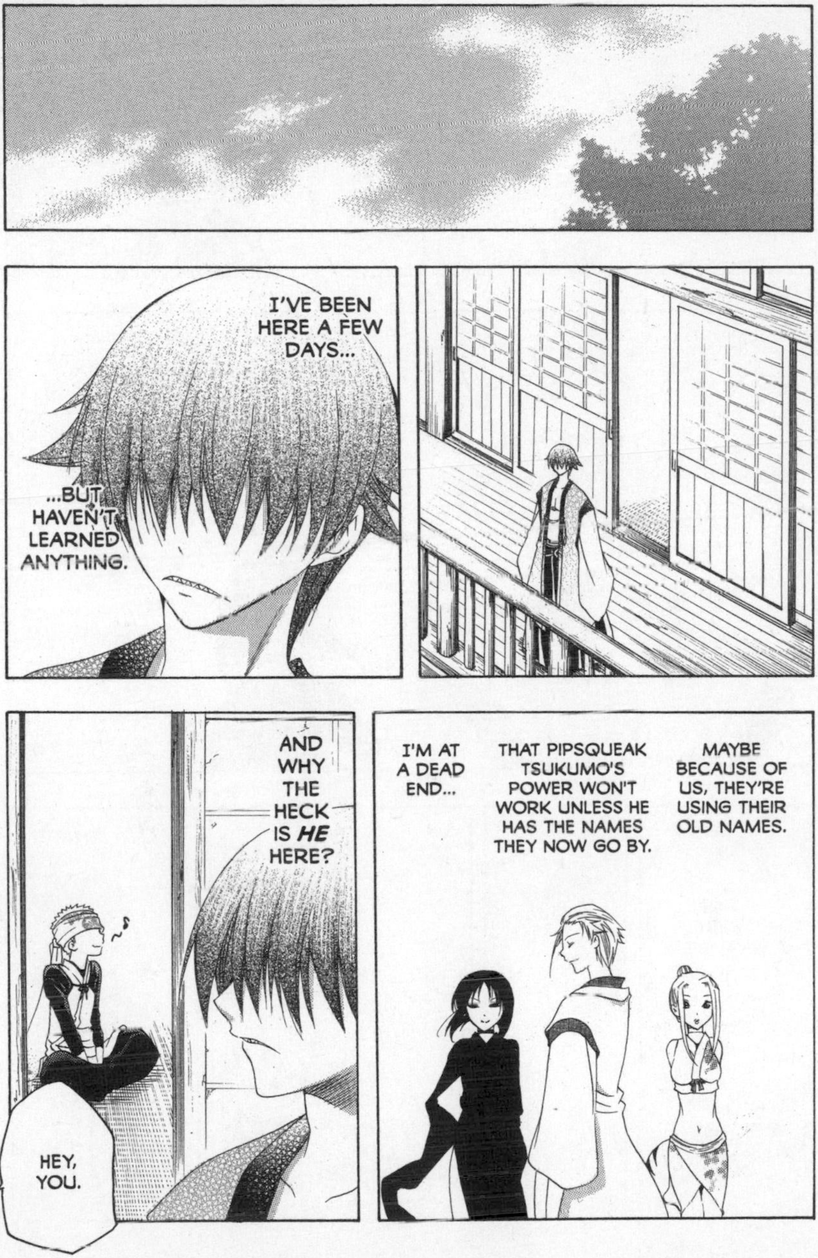
I'VE BEEN HERE A FEW DAYS...
...BUT HAVEN'T LEARNED ANYTHING.
MAYBE BECAUSE OF US, THEY'RE USING THEIR OLD NAMES.
THAT PIPSQUEAK TSUKUMO'S POWER WON'T WORK UNLESS HE HAS THE NAMES THEY NOW GO BY.
I'M AT A DEAD END...
AND WHY THE HECK IS *HE* HERE?
HEY, YOU.

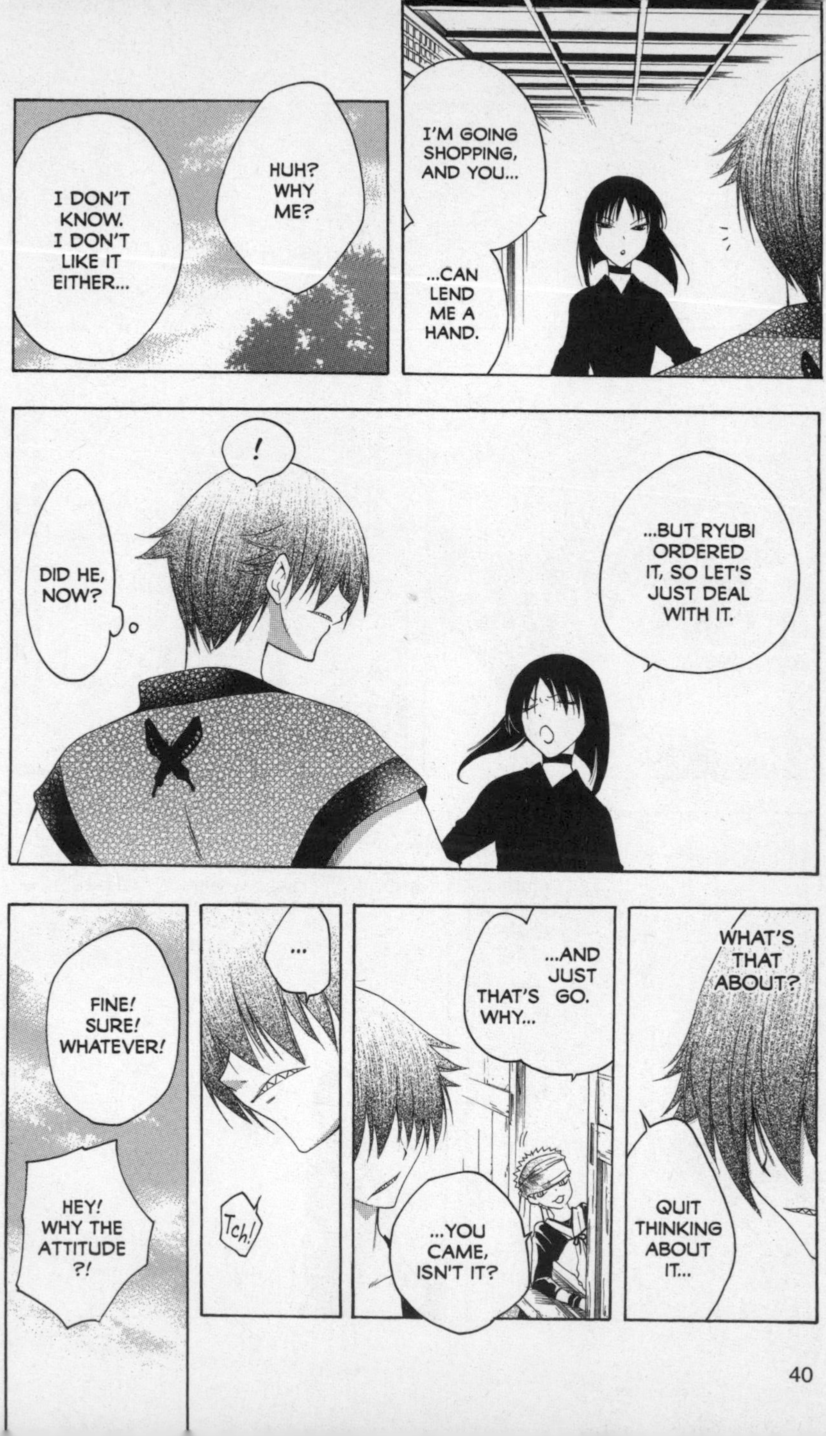
I'M GOING SHOPPING, AND YOU...
...CAN LEND ME A HAND.
HUH? WHY ME?
I DON'T KNOW. I DON'T LIKE IT EITHER...
...BUT RYUBI ORDERED IT, SO LET'S JUST DEAL WITH IT.
!
DID HE, NOW?
WHAT'S THAT ABOUT?
QUIT THINKING ABOUT IT...
...AND JUST GO.
THAT'S WHY...
...YOU CAME, ISN'T IT?
...
Tch!
FINE! SURE! WHATEVER!
HEY! WHY THE ATTITUDE ?!

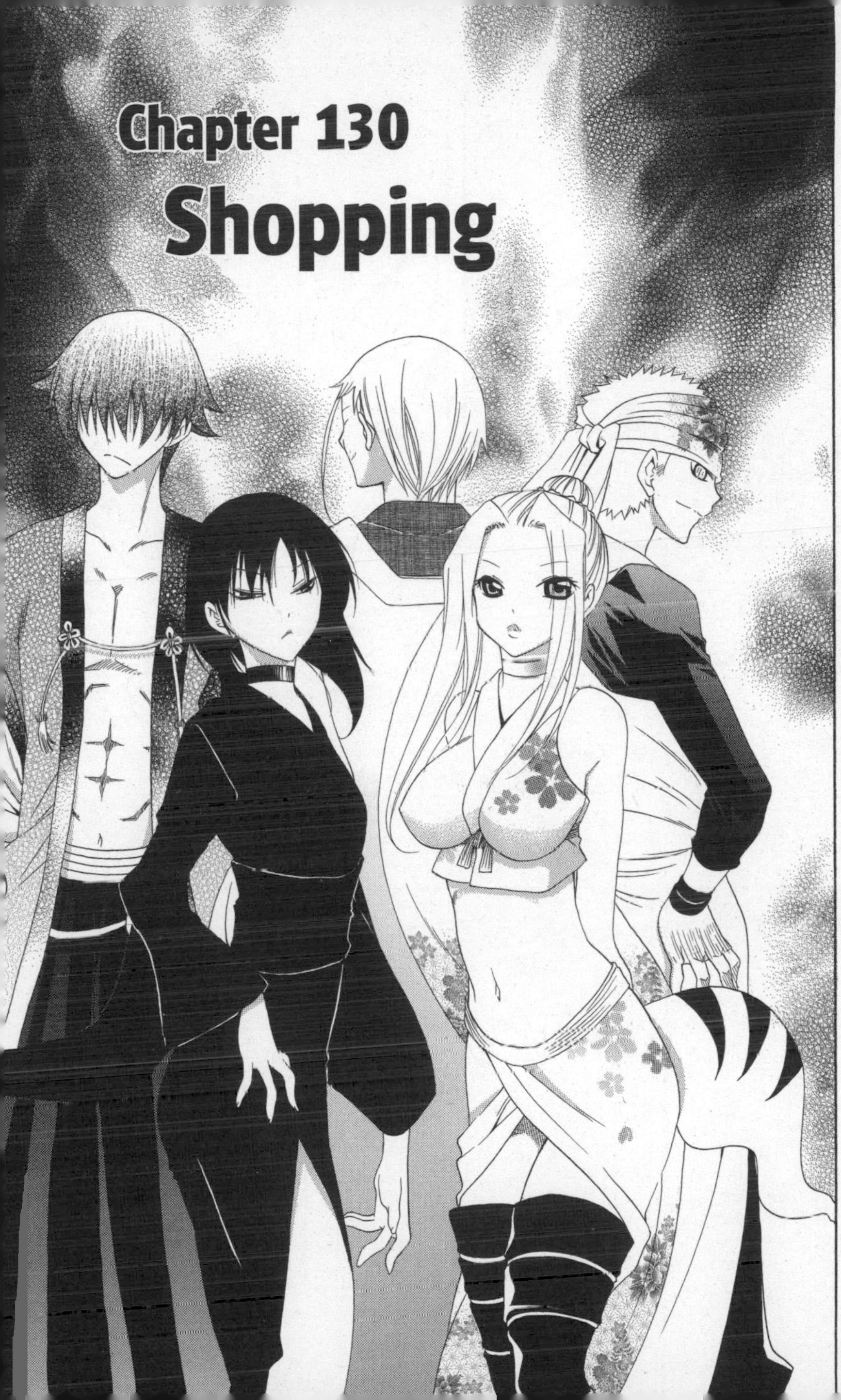
Chapter 130
Shopping

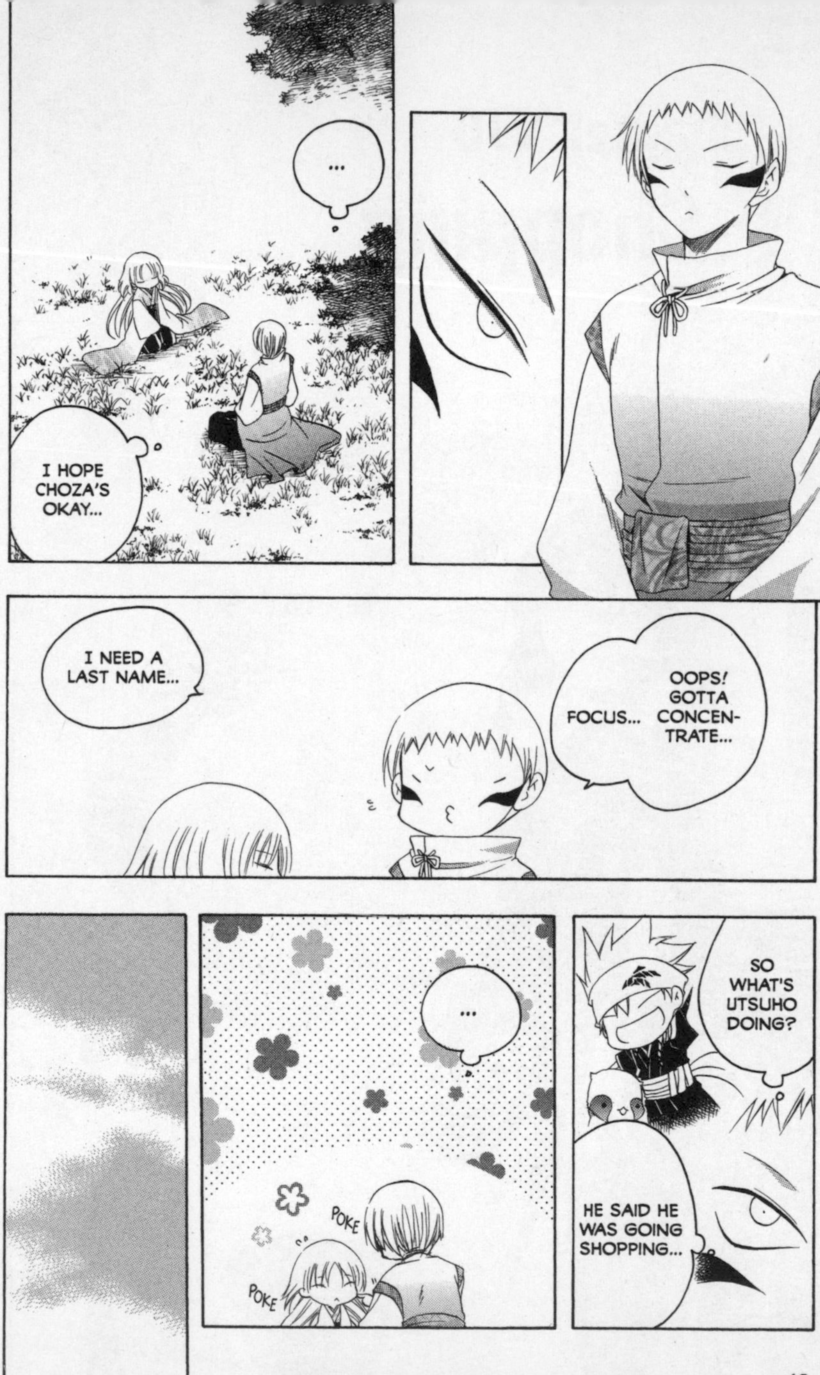
...
I HOPE CHOZA'S OKAY...
OOPS! GOTTA CONCENTRATE...
FOCUS...
I NEED A LAST NAME...
SO WHAT'S UTSUHO DOING?
HE SAID HE WAS GOING SHOPPING...
...
POKE
POKE

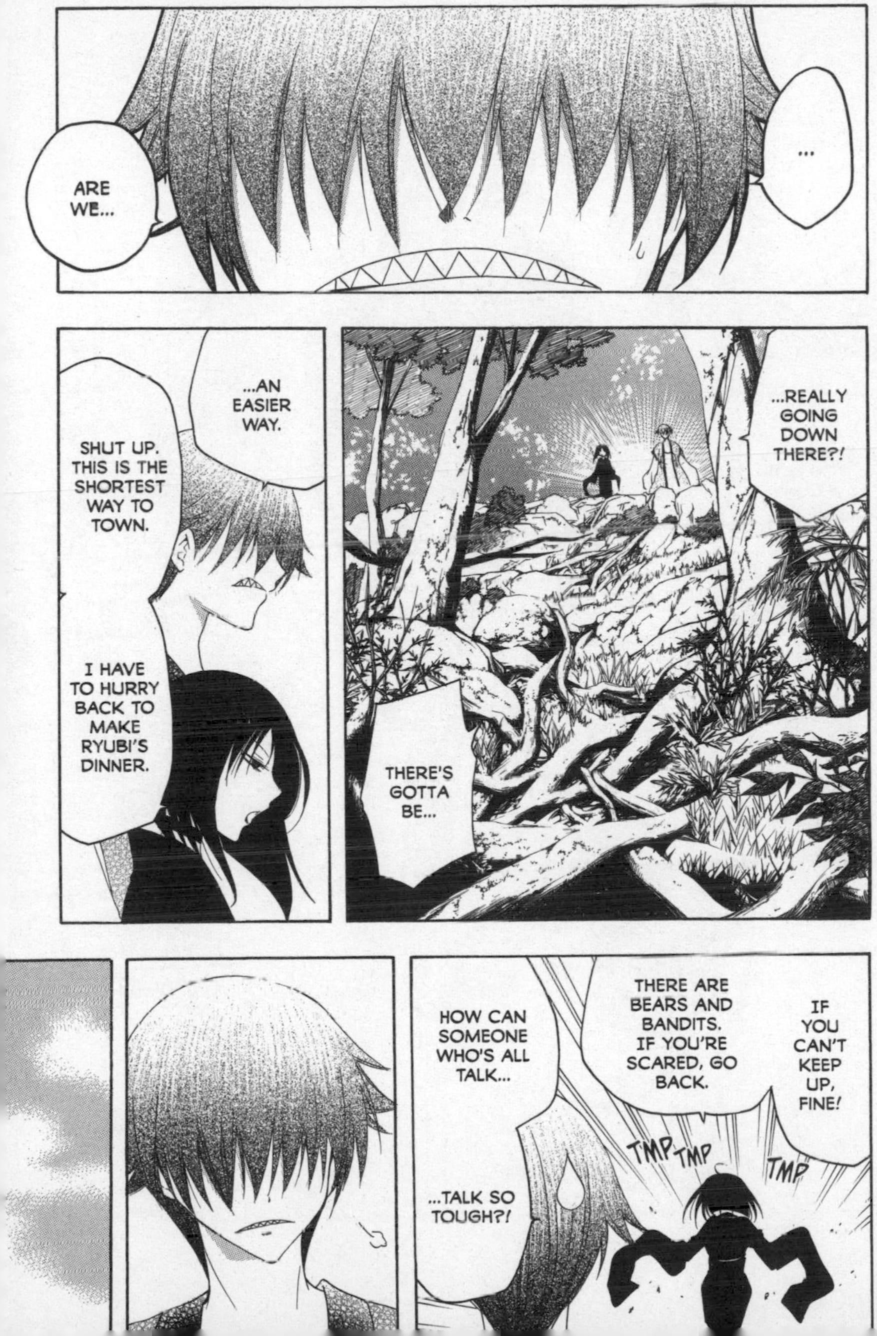
...
ARE WE...
...REALLY GOING DOWN THERE?!
THERE'S GOTTA BE...
...AN EASIER WAY.
SHUT UP. THIS IS THE SHORTEST WAY TO TOWN.
I HAVE TO HURRY BACK TO MAKE RYUBI'S DINNER.
IF YOU CAN'T KEEP UP, FINE!
THERE ARE BEARS AND BANDITS. IF YOU'RE SCARED, GO BACK.
TMP TMP TMP
HOW CAN SOMEONE WHO'S ALL TALK...
...TALK SO TOUGH?!

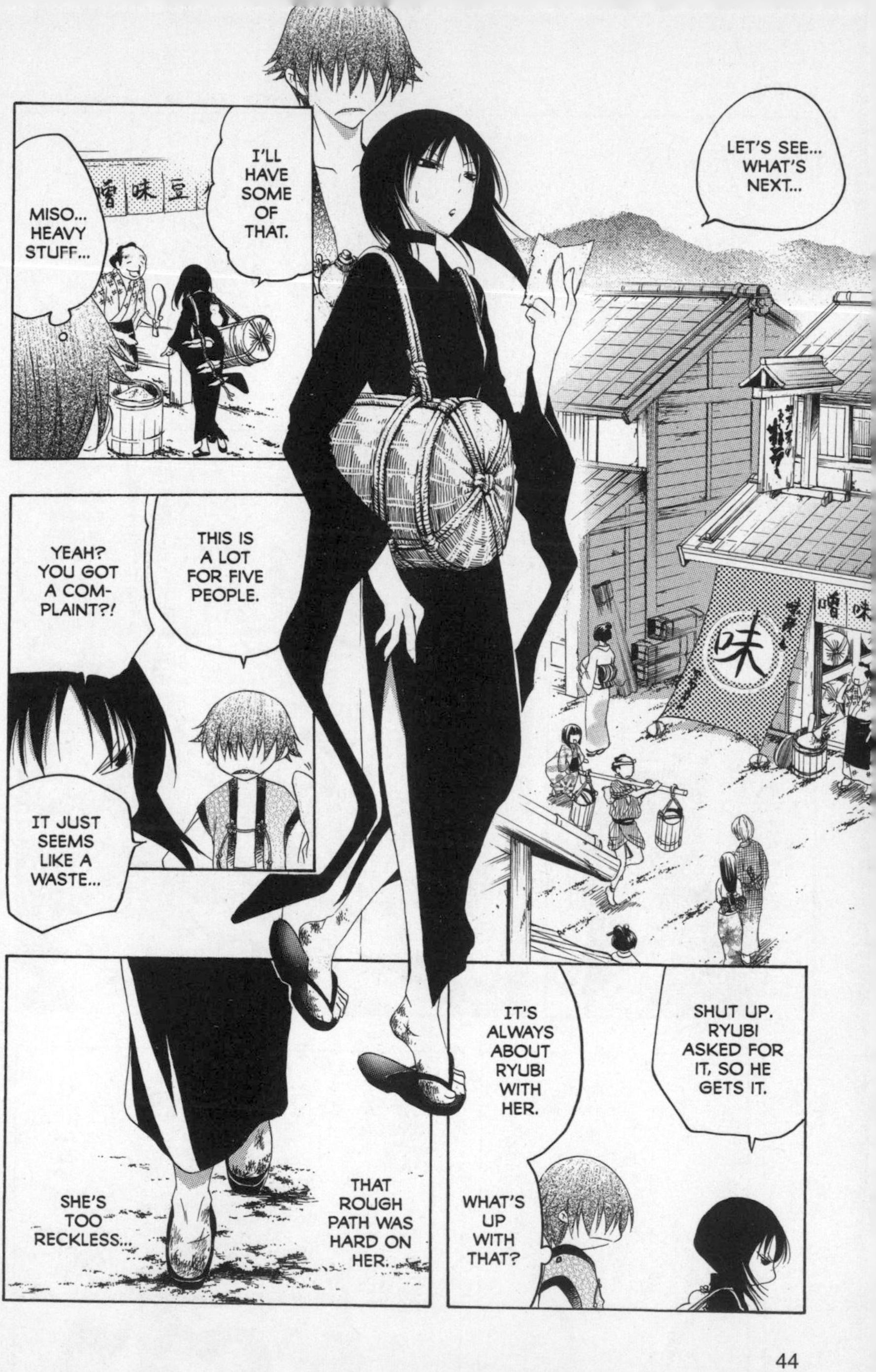
LET'S SEE... WHAT'S NEXT...
I'LL HAVE SOME OF THAT.
MISO... HEAVY STUFF...
THIS IS A LOT FOR FIVE PEOPLE.
YEAH? YOU GOT A COM-PLAINT?!
IT JUST SEEMS LIKE A WASTE...
SHUT UP. RYUBI ASKED FOR IT, SO HE GETS IT.
IT'S ALWAYS ABOUT RYUBI WITH HER.
WHAT'S UP WITH THAT?
THAT ROUGH PATH WAS HARD ON HER.
SHE'S TOO RECKLESS...

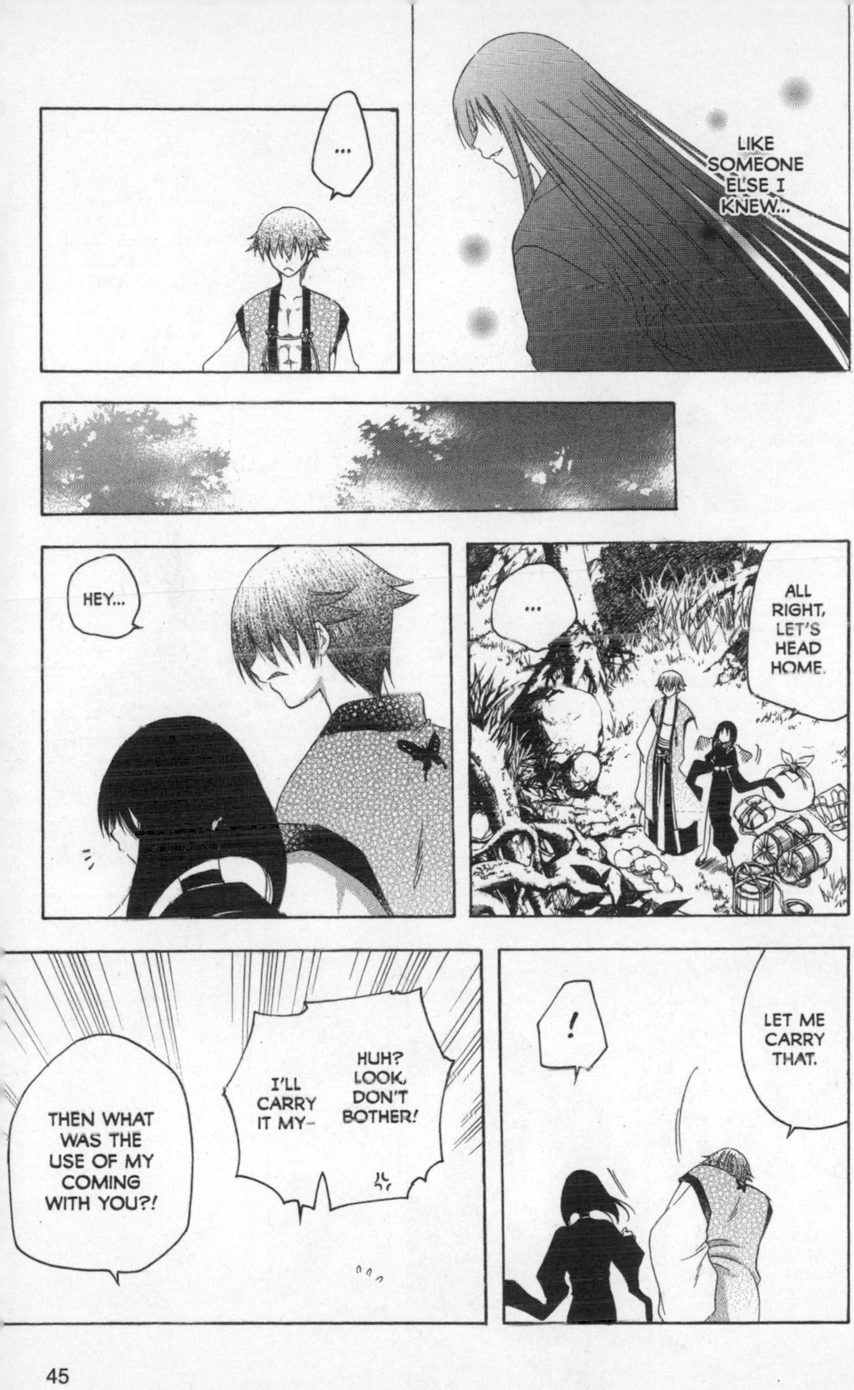
LIKE SOMEONE ELSE I KNEW...
...
ALL RIGHT, LET'S HEAD HOME.
...
HEY...
LET ME CARRY THAT.
!
HUH? LOOK, DON'T BOTHER!
I'LL CARRY IT MY-
THEN WHAT WAS THE USE OF MY COMING WITH YOU?!

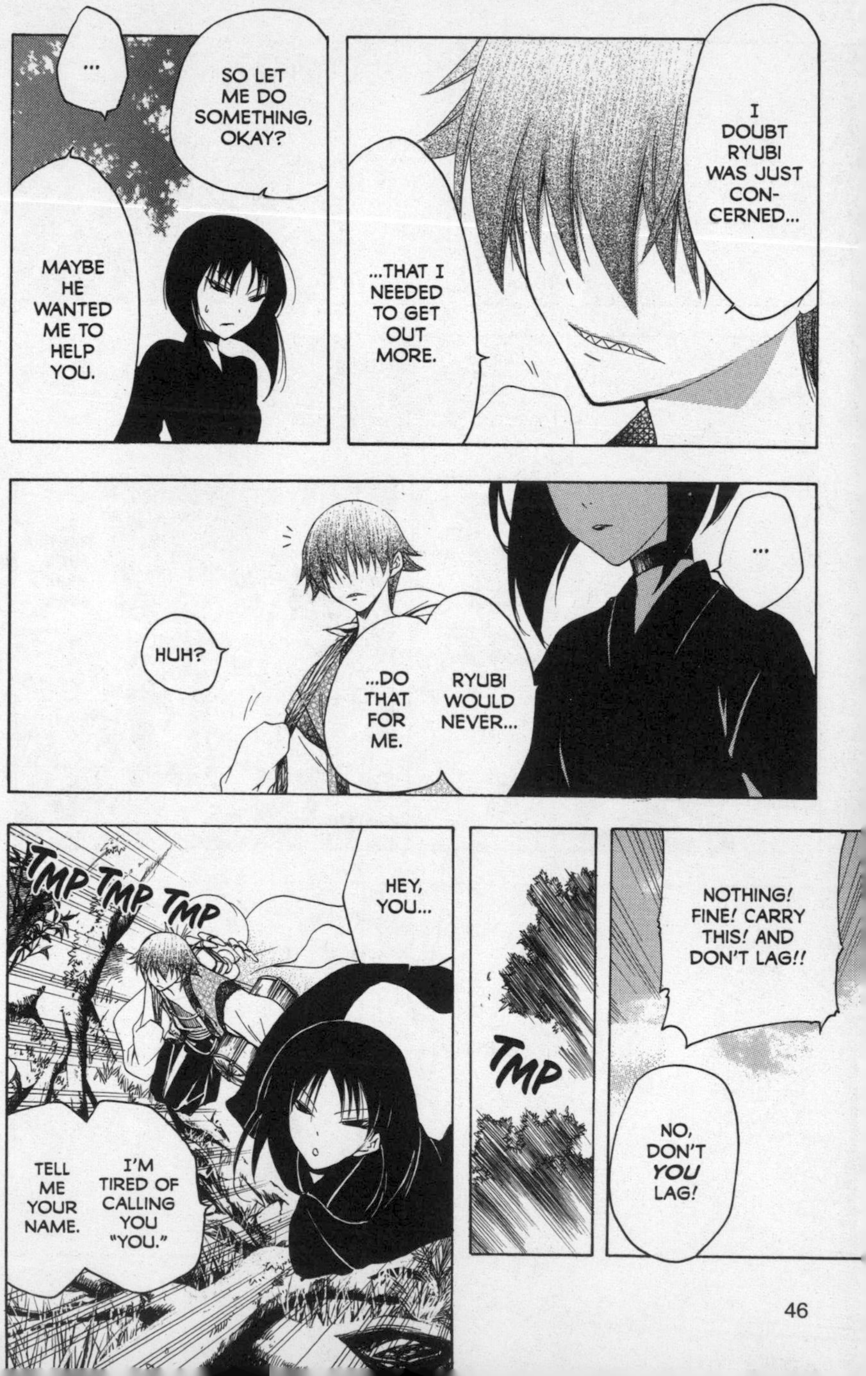
I DOUBT RYUBI WAS JUST CON-CERNED...
...THAT I NEEDED TO GET OUT MORE.
SO LET ME DO SOMETHING, OKAY?
...
MAYBE HE WANTED ME TO HELP YOU.
...
RYUBI WOULD NEVER...
...DO THAT FOR ME.
HUH?
NOTHING! FINE! CARRY THIS! AND DON'T LAG!!
NO, DON'T *YOU* LAG!
TMP
HEY, YOU...
TMP TMP TMP
I'M TIRED OF CALLING YOU "YOU."
TELL ME YOUR NAME.

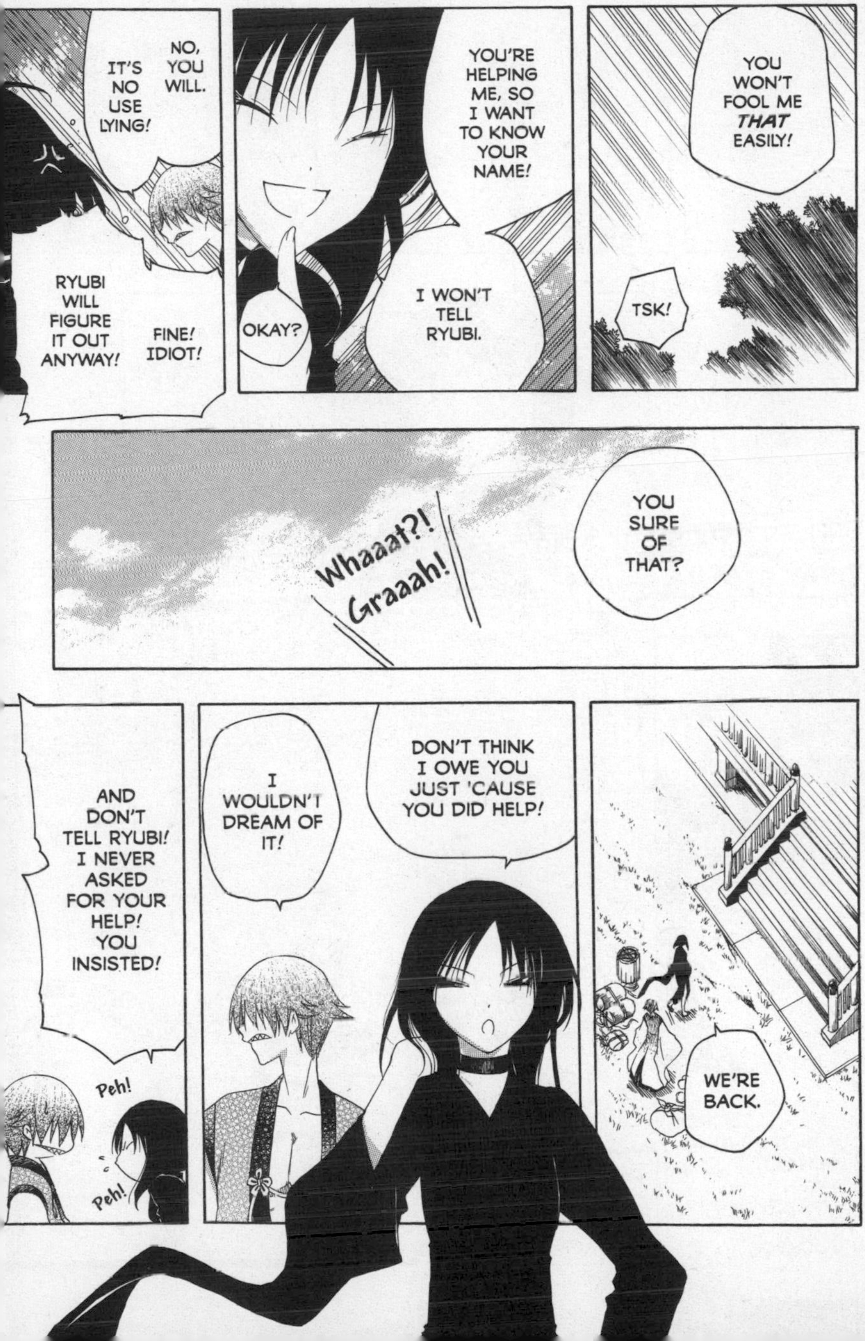
YOU WON'T FOOL ME *THAT* EASILY!
TSK!
YOU'RE HELPING ME, SO I WANT TO KNOW YOUR NAME!
I WON'T TELL RYUBI.
OKAY?
NO, YOU WILL.
IT'S NO USE LYING!
FINE! IDIOT!
RYUBI WILL FIGURE IT OUT ANYWAY!
YOU SURE OF THAT?
Whaaat?!
Graaah!
WE'RE BACK.
DON'T THINK I OWE YOU JUST 'CAUSE YOU DID HELP!
I WOULDN'T DREAM OF IT!
AND DON'T TELL RYUBI! I NEVER ASKED FOR YOUR HELP! YOU INSISTED!
Peh!
Peh!

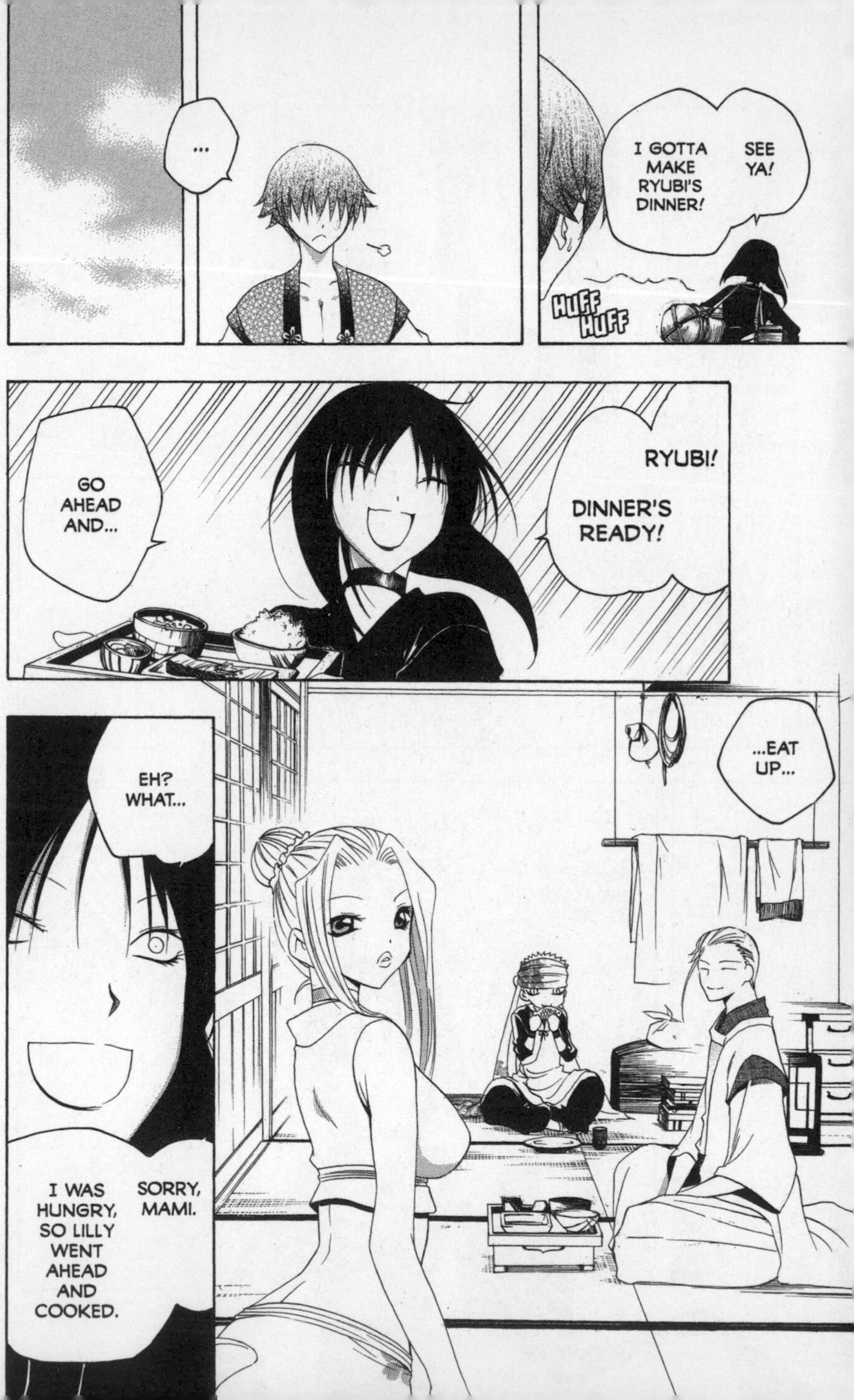
SEE YA!
I GOTTA MAKE RYUBI'S DINNER!
HUFF HUFF
...
RYUBI!
DINNER'S READY!
GO AHEAD AND...
...EAT UP...
EH? WHAT...
SORRY, MAMI.
I WAS HUNGRY, SO LILLY WENT AHEAD AND COOKED.

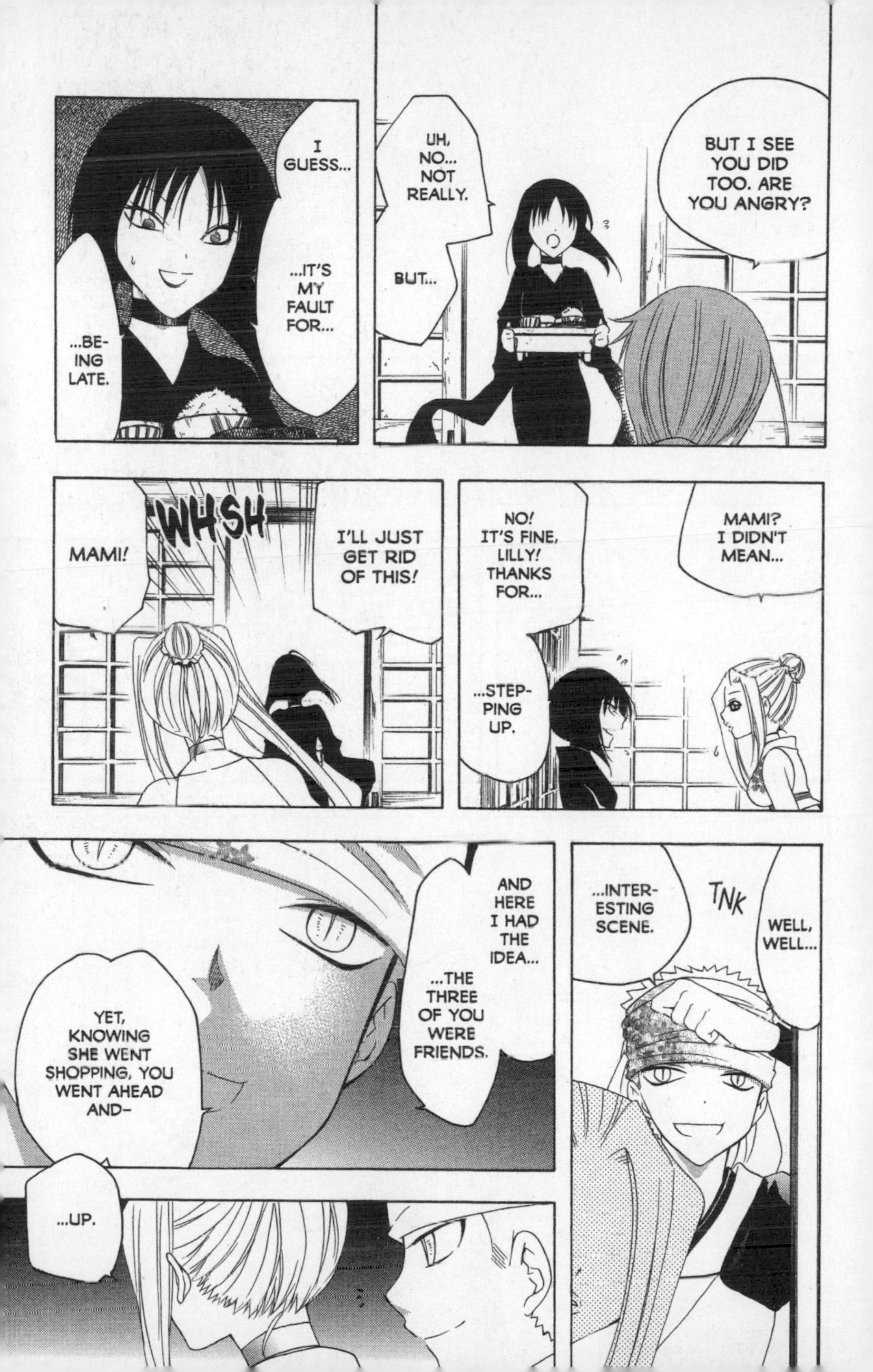
BUT I SEE YOU DID TOO. ARE YOU ANGRY?
UH, NO... NOT REALLY.
BUT...
I GUESS...
...IT'S MY FAULT FOR...
...BE-ING LATE.
MAMI? I DIDN'T MEAN...
NO! IT'S FINE, LILLY! THANKS FOR...
...STEP-PING UP.
I'LL JUST GET RID OF THIS!
WHSH
MAMI!
WELL, WELL...
TNK
...INTER-ESTING SCENE.
AND HERE I HAD THE IDEA...
...THE THREE OF YOU WERE FRIENDS.
YET, KNOWING SHE WENT SHOPPING, YOU WENT AHEAD AND–
...UP.

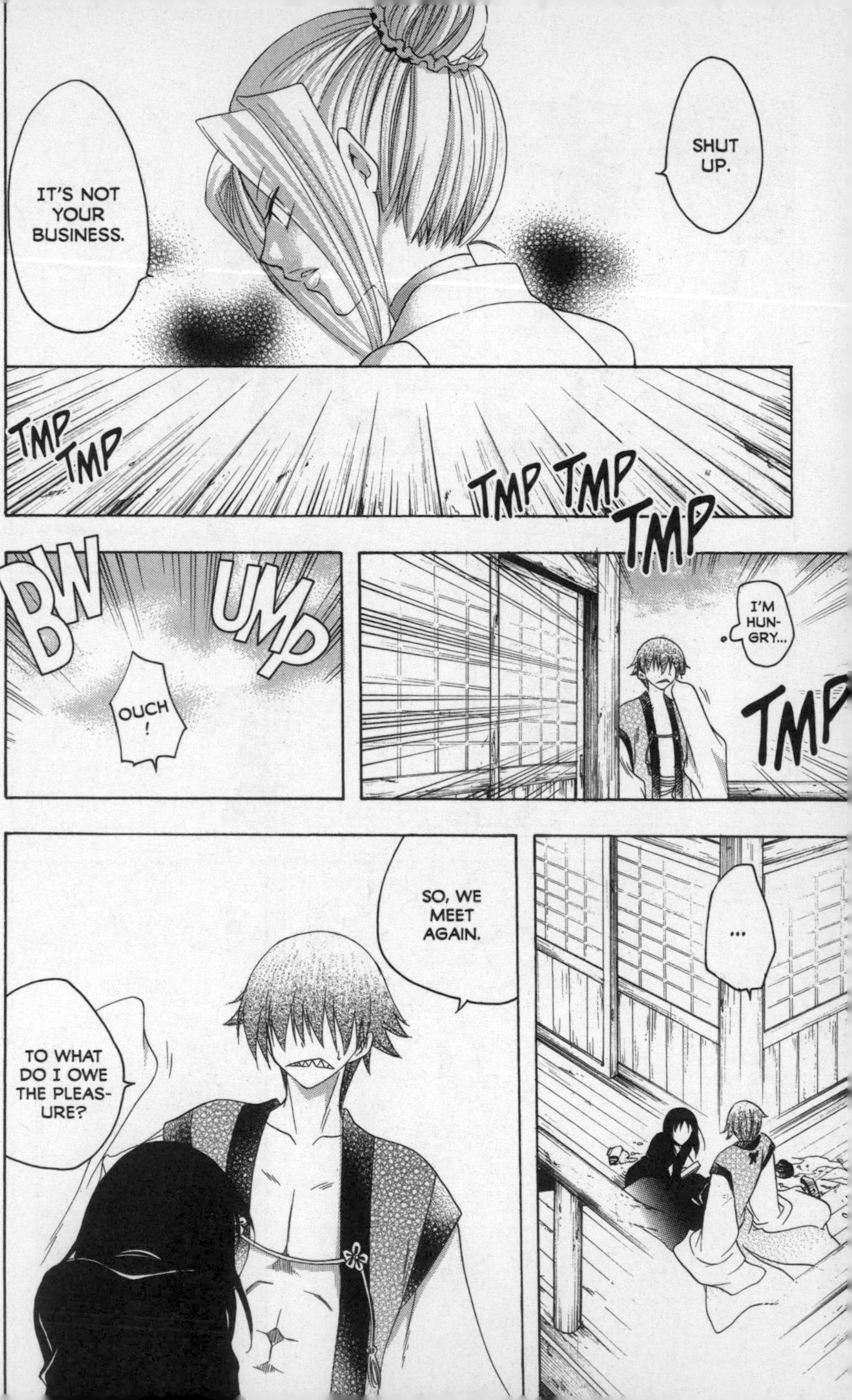
SHUT UP.
IT'S NOT YOUR BUSINESS.
TMP TMP
TMP TMP TMP
TMP
I'M HUNGRY...
BWUMP
OUCH!
...
SO, WE MEET AGAIN.
TO WHAT DO I OWE THE PLEASURE?

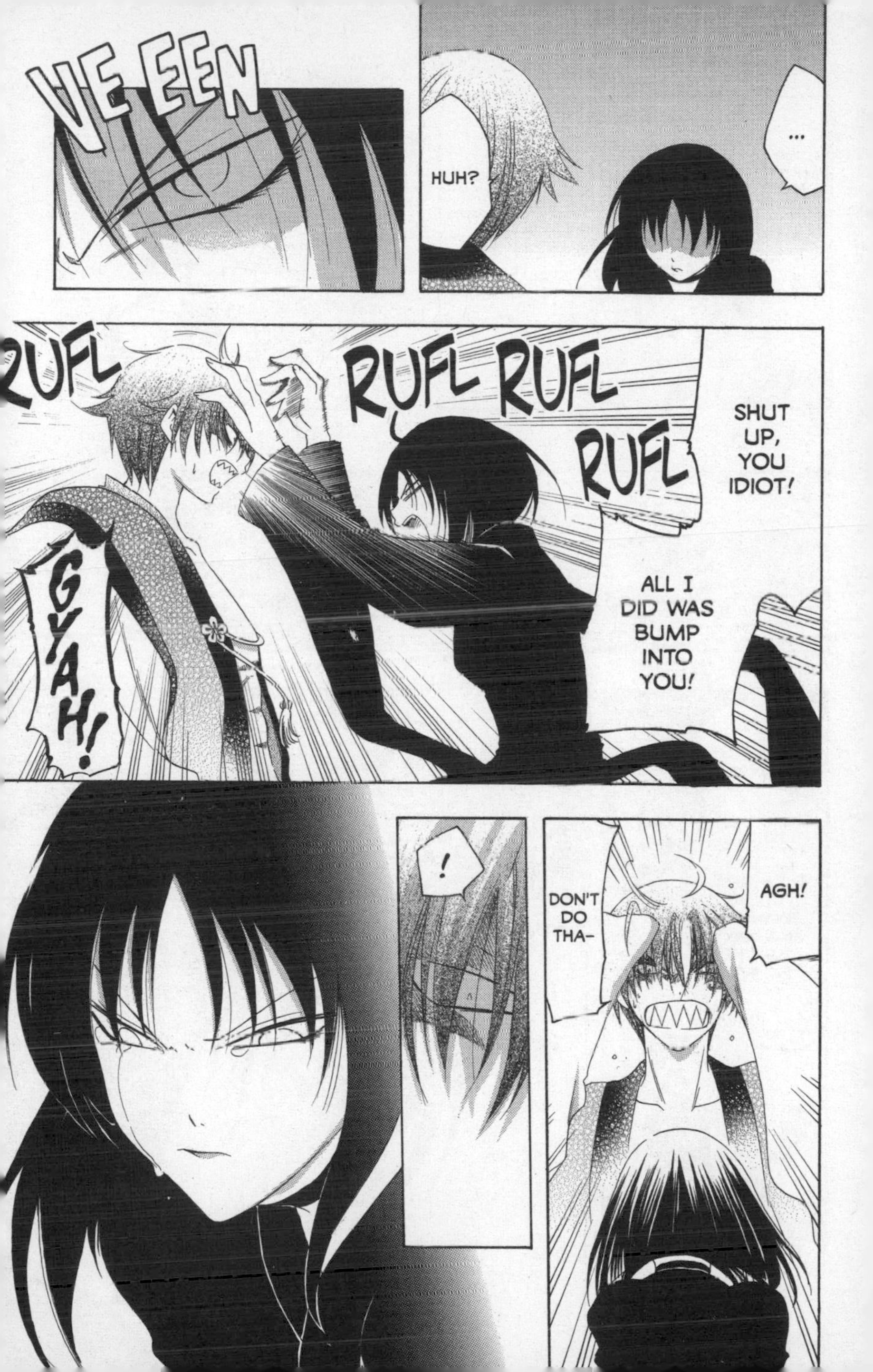
...
HUH?
VE EEN
SHUT UP, YOU IDIOT!
ALL I DID WAS BUMP INTO YOU!
RUFL RUFL RUFL RUFL
GYAH!
AGH!
DON'T DO THA-
!

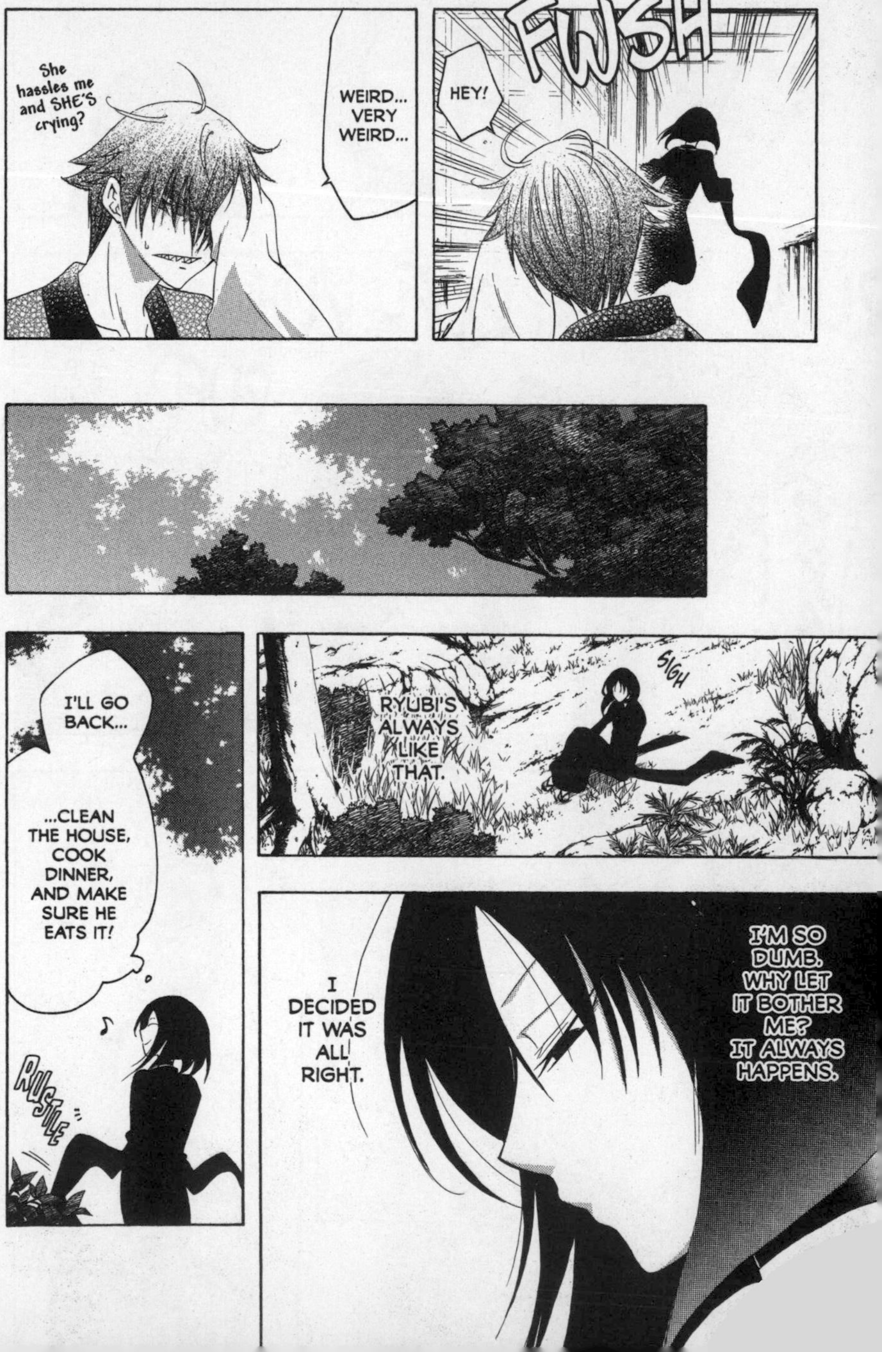
FWSH
HEY!
WEIRD... VERY WEIRD...
She hassles me and SHE'S crying?
SIGH
RYUBI'S ALWAYS LIKE THAT.
I'LL GO BACK...
...CLEAN THE HOUSE, COOK DINNER, AND MAKE SURE HE EATS IT!
RUSTLE
I'M SO DUMB. WHY LET IT BOTHER ME? IT ALWAYS HAPPENS.
I DECIDED IT WAS ALL RIGHT.

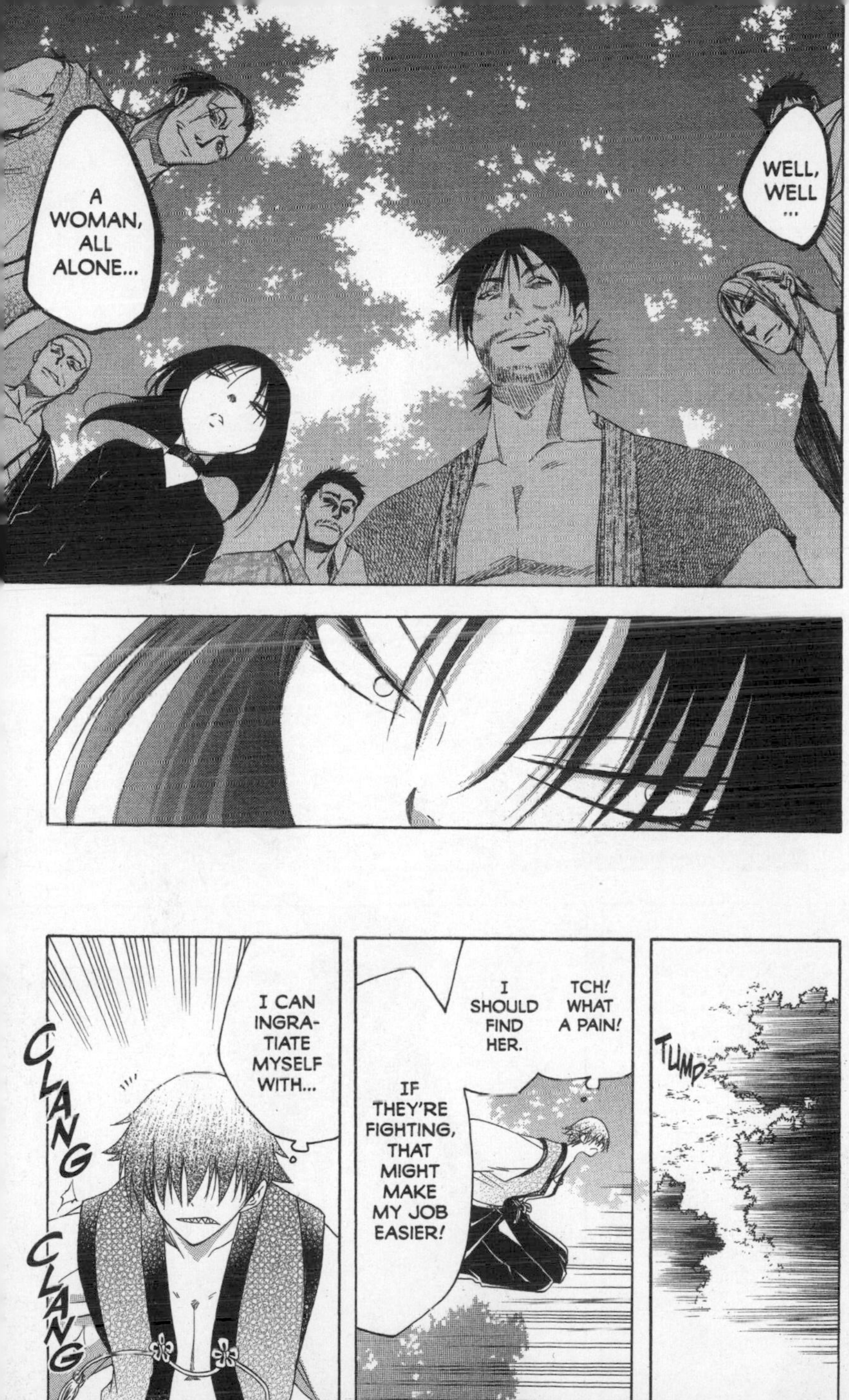
WELL, WELL ...
A WOMAN, ALL ALONE...
TUMP
TCH! WHAT A PAIN!
I SHOULD FIND HER.
IF THEY'RE FIGHTING, THAT MIGHT MAKE MY JOB EASIER!
I CAN INGRATIATE MYSELF WITH...
CLANG
CLANG
CLANG

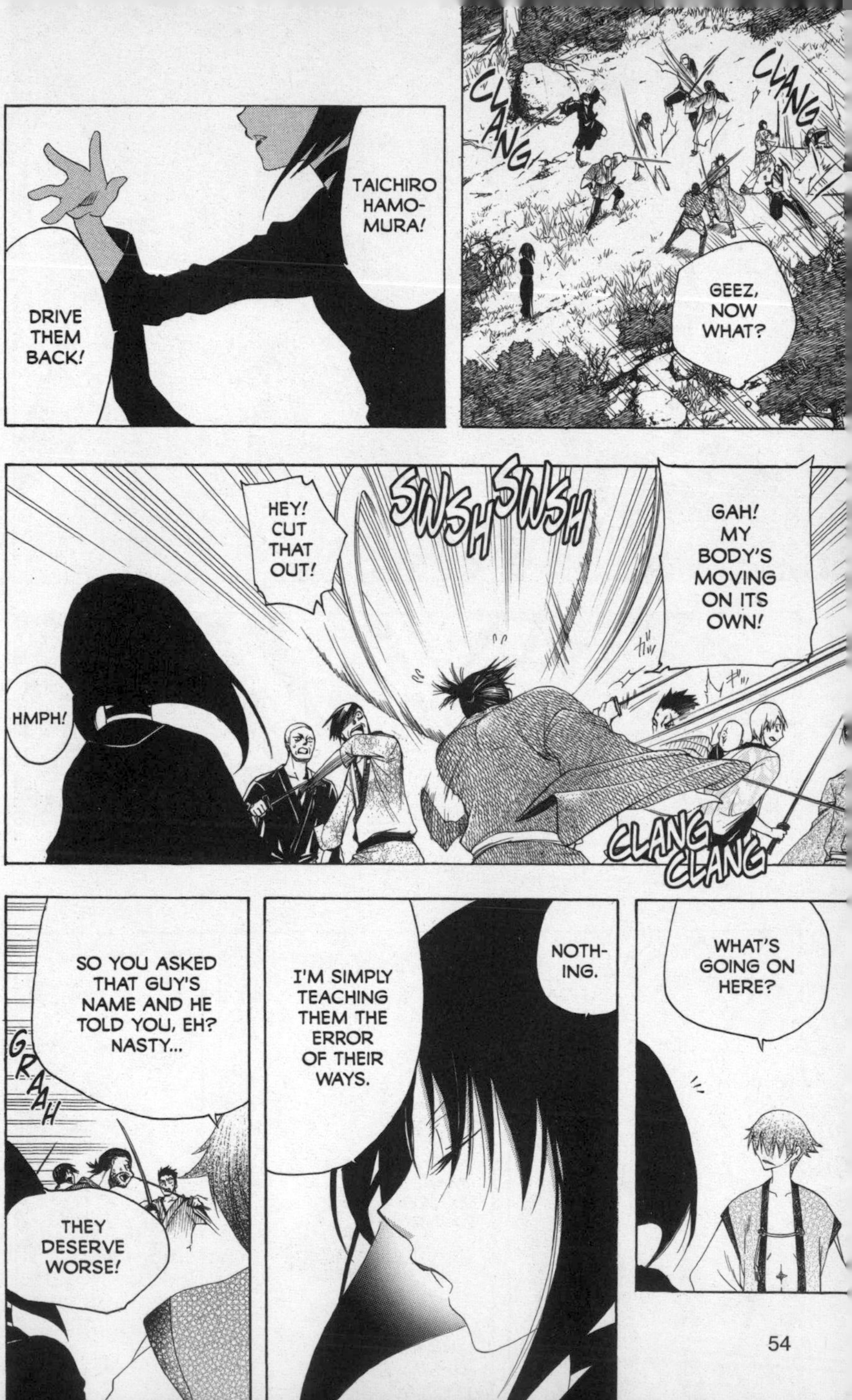
CLANG
CLANG
GEEZ, NOW WHAT?
TAICHIRO HAMO-MURA!
DRIVE THEM BACK!
GAH! MY BODY'S MOVING ON ITS OWN!
SWSH SWSH
HEY! CUT THAT OUT!
CLANG CLANG
HMPH!
WHAT'S GOING ON HERE?
NOTH-ING.
I'M SIMPLY TEACHING THEM THE ERROR OF THEIR WAYS.
SO YOU ASKED THAT GUY'S NAME AND HE TOLD YOU, EH? NASTY...
GRAAH
THEY DESERVE WORSE!

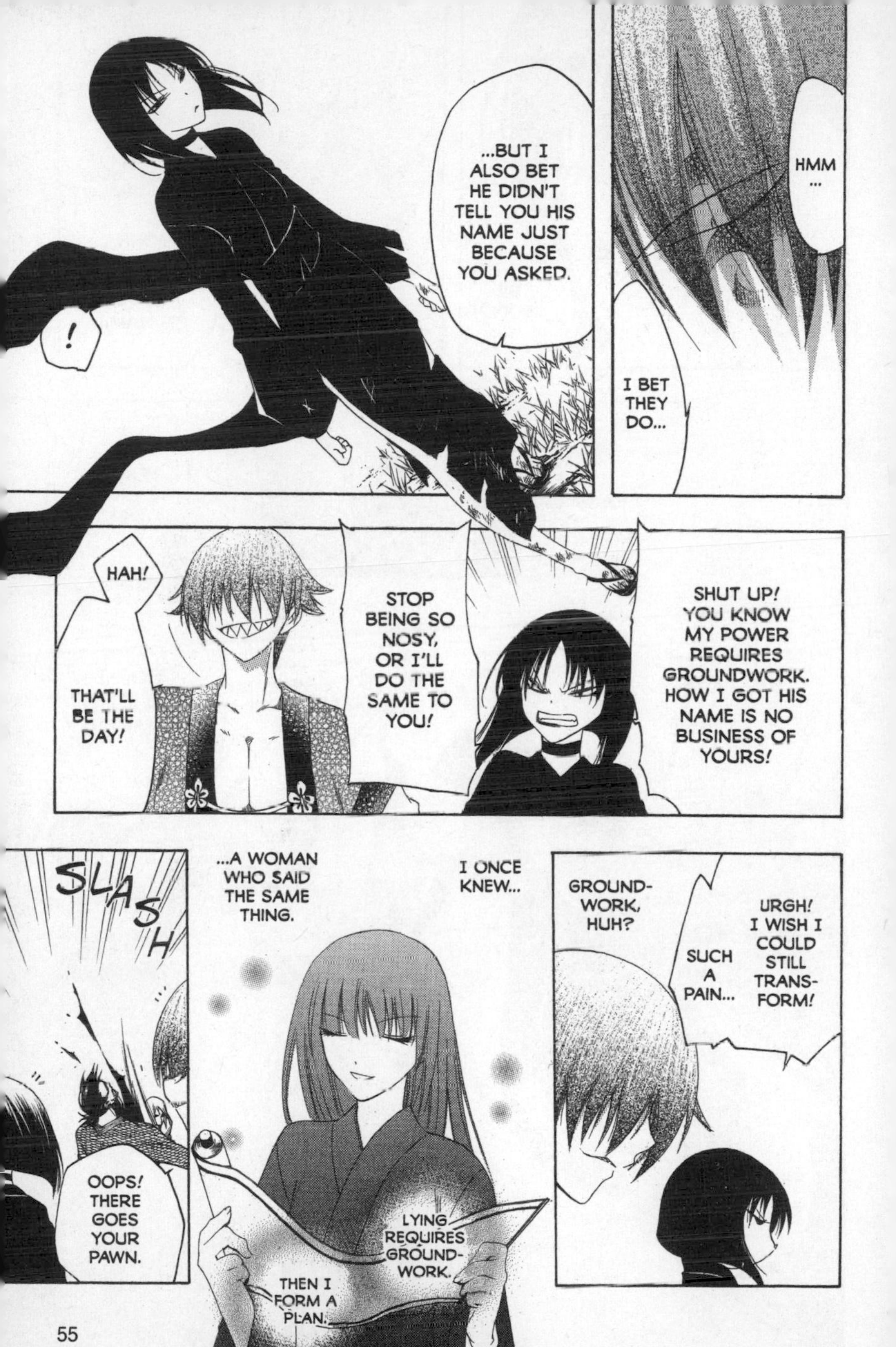
HMM ...
I BET THEY DO...
...BUT I ALSO BET HE DIDN'T TELL YOU HIS NAME JUST BECAUSE YOU ASKED.
!
SHUT UP! YOU KNOW MY POWER REQUIRES GROUNDWORK. HOW I GOT HIS NAME IS NO BUSINESS OF YOURS!
STOP BEING SO NOSY, OR I'LL DO THE SAME TO YOU!
HAH!
THAT'LL BE THE DAY!
URGH! I WISH I COULD STILL TRANS-FORM!
SUCH A PAIN...
GROUND-WORK, HUH?
I ONCE KNEW...
...A WOMAN WHO SAID THE SAME THING.
LYING REQUIRES GROUND-WORK.
THEN I FORM A PLAN.
SLASH
OOPS! THERE GOES YOUR PAWN.

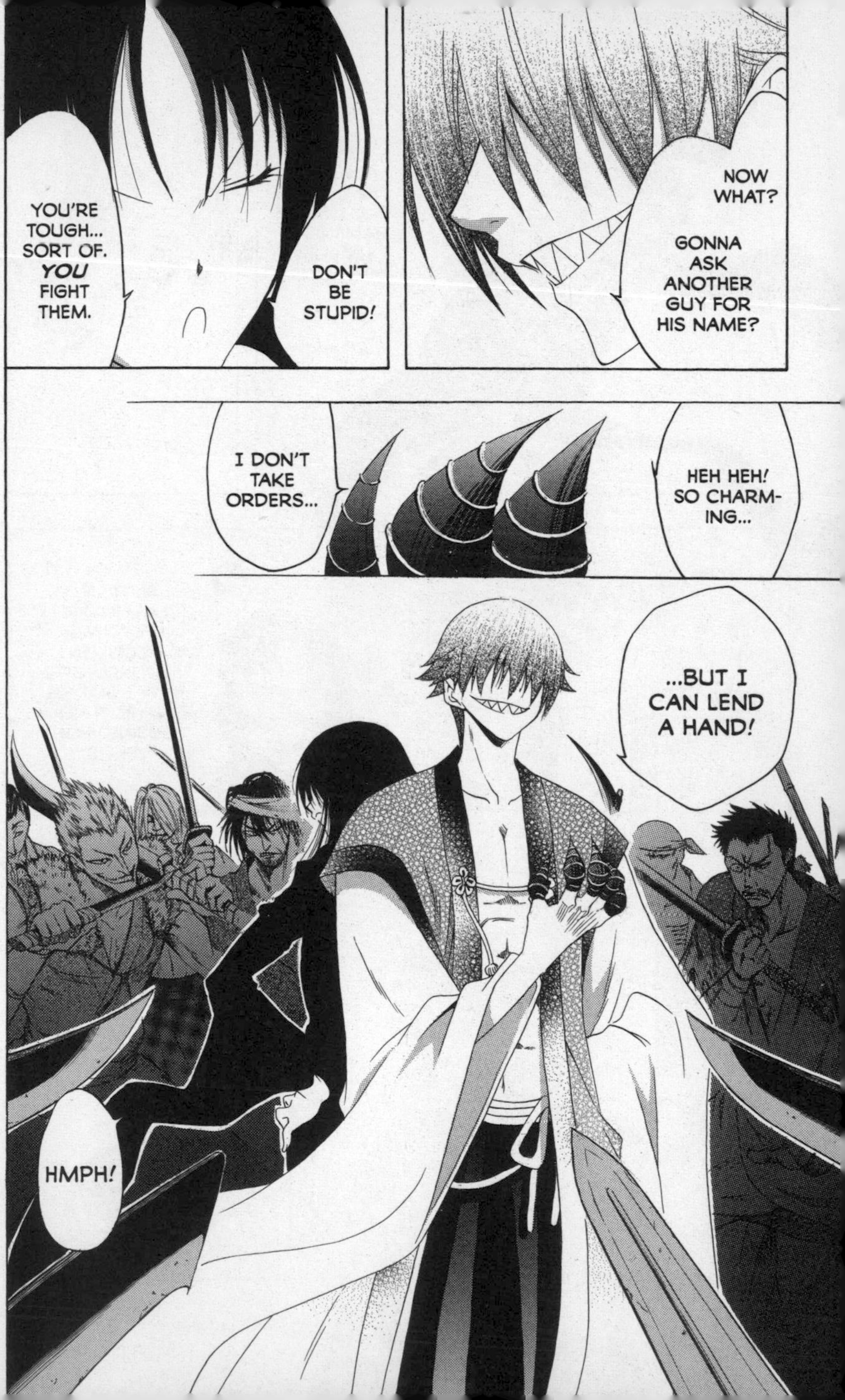
NOW WHAT?
GONNA ASK ANOTHER GUY FOR HIS NAME?
DON'T BE STUPID!
YOU'RE TOUGH... SORT OF. ***YOU*** FIGHT THEM.
HEH HEH! SO CHARM-ING...
I DON'T TAKE ORDERS...
...BUT I CAN LEND A HAND!
HMPH!

Chapter 131 Good Lies

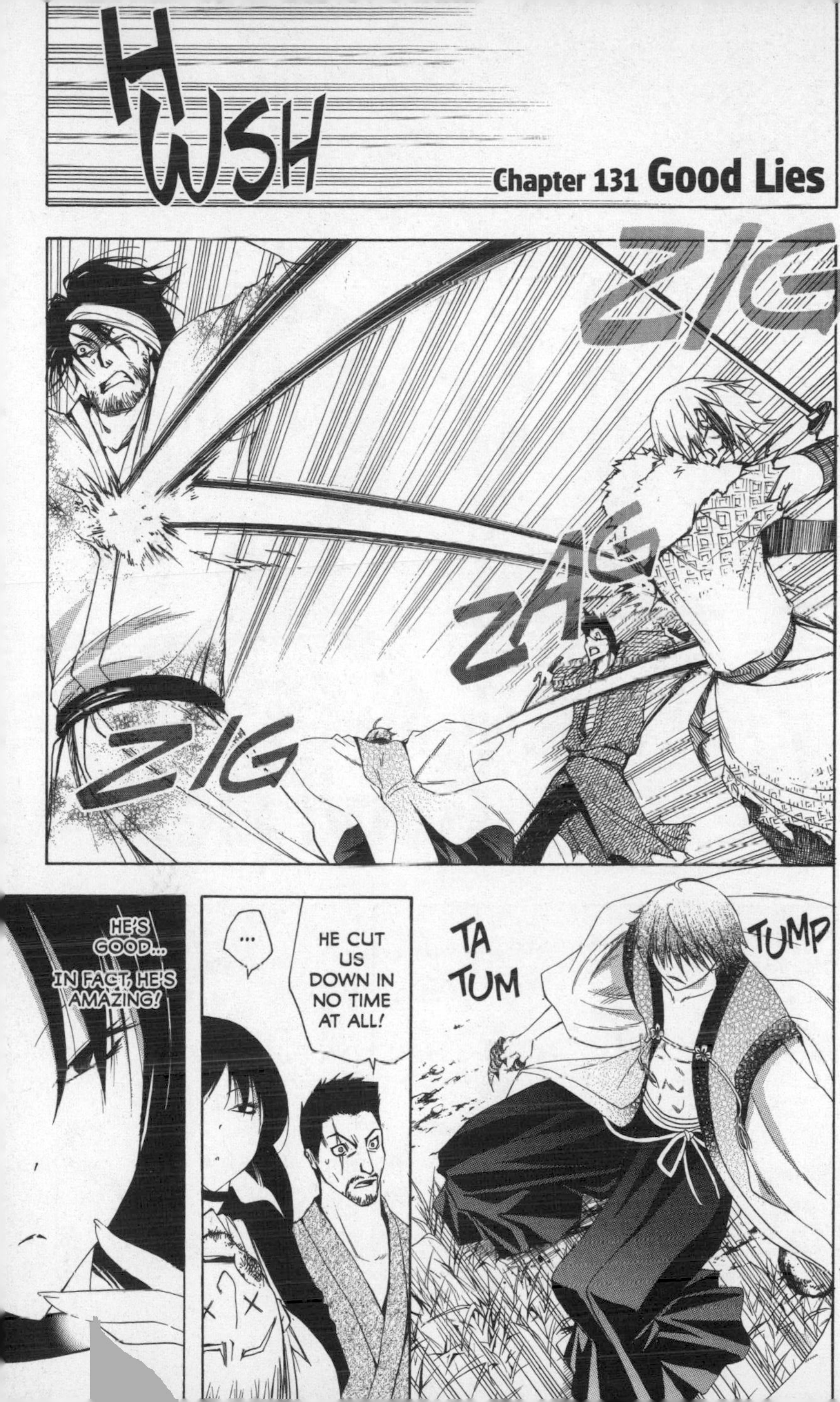
HWSH
ZIG
ZAG
ZIG
TUMP
TA TUM
...
HE CUT US DOWN IN NO TIME AT ALL!
HE'S GOOD... IN FACT, HE'S AMAZING!

Chapter 131
Good Lies

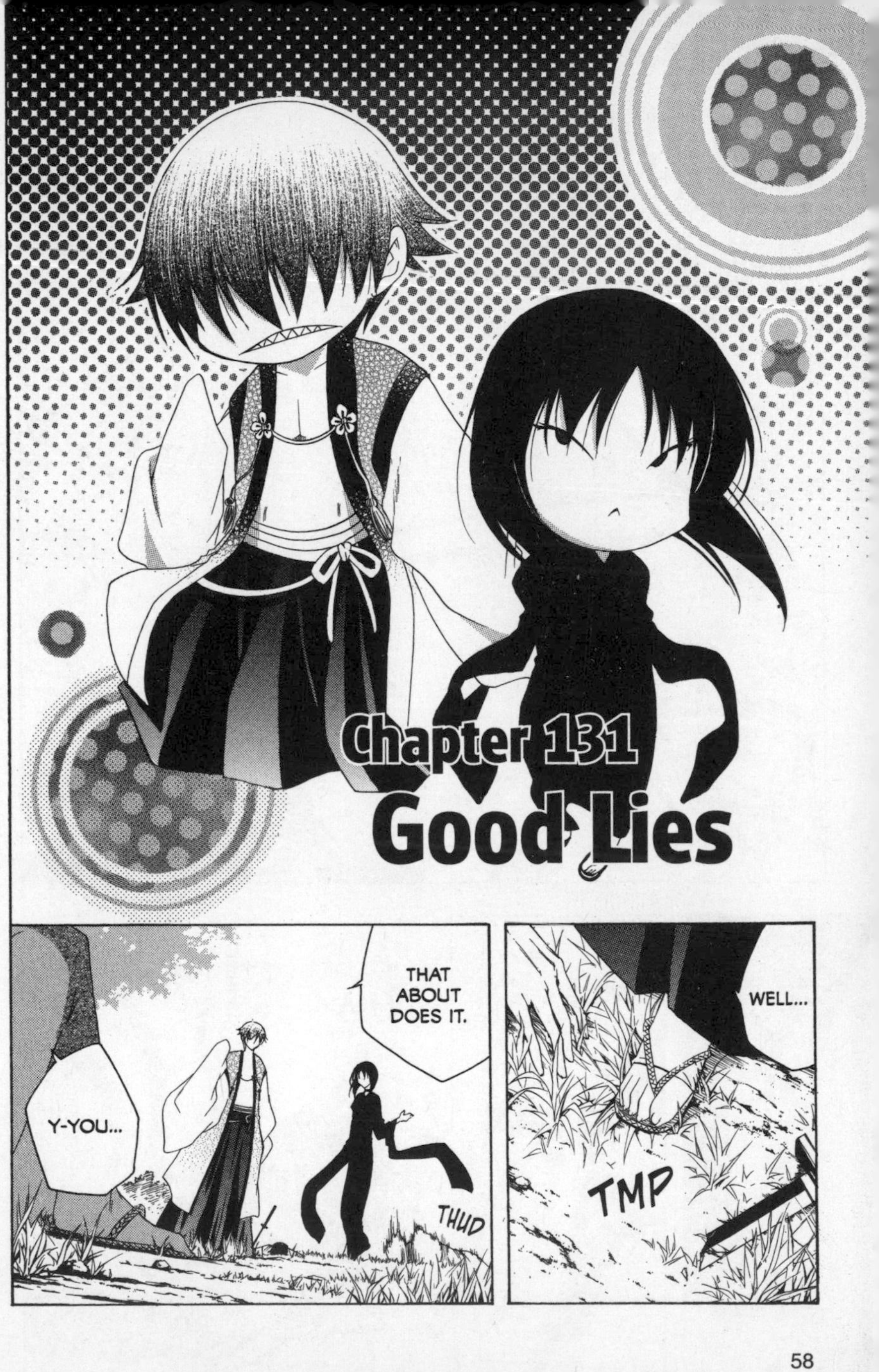
WELL...
TMP
THAT ABOUT DOES IT.
Y-YOU...
THUD

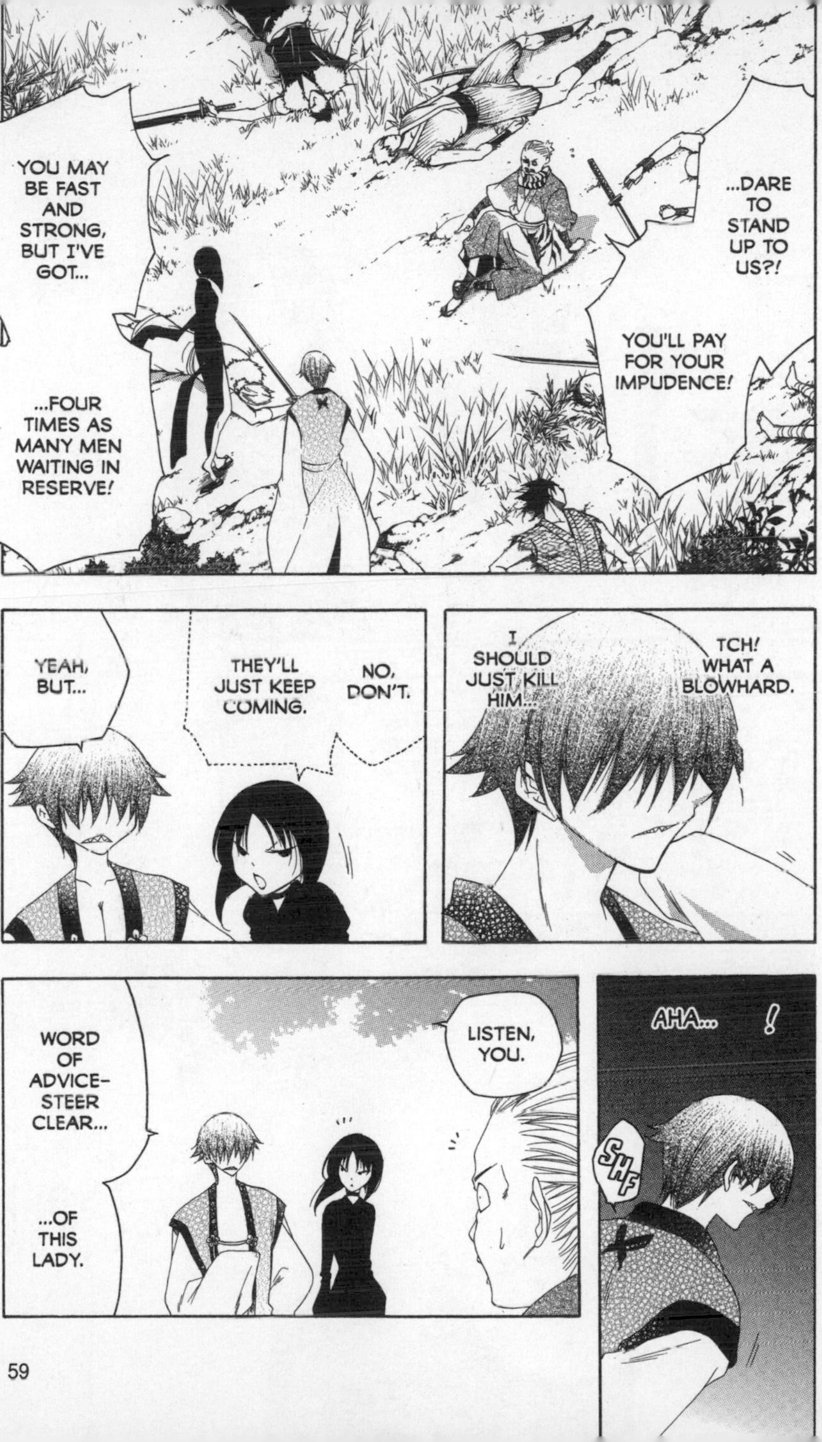
...DARE TO STAND UP TO US?!
YOU'LL PAY FOR YOUR IMPUDENCE!
YOU MAY BE FAST AND STRONG, BUT I'VE GOT...
...FOUR TIMES AS MANY MEN WAITING IN RESERVE!
TCH! WHAT A BLOWHARD.
I SHOULD JUST KILL HIM...
NO, DON'T.
THEY'LL JUST KEEP COMING.
YEAH, BUT...
AHA... !
SHF
LISTEN, YOU.
WORD OF ADVICE–STEER CLEAR...
...OF THIS LADY.

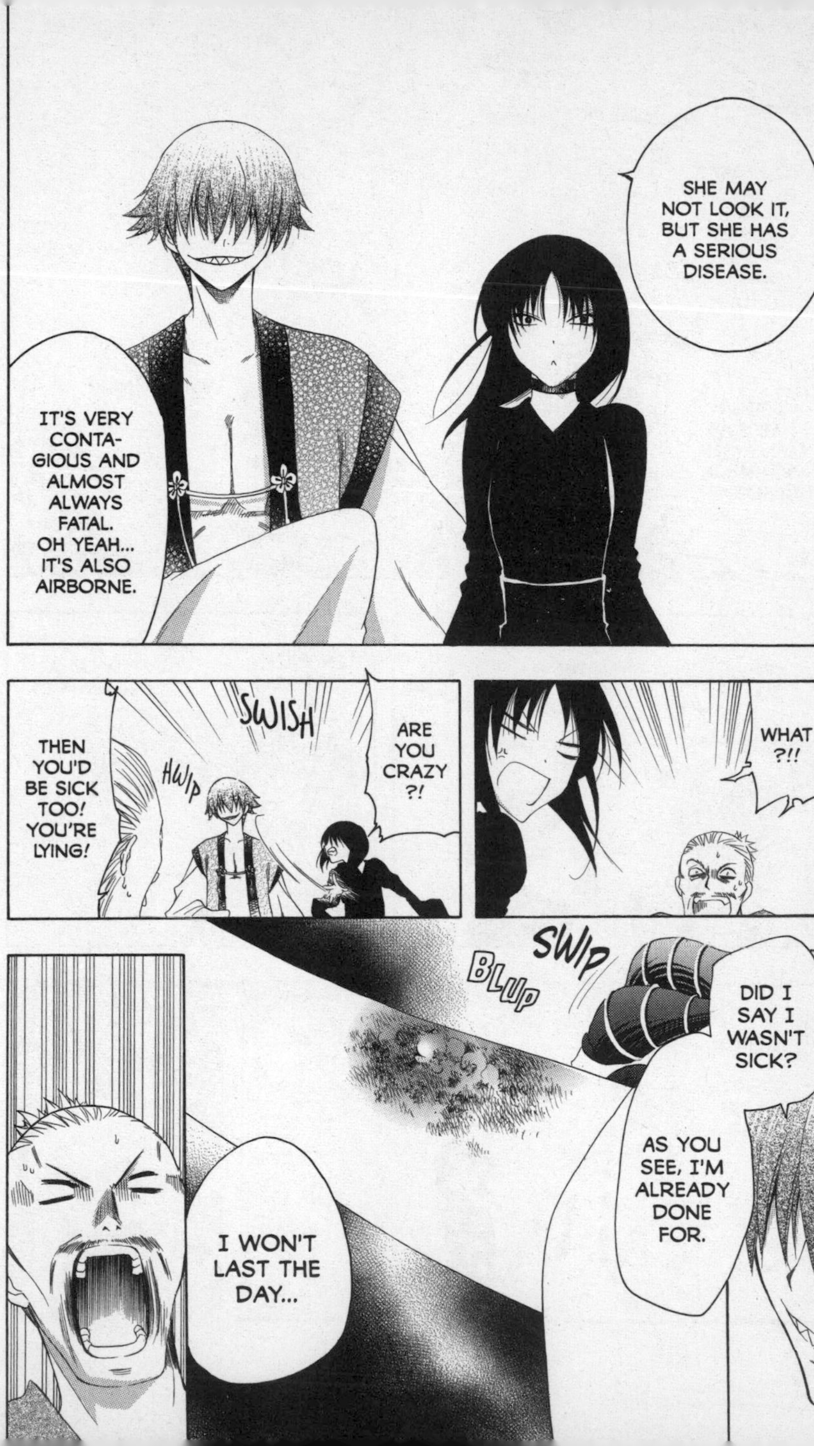
SHE MAY NOT LOOK IT, BUT SHE HAS A SERIOUS DISEASE.
IT'S VERY CONTA-GIOUS AND ALMOST ALWAYS FATAL. OH YEAH... IT'S ALSO AIRBORNE.
WHAT ?!!
ARE YOU CRAZY ?!
SWISH
HWIP
THEN YOU'D BE SICK TOO! YOU'RE LYING!
SWIP
BLUP
DID I SAY I WASN'T SICK?
AS YOU SEE, I'M ALREADY DONE FOR.
I WON'T LAST THE DAY...

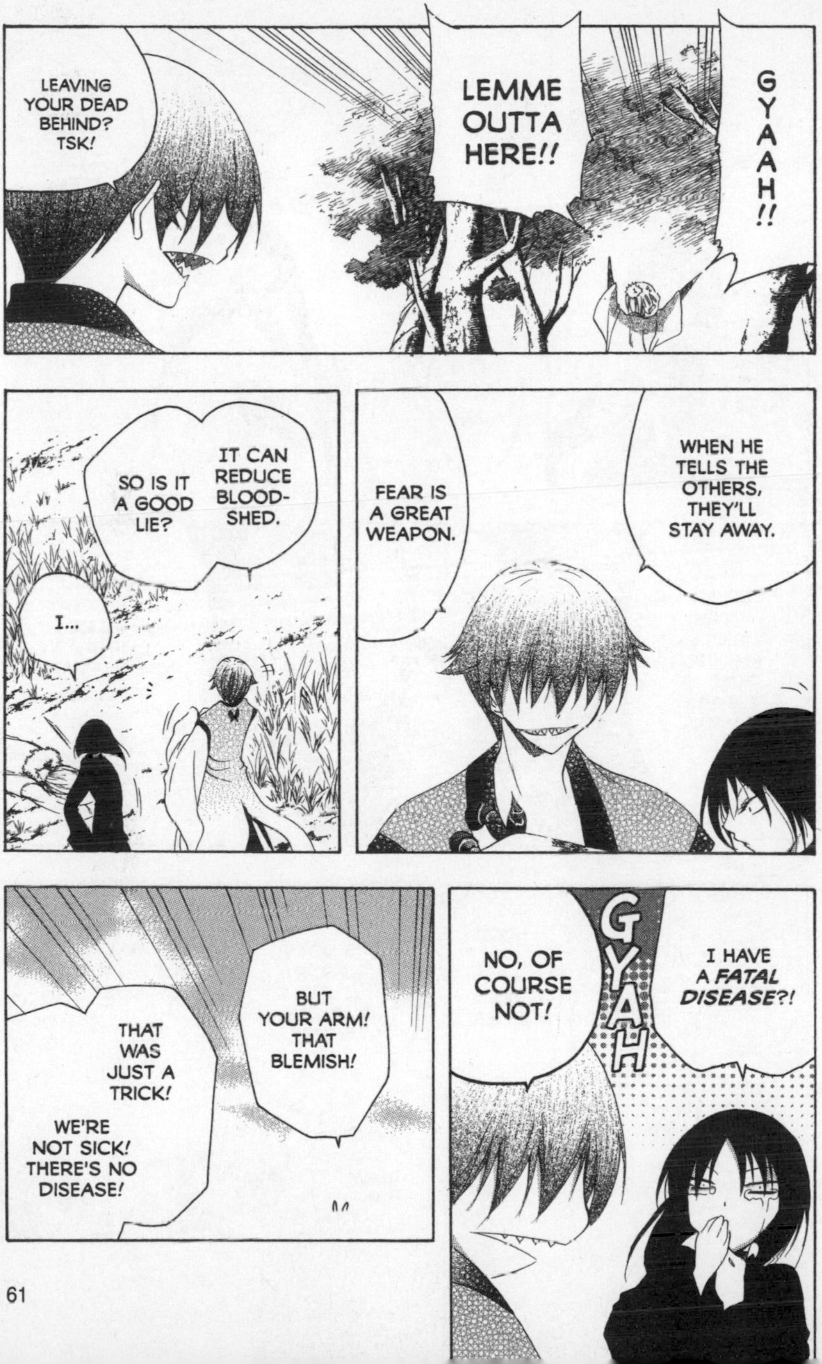
GYAAH!!
LEMME OUTTA HERE!!
LEAVING YOUR DEAD BEHIND? TSK!
WHEN HE TELLS THE OTHERS, THEY'LL STAY AWAY.
FEAR IS A GREAT WEAPON.
IT CAN REDUCE BLOODSHED.
SO IS IT A GOOD LIE?
I...
I HAVE A *FATAL DISEASE*?!
GYAH
NO, OF COURSE NOT!
BUT YOUR ARM! THAT BLEMISH!
THAT WAS JUST A TRICK!
WE'RE NOT SICK! THERE'S NO DISEASE!

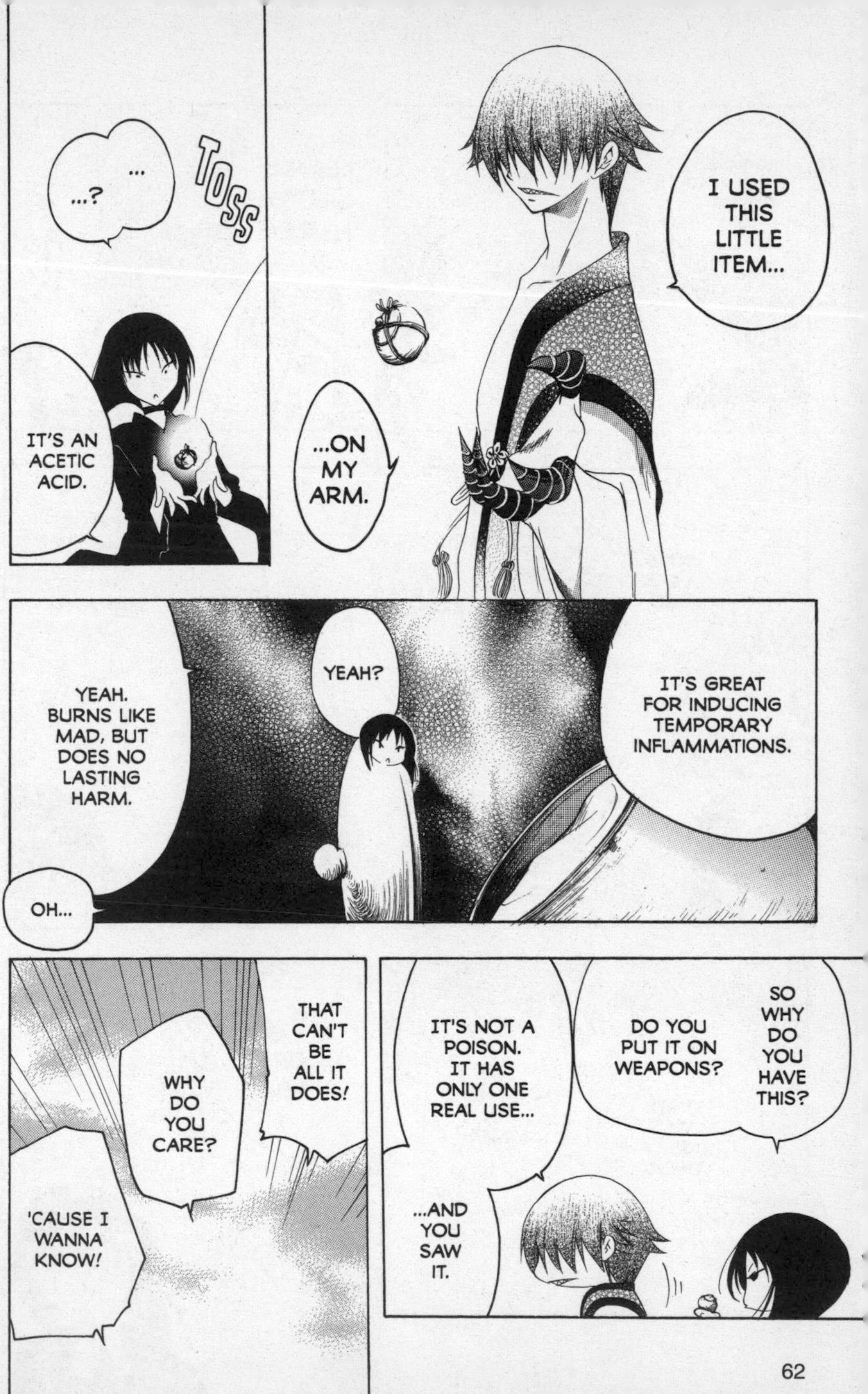
I USED THIS LITTLE ITEM...
...ON MY ARM.
...
...?
TOSS
IT'S AN ACETIC ACID.
IT'S GREAT FOR INDUCING TEMPORARY INFLAMMATIONS.
YEAH?
YEAH. BURNS LIKE MAD, BUT DOES NO LASTING HARM.
OH...
SO WHY DO YOU HAVE THIS?
DO YOU PUT IT ON WEAPONS?
IT'S NOT A POISON. IT HAS ONLY ONE REAL USE...
...AND YOU SAW IT.
THAT CAN'T BE ALL IT DOES!
WHY DO YOU CARE?
'CAUSE I WANNA KNOW!

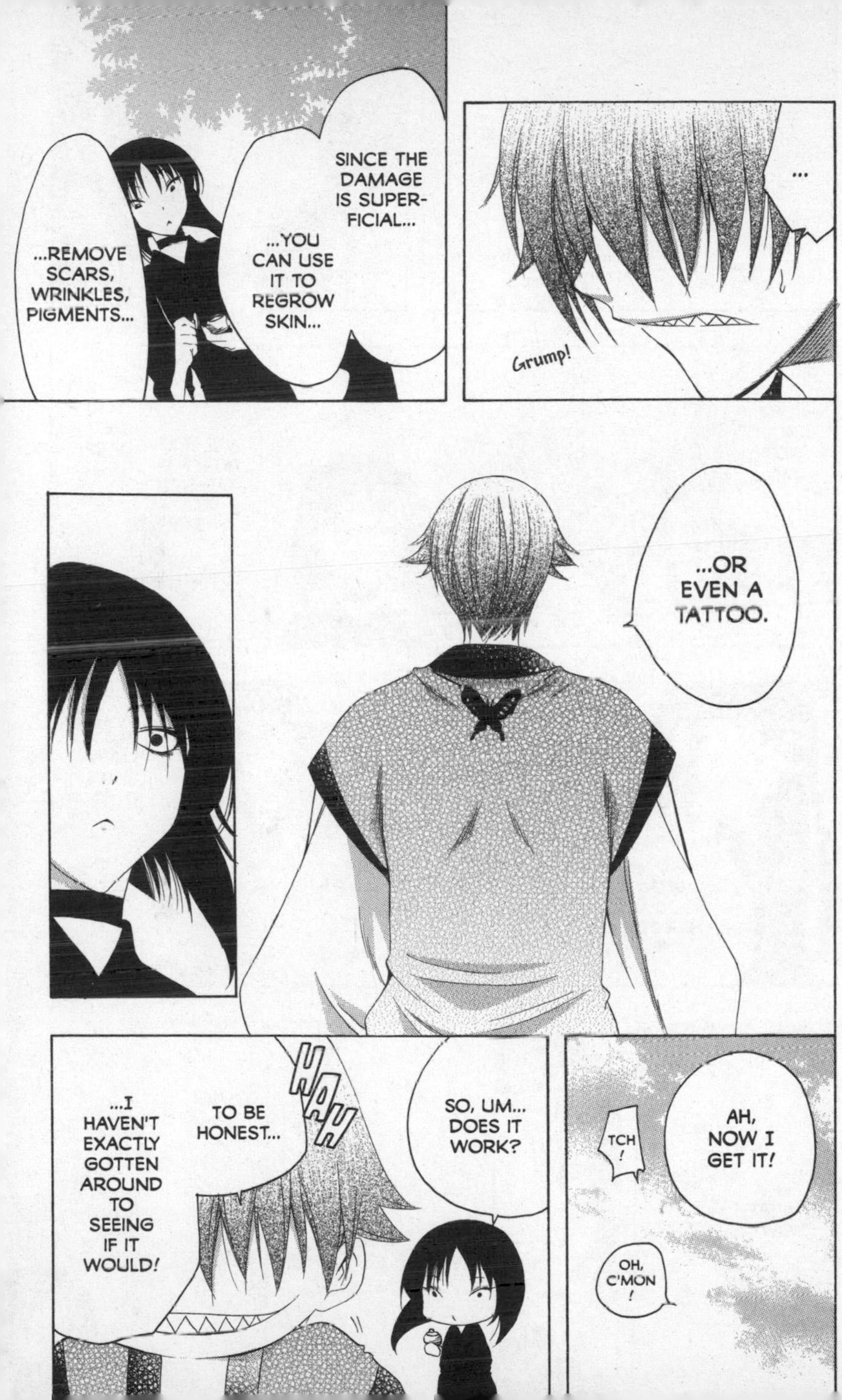
...
Grump!
SINCE THE DAMAGE IS SUPER-FICIAL...
...YOU CAN USE IT TO REGROW SKIN...
...REMOVE SCARS, WRINKLES, PIGMENTS...
...OR EVEN A TATTOO.
AH, NOW I GET IT!
TCH!
OH, C'MON!
SO, UM... DOES IT WORK?
HAH
TO BE HONEST...
...I HAVEN'T EXACTLY GOTTEN AROUND TO SEEING IF IT WOULD!

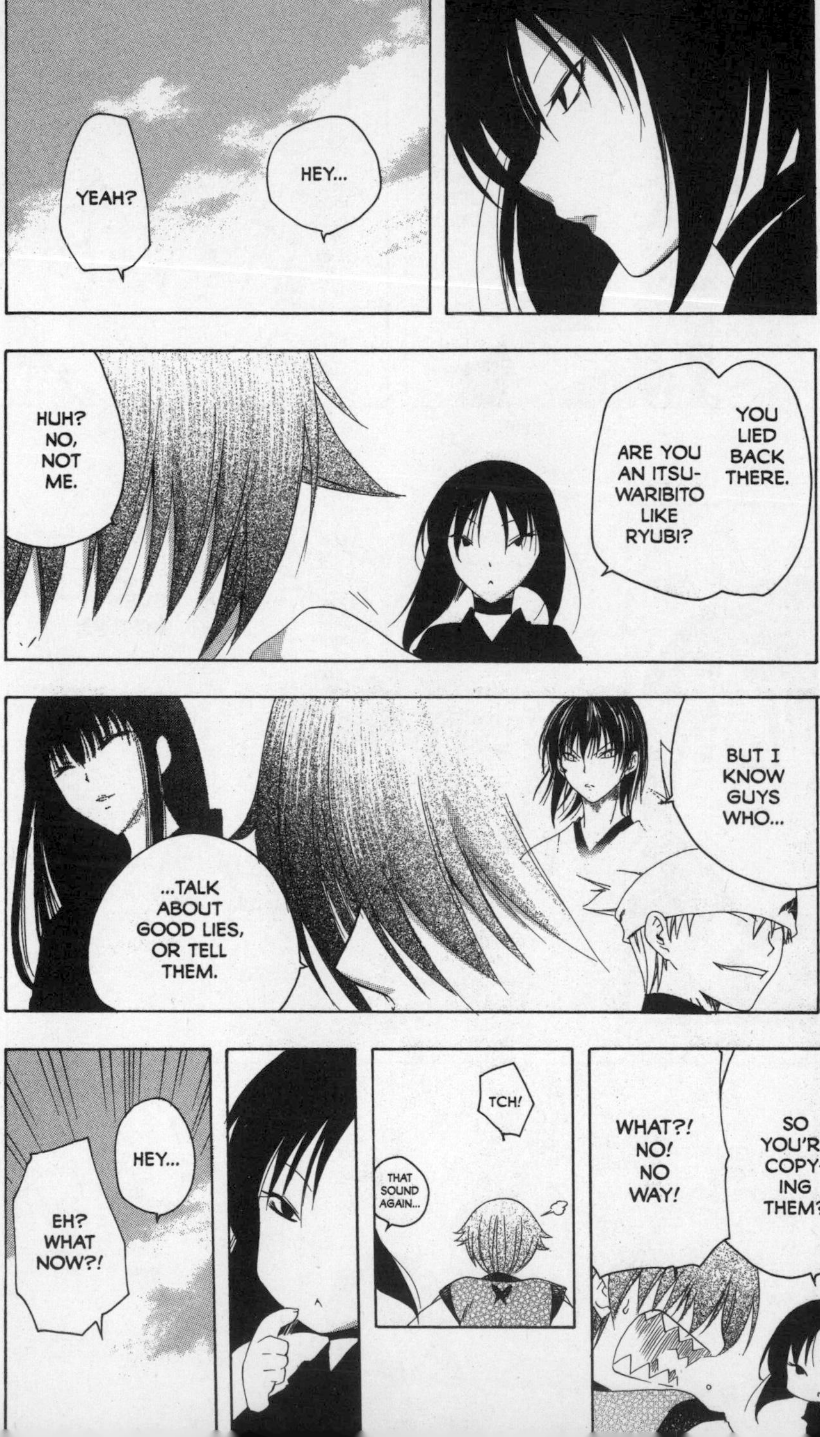
HEY...
YEAH?
YOU LIED BACK THERE.
ARE YOU AN ITSU-WARIBITO LIKE RYUBI?
HUH? NO, NOT ME.
BUT I KNOW GUYS WHO...
...TALK ABOUT GOOD LIES, OR TELL THEM.
SO YOU'RE COPY-ING THEM?
WHAT?! NO! NO WAY!
TCH!
THAT SOUND AGAIN...
HEY...
EH? WHAT NOW?!

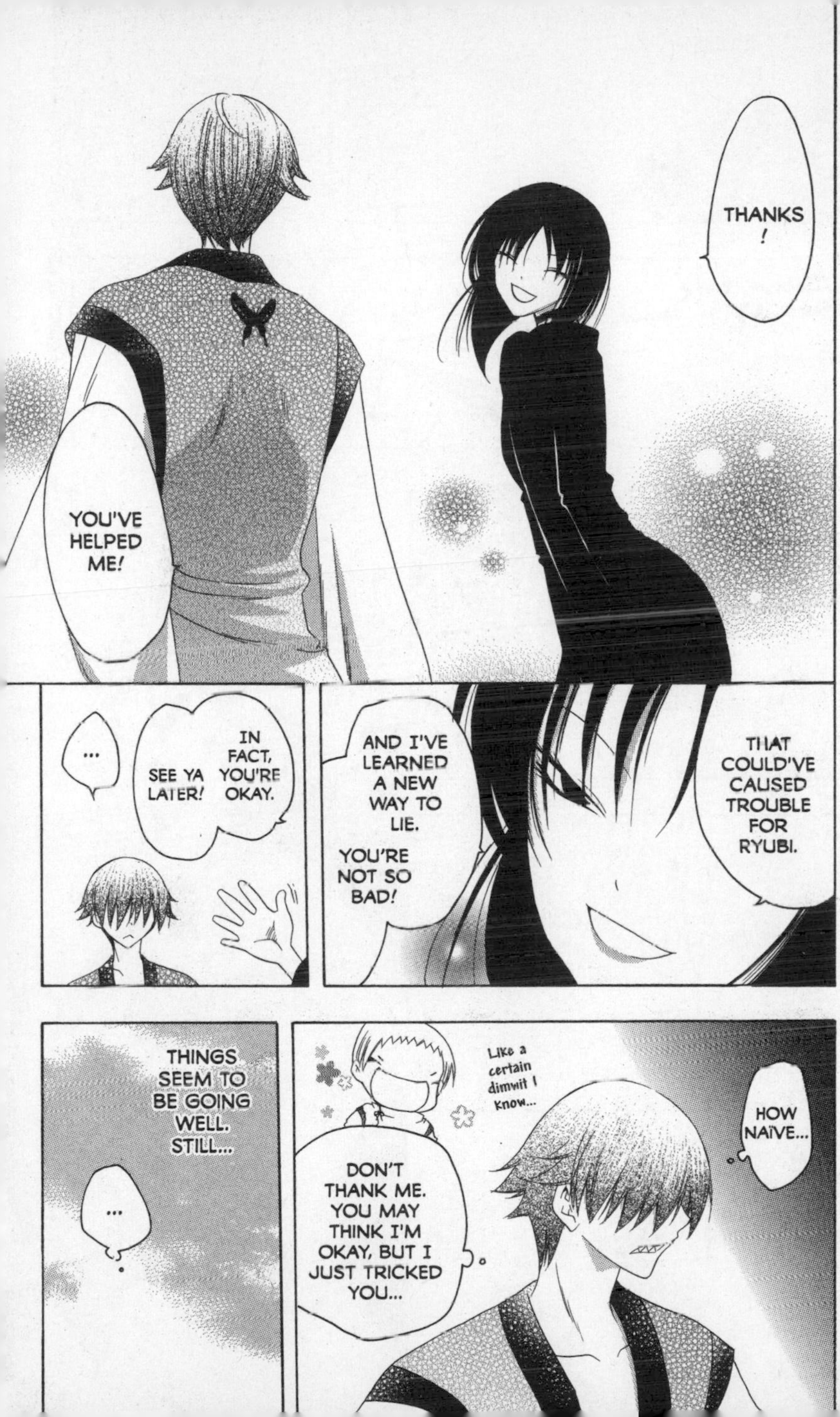
THANKS!
YOU'VE HELPED ME!
THAT COULD'VE CAUSED TROUBLE FOR RYUBI.
AND I'VE LEARNED A NEW WAY TO LIE.
YOU'RE NOT SO BAD!
IN FACT, YOU'RE OKAY.
SEE YA LATER!
...
HOW NAïVE...
Like a certain dimwit I know...
DON'T THANK ME. YOU MAY THINK I'M OKAY, BUT I JUST TRICKED YOU...
THINGS SEEM TO BE GOING WELL. STILL...
...

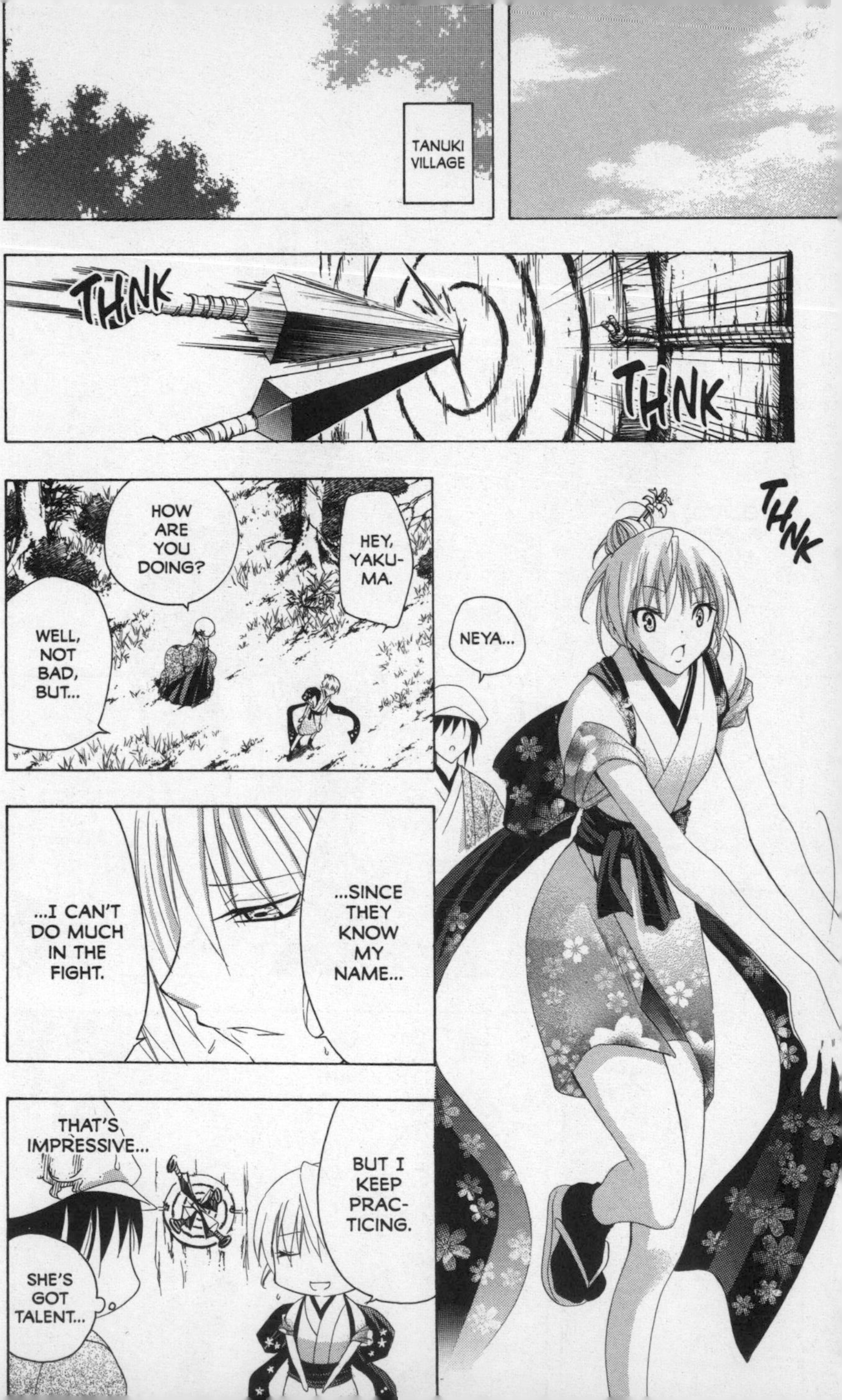
TANUKI VILLAGE
THNK
THNK
THNK
NEYA...
HEY, YAKU-MA.
HOW ARE YOU DOING?
WELL, NOT BAD, BUT...
...SINCE THEY KNOW MY NAME...
...I CAN'T DO MUCH IN THE FIGHT.
BUT I KEEP PRAC-TICING.
THAT'S IMPRESSIVE...
SHE'S GOT TALENT...

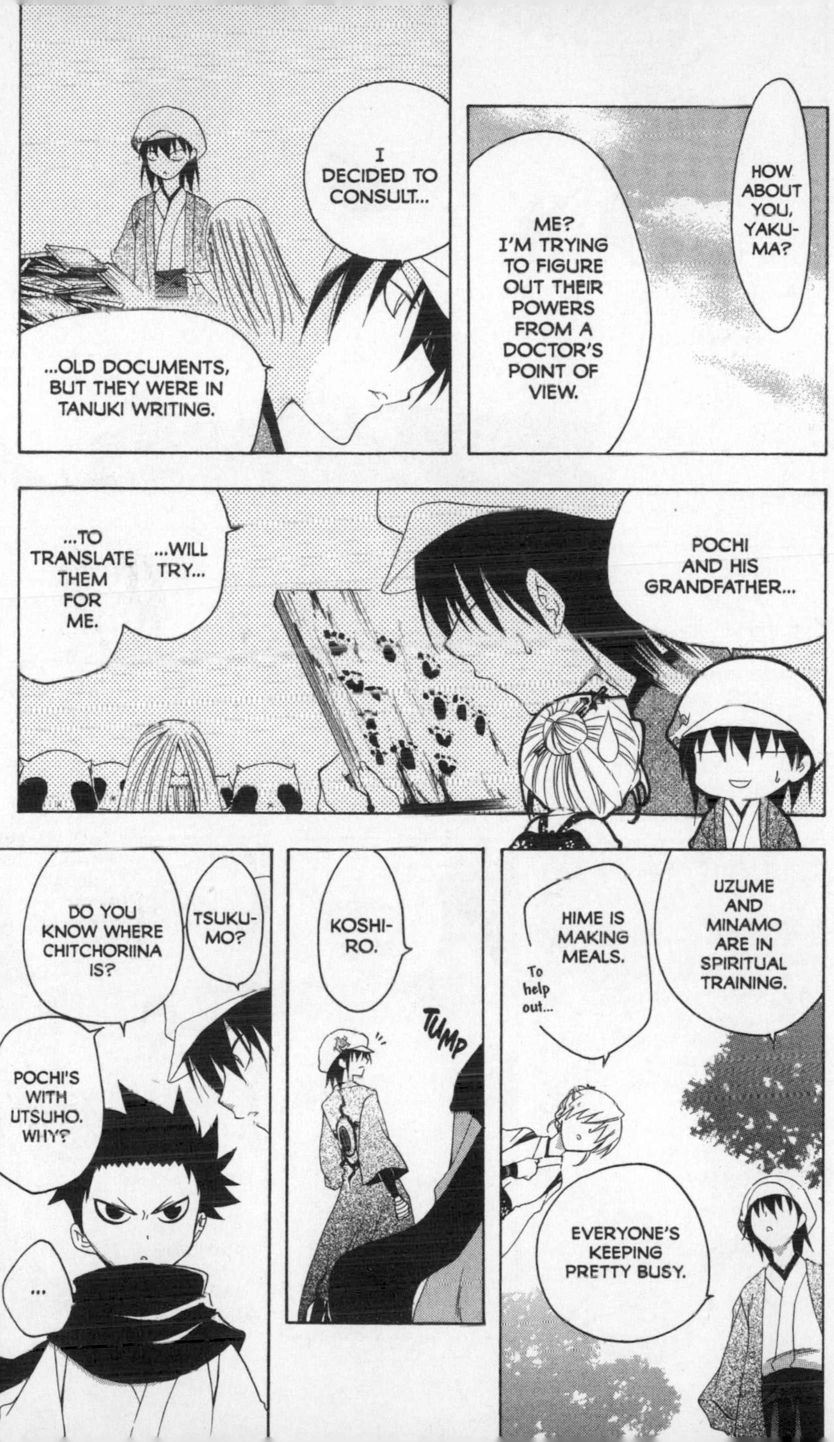
HOW ABOUT YOU, YAKU-MA?
ME? I'M TRYING TO FIGURE OUT THEIR POWERS FROM A DOCTOR'S POINT OF VIEW.
I DECIDED TO CONSULT...
...OLD DOCUMENTS, BUT THEY WERE IN TANUKI WRITING.
POCHI AND HIS GRANDFATHER...
...WILL TRY...
...TO TRANSLATE THEM FOR ME.
UZUME AND MINAMO ARE IN SPIRITUAL TRAINING.
HIME IS MAKING MEALS.
To help out...
EVERYONE'S KEEPING PRETTY BUSY.
KOSHI-RO.
TUMP
TSUKU-MO?
DO YOU KNOW WHERE CHITCHORIINA IS?
POCHI'S WITH UTSUHO. WHY?
...

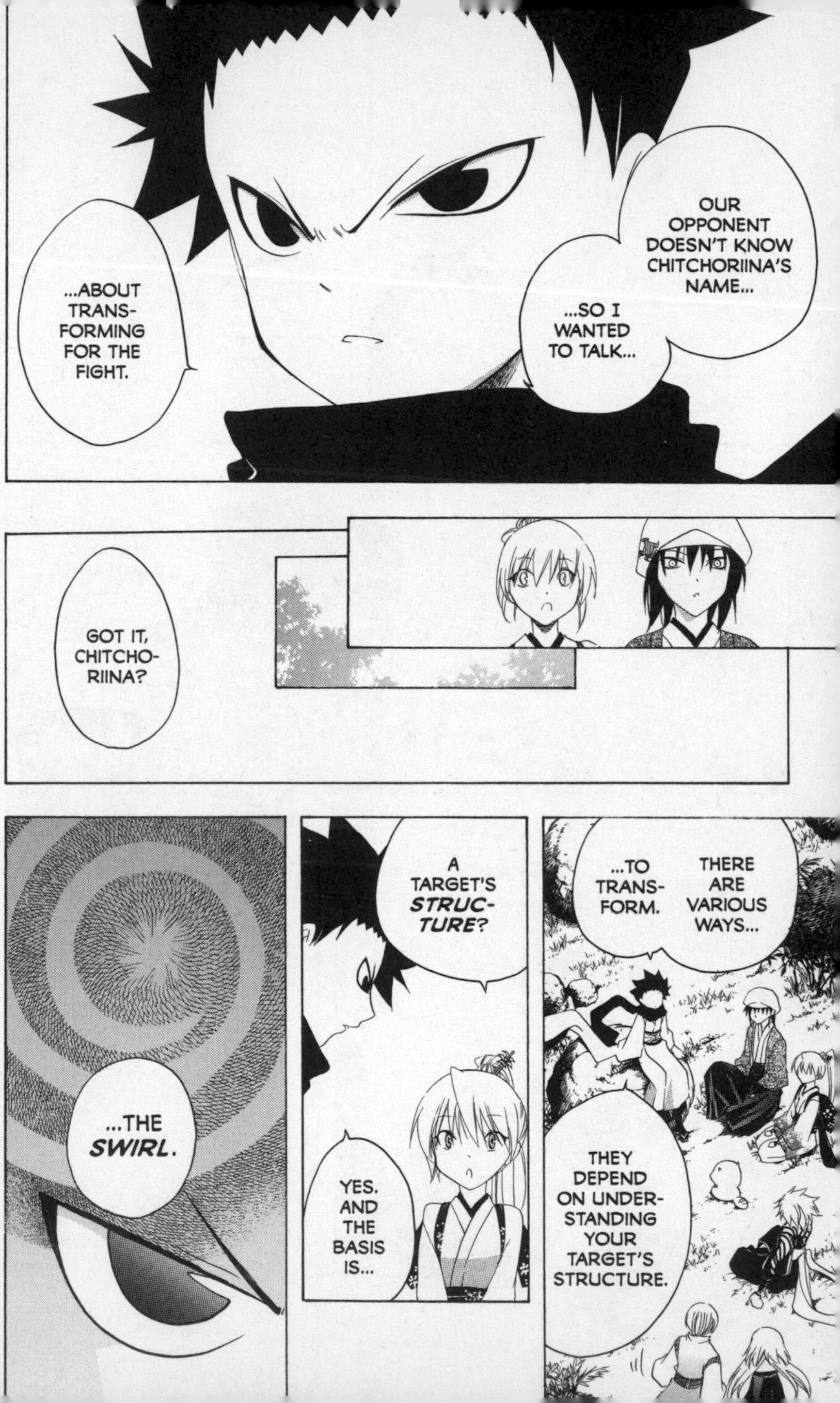
OUR OPPONENT DOESN'T KNOW CHITCHORIINA'S NAME...
...SO I WANTED TO TALK...
...ABOUT TRANS-FORMING FOR THE FIGHT.
GOT IT, CHITCHO-RIINA?
THERE ARE VARIOUS WAYS...
...TO TRANS-FORM.
THEY DEPEND ON UNDER-STANDING YOUR TARGET'S STRUCTURE.
A TARGET'S *STRUC-TURE*?
YES. AND THE BASIS IS...
...THE *SWIRL*.

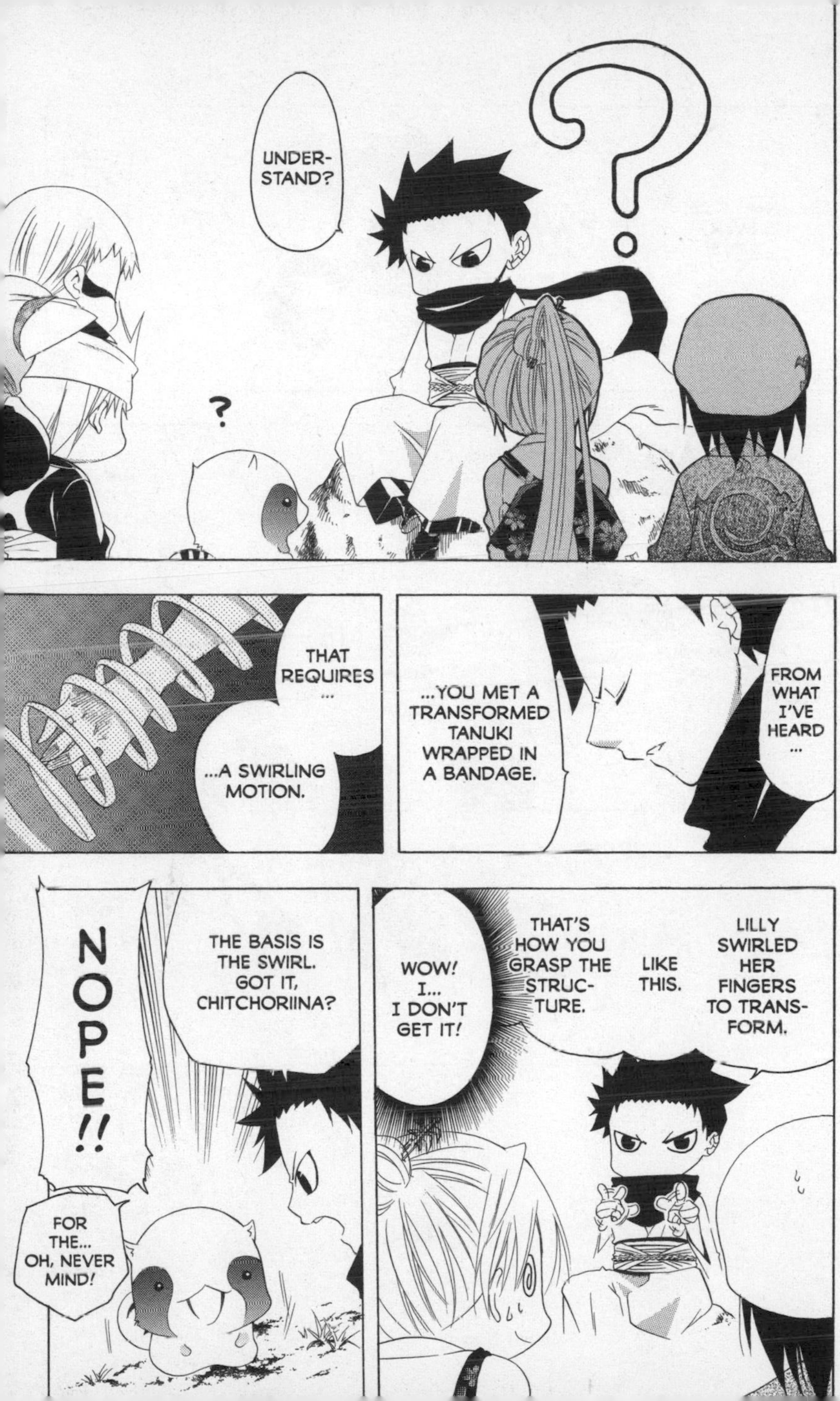
UNDER-STAND?
?
?
FROM WHAT I'VE HEARD ...
...YOU MET A TRANSFORMED TANUKI WRAPPED IN A BANDAGE.
THAT REQUIRES ...
...A SWIRLING MOTION.
LILLY SWIRLED HER FINGERS TO TRANS-FORM.
LIKE THIS.
THAT'S HOW YOU GRASP THE STRUC-TURE.
WOW! I... I DON'T GET IT!
THE BASIS IS THE SWIRL. GOT IT, CHITCHORIINA?
NOPE!!
FOR THE... OH, NEVER MIND!

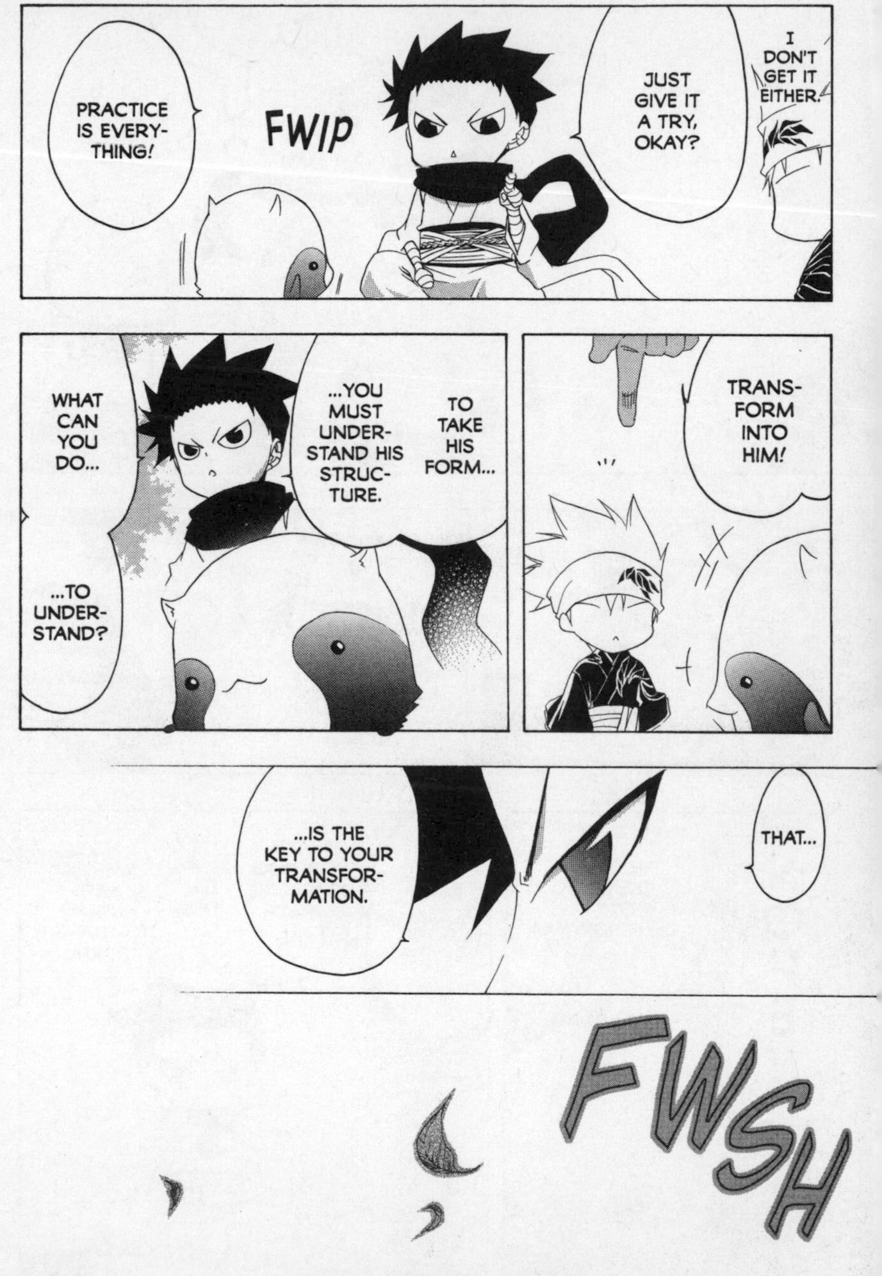
I DON'T GET IT EITHER.
JUST GIVE IT A TRY, OKAY?
FWIP
PRACTICE IS EVERYTHING!
TRANSFORM INTO HIM!
TO TAKE HIS FORM...
...YOU MUST UNDERSTAND HIS STRUCTURE.
WHAT CAN YOU DO...
...TO UNDERSTAND?
THAT...
...IS THE KEY TO YOUR TRANSFORMATION.
FWSH

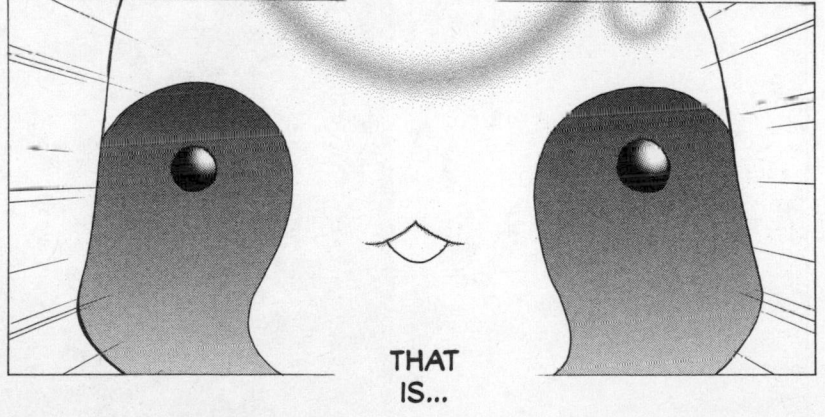

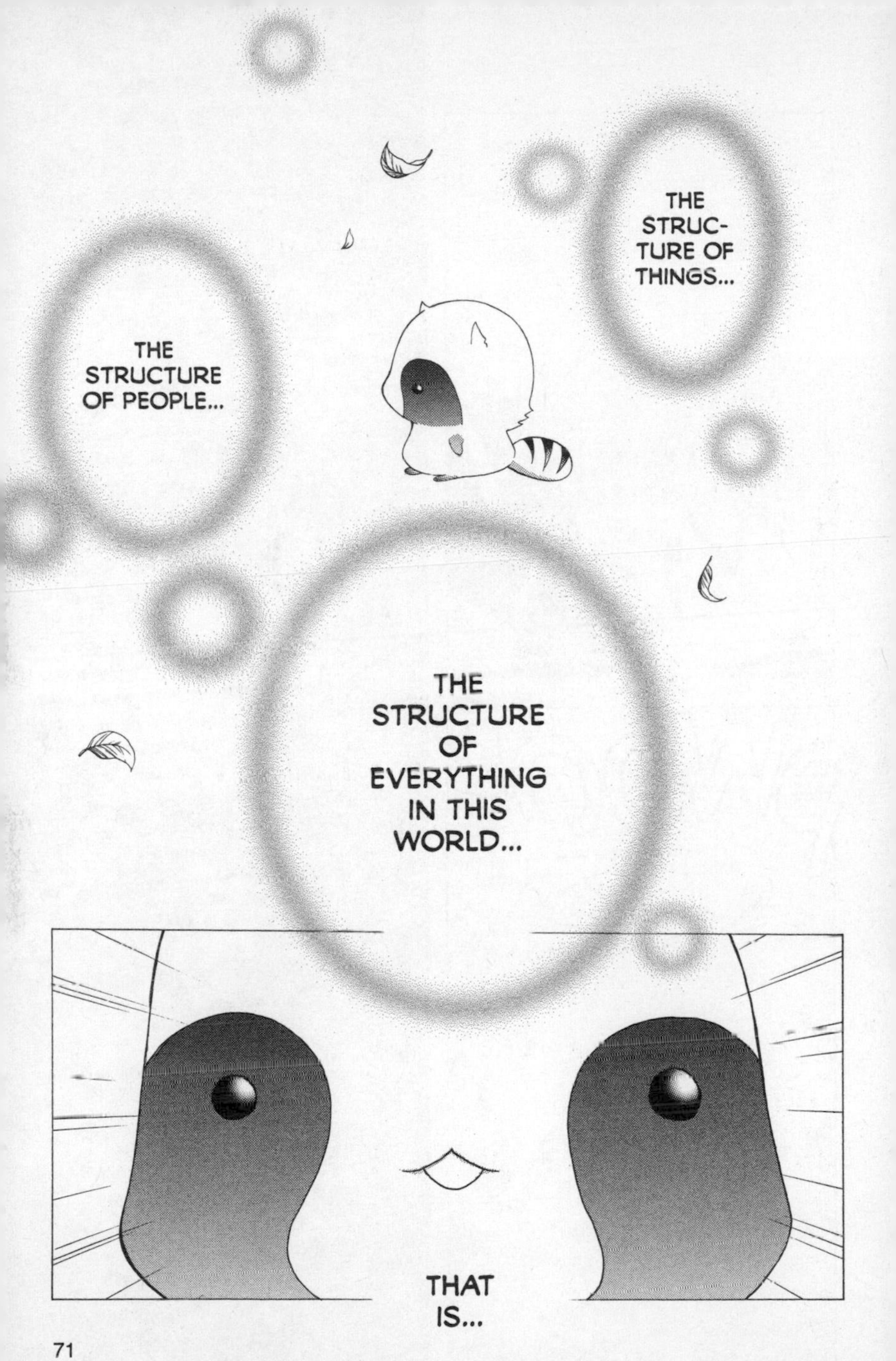

THE STRUCTURE OF THINGS...

THE STRUCTURE OF PEOPLE...

THE STRUCTURE OF EVERYTHING IN THIS WORLD...

THAT IS...

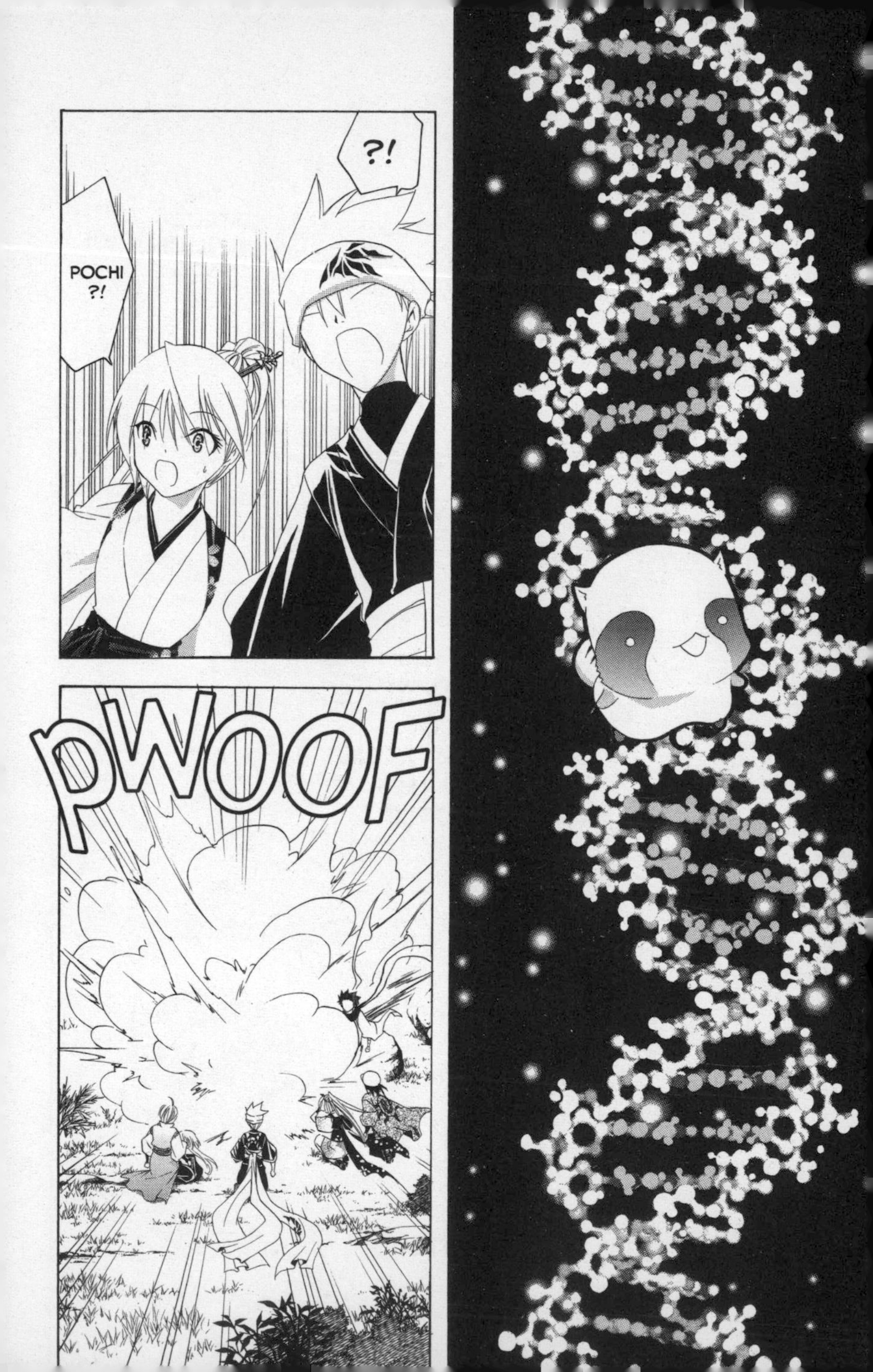
?!
POCHI ?!
pWOOF

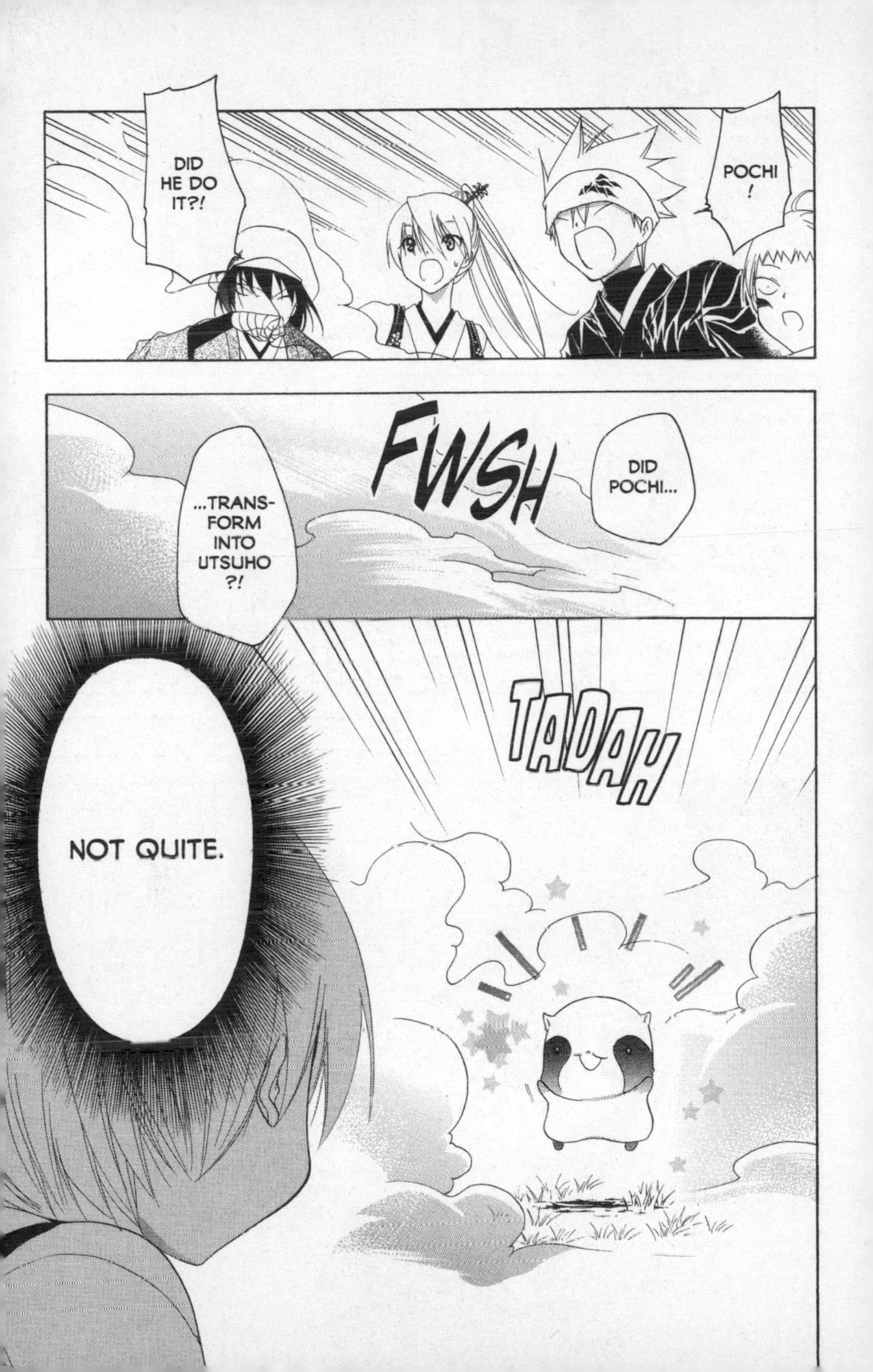
POCHI!
DID HE DO IT?!
FWSH
DID POCHI...
...TRANSFORM INTO UTSUHO?!
TADAH
NOT QUITE.

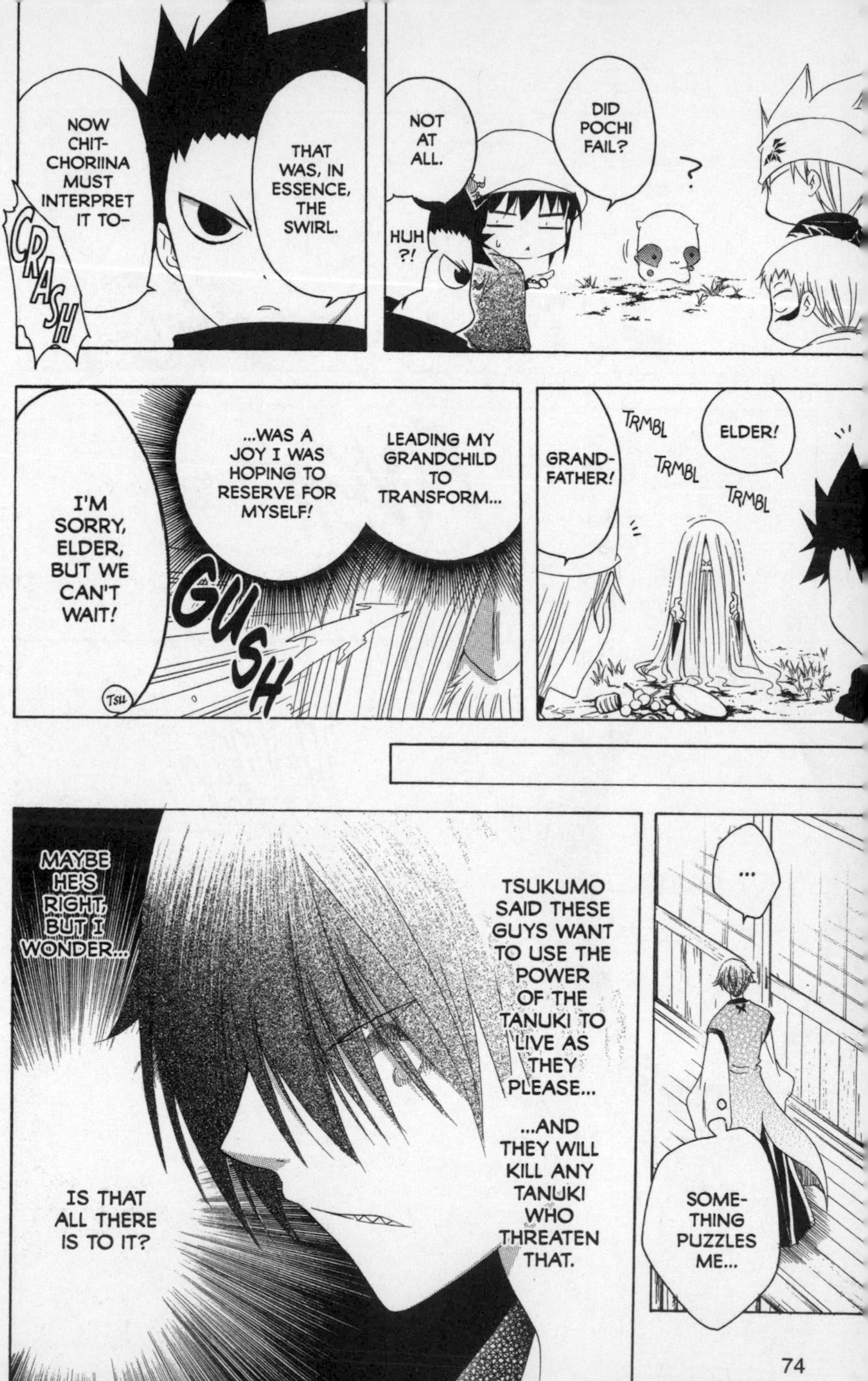
DID POCHI FAIL?
?
NOT AT ALL.
HUH ?!
THAT WAS, IN ESSENCE, THE SWIRL.
NOW CHIT-CHORIINA MUST INTERPRET IT TO–
CRASH
ELDER!
GRAND-FATHER!
TRMBL
TRMBL
TRMBL
LEADING MY GRANDCHILD TO TRANSFORM...
...WAS A JOY I WAS HOPING TO RESERVE FOR MYSELF!
GUSH
TSU
I'M SORRY, ELDER, BUT WE CAN'T WAIT!
...
SOME-THING PUZZLES ME...
TSUKUMO SAID THESE GUYS WANT TO USE THE POWER OF THE TANUKI TO LIVE AS THEY PLEASE...
...AND THEY WILL KILL ANY TANUKI WHO THREATEN THAT.
MAYBE HE'S RIGHT, BUT I WONDER...
IS THAT ALL THERE IS TO IT?

Chapter 132 The Ability to Change

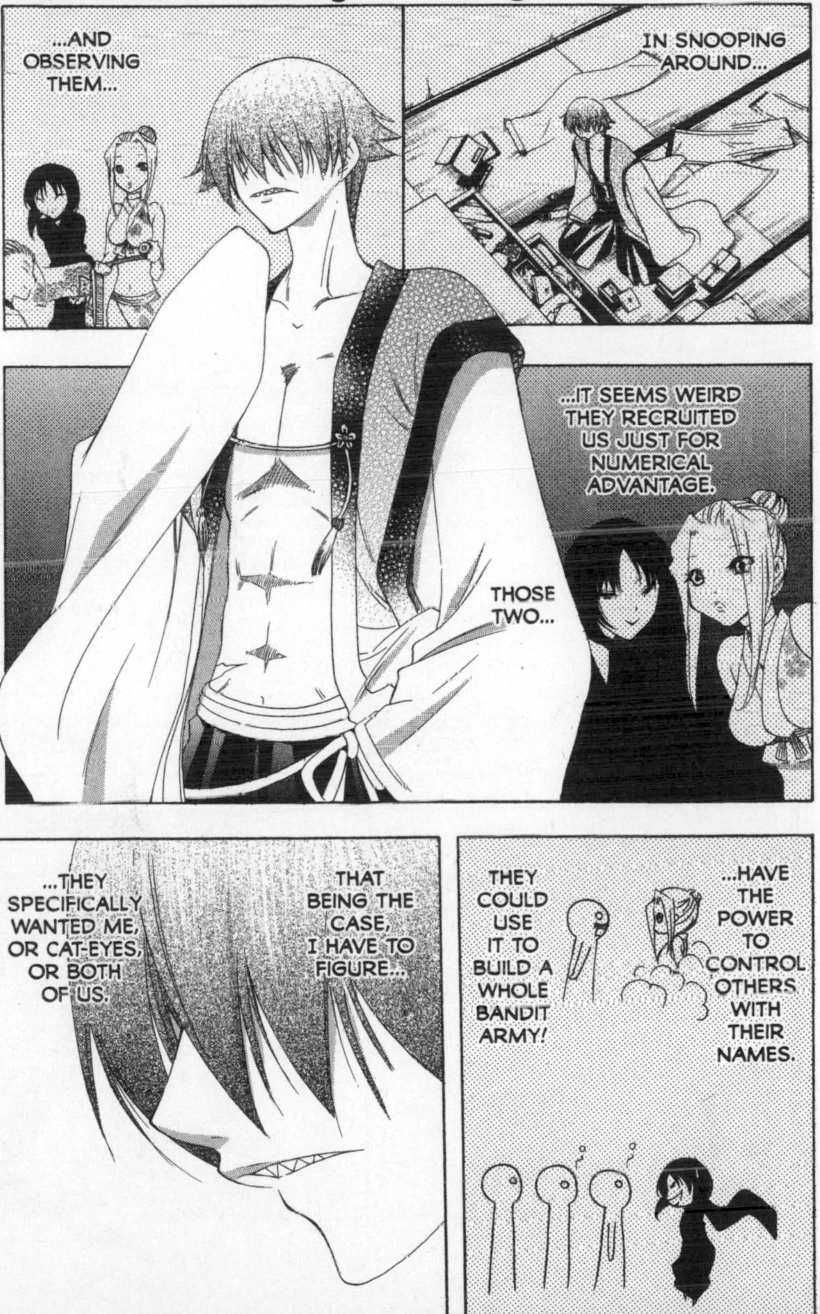
IN SNOOPING AROUND...
...AND OBSERVING THEM...
...IT SEEMS WEIRD THEY RECRUITED US JUST FOR NUMERICAL ADVANTAGE.
THOSE TWO...
...HAVE THE POWER TO CONTROL OTHERS WITH THEIR NAMES.
THEY COULD USE IT TO BUILD A WHOLE BANDIT ARMY!
THAT BEING THE CASE, I HAVE TO FIGURE...
...THEY SPECIFICALLY WANTED ME, OR CAT-EYES, OR BOTH OF US.

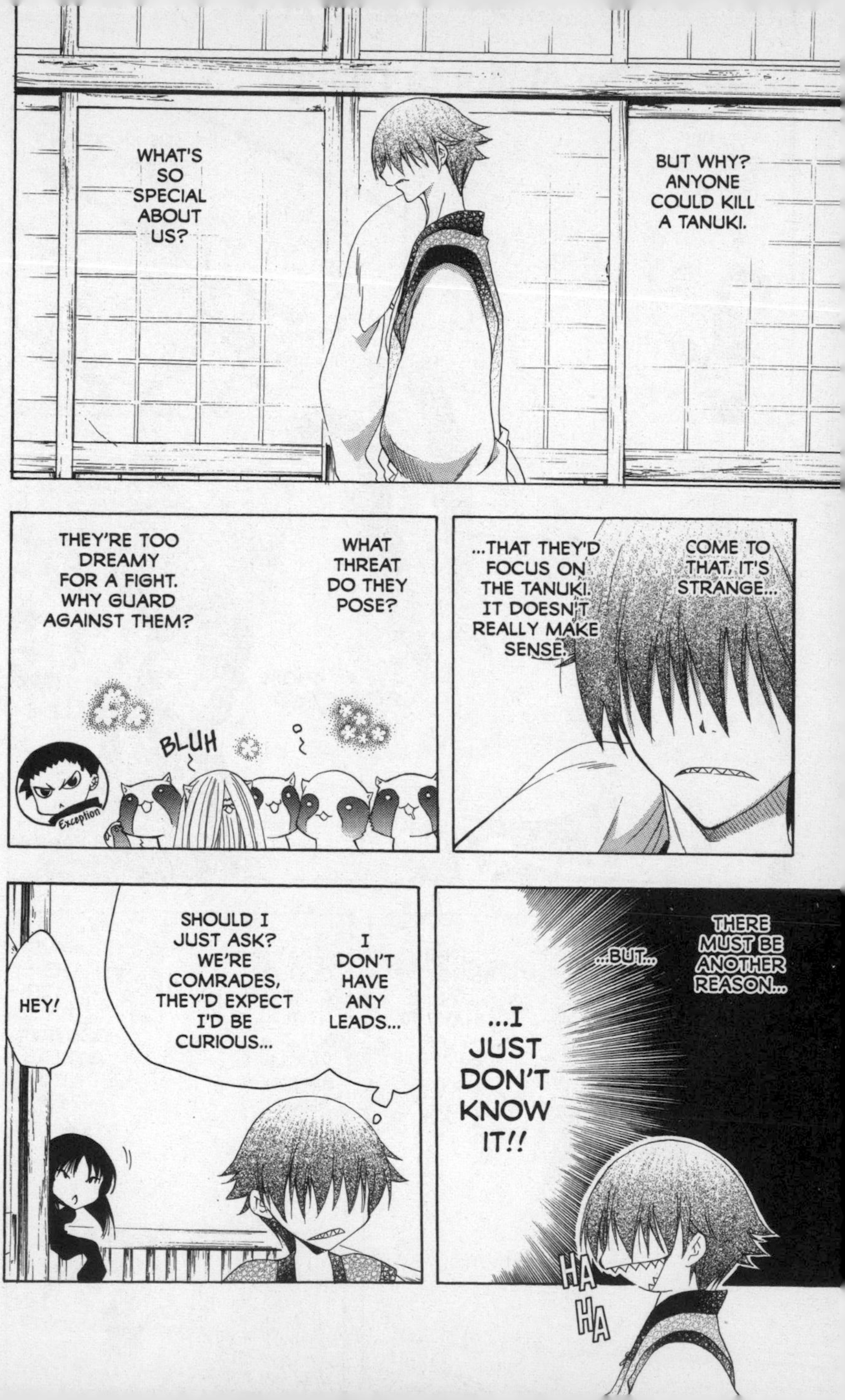
BUT WHY? ANYONE COULD KILL A TANUKI.
WHAT'S SO SPECIAL ABOUT US?
COME TO THAT, IT'S STRANGE...
...THAT THEY'D FOCUS ON THE TANUKI. IT DOESN'T REALLY MAKE SENSE.
WHAT THREAT DO THEY POSE?
THEY'RE TOO DREAMY FOR A FIGHT. WHY GUARD AGAINST THEM?
BLUH
Exception
THERE MUST BE ANOTHER REASON...
...BUT...
...I JUST DON'T KNOW IT!!
HA HA
I DON'T HAVE ANY LEADS...
SHOULD I JUST ASK? WE'RE COMRADES, THEY'D EXPECT I'D BE CURIOUS...
HEY!

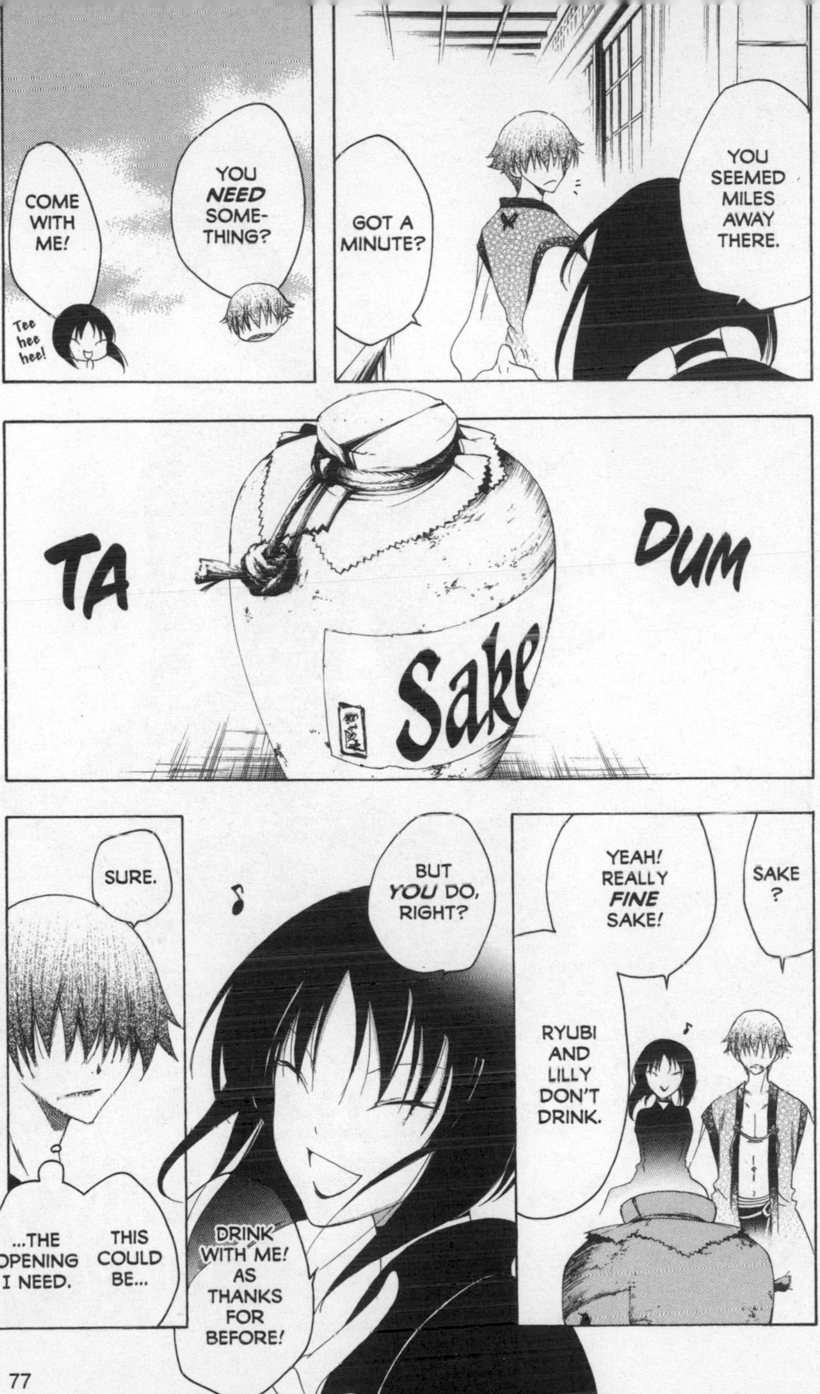
YOU SEEMED MILES AWAY THERE.
GOT A MINUTE?
YOU NEED SOME-THING?
COME WITH ME!
Tee hee hee!
DUM
TA
Sake
SAKE?
YEAH! REALLY FINE SAKE!
RYUBI AND LILLY DON'T DRINK.
BUT YOU DO, RIGHT?
DRINK WITH ME! AS THANKS FOR BEFORE!
SURE.
THIS COULD BE...
...THE OPENING I NEED.

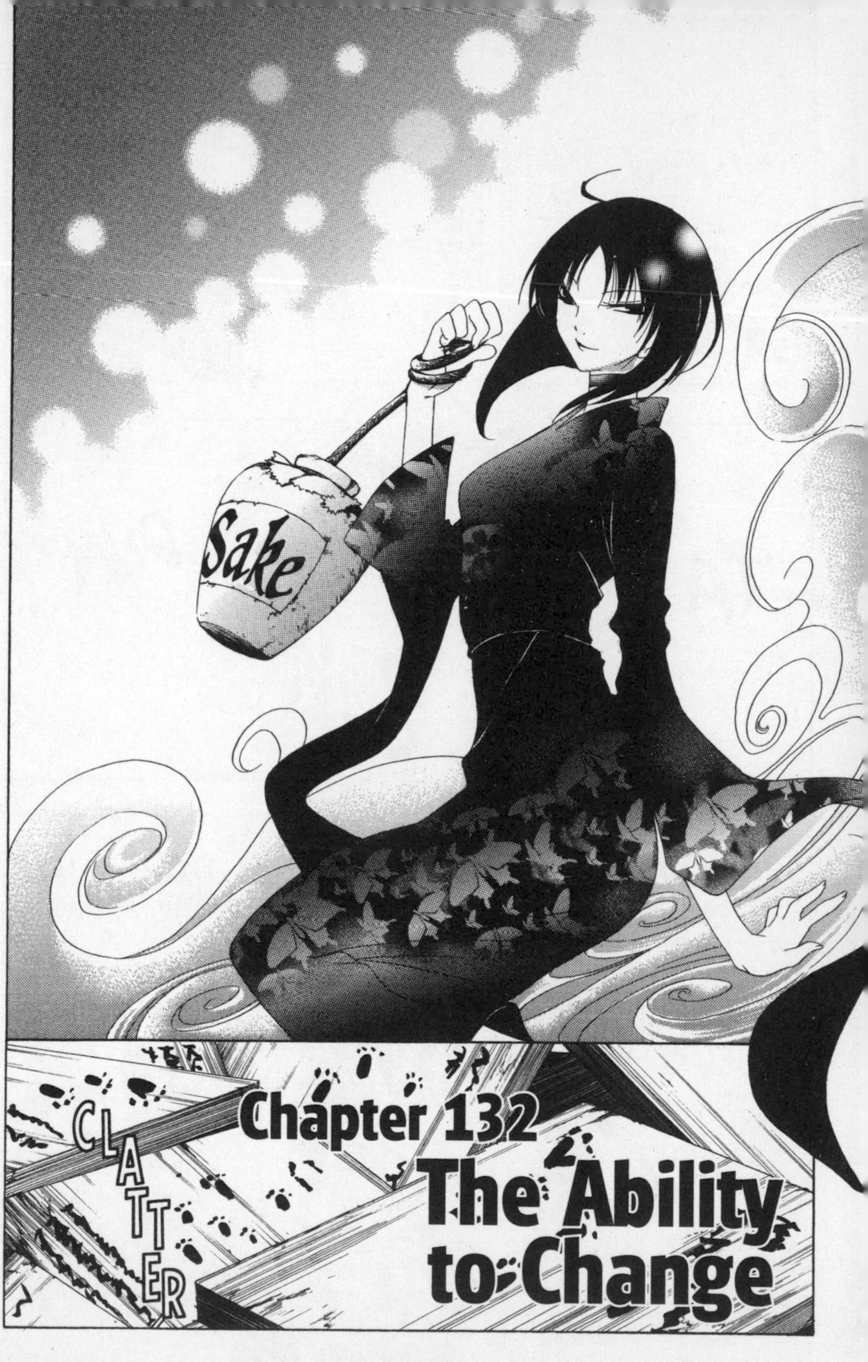
Sake
CLATTER
Chapter 132
The Ability to Change

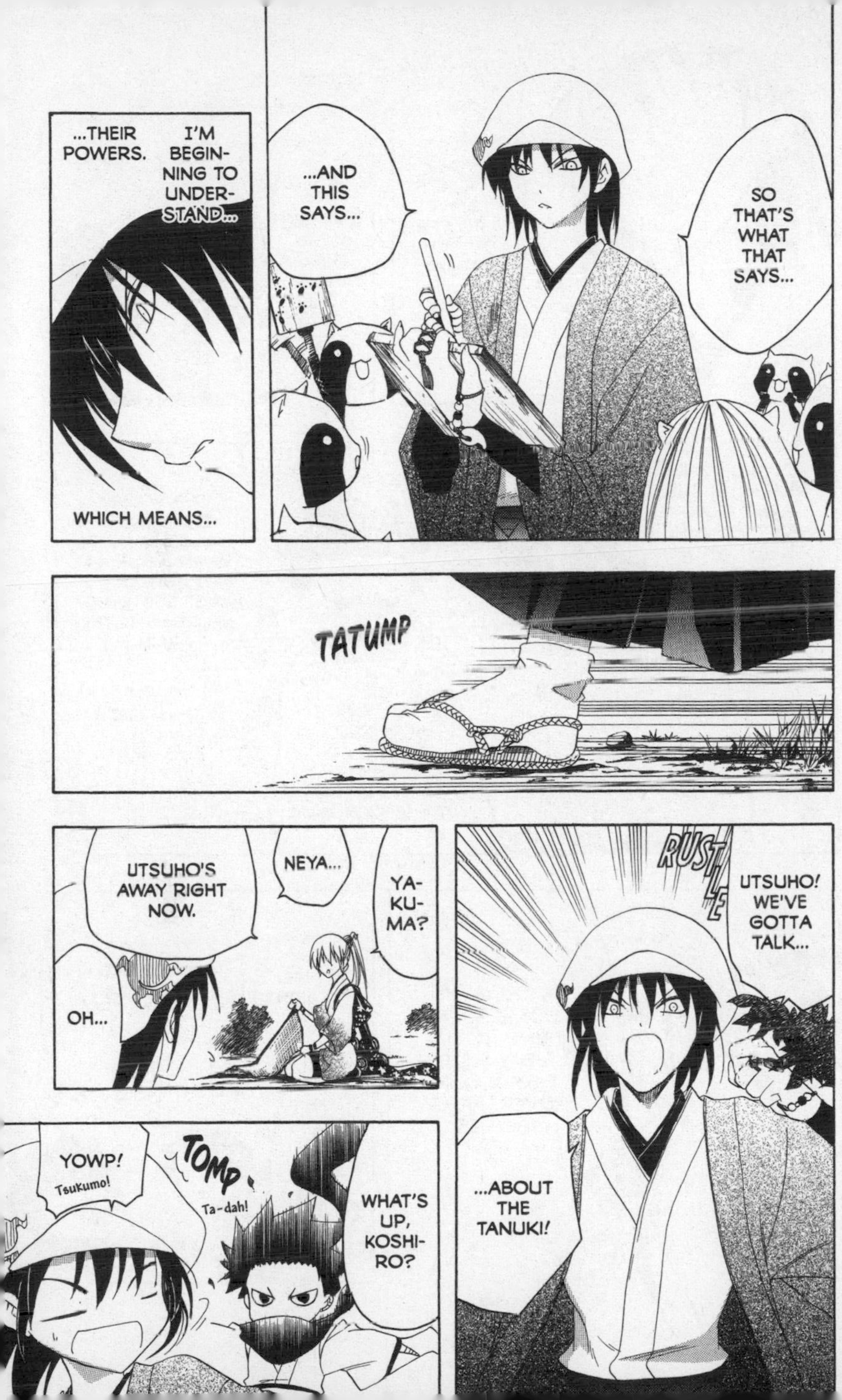
SO THAT'S WHAT THAT SAYS...
...AND THIS SAYS...
I'M BEGINNING TO UNDERSTAND...
...THEIR POWERS.
WHICH MEANS...
TATUMP
RUSTLE
UTSUHO! WE'VE GOTTA TALK...
...ABOUT THE TANUKI!
YA-KU-MA?
NEYA...
UTSUHO'S AWAY RIGHT NOW.
OH...
WHAT'S UP, KOSHIRO?
TOMP
Ta-dah!
YOWP!
Tsukumo!

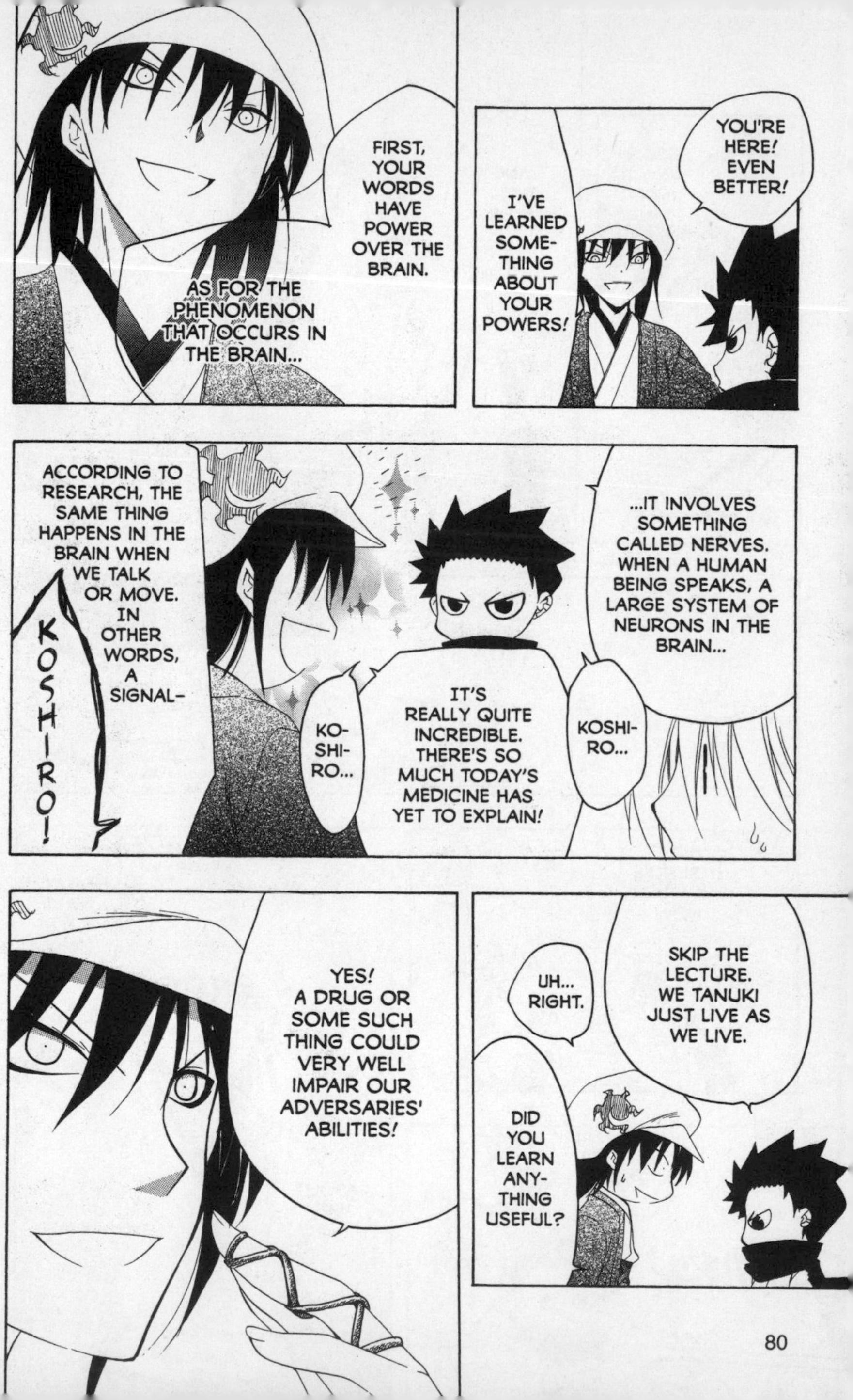
YOU'RE HERE! EVEN BETTER!
I'VE LEARNED SOME-THING ABOUT YOUR POWERS!
FIRST, YOUR WORDS HAVE POWER OVER THE BRAIN.
AS FOR THE PHENOMENON THAT OCCURS IN THE BRAIN...
...IT INVOLVES SOMETHING CALLED NERVES. WHEN A HUMAN BEING SPEAKS, A LARGE SYSTEM OF NEURONS IN THE BRAIN...
KOSHI-RO...
IT'S REALLY QUITE INCREDIBLE. THERE'S SO MUCH TODAY'S MEDICINE HAS YET TO EXPLAIN!
KO-SHI-RO...
ACCORDING TO RESEARCH, THE SAME THING HAPPENS IN THE BRAIN WHEN WE TALK OR MOVE. IN OTHER WORDS, A SIGNAL–
KOSHIRO!
SKIP THE LECTURE. WE TANUKI JUST LIVE AS WE LIVE.
UH... RIGHT.
DID YOU LEARN ANY-THING USEFUL?
YES! A DRUG OR SOME SUCH THING COULD VERY WELL IMPAIR OUR ADVERSARIES' ABILITIES!

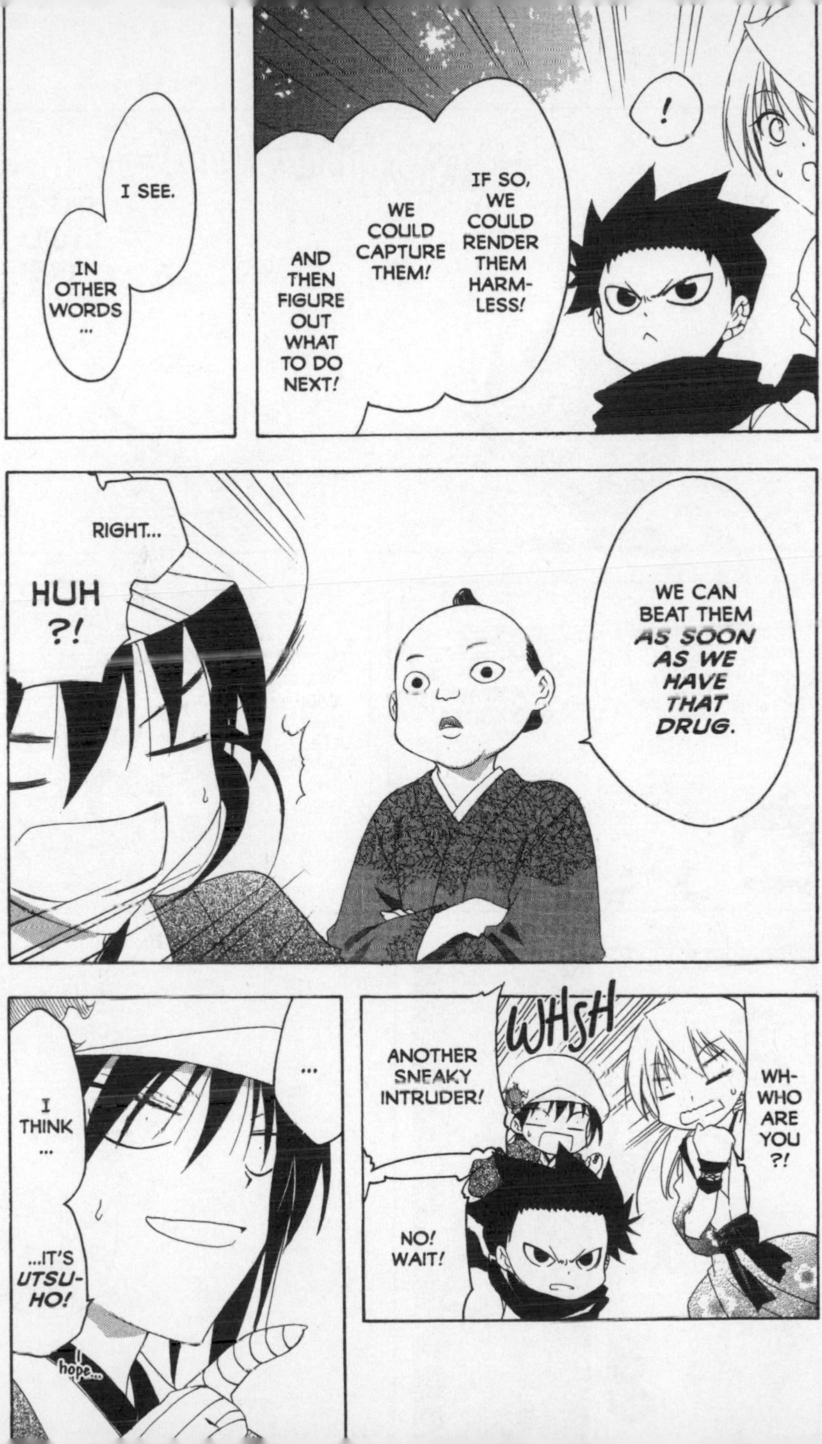
!
IF SO, WE COULD RENDER THEM HARMLESS!
WE COULD CAPTURE THEM!
AND THEN FIGURE OUT WHAT TO DO NEXT!
I SEE.
IN OTHER WORDS ...
WE CAN BEAT THEM *AS SOON AS WE HAVE THAT DRUG.*
RIGHT...
HUH ?!
WHSH
WH-WHO ARE YOU ?!
ANOTHER SNEAKY INTRUDER!
NO! WAIT!
...
I THINK ...
...IT'S *UTSU-HO!*
I hope...

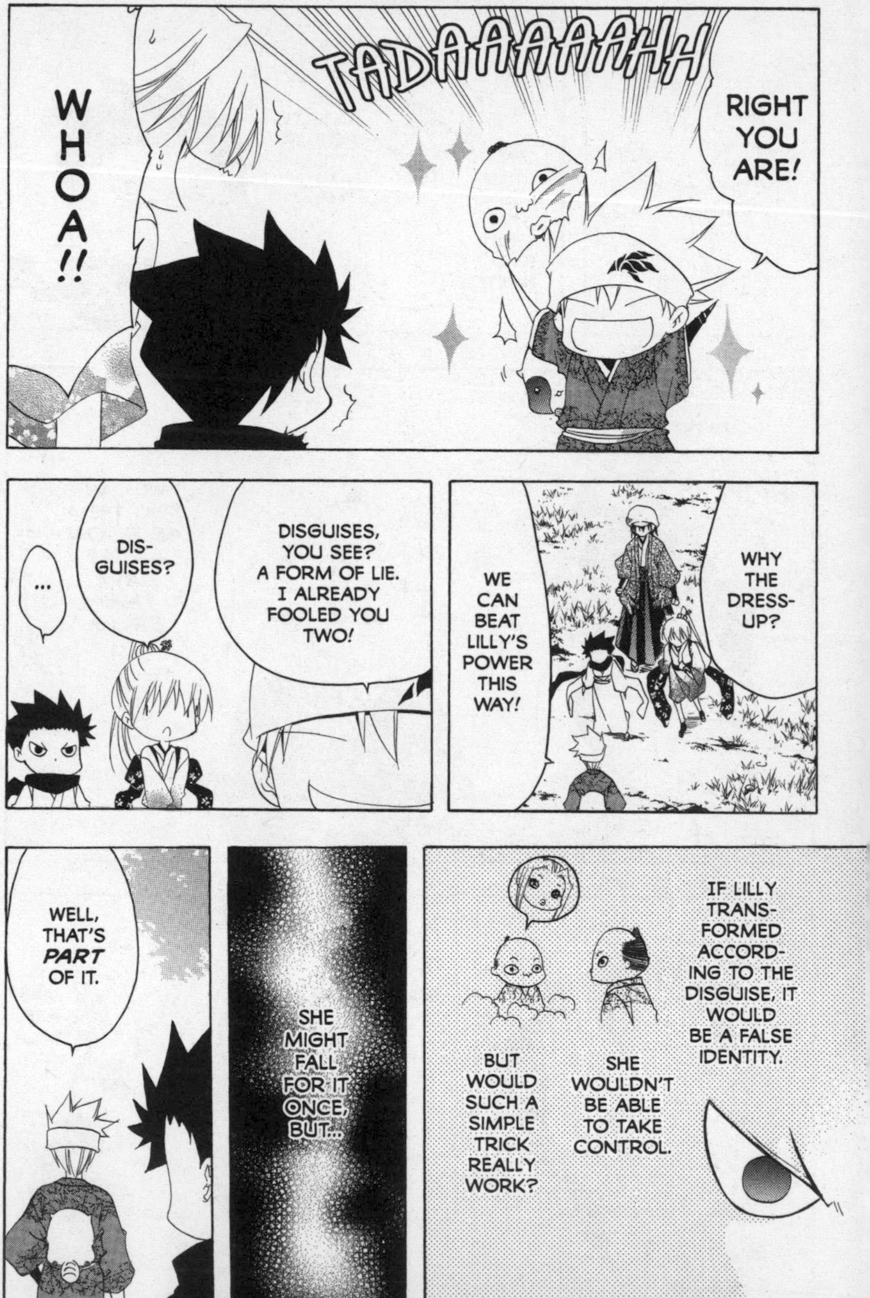
RIGHT YOU ARE!
TADAAAAAAHH
WHOA!!
WHY THE DRESS-UP?
WE CAN BEAT LILLY'S POWER THIS WAY!
DISGUISES, YOU SEE? A FORM OF LIE. I ALREADY FOOLED YOU TWO!
DIS-GUISES?
...
IF LILLY TRANS-FORMED ACCORD-ING TO THE DISGUISE, IT WOULD BE A FALSE IDENTITY.
SHE WOULDN'T BE ABLE TO TAKE CONTROL.
BUT WOULD SUCH A SIMPLE TRICK REALLY WORK?
SHE MIGHT FALL FOR IT ONCE, BUT...
WELL, THAT'S *PART* OF IT.

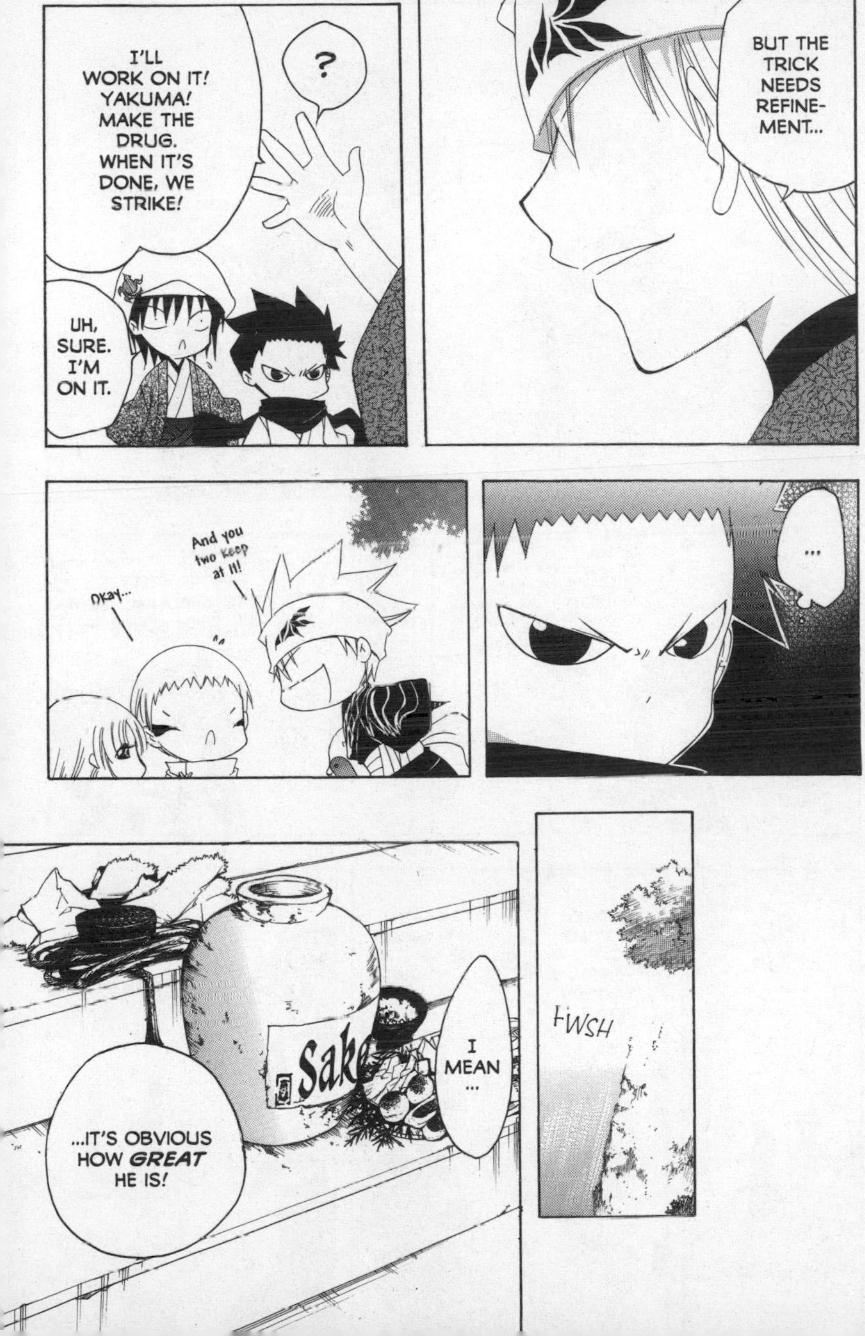
BUT THE TRICK NEEDS REFINE-MENT...
I'LL WORK ON IT! YAKUMA! MAKE THE DRUG. WHEN IT'S DONE, WE STRIKE!
?
UH, SURE. I'M ON IT.
...
And you two keep at it!
okay...
FWSH
I MEAN ...
...IT'S OBVIOUS HOW ***GREAT*** HE IS!
Sake

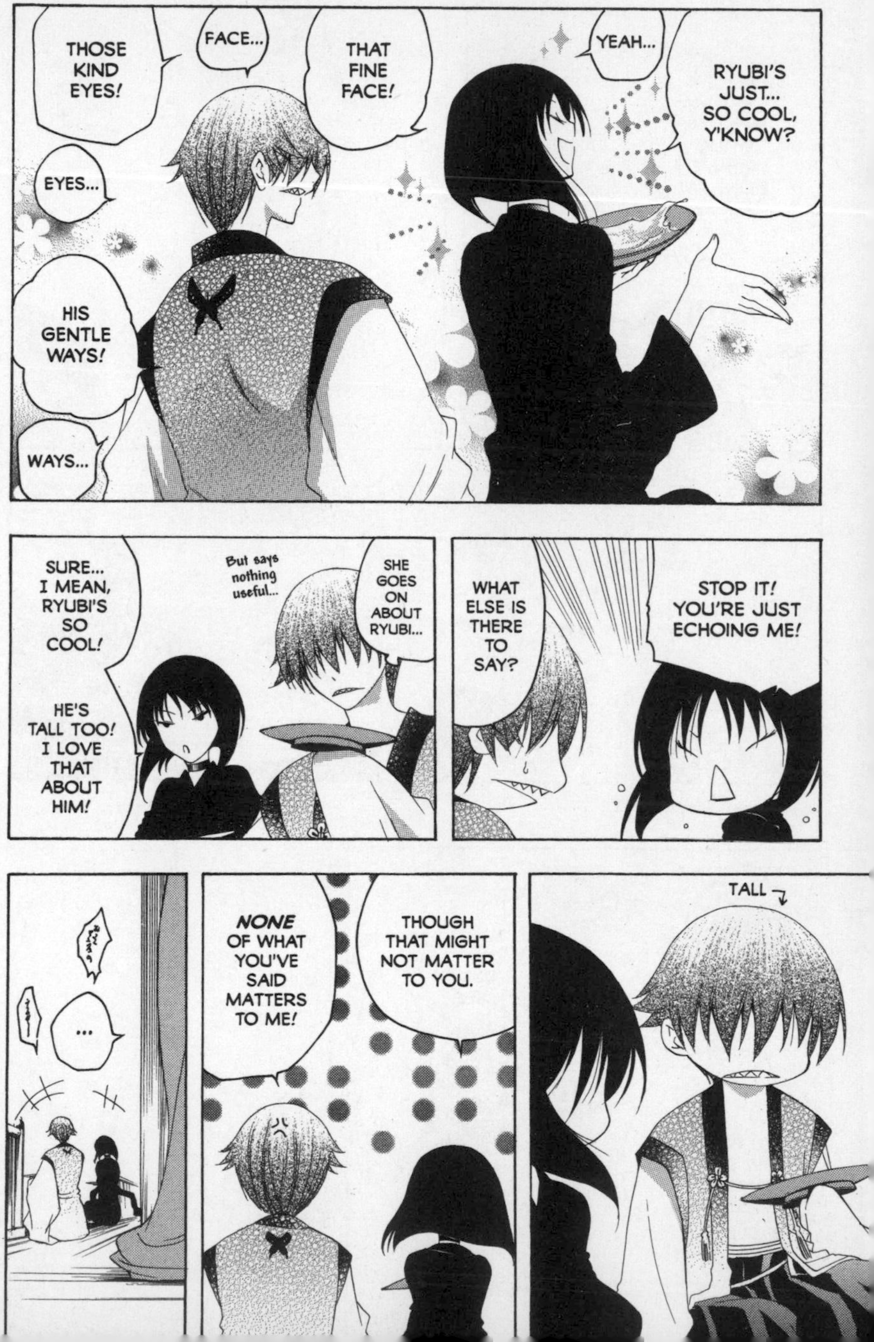
RYUBI'S JUST... SO COOL, Y'KNOW?
YEAH...
THAT FINE FACE!
FACE...
THOSE KIND EYES!
EYES...
HIS GENTLE WAYS!
WAYS...
STOP IT! YOU'RE JUST ECHOING ME!
WHAT ELSE IS THERE TO SAY?
SHE GOES ON ABOUT RYUBI...
But says nothing useful...
SURE... I MEAN, RYUBI'S SO COOL!
HE'S TALL TOO! I LOVE THAT ABOUT HIM!
TALL
THOUGH THAT MIGHT NOT MATTER TO YOU.
NONE OF WHAT YOU'VE SAID MATTERS TO ME!
...

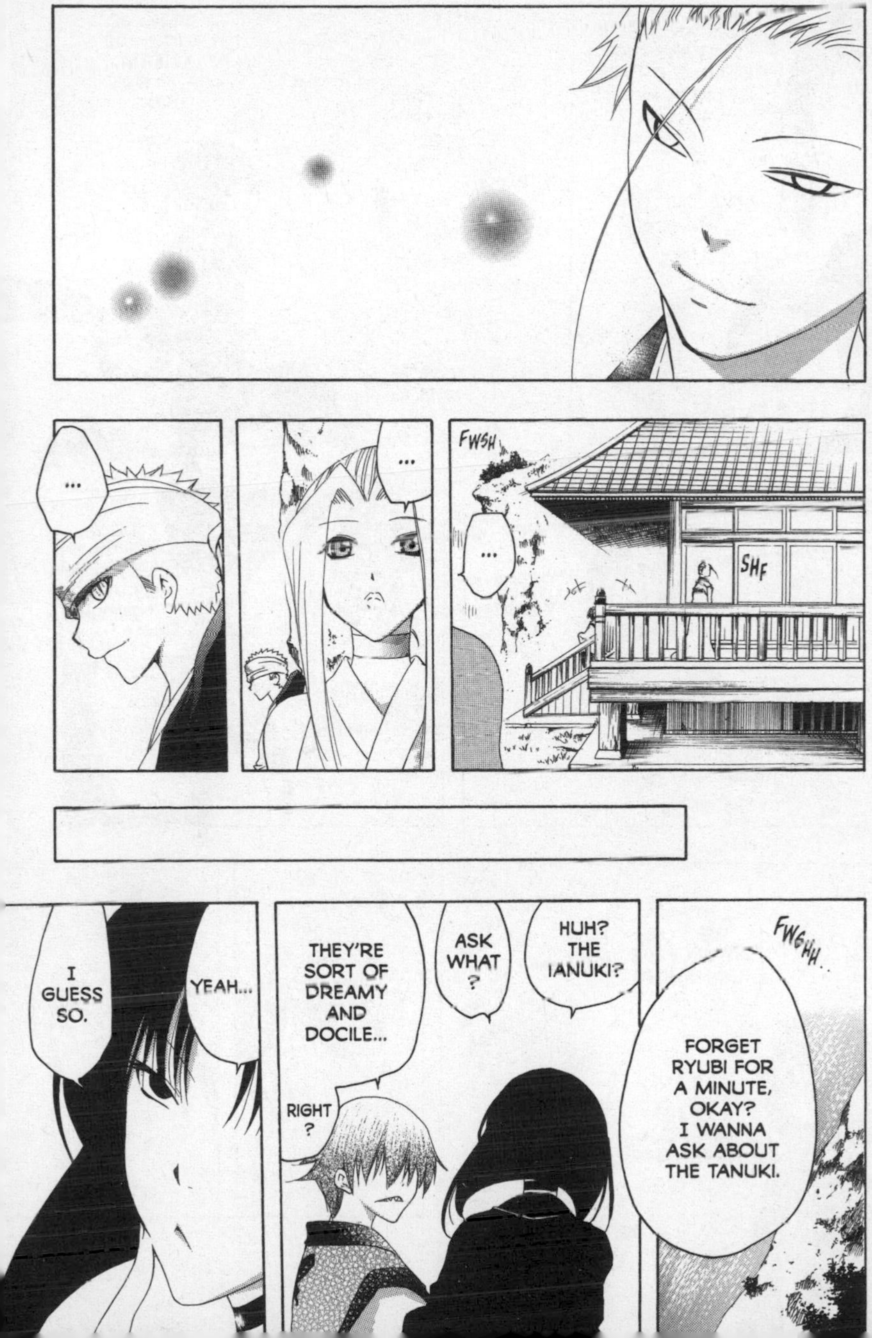
FWSH
SHF
...
...
...
FWGHH..
FORGET RYUBI FOR A MINUTE, OKAY? I WANNA ASK ABOUT THE TANUKI.
HUH? THE IANUKI?
ASK WHAT?
THEY'RE SORT OF DREAMY AND DOCILE...
RIGHT?
YEAH...
I GUESS SO.

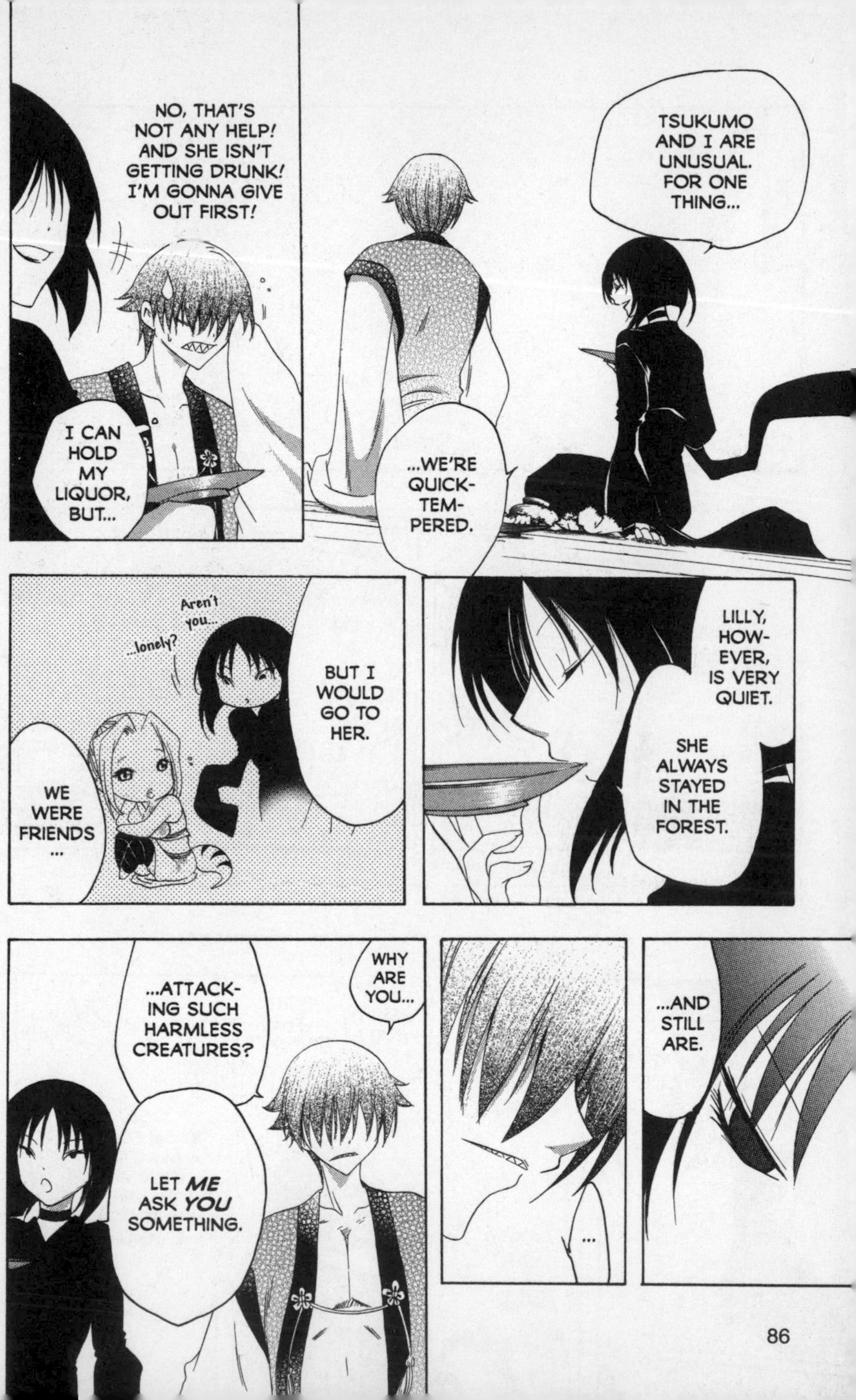
TSUKUMO AND I ARE UNUSUAL. FOR ONE THING...
...WE'RE QUICK-TEM-PERED.
NO, THAT'S NOT ANY HELP! AND SHE ISN'T GETTING DRUNK! I'M GONNA GIVE OUT FIRST!
I CAN HOLD MY LIQUOR, BUT...
LILLY, HOW-EVER, IS VERY QUIET.
SHE ALWAYS STAYED IN THE FOREST.
BUT I WOULD GO TO HER.
Aren't you...
...lonely?
WE WERE FRIENDS ...
...AND STILL ARE.
...
WHY ARE YOU...
...ATTACK-ING SUCH HARMLESS CREATURES?
LET *ME* ASK *YOU* SOMETHING.

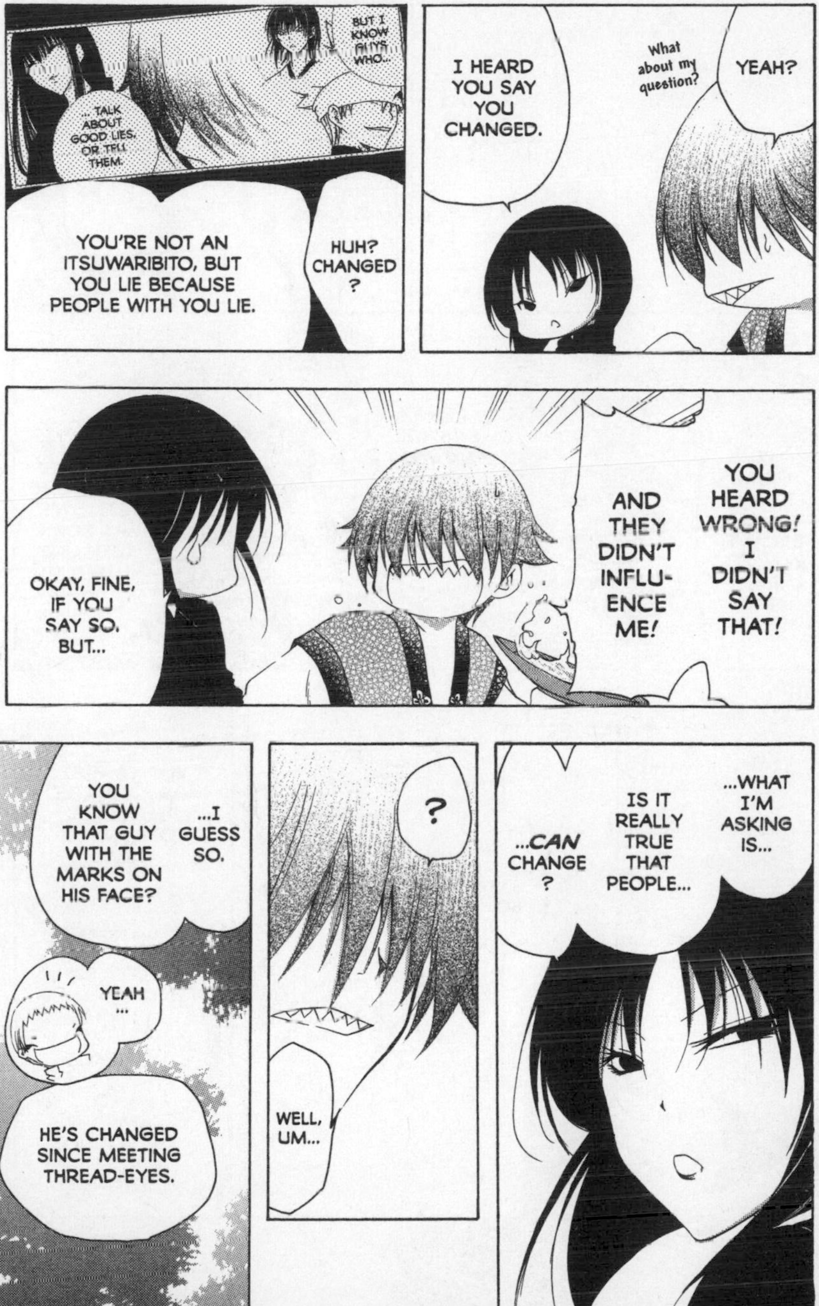
YEAH?
What about my question?
I HEARD YOU SAY YOU CHANGED.
BUT I KNOW GUYS WHO...
...TALK ABOUT GOOD LIES, OR TELL THEM.
HUH? CHANGED ?
YOU'RE NOT AN ITSUWARIBITO, BUT YOU LIE BECAUSE PEOPLE WITH YOU LIE.
YOU HEARD WRONG! I DIDN'T SAY THAT!
AND THEY DIDN'T INFLU- ENCE ME!
OKAY, FINE, IF YOU SAY SO. BUT...
...WHAT I'M ASKING IS...
IS IT REALLY TRUE THAT PEOPLE...
...CAN CHANGE ?
?
WELL, UM...
...I GUESS SO.
YOU KNOW THAT GUY WITH THE MARKS ON HIS FACE?
YEAH ...
HE'S CHANGED SINCE MEETING THREAD-EYES.

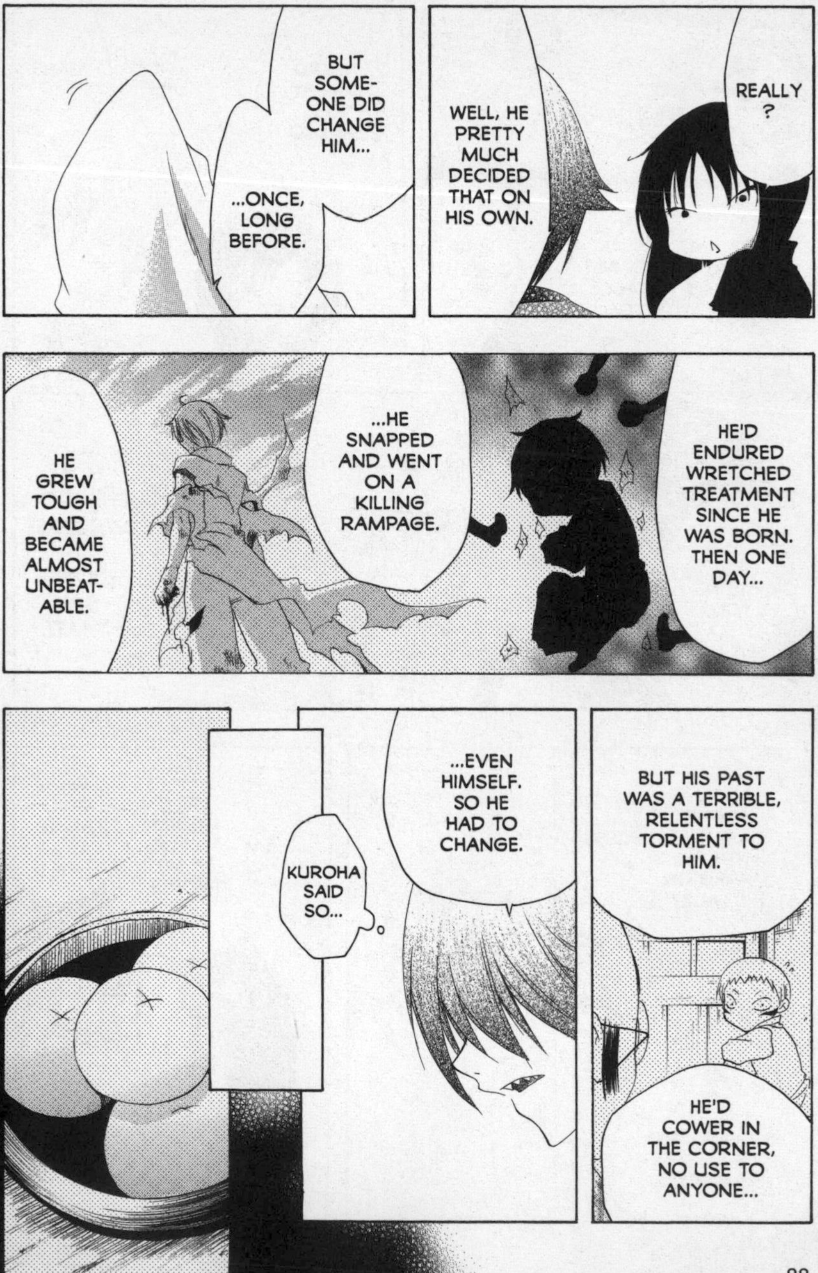
REALLY?
WELL, HE PRETTY MUCH DECIDED THAT ON HIS OWN.
BUT SOME-ONE DID CHANGE HIM...
...ONCE, LONG BEFORE.
HE'D ENDURED WRETCHED TREATMENT SINCE HE WAS BORN. THEN ONE DAY...
...HE SNAPPED AND WENT ON A KILLING RAMPAGE.
HE GREW TOUGH AND BECAME ALMOST UNBEAT-ABLE.
BUT HIS PAST WAS A TERRIBLE, RELENTLESS TORMENT TO HIM.
HE'D COWER IN THE CORNER, NO USE TO ANYONE...
...EVEN HIMSELF. SO HE HAD TO CHANGE.
KUROHA SAID SO...

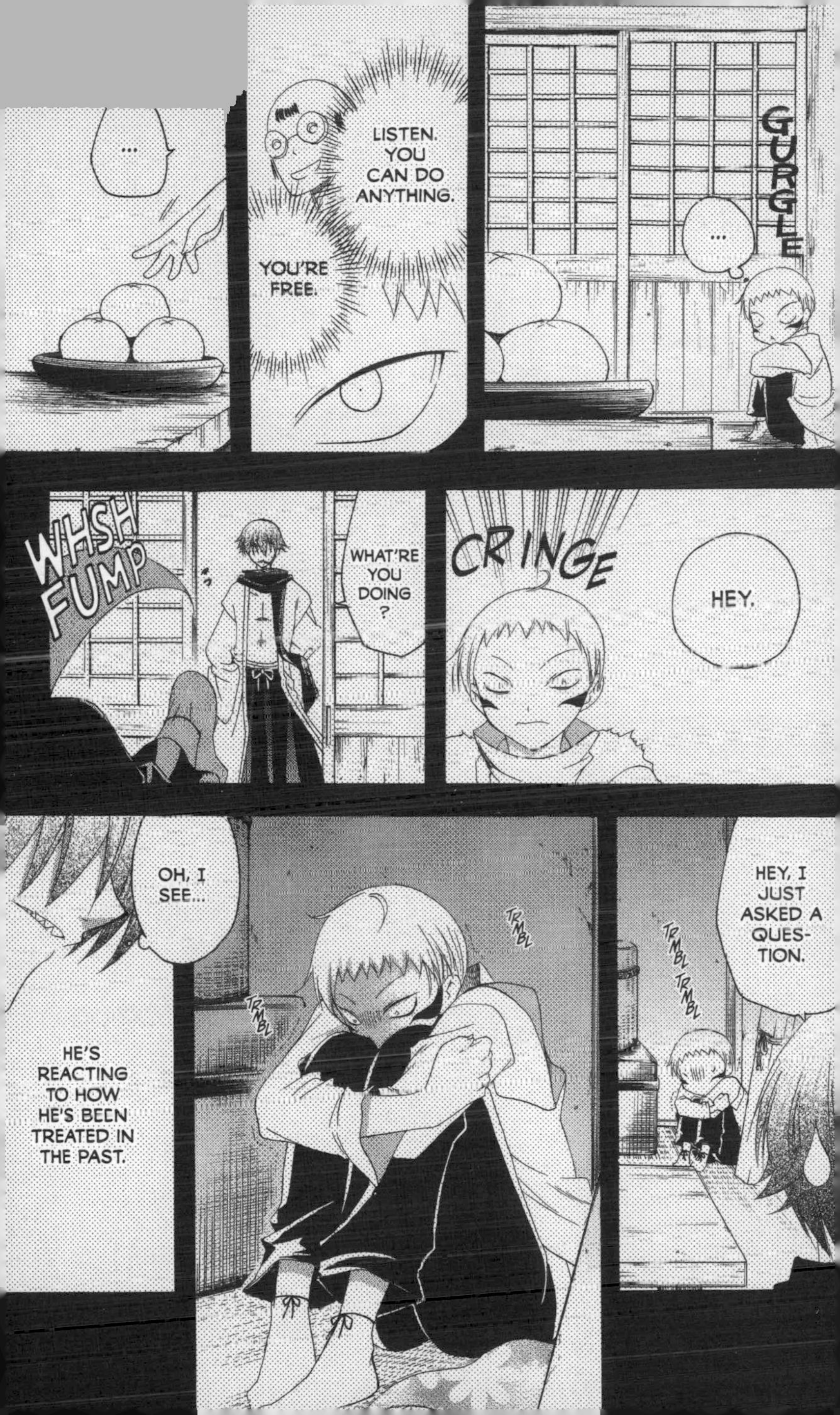
GURGLE
...
LISTEN. YOU CAN DO ANYTHING.
YOU'RE FREE.
...
HEY.
CRINGE
WHAT'RE YOU DOING?
WHSH FUMP
HEY, I JUST ASKED A QUES-TION.
TRMBL TRMBL
TRMBL
TRMBL
OH, I SEE...
HE'S REACTING TO HOW HE'S BEEN TREATED IN THE PAST.

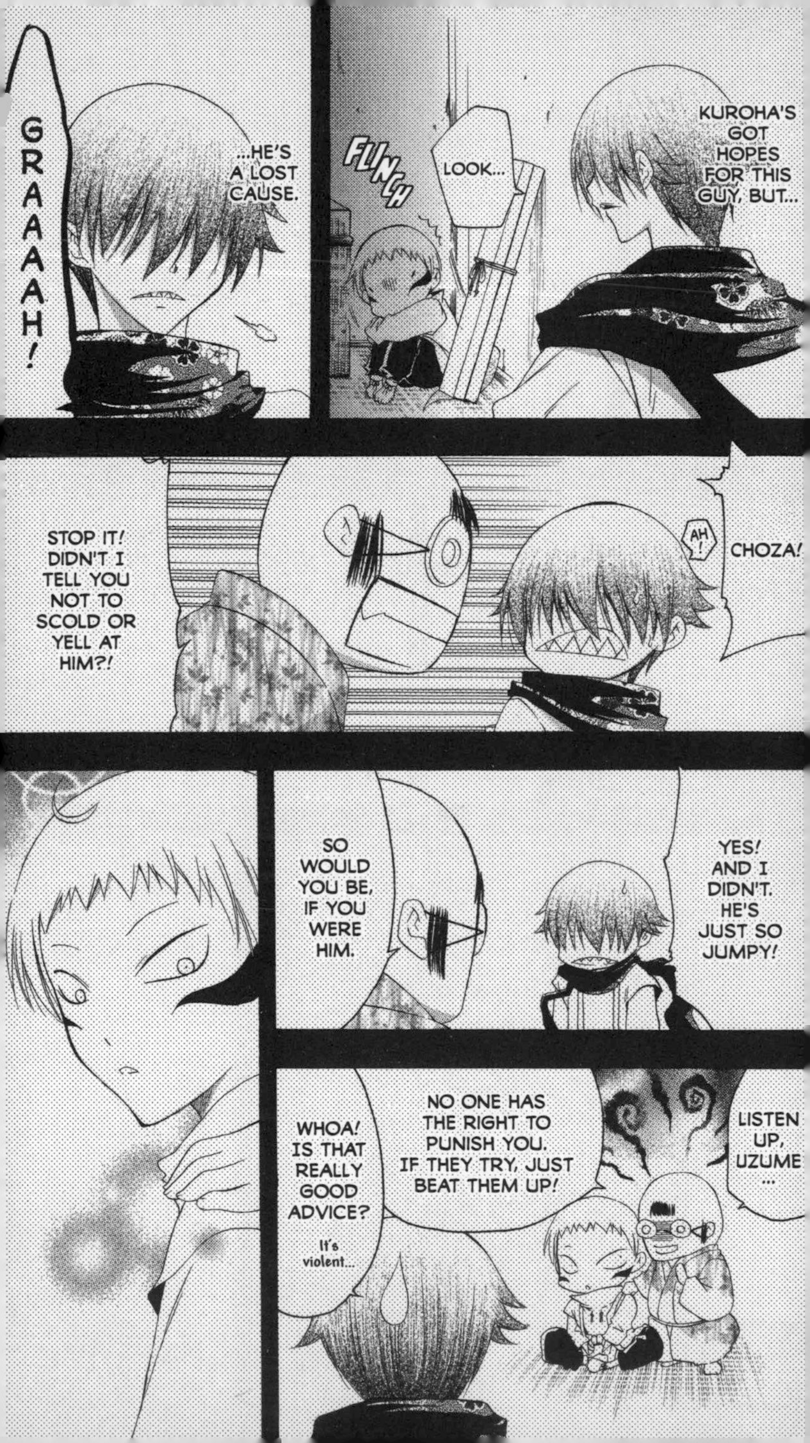
KUROHA'S GOT HOPES FOR THIS GUY, BUT...
LOOK...
FLINCH
...HE'S A LOST CAUSE.
GRAAAAAH!
CHOZA!
AH!
STOP IT! DIDN'T I TELL YOU NOT TO SCOLD OR YELL AT HIM?!
YES! AND I DIDN'T. HE'S JUST SO JUMPY!
SO WOULD YOU BE, IF YOU WERE HIM.
LISTEN UP, UZUME ...
NO ONE HAS THE RIGHT TO PUNISH YOU. IF THEY TRY, JUST BEAT THEM UP!
WHOA! IS THAT REALLY GOOD ADVICE?
It's violent...

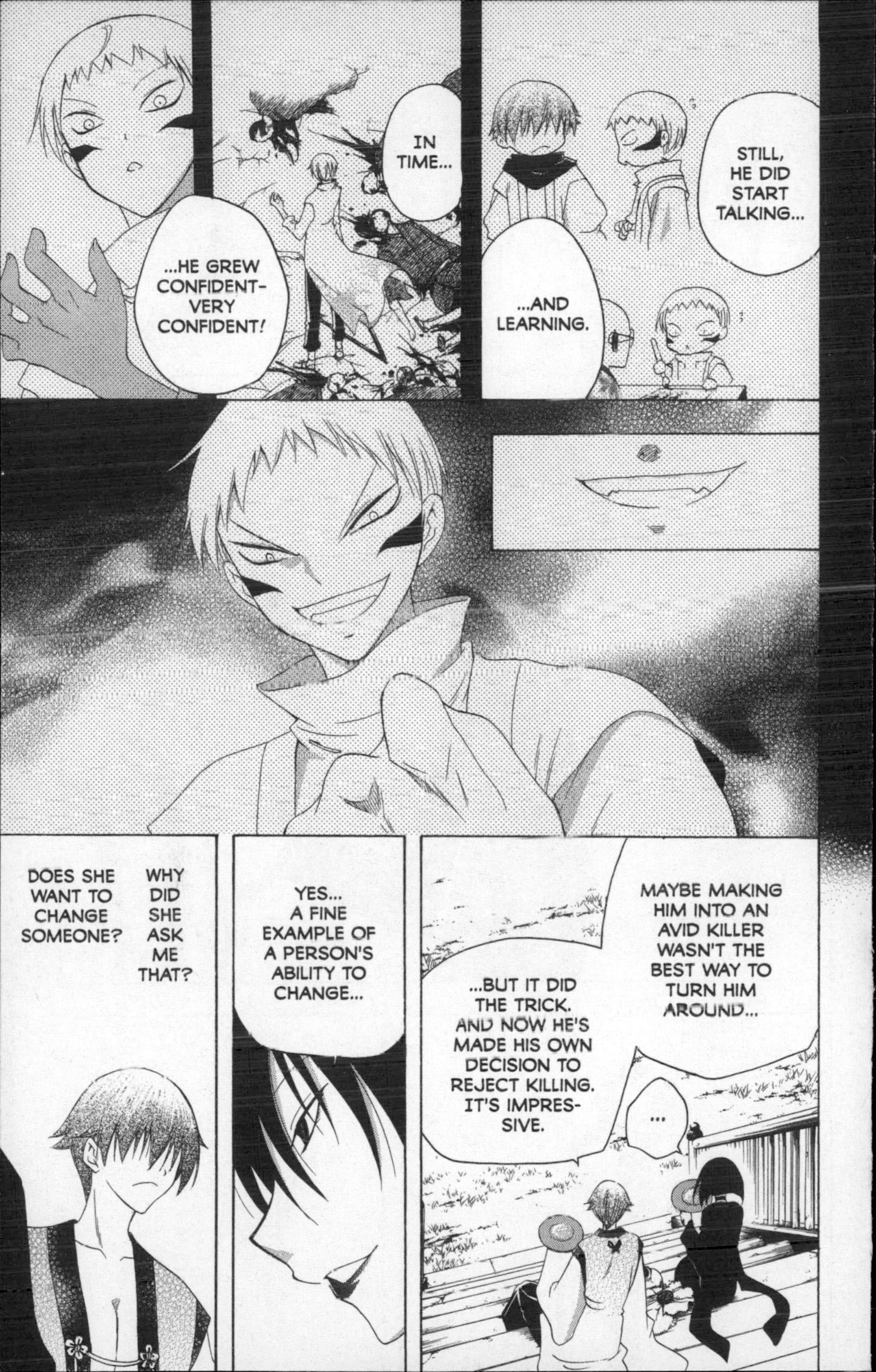
STILL, HE DID START TALKING...
...AND LEARNING.
IN TIME...
...HE GREW CONFIDENT- VERY CONFIDENT!
MAYBE MAKING HIM INTO AN AVID KILLER WASN'T THE BEST WAY TO TURN HIM AROUND...
...BUT IT DID THE TRICK. AND NOW HE'S MADE HIS OWN DECISION TO REJECT KILLING. IT'S IMPRES-SIVE.
...
YES... A FINE EXAMPLE OF A PERSON'S ABILITY TO CHANGE...
WHY DID SHE ASK ME THAT?
DOES SHE WANT TO CHANGE SOMEONE?

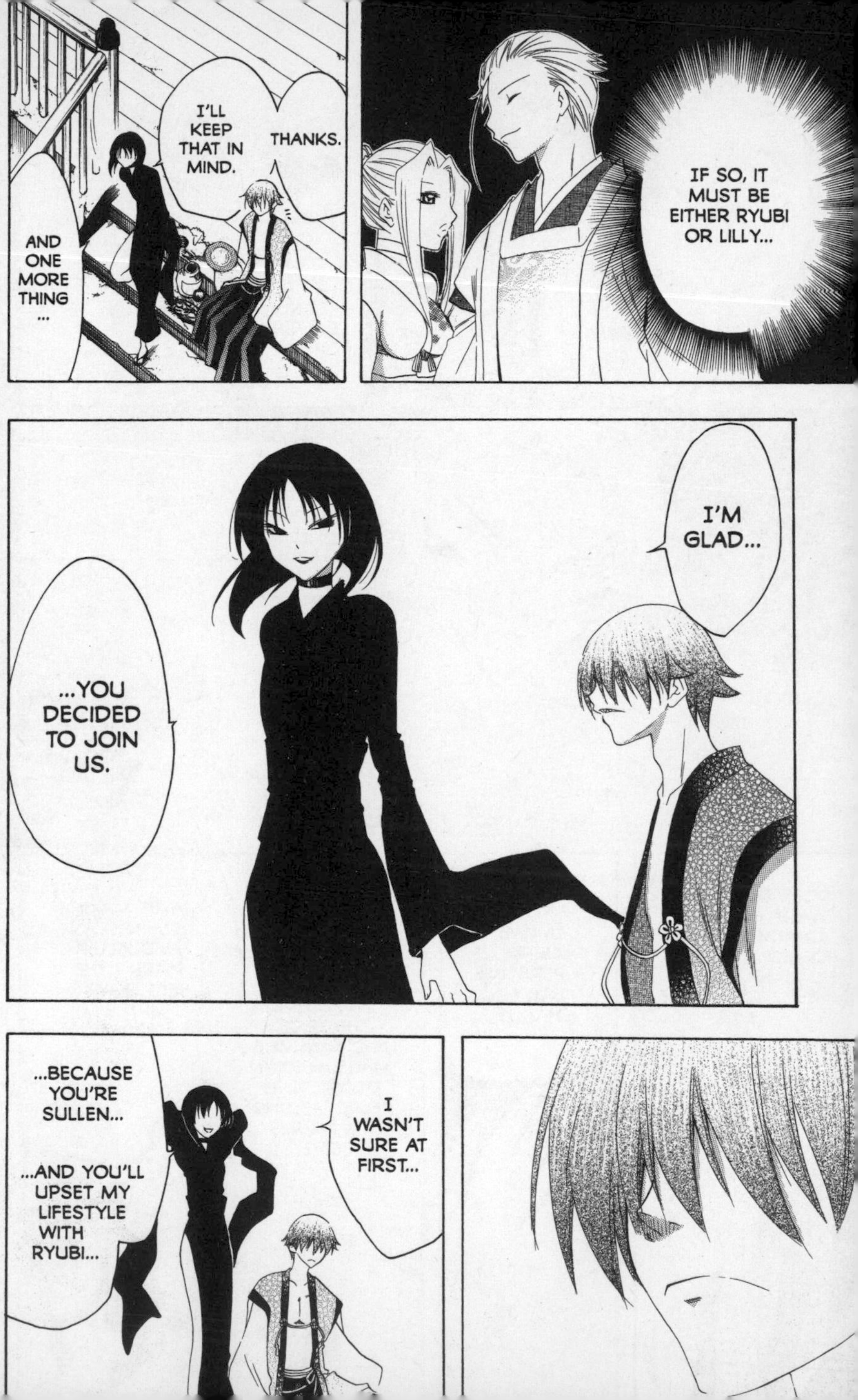
IF SO, IT MUST BE EITHER RYUBI OR LILLY...
THANKS.
I'LL KEEP THAT IN MIND.
AND ONE MORE THING ...
I'M GLAD...
...YOU DECIDED TO JOIN US.
I WASN'T SURE AT FIRST...
...BECAUSE YOU'RE SULLEN...
...AND YOU'LL UPSET MY LIFESTYLE WITH RYUBI...

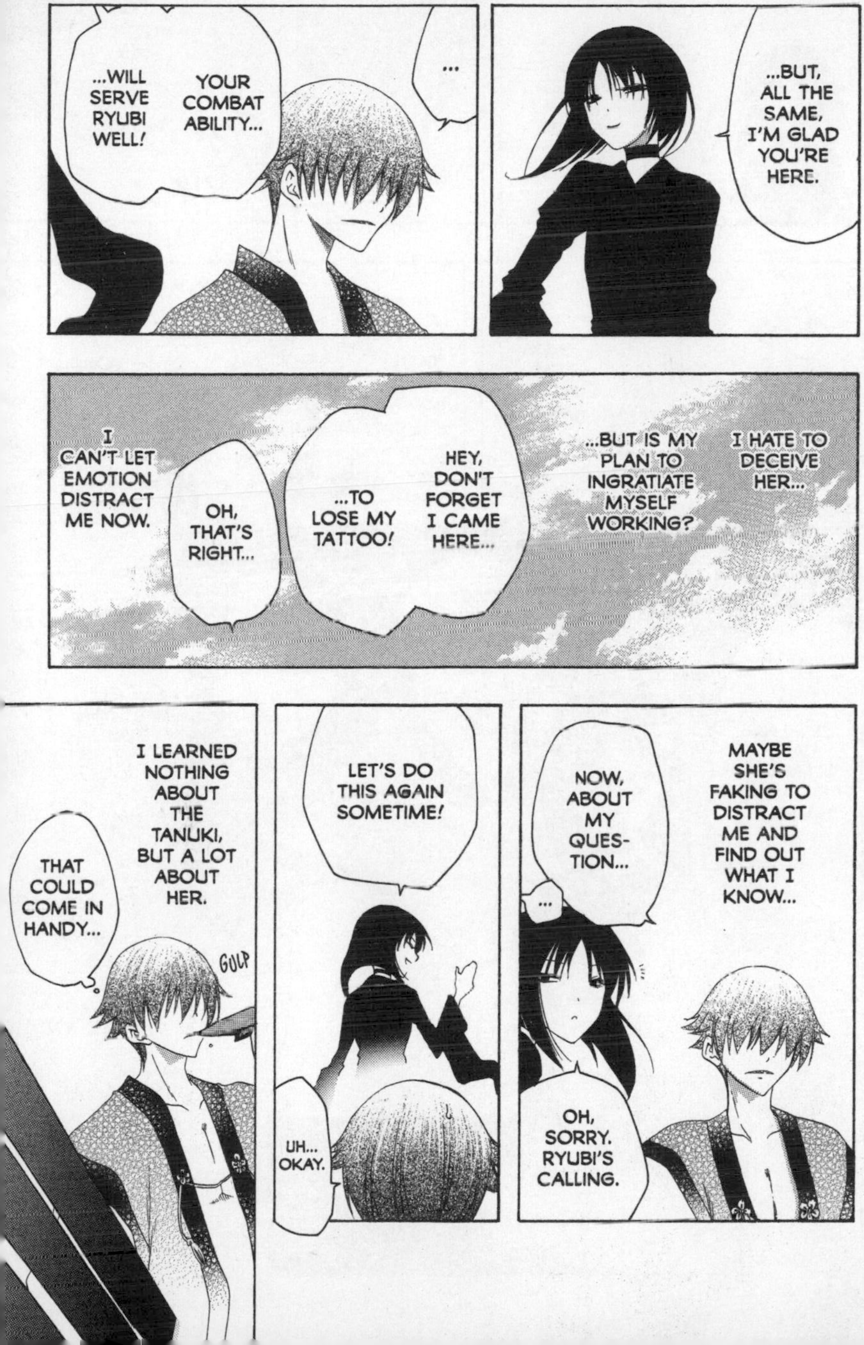
...BUT, ALL THE SAME, I'M GLAD YOU'RE HERE.
...
YOUR COMBAT ABILITY...
...WILL SERVE RYUBI WELL!
I HATE TO DECEIVE HER...
...BUT IS MY PLAN TO INGRATIATE MYSELF WORKING?
HEY, DON'T FORGET I CAME HERE...
...TO LOSE MY TATTOO!
OH, THAT'S RIGHT...
I CAN'T LET EMOTION DISTRACT ME NOW.
MAYBE SHE'S FAKING TO DISTRACT ME AND FIND OUT WHAT I KNOW...
NOW, ABOUT MY QUES-TION...
...
OH, SORRY. RYUBI'S CALLING.
LET'S DO THIS AGAIN SOMETIME!
UH... OKAY.
I LEARNED NOTHING ABOUT THE TANUKI, BUT A LOT ABOUT HER.
THAT COULD COME IN HANDY...
GULP

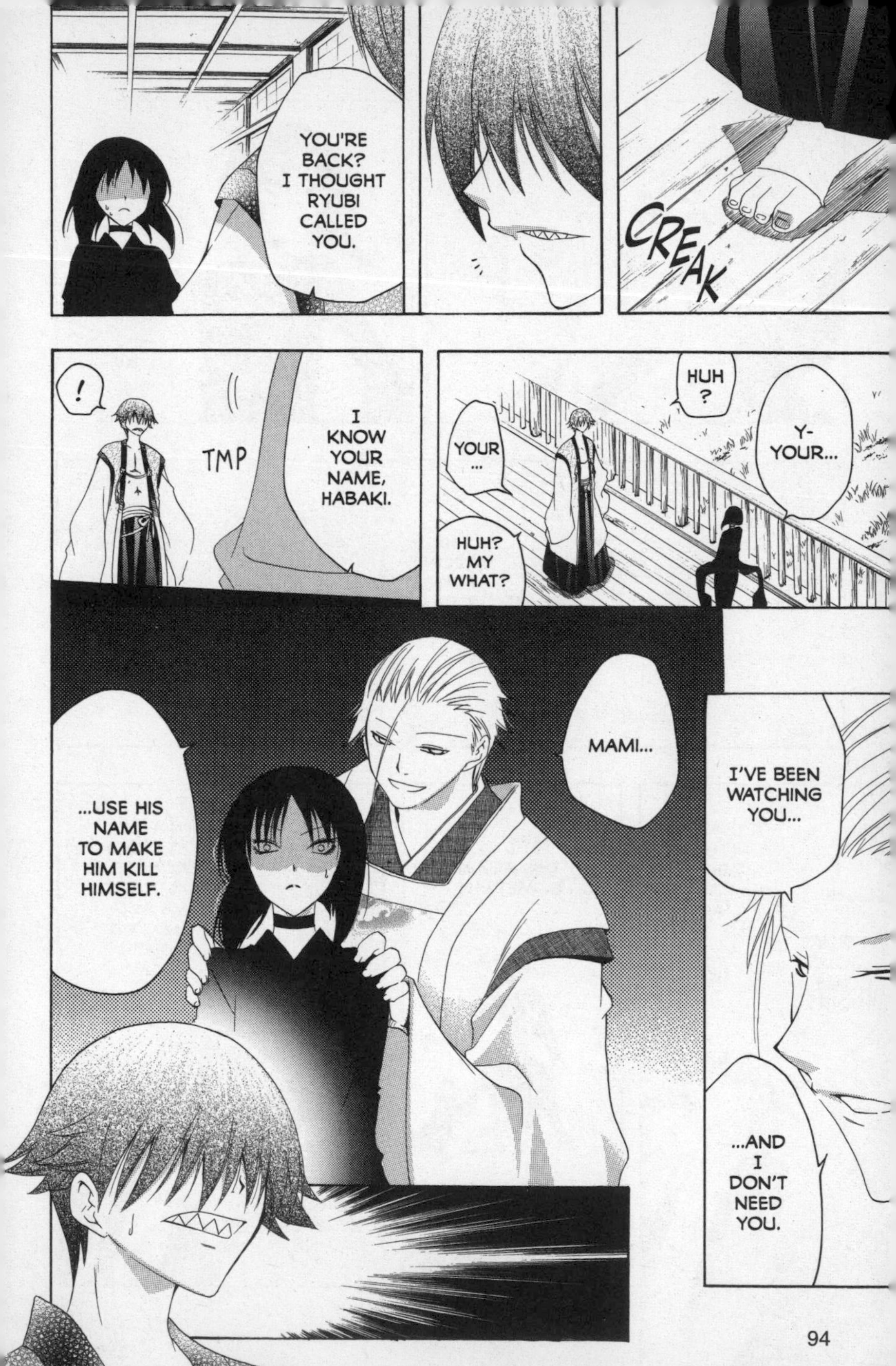
CREAK
YOU'RE BACK? I THOUGHT RYUBI CALLED YOU.
Y-YOUR...
HUH?
YOUR...
HUH? MY WHAT?
I KNOW YOUR NAME, HABAKI.
TMP
!
I'VE BEEN WATCHING YOU...
...AND I DON'T NEED YOU.
MAMI...
...USE HIS NAME TO MAKE HIM KILL HIMSELF.

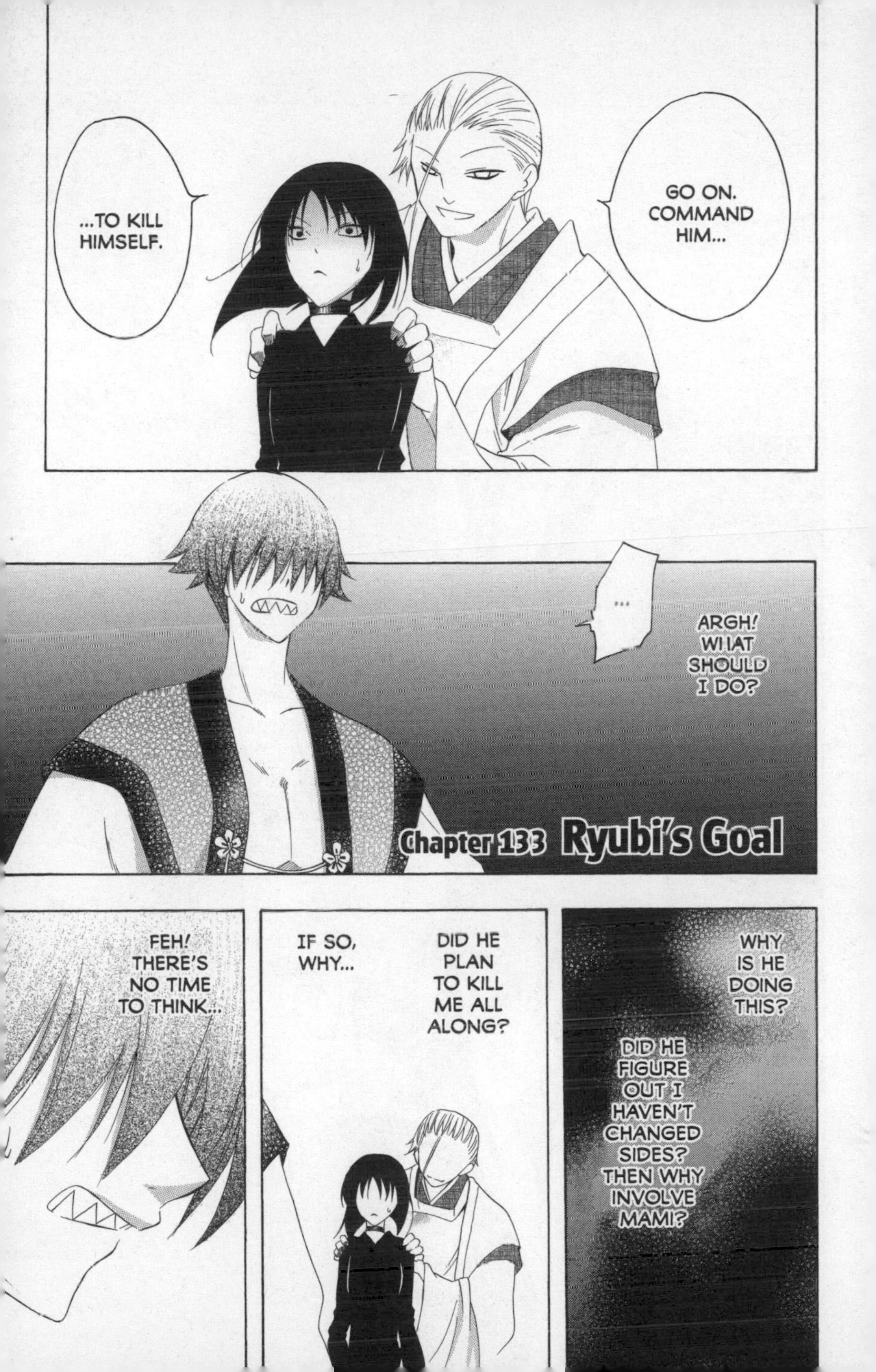
GO ON. COMMAND HIM...
...TO KILL HIMSELF.
...
ARGH! WHAT SHOULD I DO?
Chapter 133 Ryubi's Goal
WHY IS HE DOING THIS?
DID HE FIGURE OUT I HAVEN'T CHANGED SIDES? THEN WHY INVOLVE MAMI?
DID HE PLAN TO KILL ME ALL ALONG?
IF SO, WHY...
FEH! THERE'S NO TIME TO THINK...

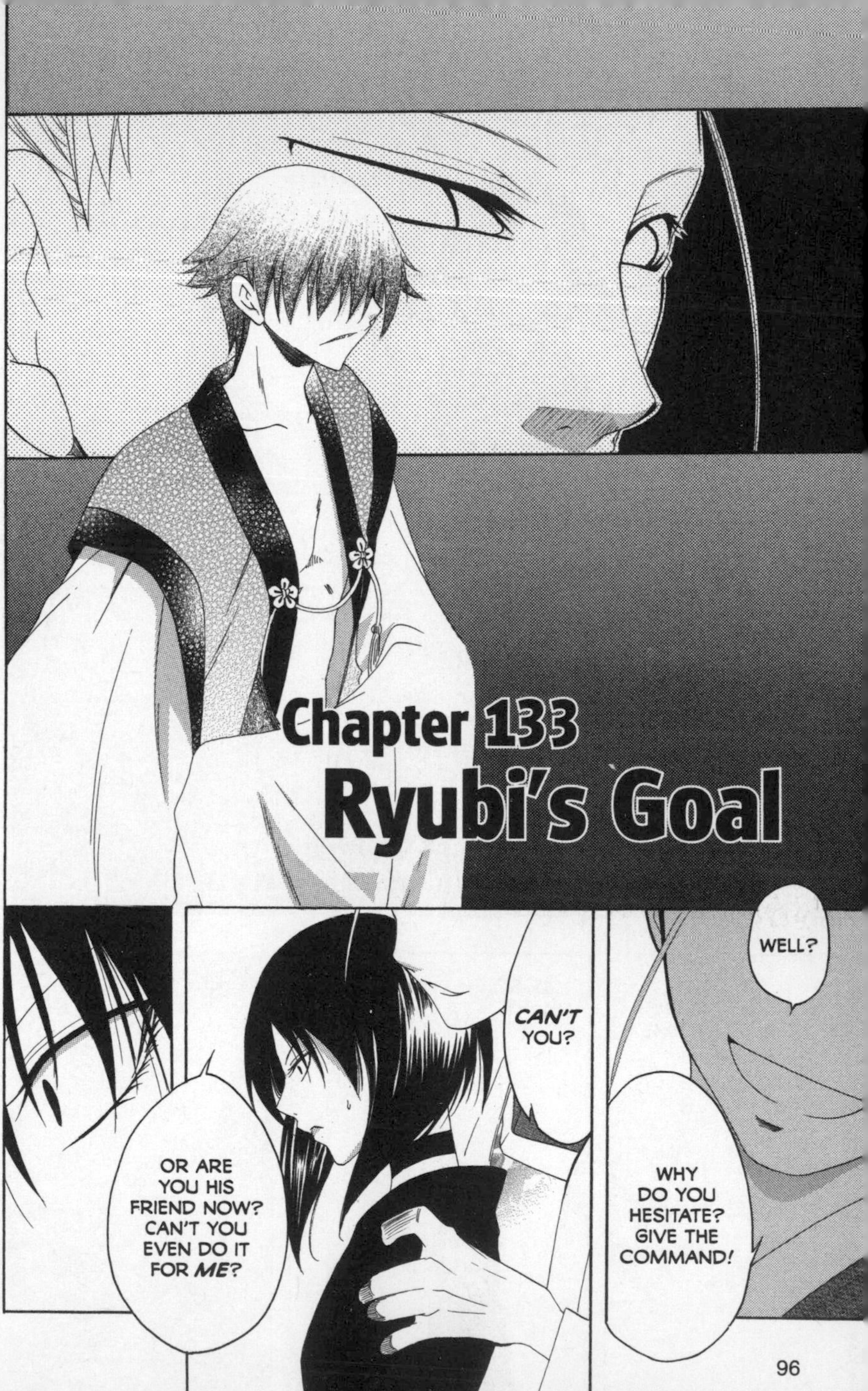
Chapter 133
Ryubi's Goal
WELL?
WHY DO YOU HESITATE? GIVE THE COMMAND!
CAN'T YOU?
OR ARE YOU HIS FRIEND NOW? CAN'T YOU EVEN DO IT FOR ME?

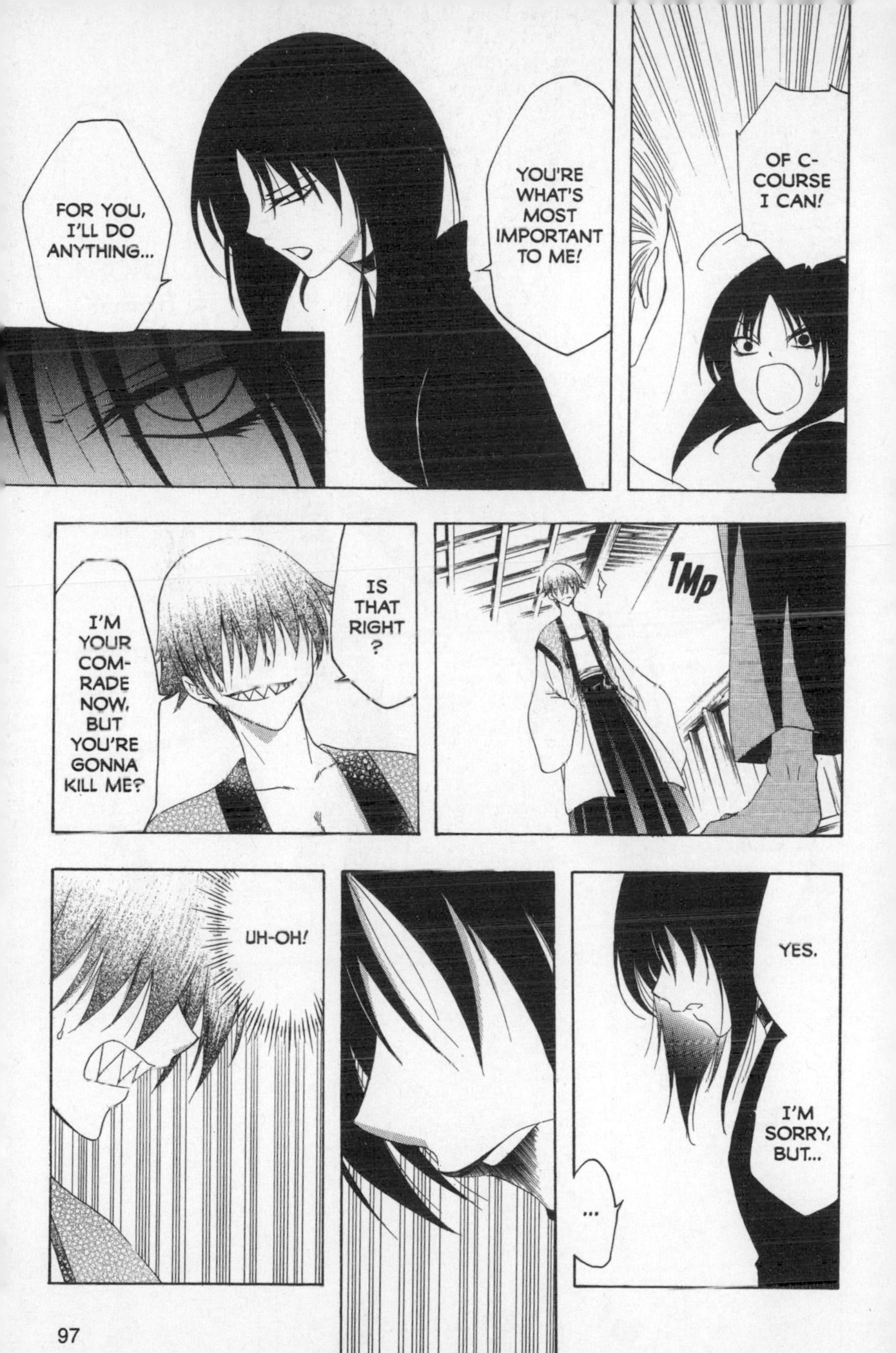
OF C-COURSE I CAN!
YOU'RE WHAT'S MOST IMPORTANT TO ME!
FOR YOU, I'LL DO ANYTHING...
TMP
IS THAT RIGHT?
I'M YOUR COM-RADE NOW, BUT YOU'RE GONNA KILL ME?
YES.
I'M SORRY, BUT...
...
UH-OH!

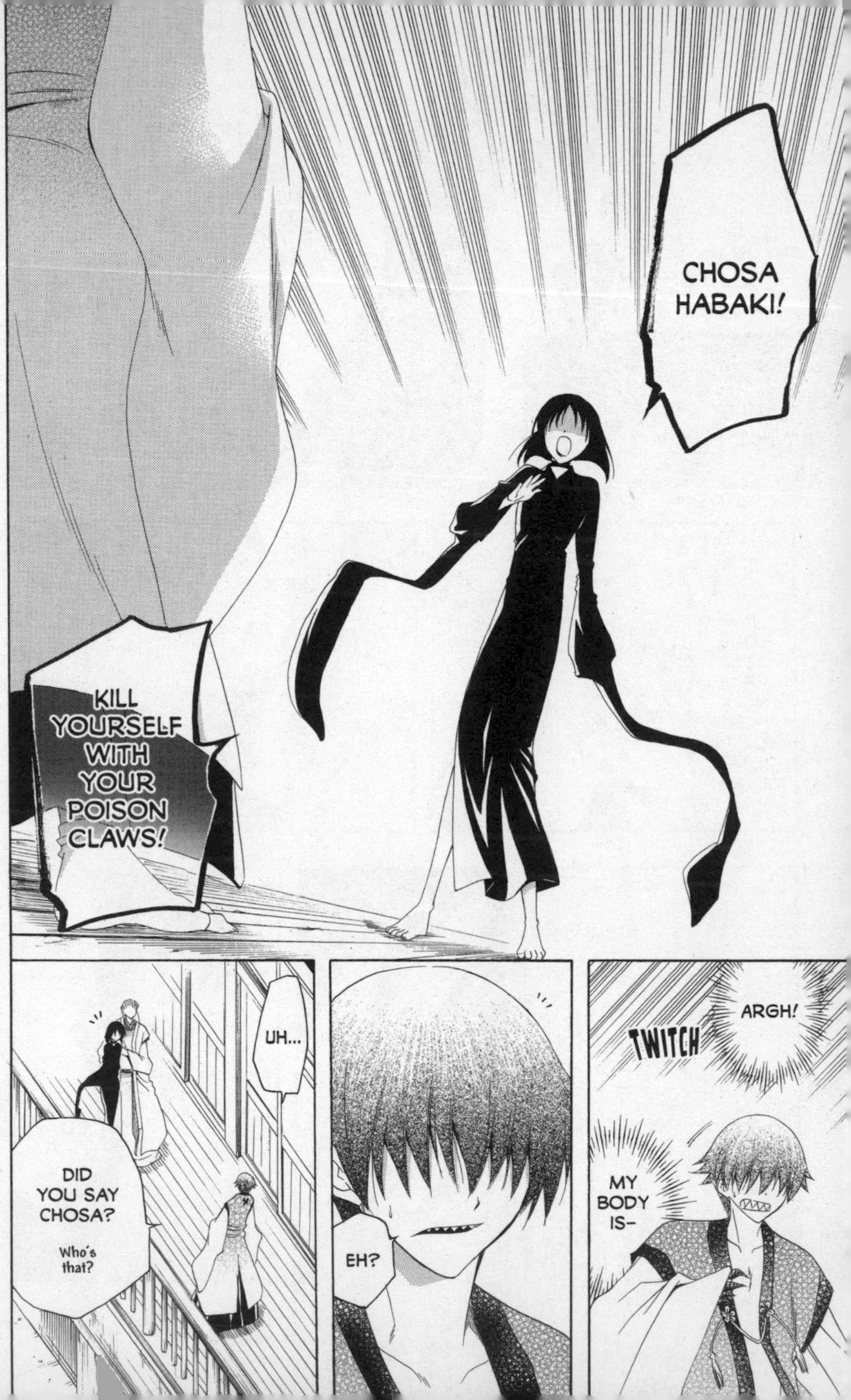
CHOSA HABAKI!
KILL YOURSELF WITH YOUR POISON CLAWS!
ARGH!
TWITCH
MY BODY IS-
EH?
UH...
DID YOU SAY CHOSA?
Who's that?

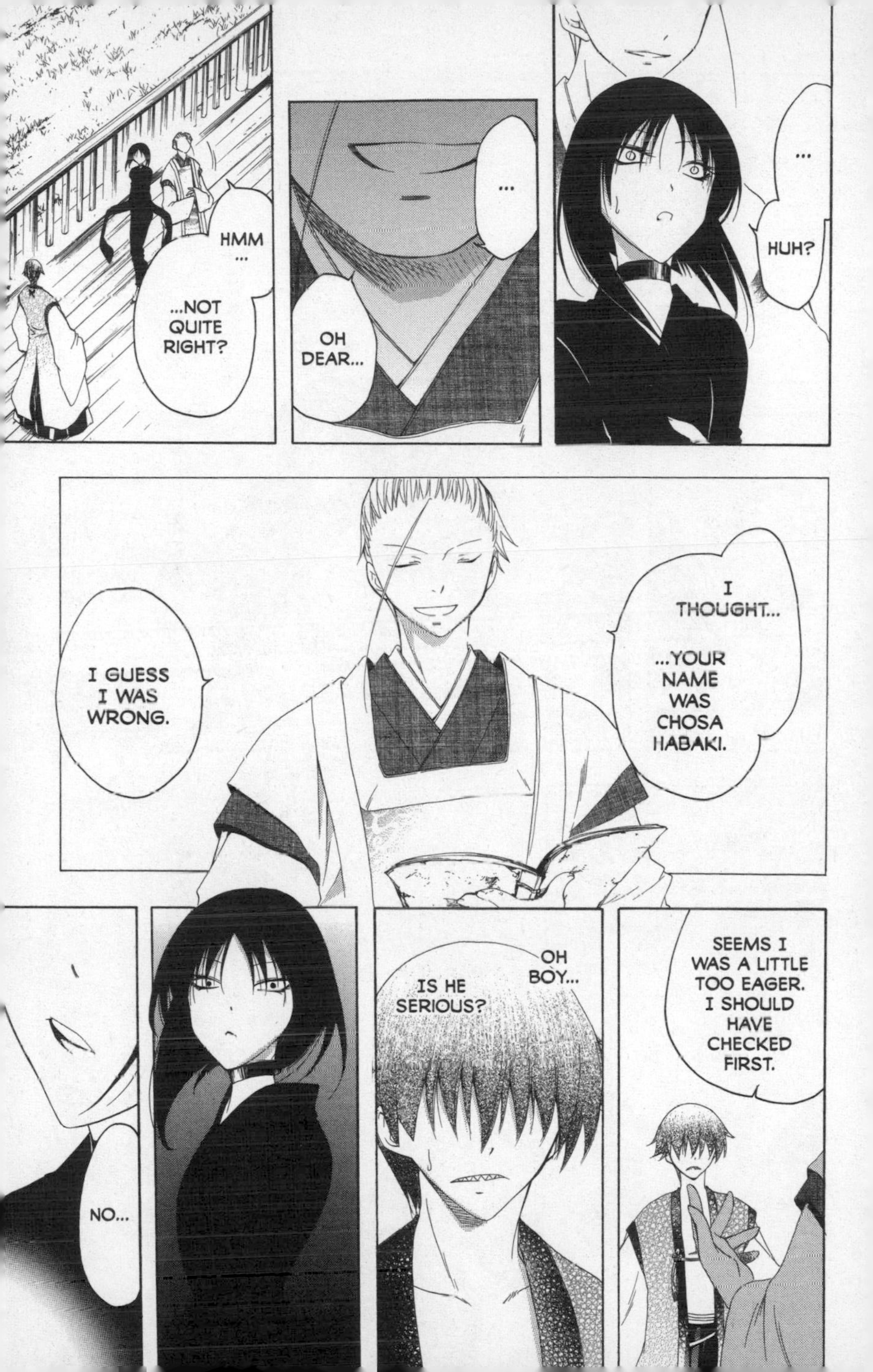
...
HUH?
...
OH DEAR...
HMM ...
...NOT QUITE RIGHT?
I THOUGHT...
...YOUR NAME WAS CHOSA HABAKI.
I GUESS I WAS WRONG.
SEEMS I WAS A LITTLE TOO EAGER. I SHOULD HAVE CHECKED FIRST.
OH BOY...
IS HE SERIOUS?
NO...

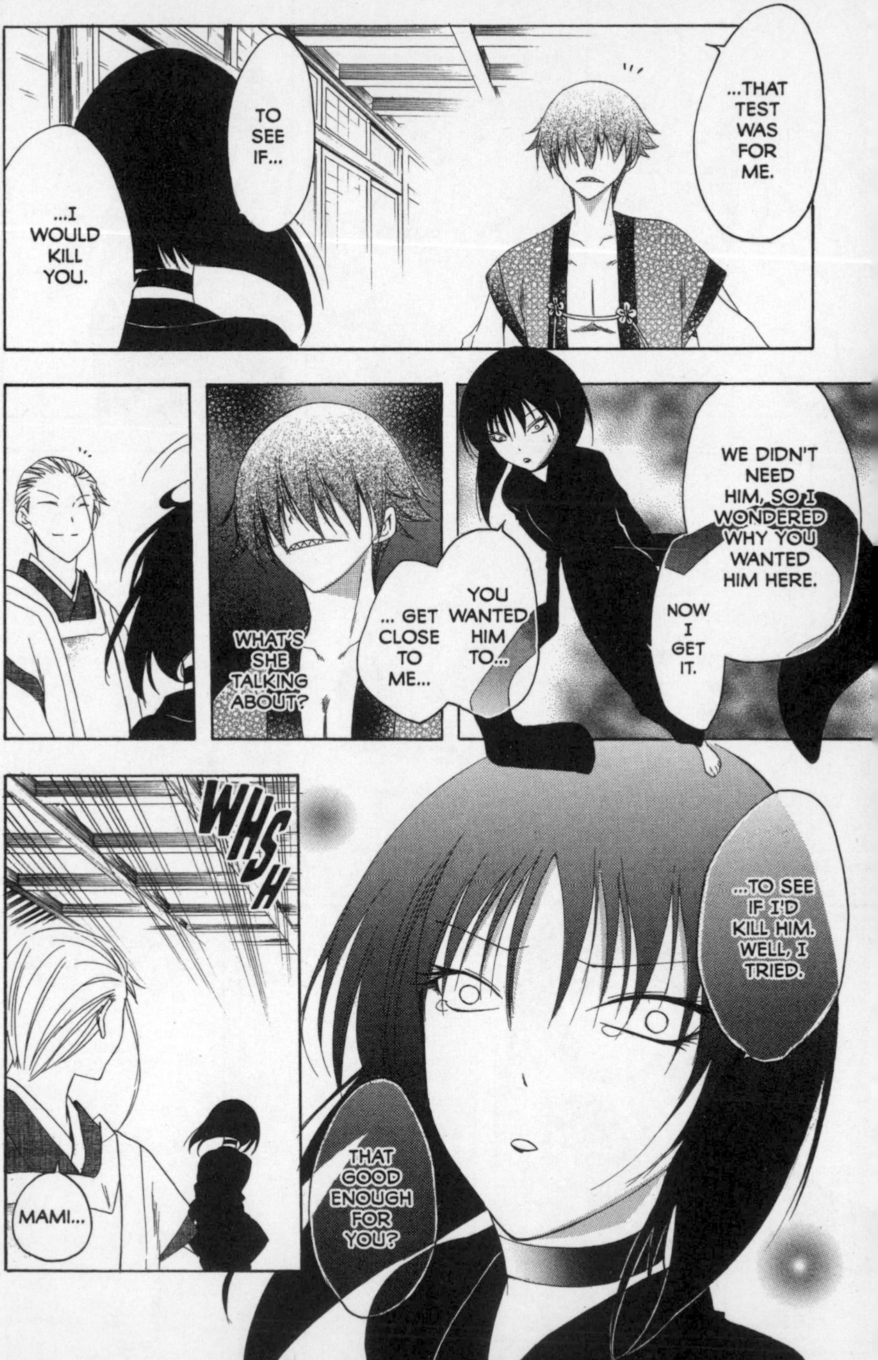
...THAT TEST WAS FOR ME.
TO SEE IF...
...I WOULD KILL YOU.
WE DIDN'T NEED HIM, SO I WONDERED WHY YOU WANTED HIM HERE.
NOW I GET IT.
YOU WANTED HIM TO...
... GET CLOSE TO ME...
WHAT'S SHE TALKING ABOUT?
...TO SEE IF I'D KILL HIM. WELL, I TRIED.
THAT GOOD ENOUGH FOR YOU?
WHSH
MAMI...

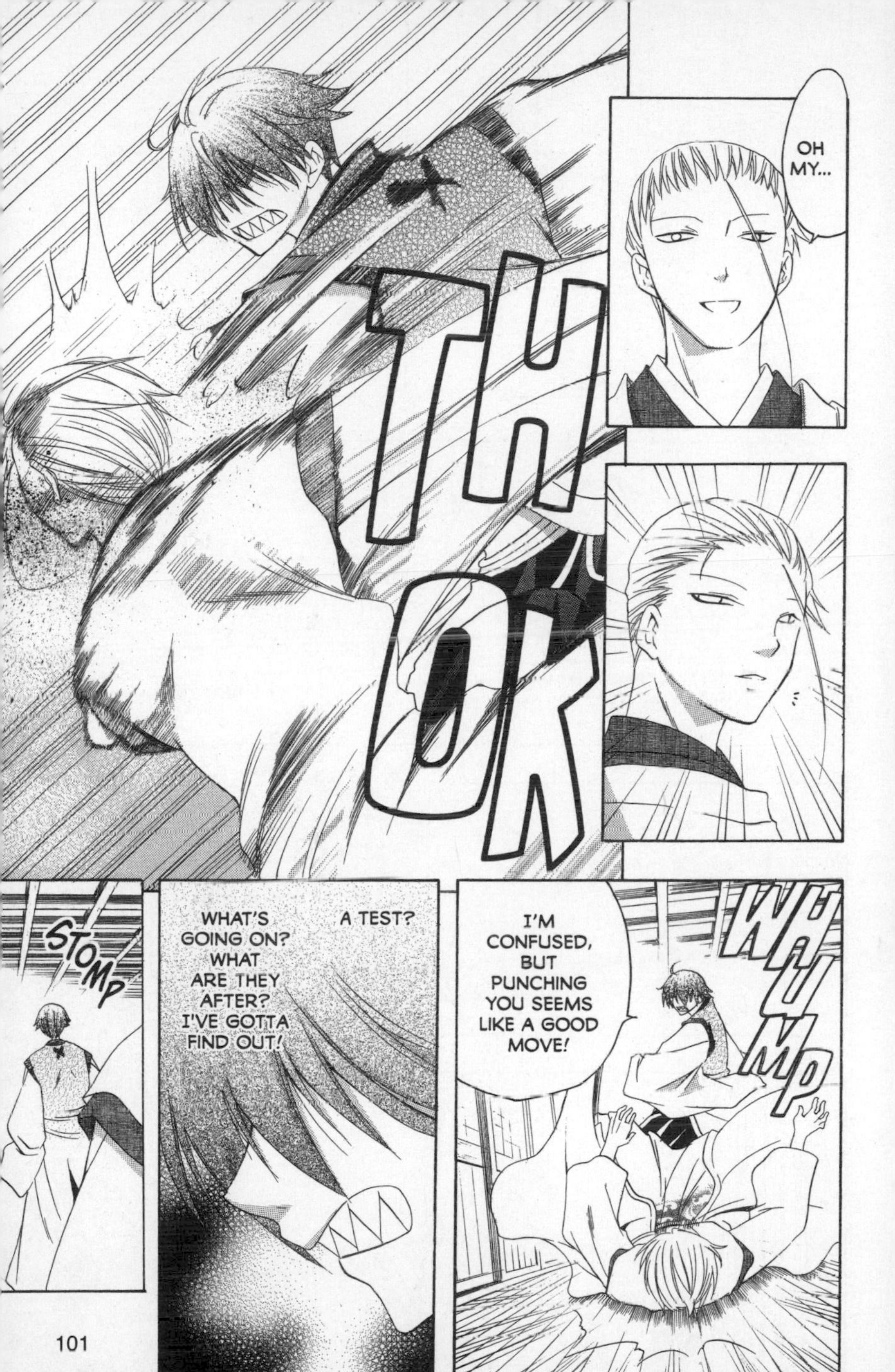
OH MY...
THOK
WHUMP
I'M CONFUSED, BUT PUNCHING YOU SEEMS LIKE A GOOD MOVE!
A TEST?
WHAT'S GOING ON? WHAT ARE THEY AFTER? I'VE GOTTA FIND OUT!
STOMP

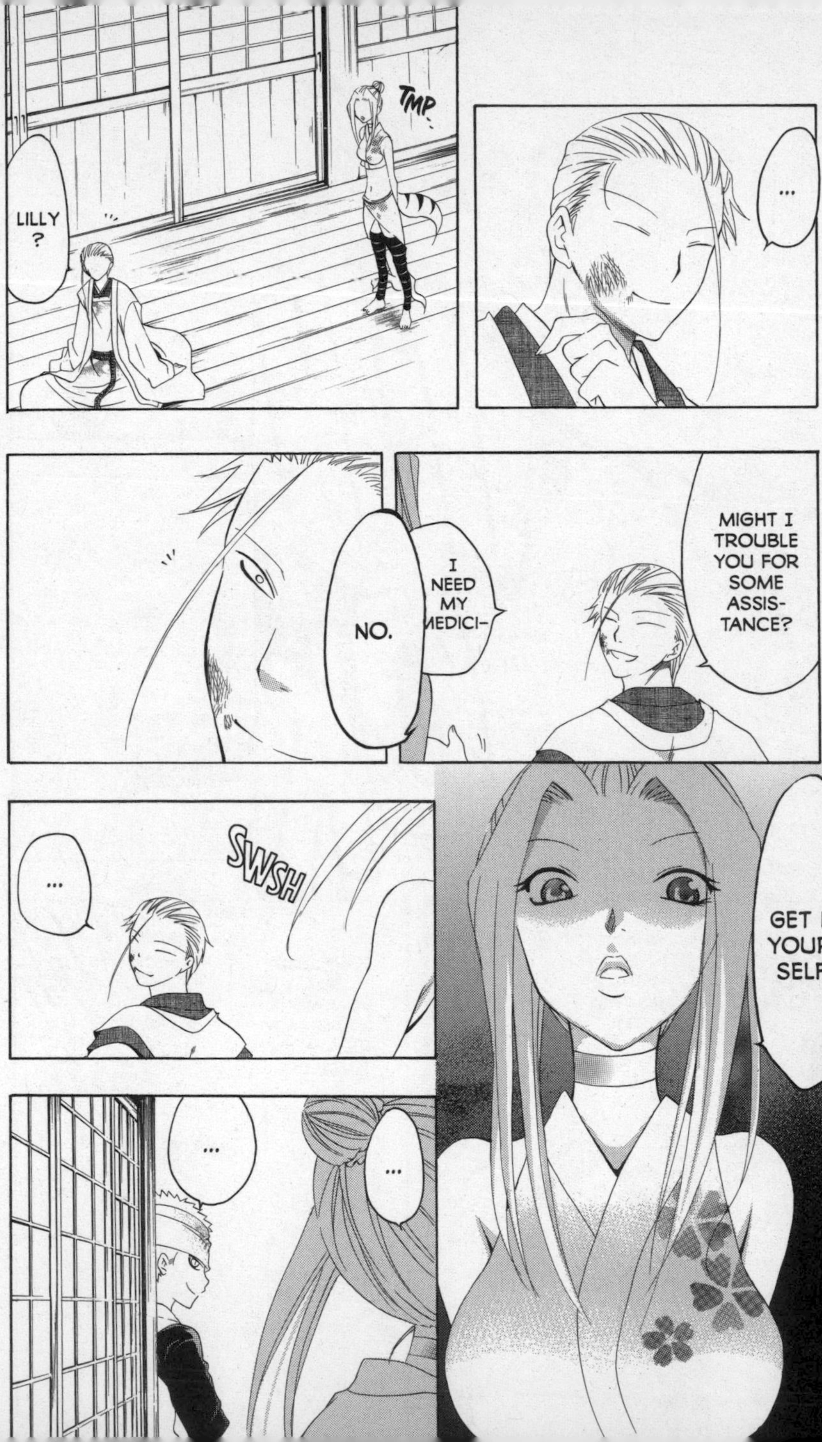
...
TMP
LILLY?
MIGHT I TROUBLE YOU FOR SOME ASSIS-TANCE?
I NEED MY MEDICI–
NO.
GET IT YOUR-SELF.
SWSH
...
...
...

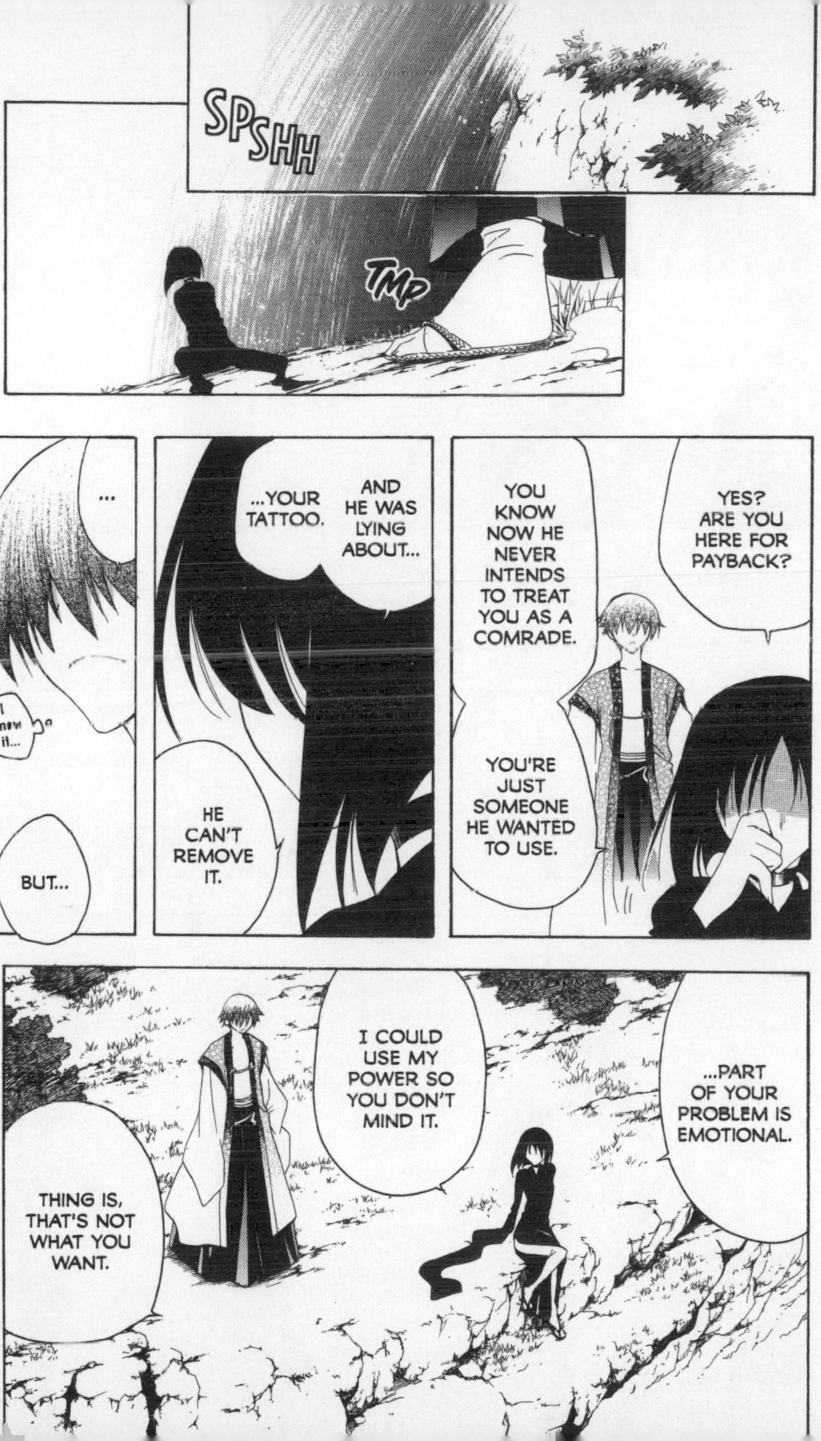
SPSHH
TMP
YES? ARE YOU HERE FOR PAYBACK?
YOU KNOW NOW HE NEVER INTENDS TO TREAT YOU AS A COMRADE.
YOU'RE JUST SOMEONE HE WANTED TO USE.
AND HE WAS LYING ABOUT...
...YOUR TATTOO.
HE CAN'T REMOVE IT.
...
I know it...
BUT...
...PART OF YOUR PROBLEM IS EMOTIONAL.
I COULD USE MY POWER SO YOU DON'T MIND IT.
THING IS, THAT'S NOT WHAT YOU WANT.

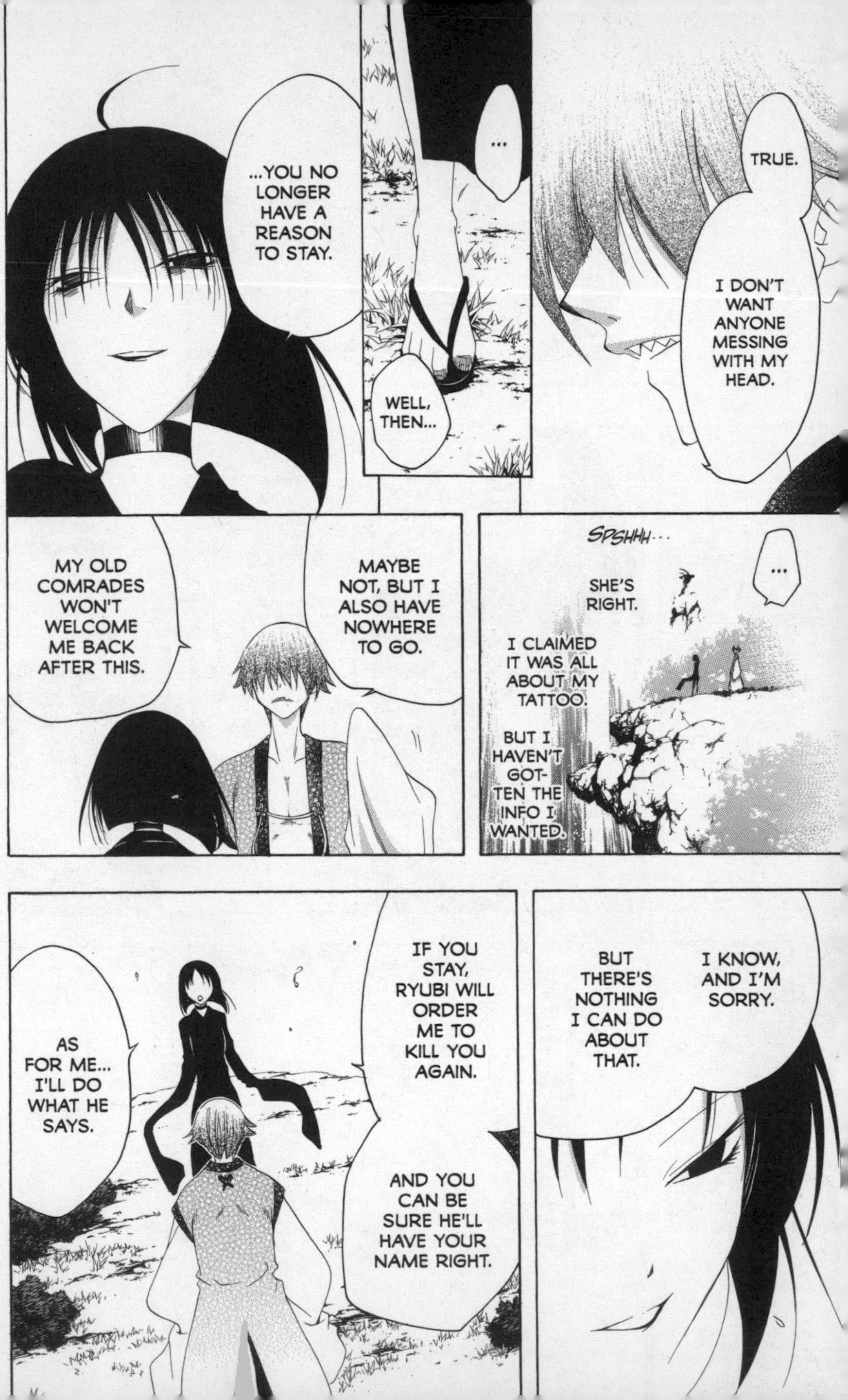
TRUE.
I DON'T WANT ANYONE MESSING WITH MY HEAD.
...
WELL, THEN...
...YOU NO LONGER HAVE A REASON TO STAY.
SPSHHH...
...
SHE'S RIGHT.
I CLAIMED IT WAS ALL ABOUT MY TATTOO.
BUT I HAVEN'T GOT-TEN THE INFO I WANTED.
MAYBE NOT, BUT I ALSO HAVE NOWHERE TO GO.
MY OLD COMRADES WON'T WELCOME ME BACK AFTER THIS.
I KNOW, AND I'M SORRY.
BUT THERE'S NOTHING I CAN DO ABOUT THAT.
IF YOU STAY, RYUBI WILL ORDER ME TO KILL YOU AGAIN.
AND YOU CAN BE SURE HE'LL HAVE YOUR NAME RIGHT.
AS FOR ME... I'LL DO WHAT HE SAYS.

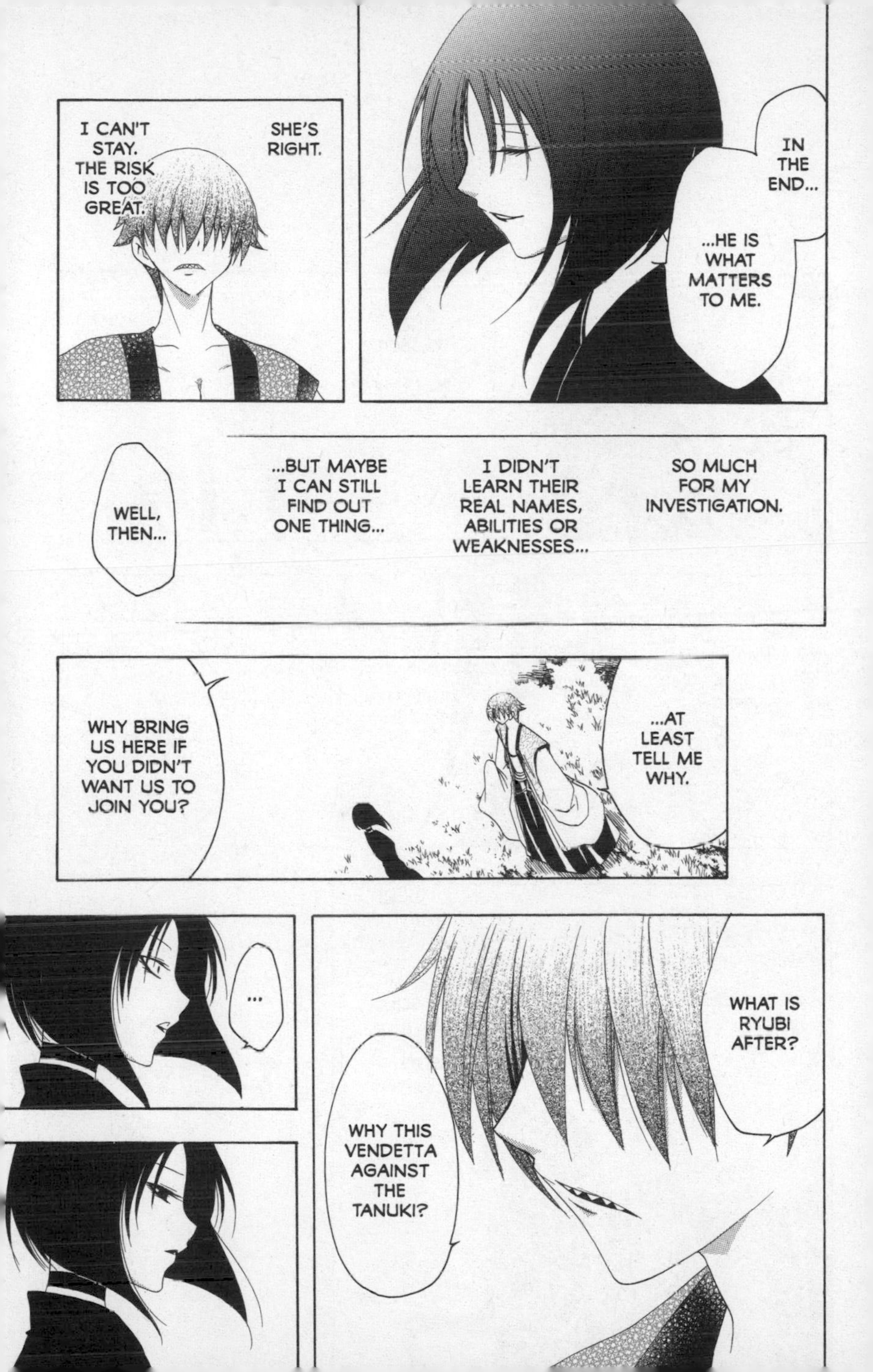
IN THE END...
...HE IS WHAT MATTERS TO ME.
SHE'S RIGHT.
I CAN'T STAY. THE RISK IS TOO GREAT.
SO MUCH FOR MY INVESTIGATION.
I DIDN'T LEARN THEIR REAL NAMES, ABILITIES OR WEAKNESSES...
...BUT MAYBE I CAN STILL FIND OUT ONE THING...
WELL, THEN...
...AT LEAST TELL ME WHY.
WHY BRING US HERE IF YOU DIDN'T WANT US TO JOIN YOU?
WHAT IS RYUBI AFTER?
WHY THIS VENDETTA AGAINST THE TANUKI?
...

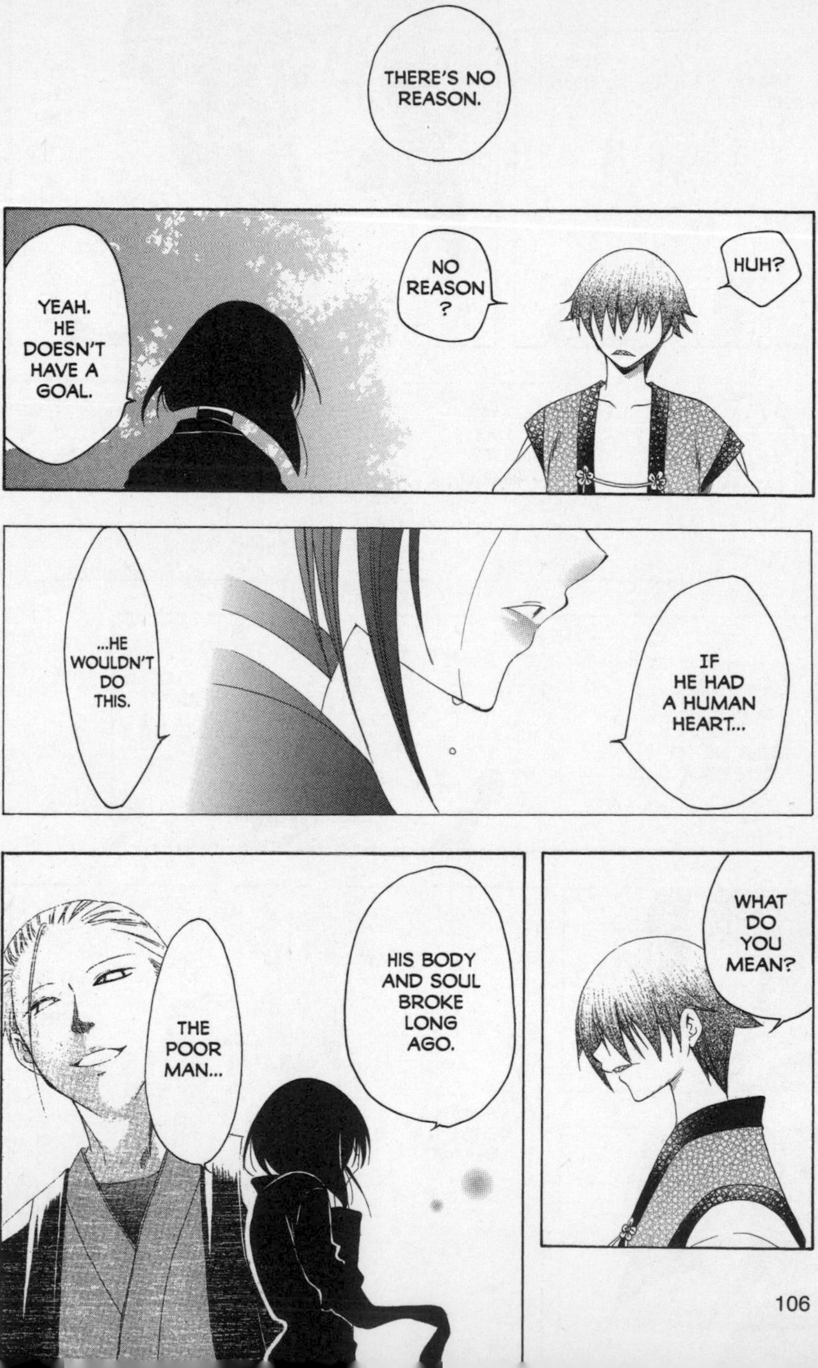
THERE'S NO REASON.
HUH?
NO REASON ?
YEAH. HE DOESN'T HAVE A GOAL.
IF HE HAD A HUMAN HEART...
...HE WOULDN'T DO THIS.
WHAT DO YOU MEAN?
HIS BODY AND SOUL BROKE LONG AGO.
THE POOR MAN...

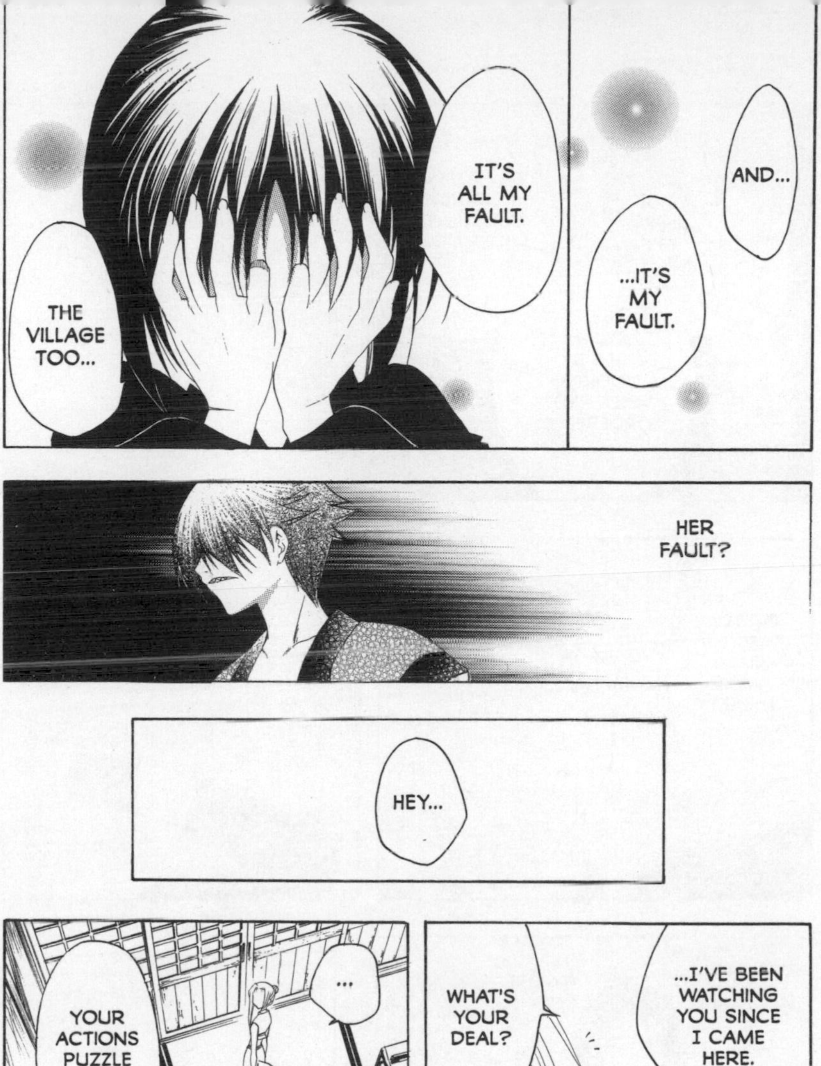
AND...
...IT'S MY FAULT.
IT'S ALL MY FAULT.
THE VILLAGE TOO...
HER FAULT?
HEY...
...I'VE BEEN WATCHING YOU SINCE I CAME HERE.
WHAT'S YOUR DEAL?
...
YOUR ACTIONS PUZZLE ME.

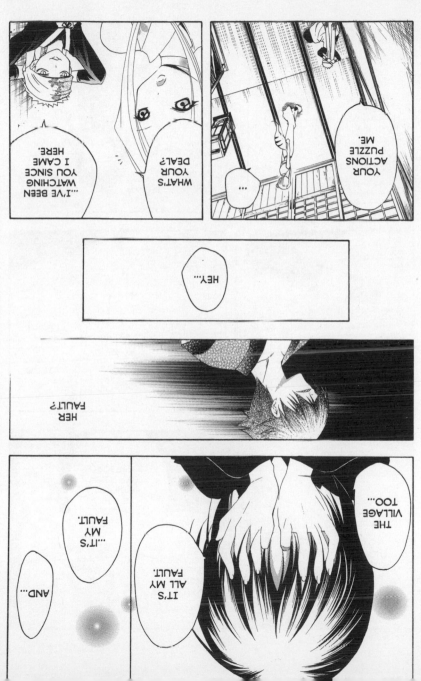

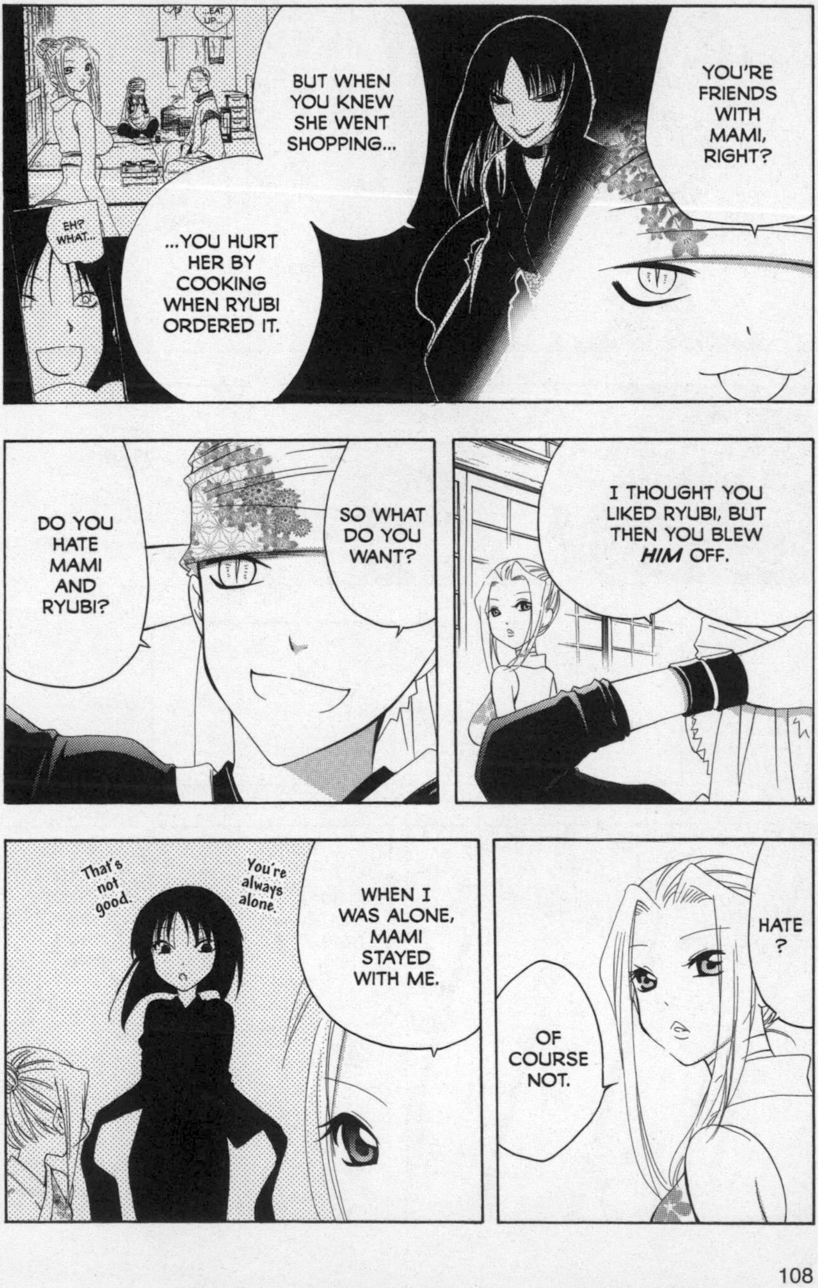
YOU'RE FRIENDS WITH MAMI, RIGHT?
BUT WHEN YOU KNEW SHE WENT SHOPPING...
...EAT UP...
...YOU HURT HER BY COOKING WHEN RYUBI ORDERED IT.
EH? WHAT...
I THOUGHT YOU LIKED RYUBI, BUT THEN YOU BLEW *HIM* OFF.
SO WHAT DO YOU WANT?
DO YOU HATE MAMI AND RYUBI?
HATE ?
OF COURSE NOT.
WHEN I WAS ALONE, MAMI STAYED WITH ME.
You're always alone.
That's not good.

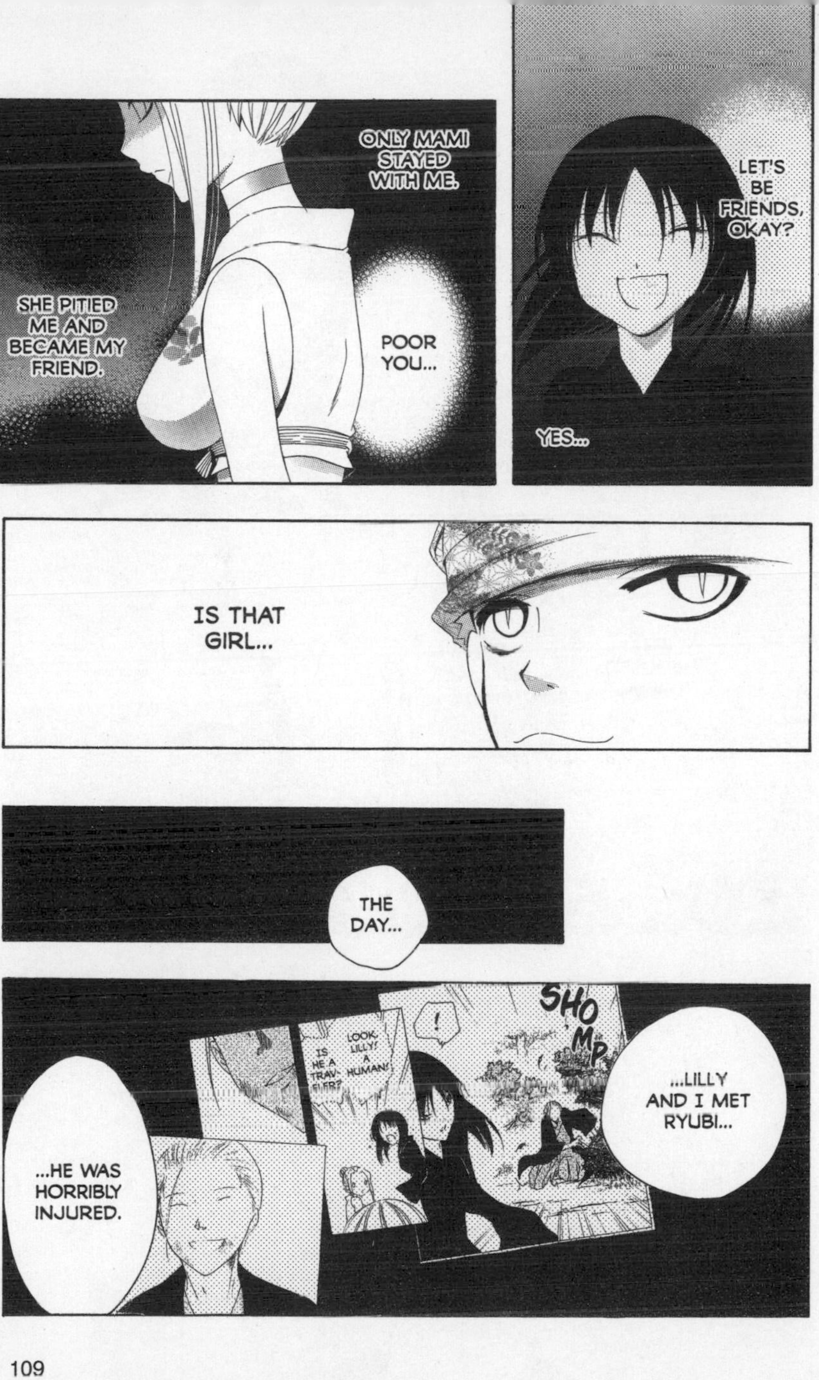
LET'S BE FRIENDS, OKAY?
YES...
ONLY MAMI STAYED WITH ME.
POOR YOU...
SHE PITIED ME AND BECAME MY FRIEND.
IS THAT GIRL...
THE DAY...
...LILLY AND I MET RYUBI...
SHOMP
!
LOOK, LILLY! A HUMAN!
IS HE A TRAV- ELER?
...HE WAS HORRIBLY INJURED.

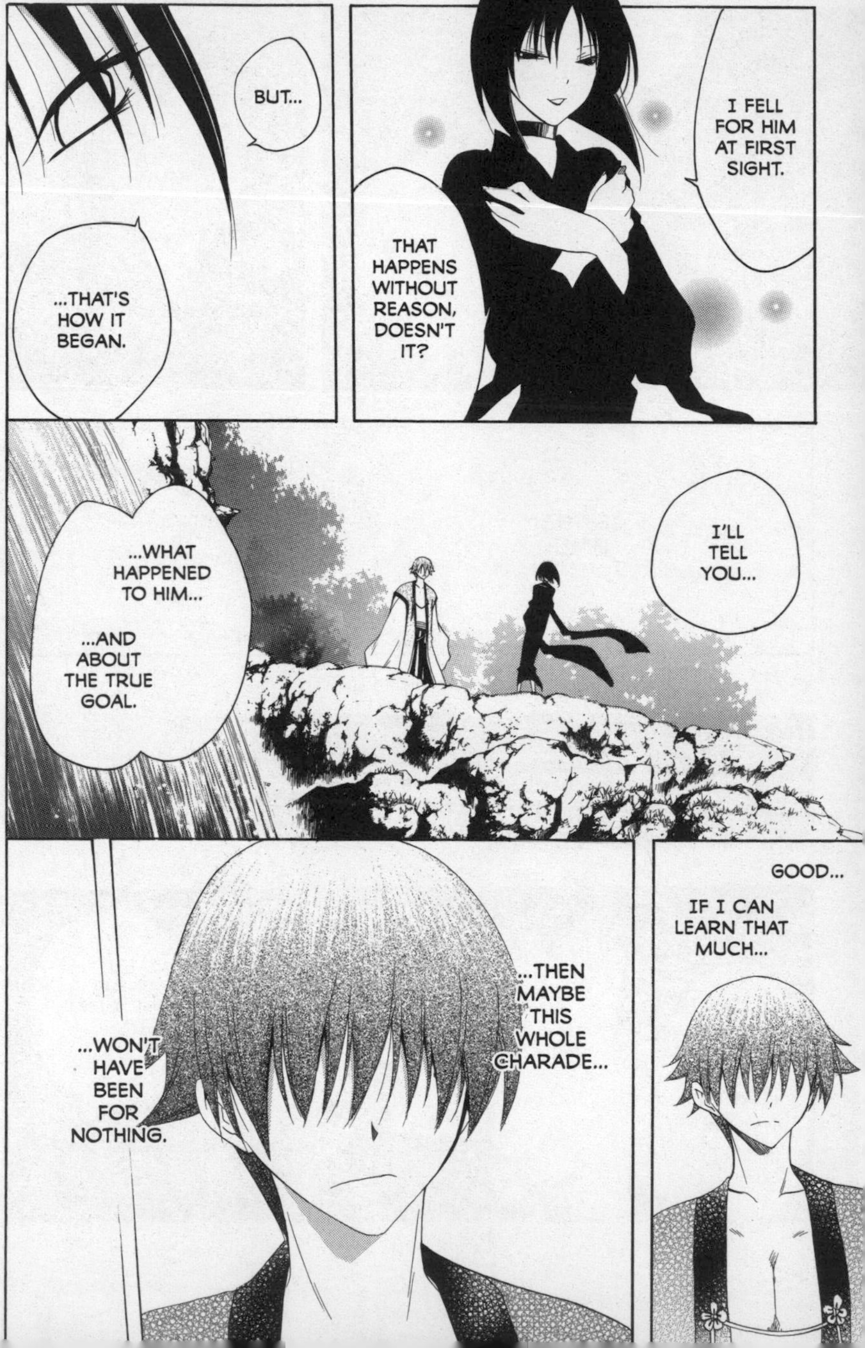
I FELL FOR HIM AT FIRST SIGHT.
THAT HAPPENS WITHOUT REASON, DOESN'T IT?
BUT...
...THAT'S HOW IT BEGAN.
I'LL TELL YOU...
...WHAT HAPPENED TO HIM...
...AND ABOUT THE TRUE GOAL.
GOOD...
IF I CAN LEARN THAT MUCH...
...THEN MAYBE THIS WHOLE CHARADE...
...WON'T HAVE BEEN FOR NOTHING.

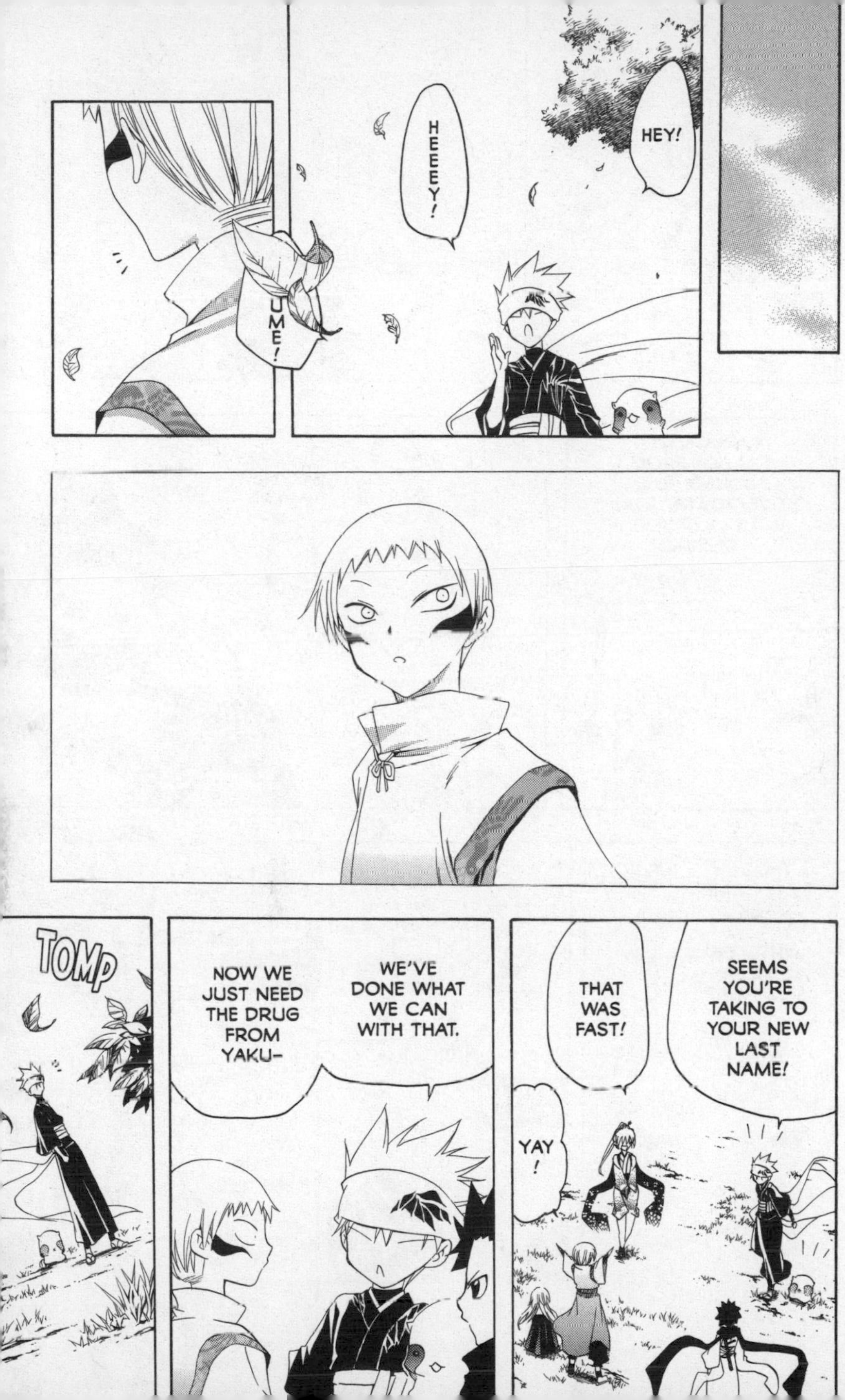
HEY!
HEEEEY!
UME!
SEEMS YOU'RE TAKING TO YOUR NEW LAST NAME!
THAT WAS FAST!
YAY!
WE'VE DONE WHAT WE CAN WITH THAT.
NOW WE JUST NEED THE DRUG FROM YAKU-
TOMP

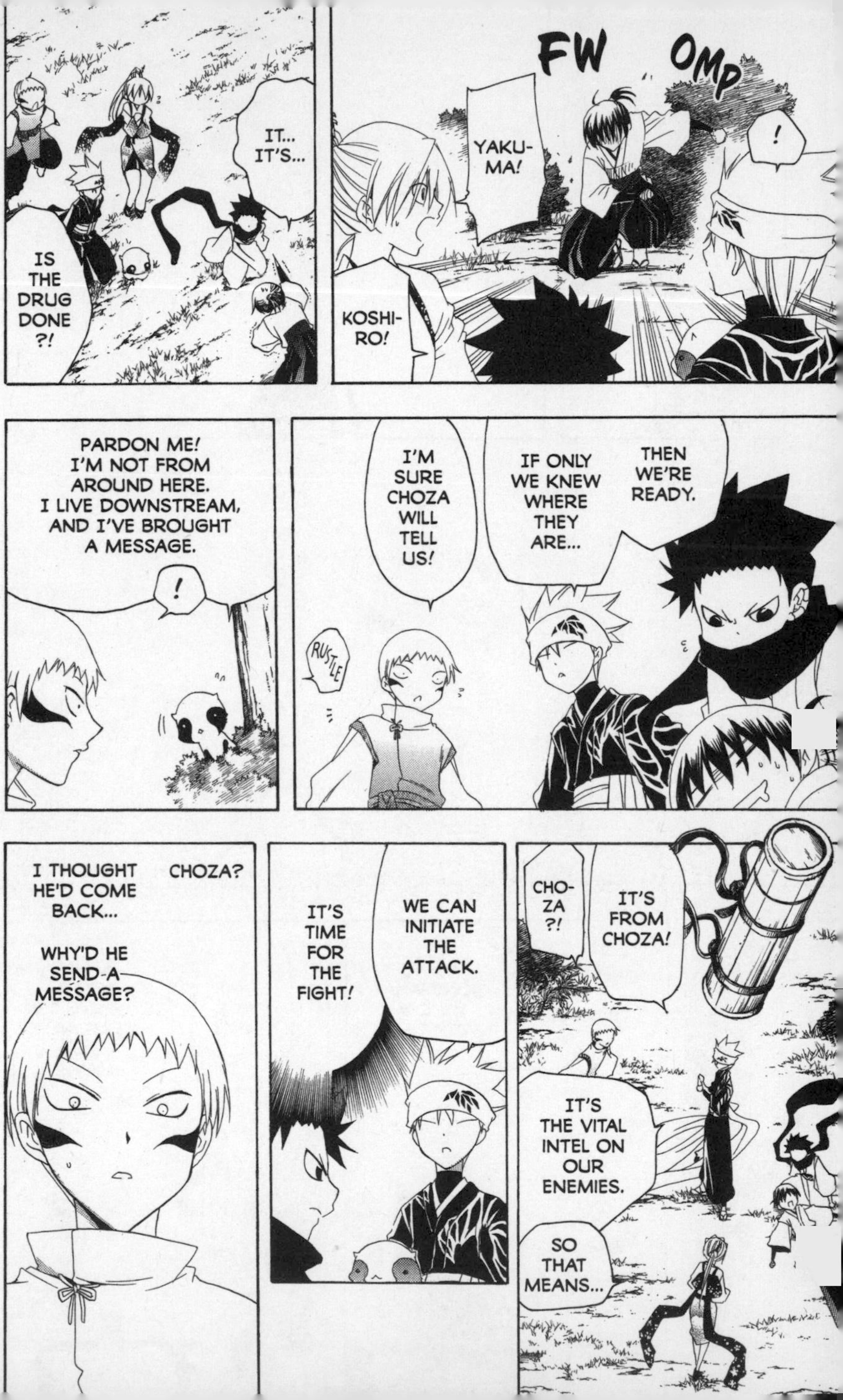
!
FW OMP
YAKU-MA!
KOSHI-RO!
IT... IT'S...
IS THE DRUG DONE?!
THEN WE'RE READY.
IF ONLY WE KNEW WHERE THEY ARE...
I'M SURE CHOZA WILL TELL US!
RUSTLE
PARDON ME! I'M NOT FROM AROUND HERE. I LIVE DOWNSTREAM, AND I'VE BROUGHT A MESSAGE.
!
IT'S FROM CHOZA!
CHO-ZA?!
IT'S THE VITAL INTEL ON OUR ENEMIES.
SO THAT MEANS...
WE CAN INITIATE THE ATTACK.
IT'S TIME FOR THE FIGHT!
CHOZA?
I THOUGHT HE'D COME BACK...
WHY'D HE SEND-A MESSAGE?

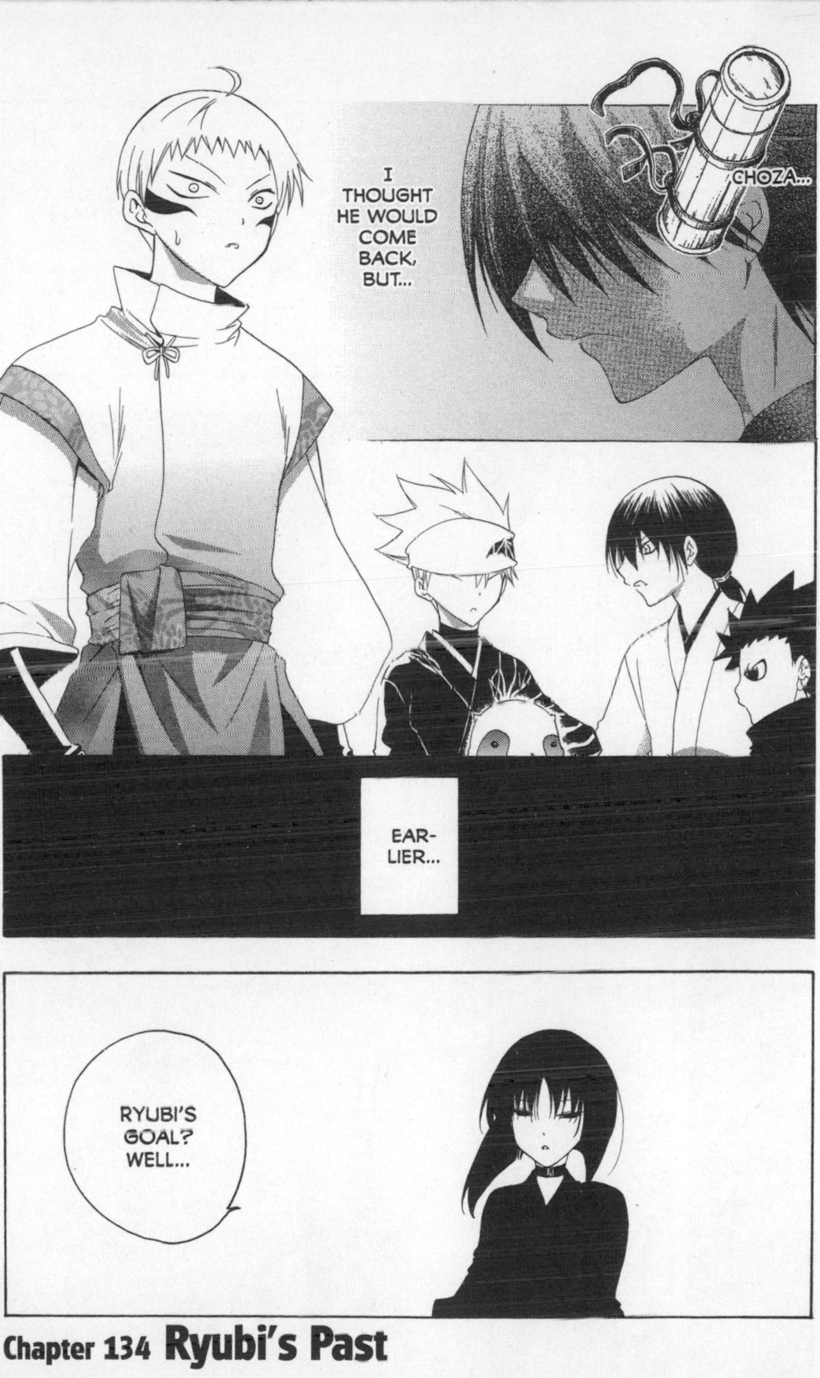
CHOZA...
I THOUGHT HE WOULD COME BACK, BUT...
EAR-LIER...
RYUBI'S GOAL? WELL...

Chapter 134 Ryubi's Past

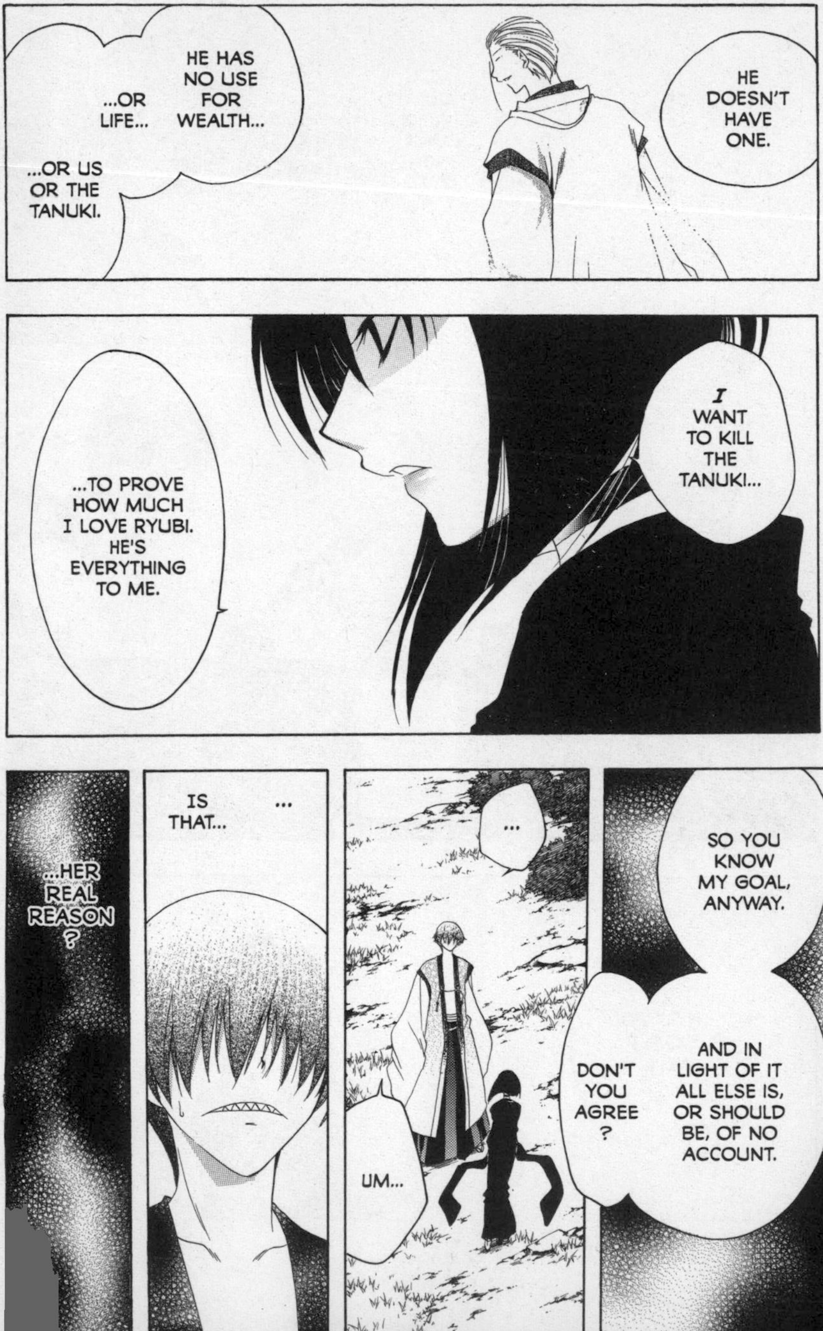
HE DOESN'T HAVE ONE.
HE HAS NO USE FOR WEALTH...
...OR LIFE...
...OR US OR THE TANUKI.
I WANT TO KILL THE TANUKI...
...TO PROVE HOW MUCH I LOVE RYUBI. HE'S EVERYTHING TO ME.
SO YOU KNOW MY GOAL, ANYWAY.
AND IN LIGHT OF IT ALL ELSE IS, OR SHOULD BE, OF NO ACCOUNT.
DON'T YOU AGREE ?
UM...
...
IS THAT...
...
...HER REAL REASON ?

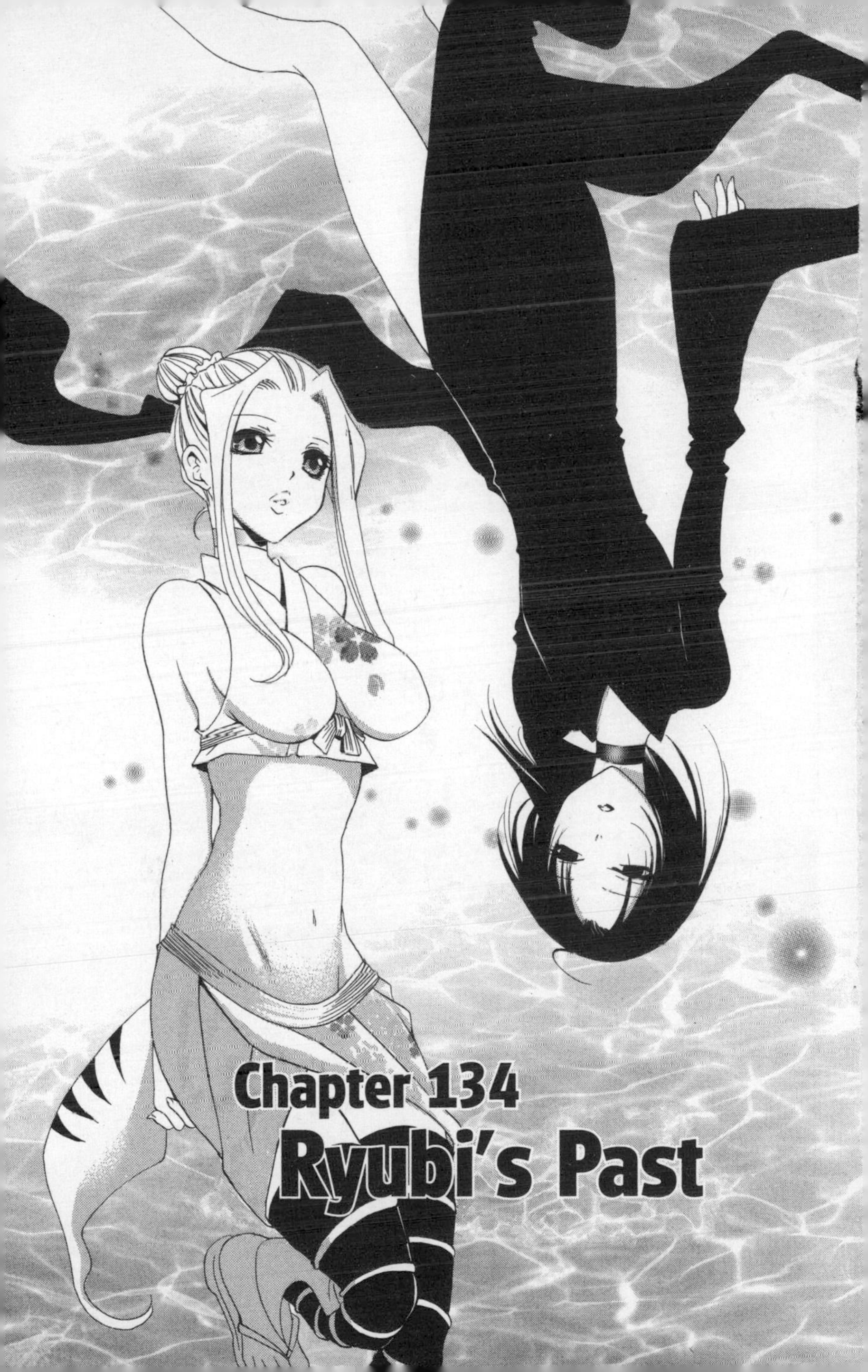
Chapter 134
Ryubi's Past

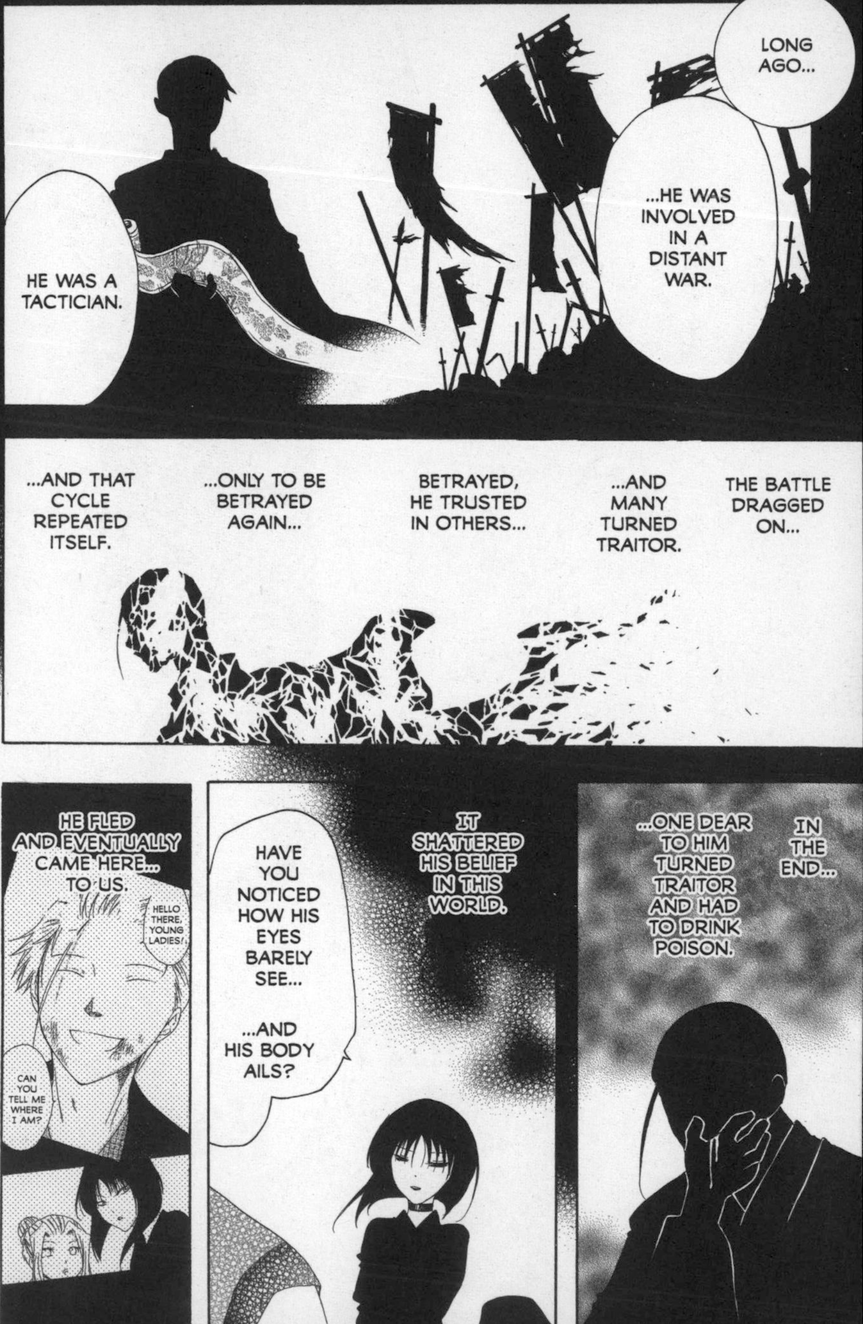
LONG AGO...
...HE WAS INVOLVED IN A DISTANT WAR.
HE WAS A TACTICIAN.
THE BATTLE DRAGGED ON...
...AND MANY TURNED TRAITOR.
BETRAYED, HE TRUSTED IN OTHERS...
...ONLY TO BE BETRAYED AGAIN...
...AND THAT CYCLE REPEATED ITSELF.
IN THE END...
...ONE DEAR TO HIM TURNED TRAITOR AND HAD TO DRINK POISON.
IT SHATTERED HIS BELIEF IN THIS WORLD.
HAVE YOU NOTICED HOW HIS EYES BARELY SEE...
...AND HIS BODY AILS?
HE FLED AND EVENTUALLY CAME HERE... TO US.
HELLO THERE, YOUNG LADIES!
CAN YOU TELL ME WHERE I AM?

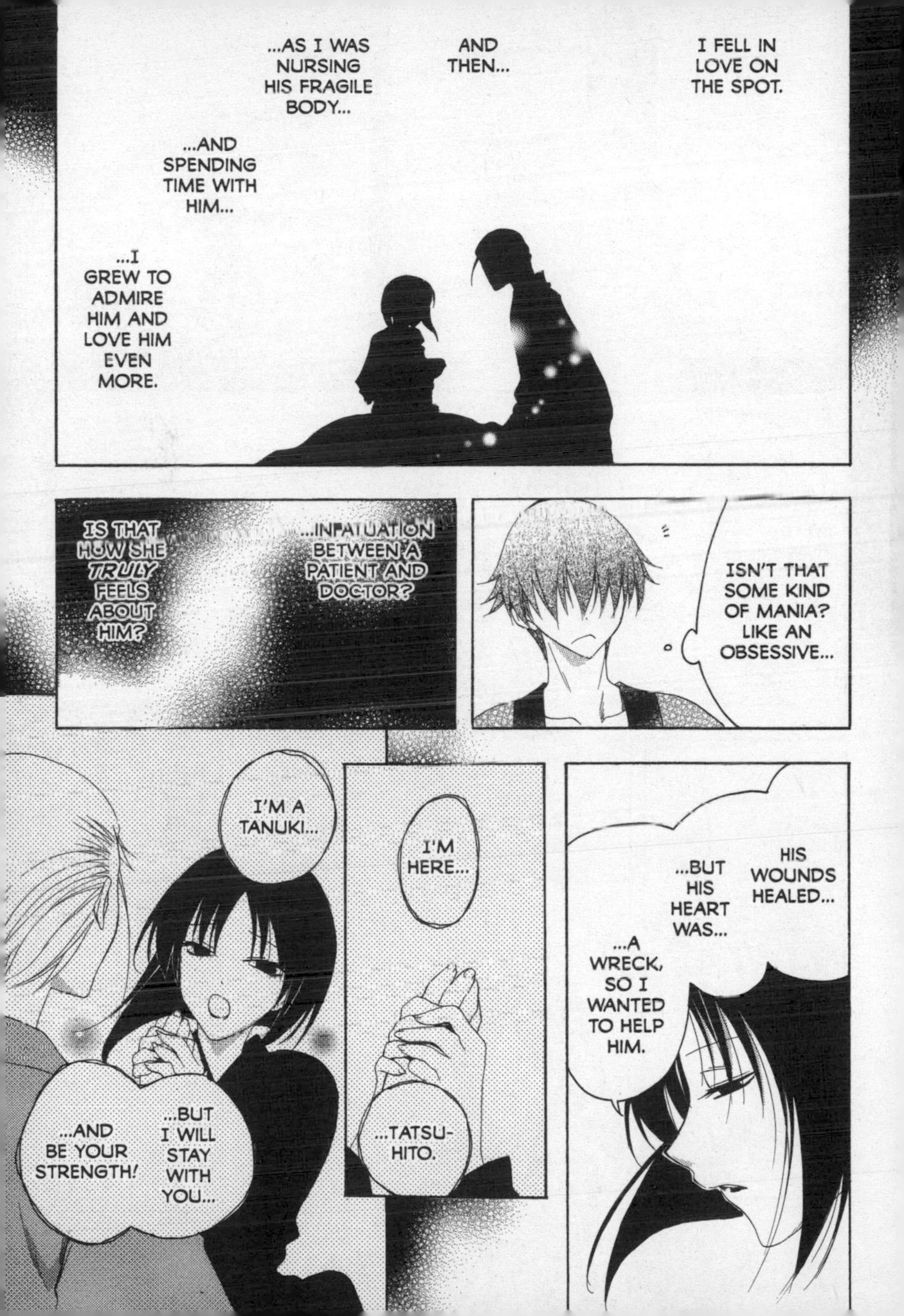
I FELL IN LOVE ON THE SPOT.
AND THEN...
...AS I WAS NURSING HIS FRAGILE BODY...
...AND SPENDING TIME WITH HIM...
...I GREW TO ADMIRE HIM AND LOVE HIM EVEN MORE.
ISN'T THAT SOME KIND OF MANIA? LIKE AN OBSESSIVE...
...INFATUATION BETWEEN A PATIENT AND DOCTOR?
IS THAT HOW SHE *TRULY* FEELS ABOUT HIM?
HIS WOUNDS HEALED...
...BUT HIS HEART WAS...
...A WRECK, SO I WANTED TO HELP HIM.
I'M HERE...
...TATSU-HITO.
I'M A TANUKI...
...BUT I WILL STAY WITH YOU...
...AND BE YOUR STRENGTH!

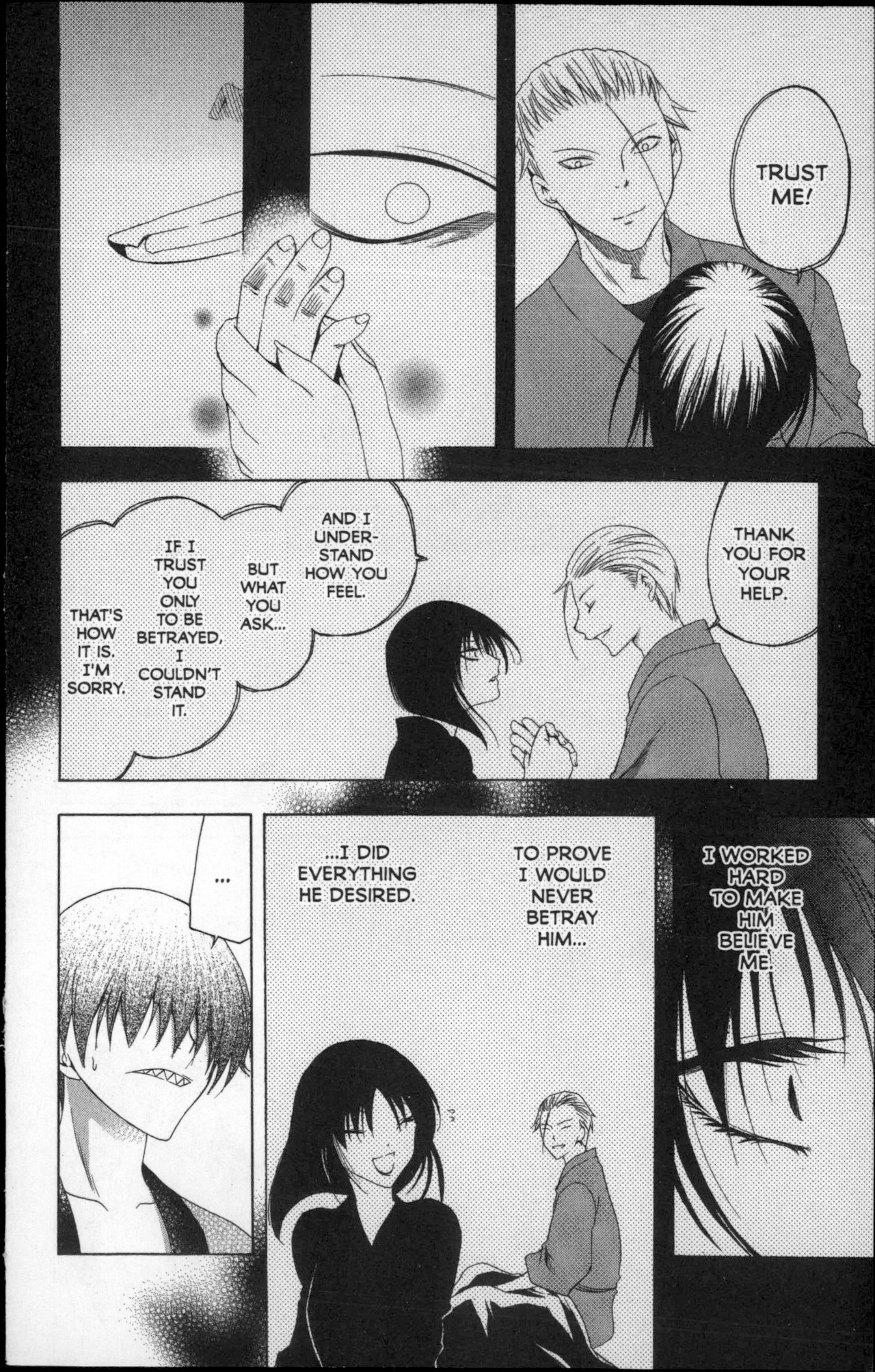
TRUST ME!
THANK YOU FOR YOUR HELP.
AND I UNDERSTAND HOW YOU FEEL.
BUT WHAT YOU ASK...
IF I TRUST YOU ONLY TO BE BETRAYED, I COULDN'T STAND IT.
THAT'S HOW IT IS. I'M SORRY.
I WORKED HARD TO MAKE HIM BELIEVE ME.
TO PROVE I WOULD NEVER BETRAY HIM...
...I DID EVERYTHING HE DESIRED.
...

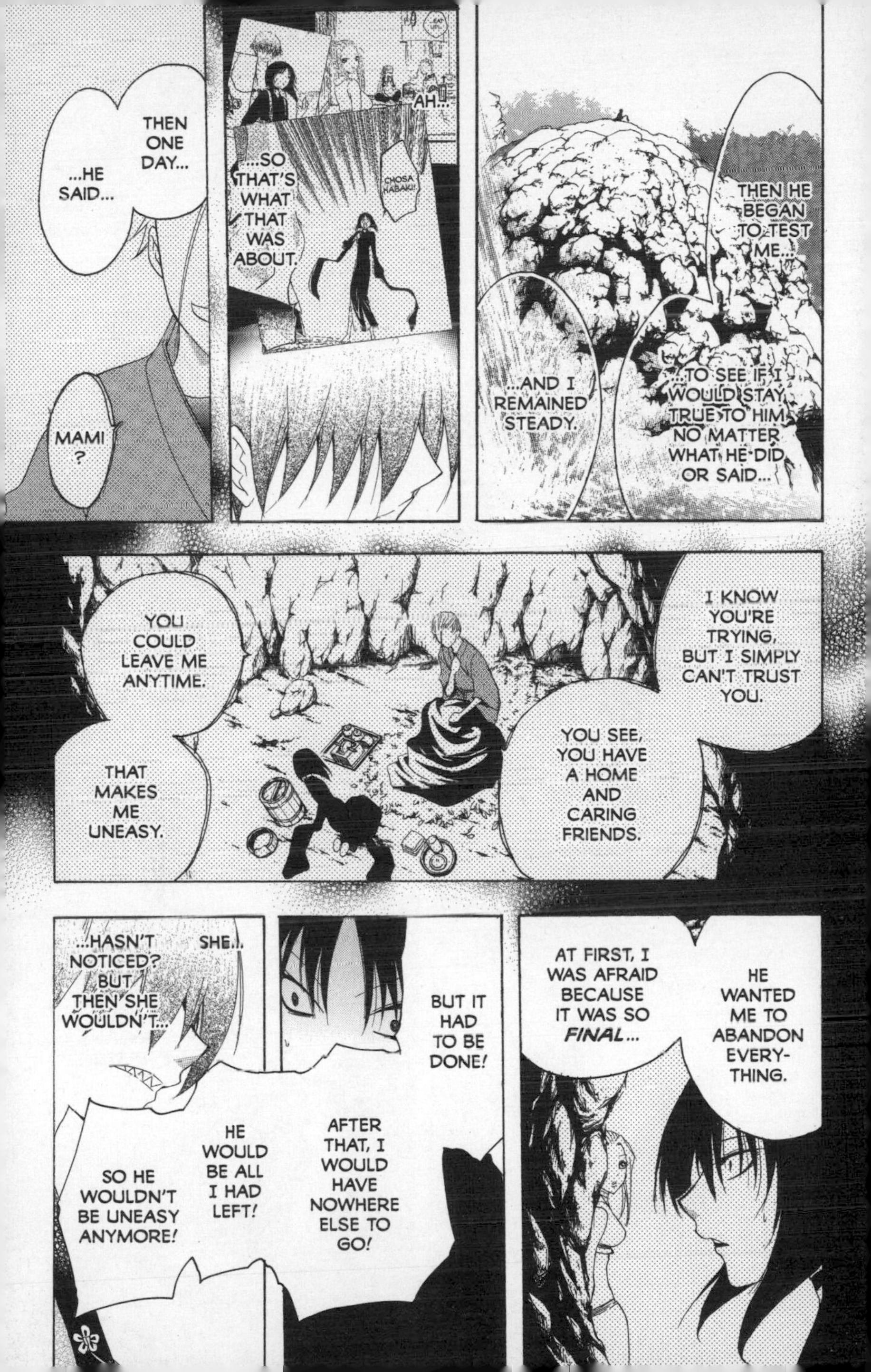
THEN HE BEGAN TO TEST ME...
...TO SEE IF I WOULD STAY TRUE TO HIM NO MATTER WHAT HE DID OR SAID...
...AND I REMAINED STEADY.
AH...
CHOSA HABAKI!
...SO THAT'S WHAT THAT WAS ABOUT.
THEN ONE DAY...
...HE SAID...
MAMI ?
I KNOW YOU'RE TRYING, BUT I SIMPLY CAN'T TRUST YOU.
YOU SEE, YOU HAVE A HOME AND CARING FRIENDS.
YOU COULD LEAVE ME ANYTIME.
THAT MAKES ME UNEASY.
HE WANTED ME TO ABANDON EVERY-THING.
AT FIRST, I WAS AFRAID BECAUSE IT WAS SO *FINAL*...
BUT IT HAD TO BE DONE!
AFTER THAT, I WOULD HAVE NOWHERE ELSE TO GO!
HE WOULD BE ALL I HAD LEFT!
SO HE WOULDN'T BE UNEASY ANYMORE!
SHE...
...HASN'T NOTICED? BUT THEN SHE WOULDN'T...

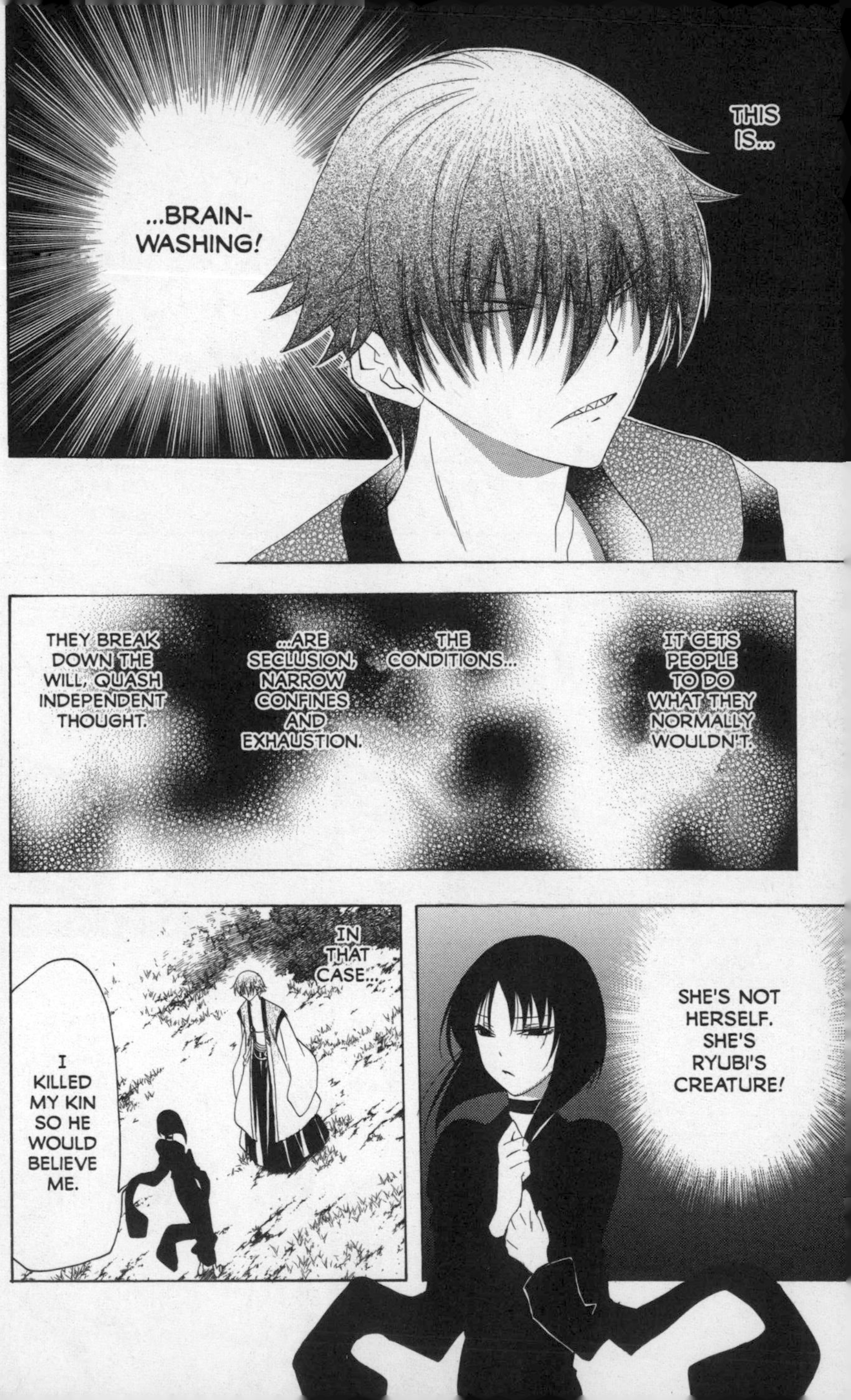
THIS IS...
...BRAIN-WASHING!
IT GETS PEOPLE TO DO WHAT THEY NORMALLY WOULDN'T.
THE CONDITIONS...
...ARE SECLUSION, NARROW CONFINES AND EXHAUSTION.
THEY BREAK DOWN THE WILL, QUASH INDEPENDENT THOUGHT.
SHE'S NOT HERSELF. SHE'S RYUBI'S CREATURE!
IN THAT CASE...
I KILLED MY KIN SO HE WOULD BELIEVE ME.

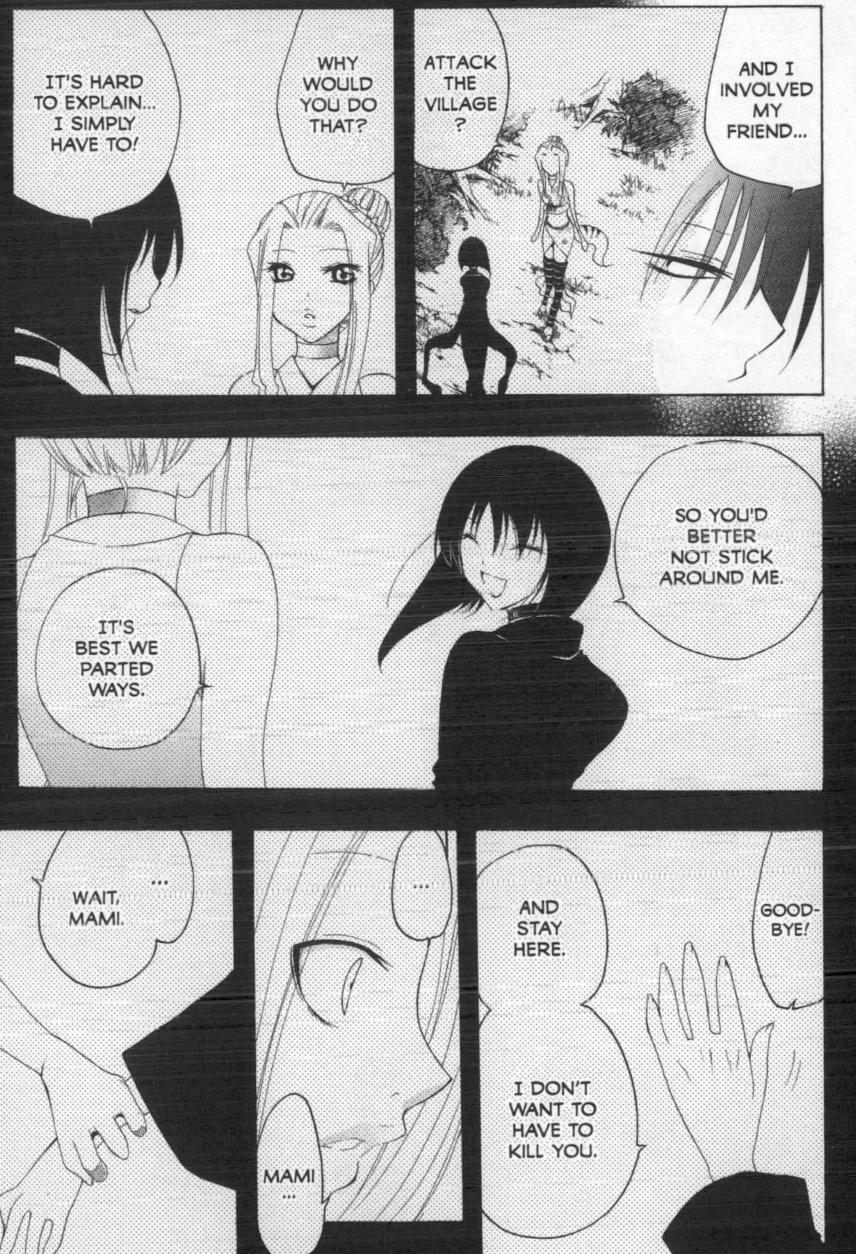
AND I INVOLVED MY FRIEND...
ATTACK THE VILLAGE ?
WHY WOULD YOU DO THAT?
IT'S HARD TO EXPLAIN... I SIMPLY HAVE TO!
SO YOU'D BETTER NOT STICK AROUND ME.
IT'S BEST WE PARTED WAYS.
GOOD-BYE!
AND STAY HERE.
I DON'T WANT TO HAVE TO KILL YOU.
...
MAMI ...
...
WAIT, MAMI.

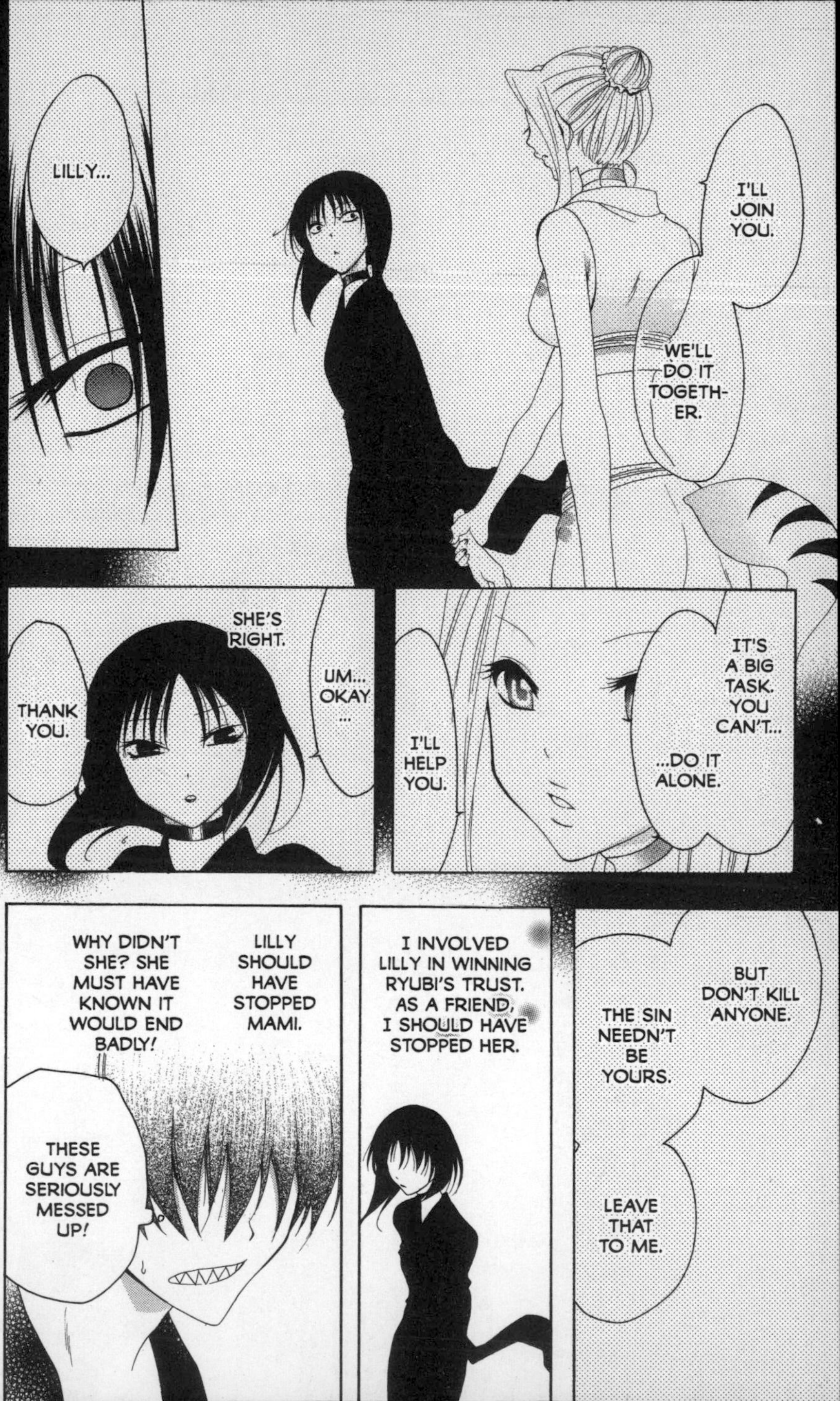
I'LL JOIN YOU.
WE'LL DO IT TOGETH-ER.
LILLY...
IT'S A BIG TASK. YOU CAN'T...
...DO IT ALONE.
I'LL HELP YOU.
UM... OKAY ...
SHE'S RIGHT.
THANK YOU.
BUT DON'T KILL ANYONE.
THE SIN NEEDN'T BE YOURS.
LEAVE THAT TO ME.
I INVOLVED LILLY IN WINNING RYUBI'S TRUST. AS A FRIEND, I SHOULD HAVE STOPPED HER.
LILLY SHOULD HAVE STOPPED MAMI.
WHY DIDN'T SHE? SHE MUST HAVE KNOWN IT WOULD END BADLY!
THESE GUYS ARE SERIOUSLY MESSED UP!

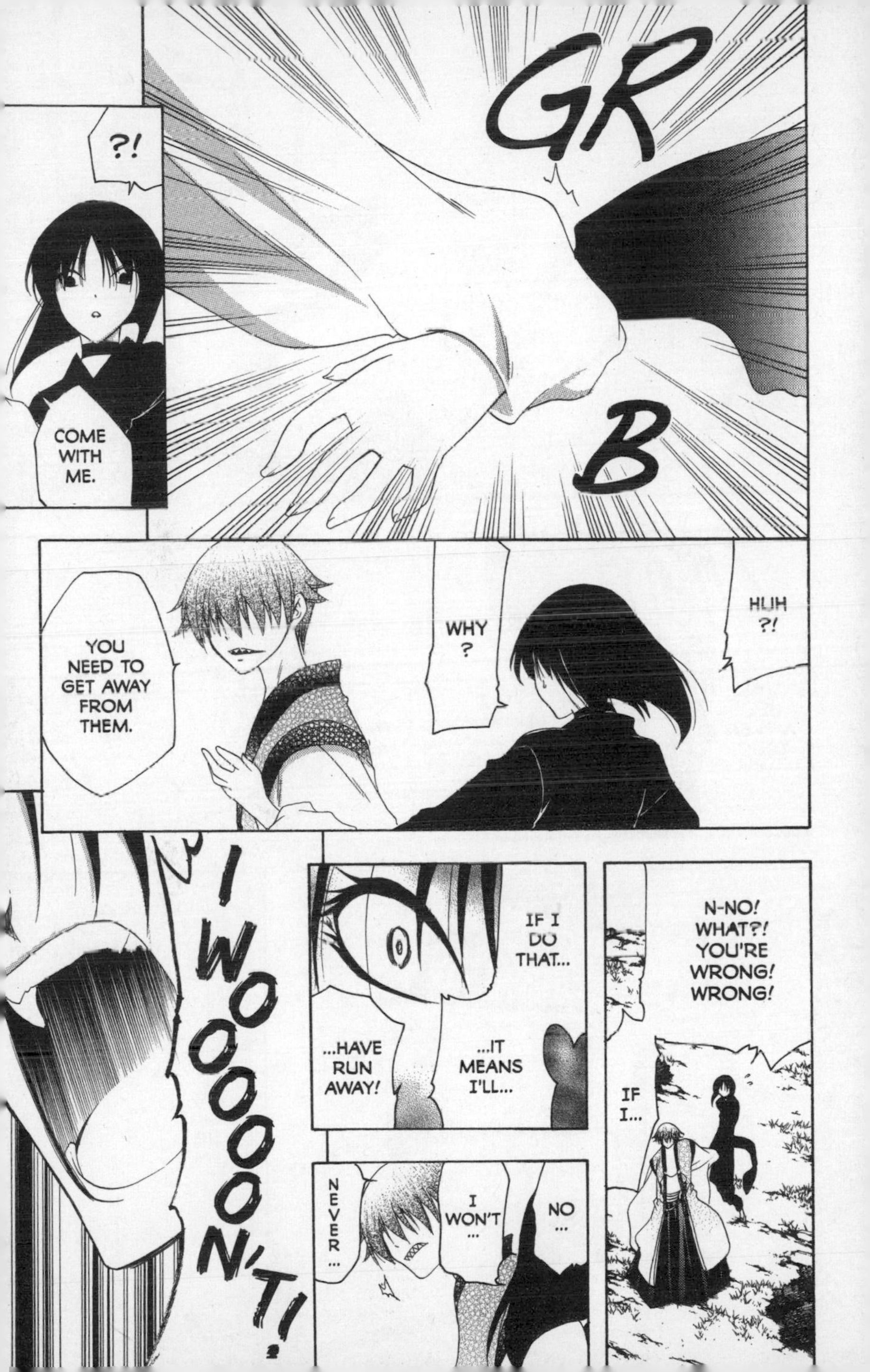
GR B
?!
COME WITH ME.
HUH ?!
WHY ?
YOU NEED TO GET AWAY FROM THEM.
N-NO! WHAT?! YOU'RE WRONG! WRONG!
IF I...
IF I DO THAT...
...IT MEANS I'LL...
...HAVE RUN AWAY!
NO ...
I WON'T ...
NEVER ...
I WOOOOON'T!

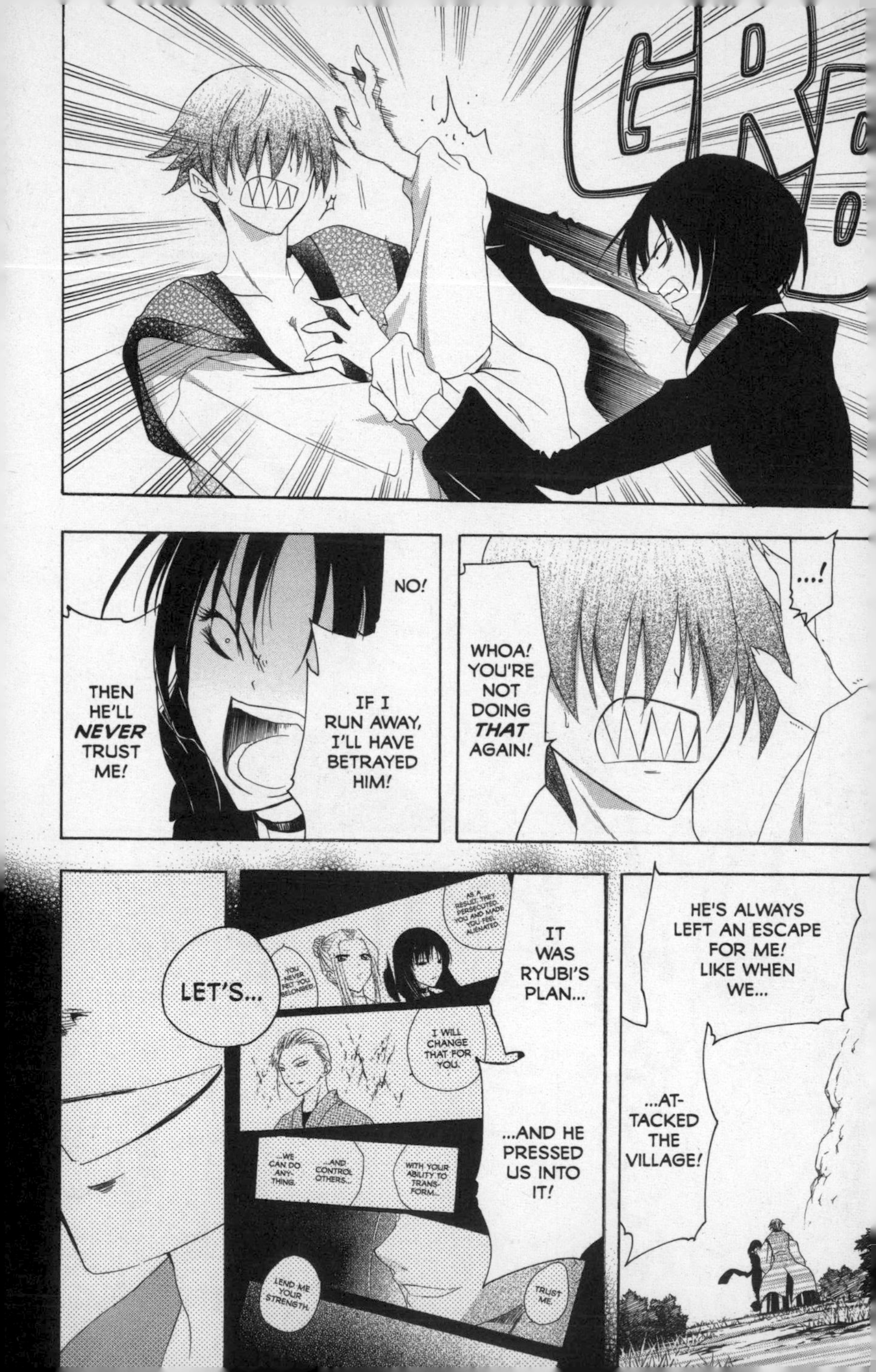
GRR
...!
WHOA! YOU'RE NOT DOING *THAT* AGAIN!
NO!
IF I RUN AWAY, I'LL HAVE BETRAYED HIM!
THEN HE'LL ***NEVER*** TRUST ME!
HE'S ALWAYS LEFT AN ESCAPE FOR ME! LIKE WHEN WE...
...AT-TACKED THE VILLAGE!
IT WAS RYUBI'S PLAN...
AS A RESULT, THEY PERSECUTED YOU AND MADE YOU FEEL ALIENATED.
YOU NEVER FELT YOU BELONGED.
I WILL CHANGE THAT FOR YOU.
WITH YOUR ABILITY TO TRANS-FORM...
...AND CONTROL OTHERS...
...WE CAN DO ANY-THING.
...AND HE PRESSED US INTO IT!
TRUST ME.
LEND ME YOUR STRENGTH.
LET'S...

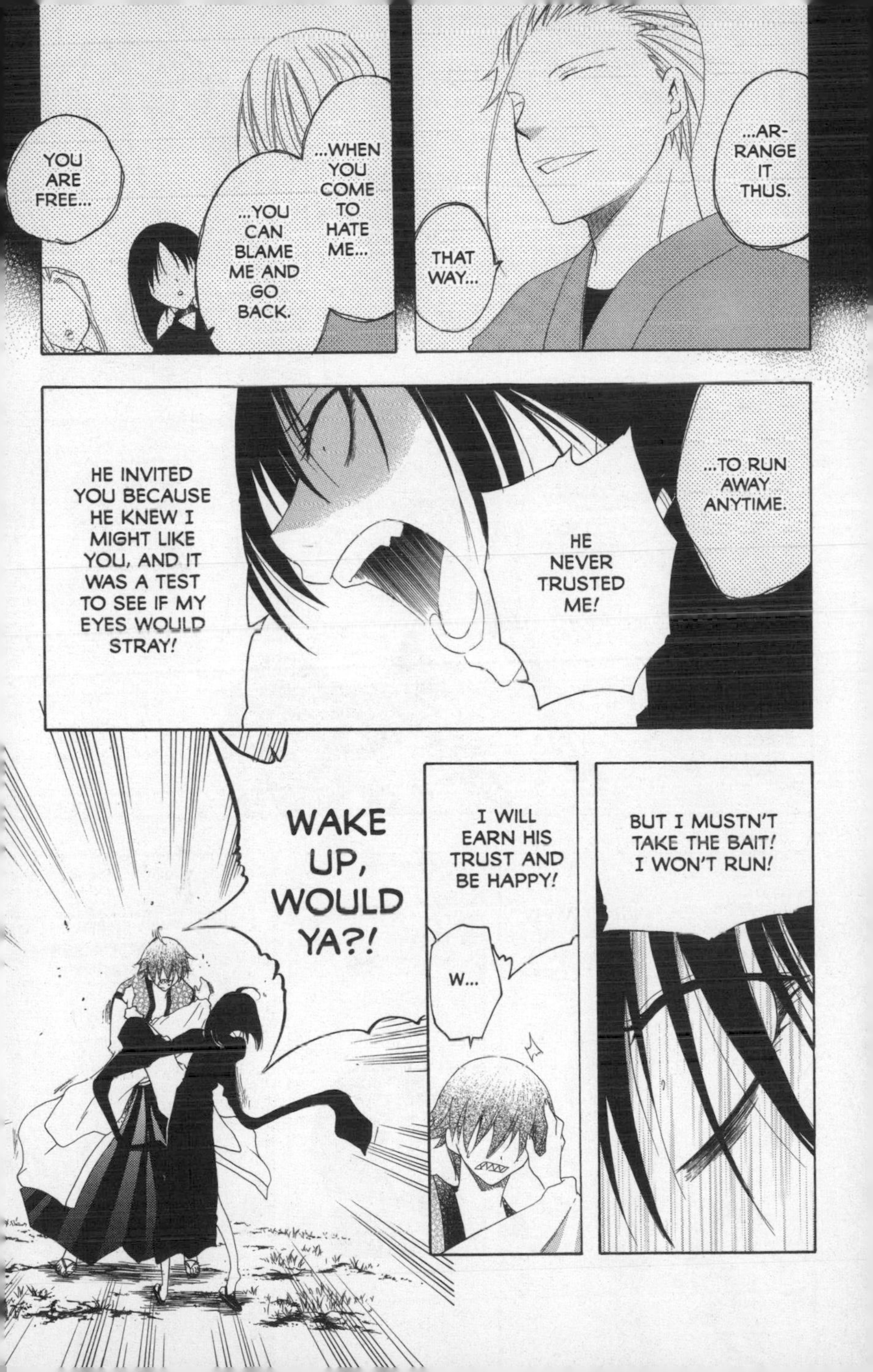
...AR-RANGE IT THUS.
THAT WAY...
...WHEN YOU COME TO HATE ME...
...YOU CAN BLAME ME AND GO BACK.
YOU ARE FREE...
...TO RUN AWAY ANYTIME.
HE NEVER TRUSTED ME!
HE INVITED YOU BECAUSE HE KNEW I MIGHT LIKE YOU, AND IT WAS A TEST TO SEE IF MY EYES WOULD STRAY!
BUT I MUSTN'T TAKE THE BAIT! I WON'T RUN!
I WILL EARN HIS TRUST AND BE HAPPY!
W...
WAKE UP, WOULD YA?!

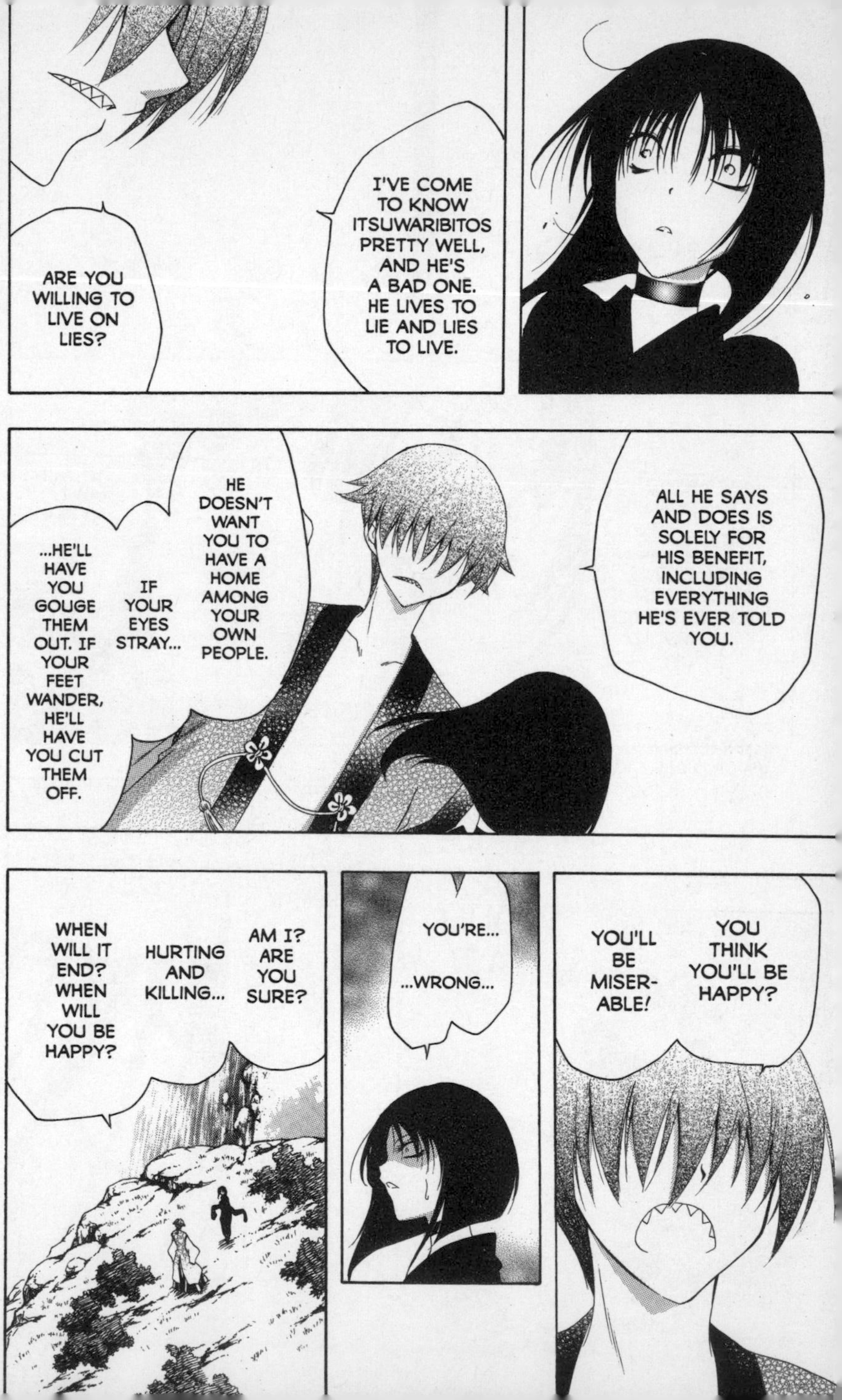
I'VE COME TO KNOW ITSUWARIBITOS PRETTY WELL, AND HE'S A BAD ONE. HE LIVES TO LIE AND LIES TO LIVE.
ARE YOU WILLING TO LIVE ON LIES?
ALL HE SAYS AND DOES IS SOLELY FOR HIS BENEFIT, INCLUDING EVERYTHING HE'S EVER TOLD YOU.
HE DOESN'T WANT YOU TO HAVE A HOME AMONG YOUR OWN PEOPLE.
IF YOUR EYES STRAY...
...HE'LL HAVE YOU GOUGE THEM OUT. IF YOUR FEET WANDER, HE'LL HAVE YOU CUT THEM OFF.
YOU THINK YOU'LL BE HAPPY?
YOU'LL BE MISER-ABLE!
YOU'RE...
...WRONG...
AM I? ARE YOU SURE?
HURTING AND KILLING...
WHEN WILL IT END? WHEN WILL YOU BE HAPPY?

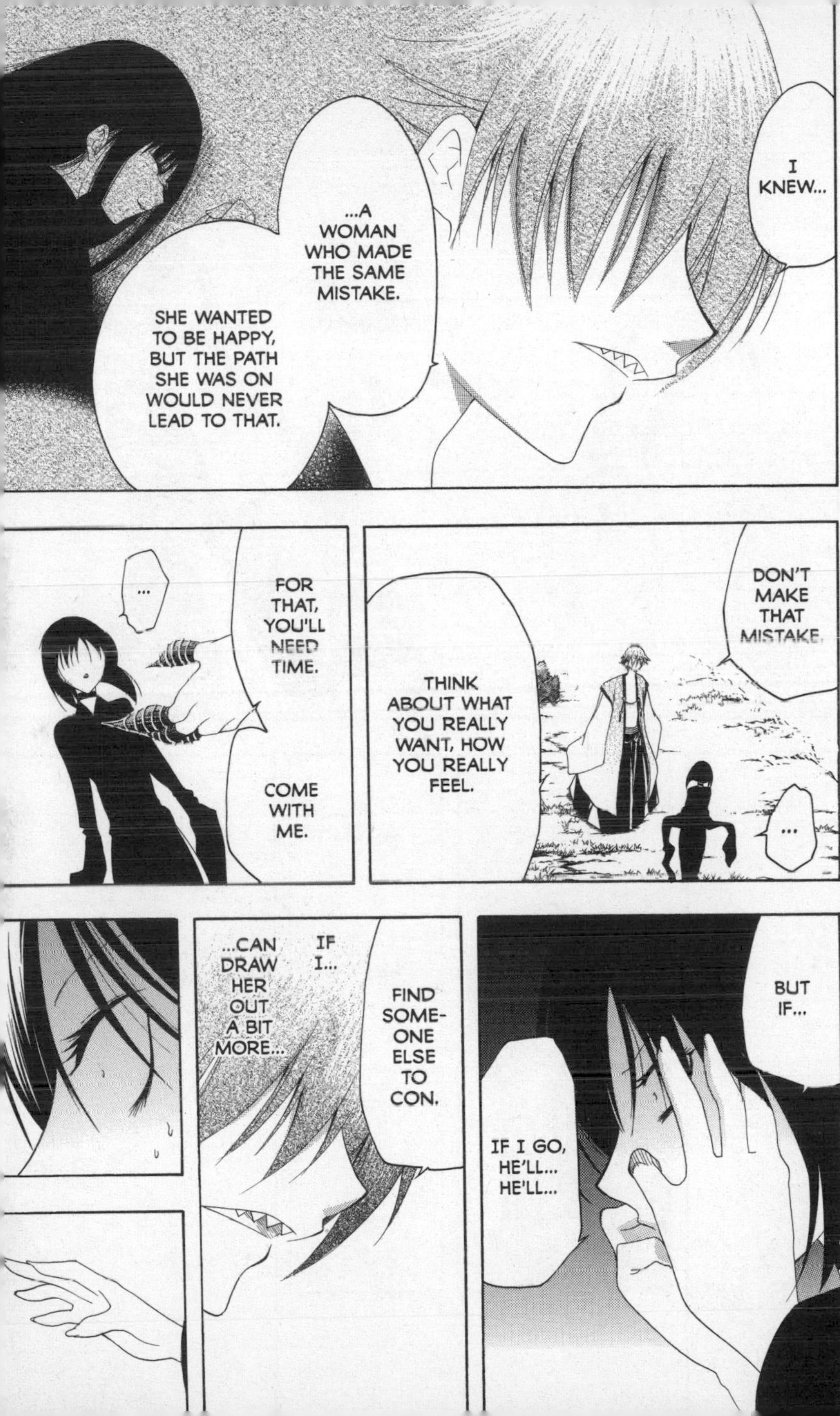
I KNEW...
...A WOMAN WHO MADE THE SAME MISTAKE.
SHE WANTED TO BE HAPPY, BUT THE PATH SHE WAS ON WOULD NEVER LEAD TO THAT.
DON'T MAKE THAT MISTAKE.
THINK ABOUT WHAT YOU REALLY WANT, HOW YOU REALLY FEEL.
...
FOR THAT, YOU'LL NEED TIME.
COME WITH ME.
...
BUT IF...
IF I GO, HE'LL... HE'LL...
FIND SOME-ONE ELSE TO CON.
IF I...
...CAN DRAW HER OUT A BIT MORE...

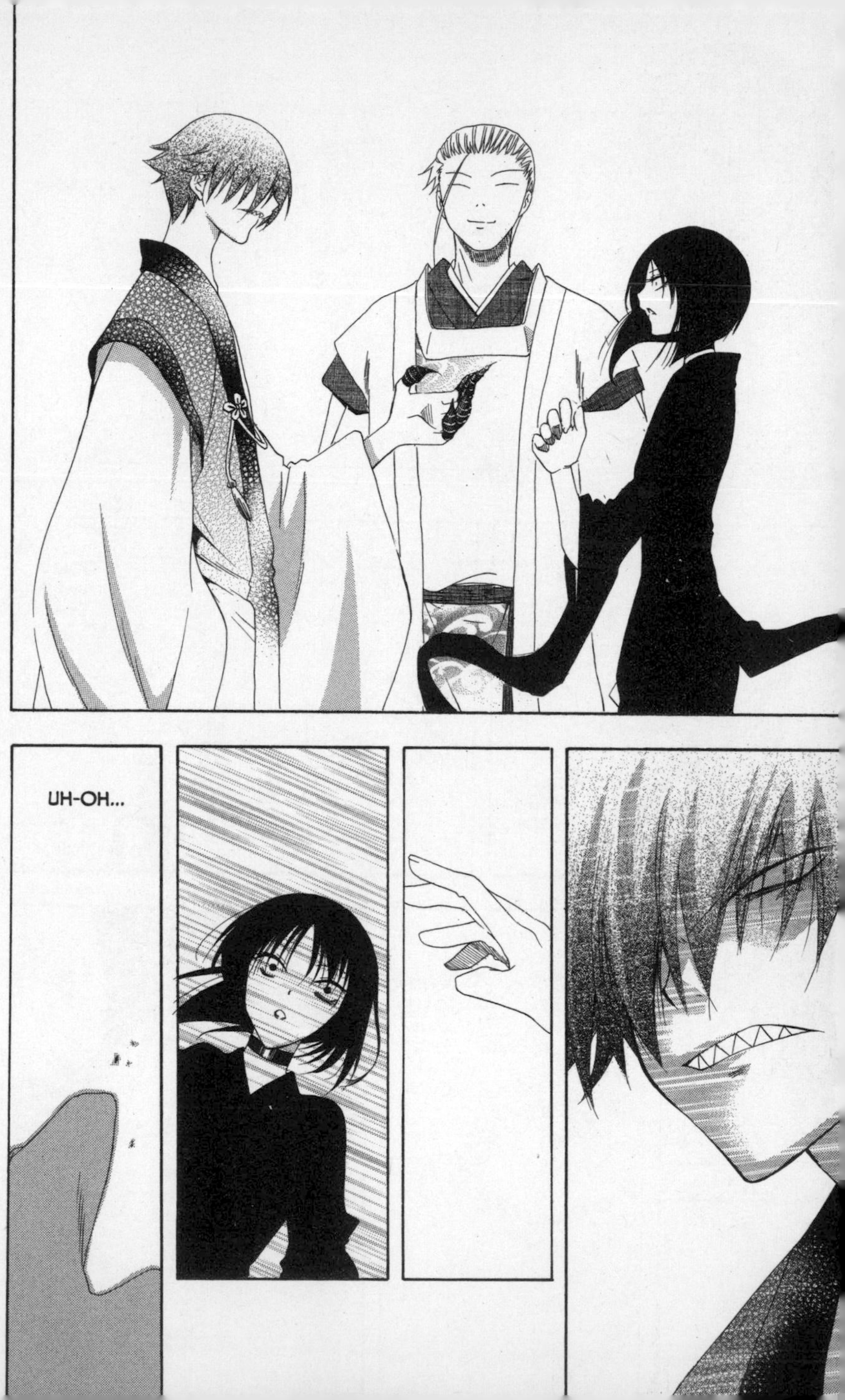
UH-OH...

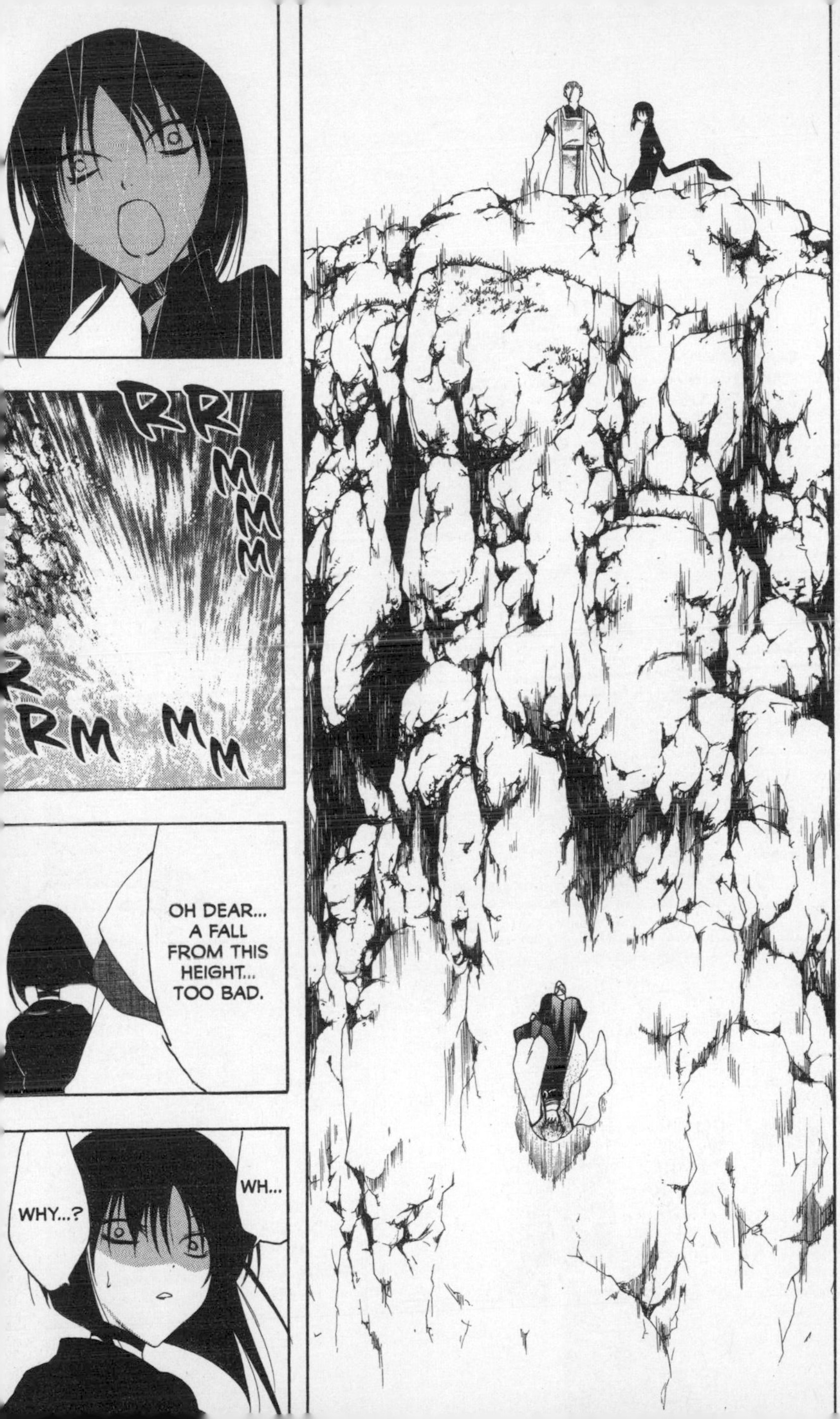
RRRMMMM
RRRM MMM
OH DEAR... A FALL FROM THIS HEIGHT... TOO BAD.
WH...
WHY...?

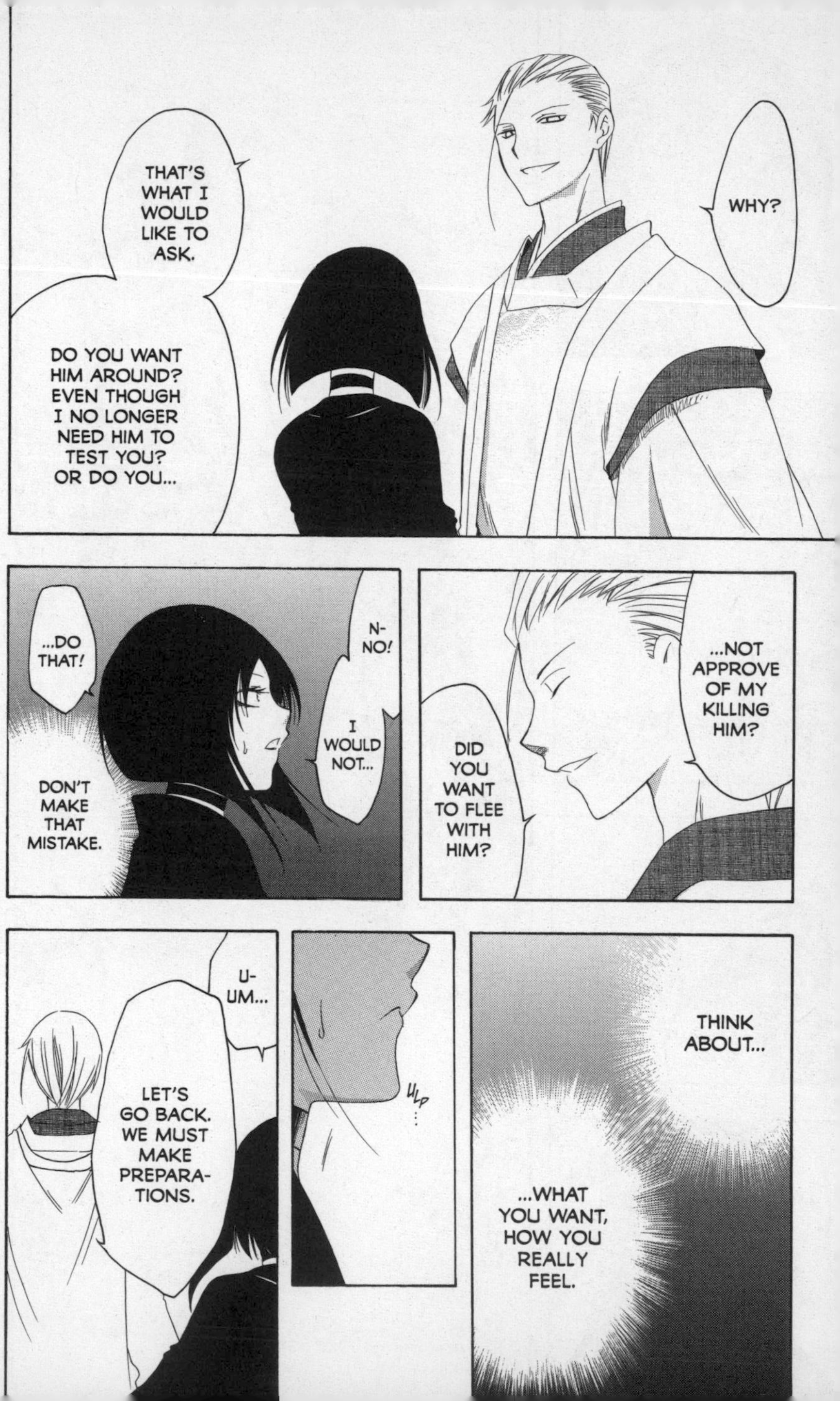
WHY?
THAT'S WHAT I WOULD LIKE TO ASK.
DO YOU WANT HIM AROUND? EVEN THOUGH I NO LONGER NEED HIM TO TEST YOU? OR DO YOU...
...NOT APPROVE OF MY KILLING HIM?
DID YOU WANT TO FLEE WITH HIM?
N-NO!
I WOULD NOT...
...DO THAT!
DON'T MAKE THAT MISTAKE.
THINK ABOUT...
...WHAT YOU WANT, HOW YOU REALLY FEEL.
ULP...
U-UM...
LET'S GO BACK. WE MUST MAKE PREPARATIONS.

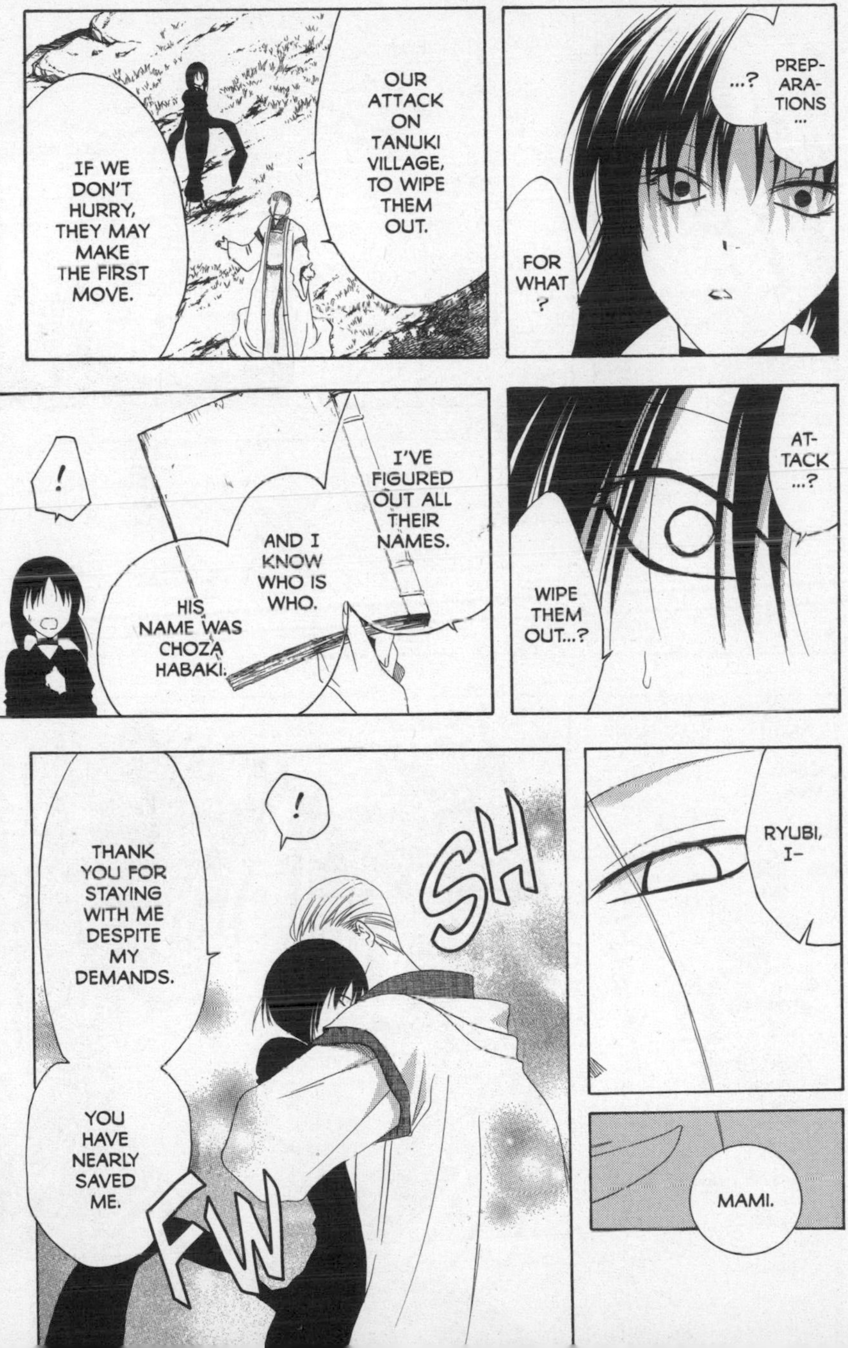
PREPARATIONS...
...?
FOR WHAT?
OUR ATTACK ON TANUKI VILLAGE, TO WIPE THEM OUT.
IF WE DON'T HURRY, THEY MAY MAKE THE FIRST MOVE.
ATTACK...?
WIPE THEM OUT...?
I'VE FIGURED OUT ALL THEIR NAMES.
AND I KNOW WHO IS WHO.
HIS NAME WAS CHOZA HABAKI.
!
RYUBI, I–
MAMI.
!
SH
THANK YOU FOR STAYING WITH ME DESPITE MY DEMANDS.
FW
YOU HAVE NEARLY SAVED ME.

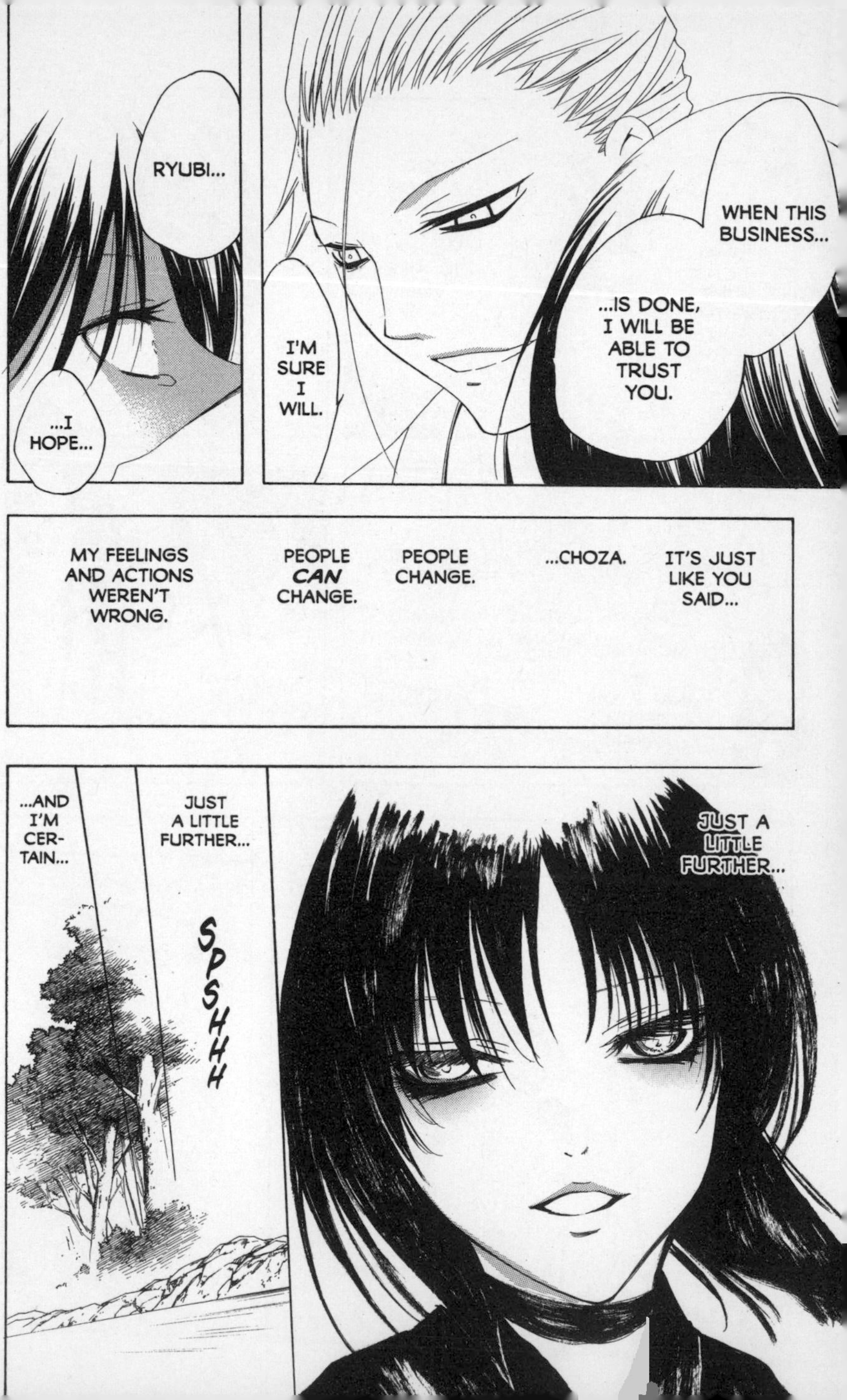
WHEN THIS BUSINESS...
...IS DONE, I WILL BE ABLE TO TRUST YOU.
I'M SURE I WILL.
RYUBI...
...I HOPE...
IT'S JUST LIKE YOU SAID...
...CHOZA.
PEOPLE CHANGE.
PEOPLE *CAN* CHANGE.
MY FEELINGS AND ACTIONS WEREN'T WRONG.
JUST A LITTLE FURTHER...
SPSHHH
JUST A LITTLE FURTHER...
...AND I'M CER-TAIN...

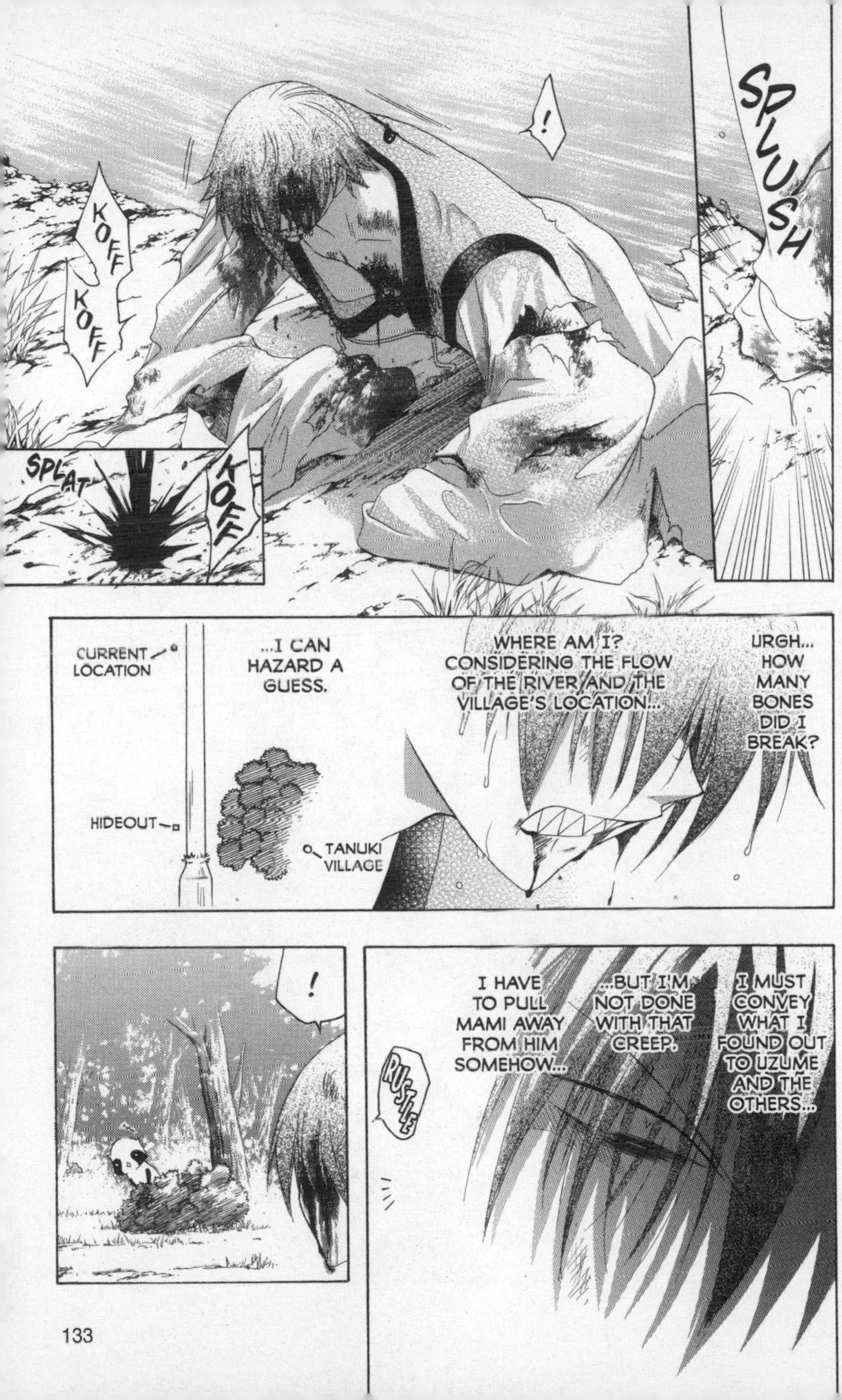
SPLUSH
!
KOFF
KOFF
KOFF
SPLAT
URGH... HOW MANY BONES DID I BREAK?
WHERE AM I? CONSIDERING THE FLOW OF THE RIVER AND THE VILLAGE'S LOCATION...
...I CAN HAZARD A GUESS.
CURRENT LOCATION
HIDEOUT
TANUKI VILLAGE
I MUST CONVEY WHAT I FOUND OUT TO UZUME AND THE OTHERS...
...BUT I'M NOT DONE WITH THAT CREEP.
I HAVE TO PULL MAMI AWAY FROM HIM SOMEHOW...
RUSTLE
!

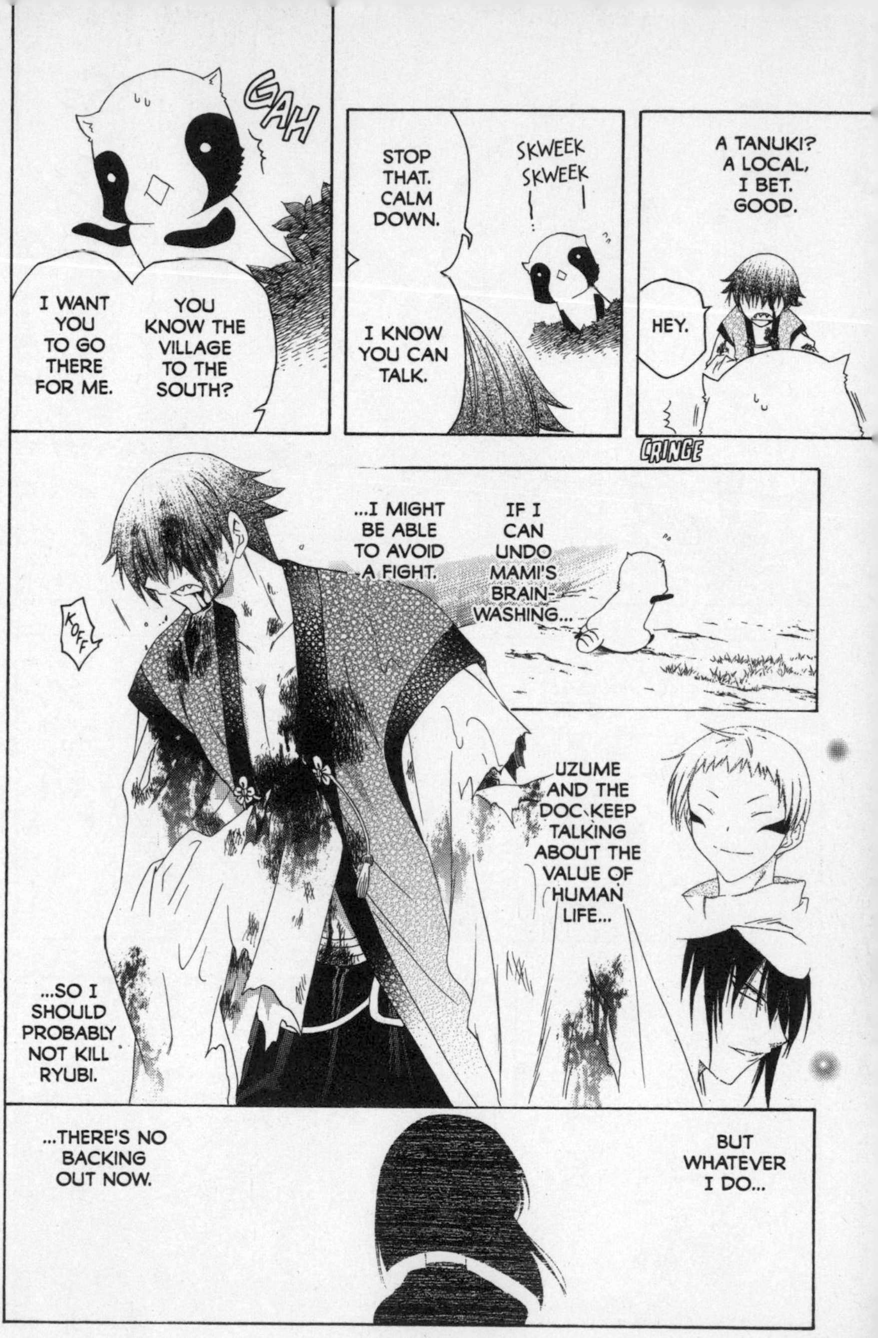
A TANUKI? A LOCAL, I BET. GOOD.
HEY.
CRINGE
SKWEEK SKWEEK
STOP THAT. CALM DOWN.
I KNOW YOU CAN TALK.
GAH
YOU KNOW THE VILLAGE TO THE SOUTH?
I WANT YOU TO GO THERE FOR ME.
IF I CAN UNDO MAMI'S BRAIN-WASHING...
...I MIGHT BE ABLE TO AVOID A FIGHT.
KOFF
UZUME AND THE DOC KEEP TALKING ABOUT THE VALUE OF HUMAN LIFE...
...SO I SHOULD PROBABLY NOT KILL RYUBI.
BUT WHATEVER I DO...
...THERE'S NO BACKING OUT NOW.

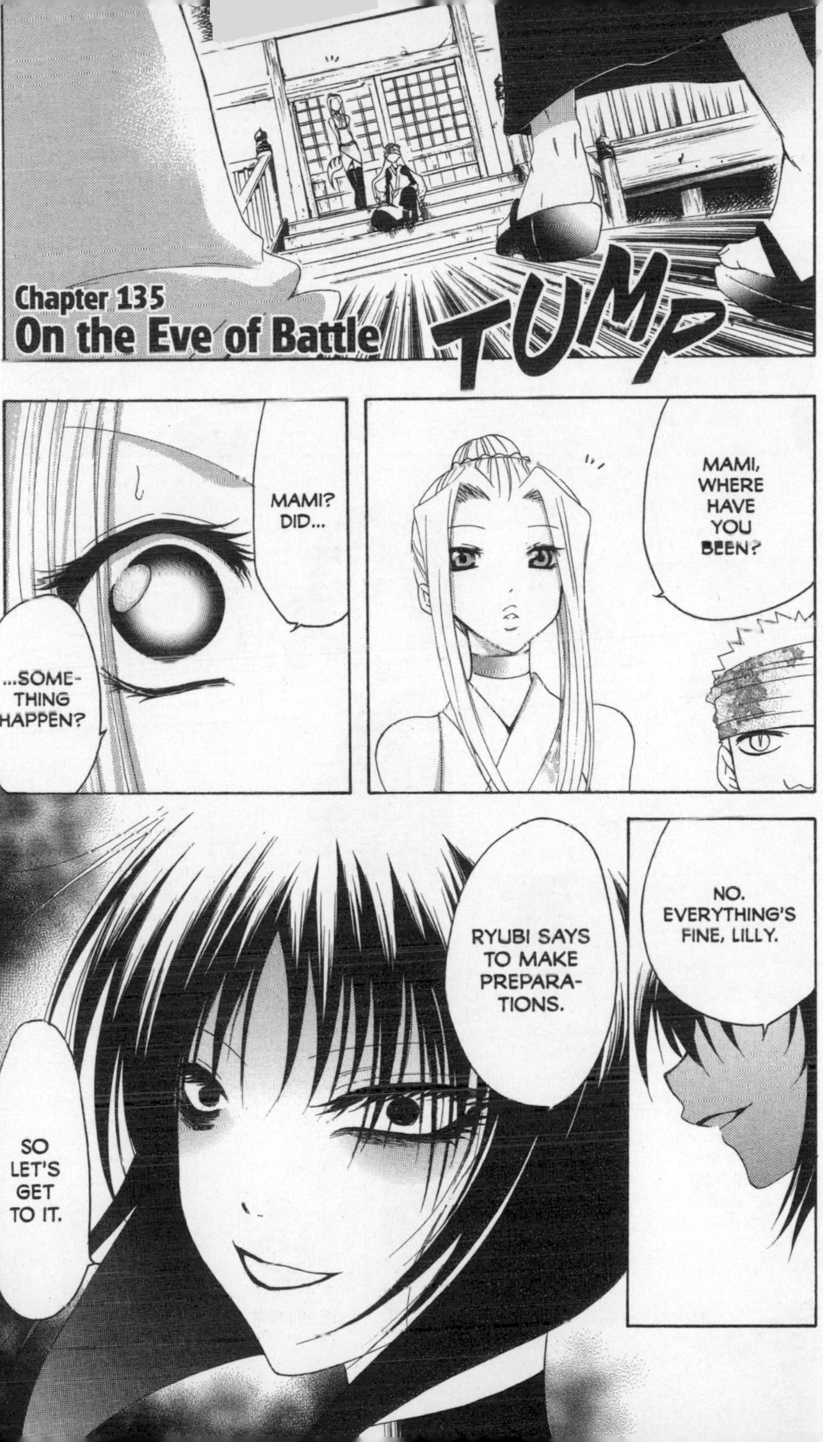
Chapter 135
On the Eve of Battle
TUMP
MAMI, WHERE HAVE YOU BEEN?
MAMI? DID...
...SOME-THING HAPPEN?
NO. EVERYTHING'S FINE, LILLY.
RYUBI SAYS TO MAKE PREPARA-TIONS.
SO LET'S GET TO IT.

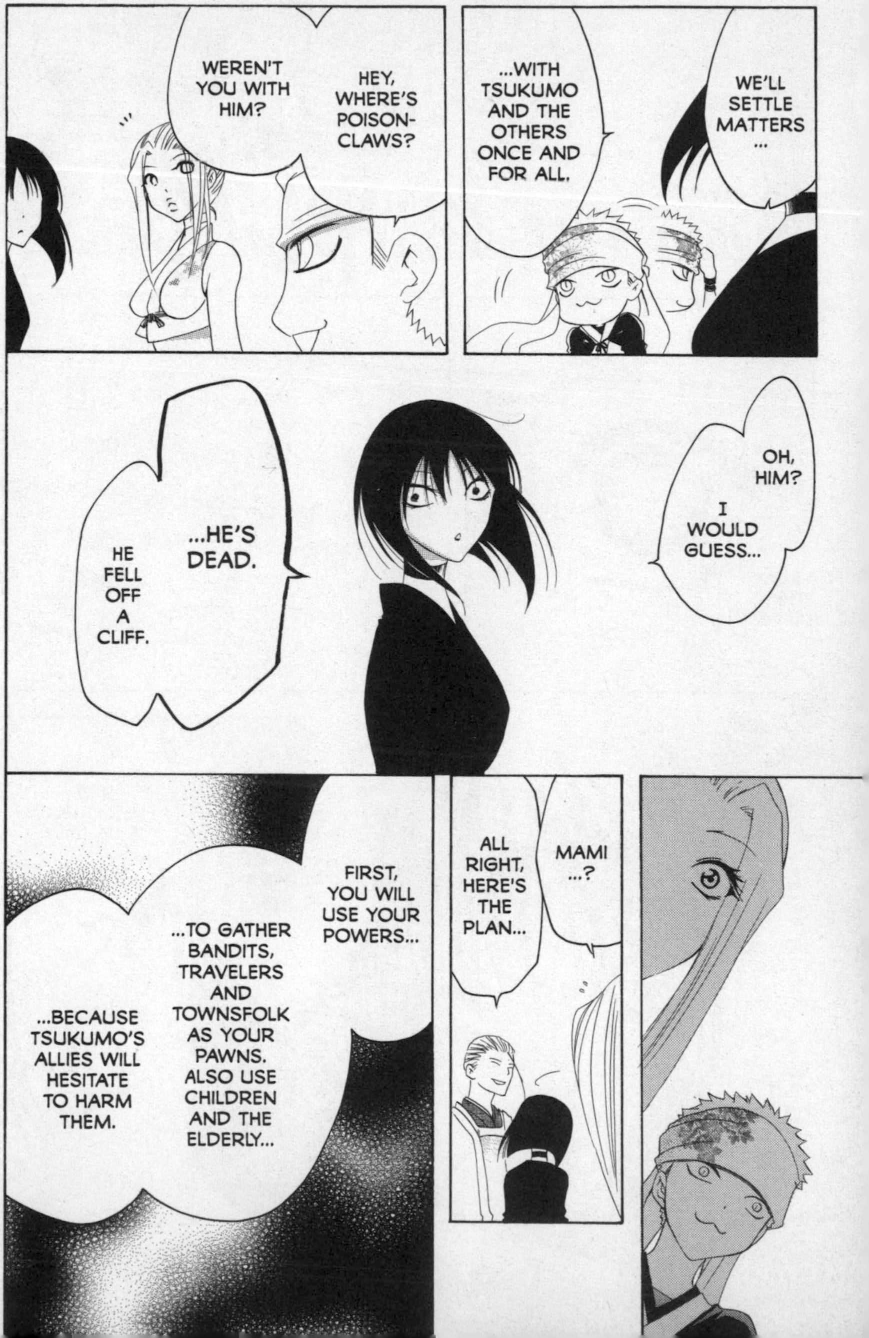
WE'LL SETTLE MATTERS ...
...WITH TSUKUMO AND THE OTHERS ONCE AND FOR ALL.
HEY, WHERE'S POISON-CLAWS?
WEREN'T YOU WITH HIM?
OH, HIM?
I WOULD GUESS...
...HE'S DEAD.
HE FELL OFF A CLIFF.
MAMI ...?
ALL RIGHT, HERE'S THE PLAN...
FIRST, YOU WILL USE YOUR POWERS...
...TO GATHER BANDITS, TRAVELERS AND TOWNSFOLK AS YOUR PAWNS. ALSO USE CHILDREN AND THE ELDERLY...
...BECAUSE TSUKUMO'S ALLIES WILL HESITATE TO HARM THEM.

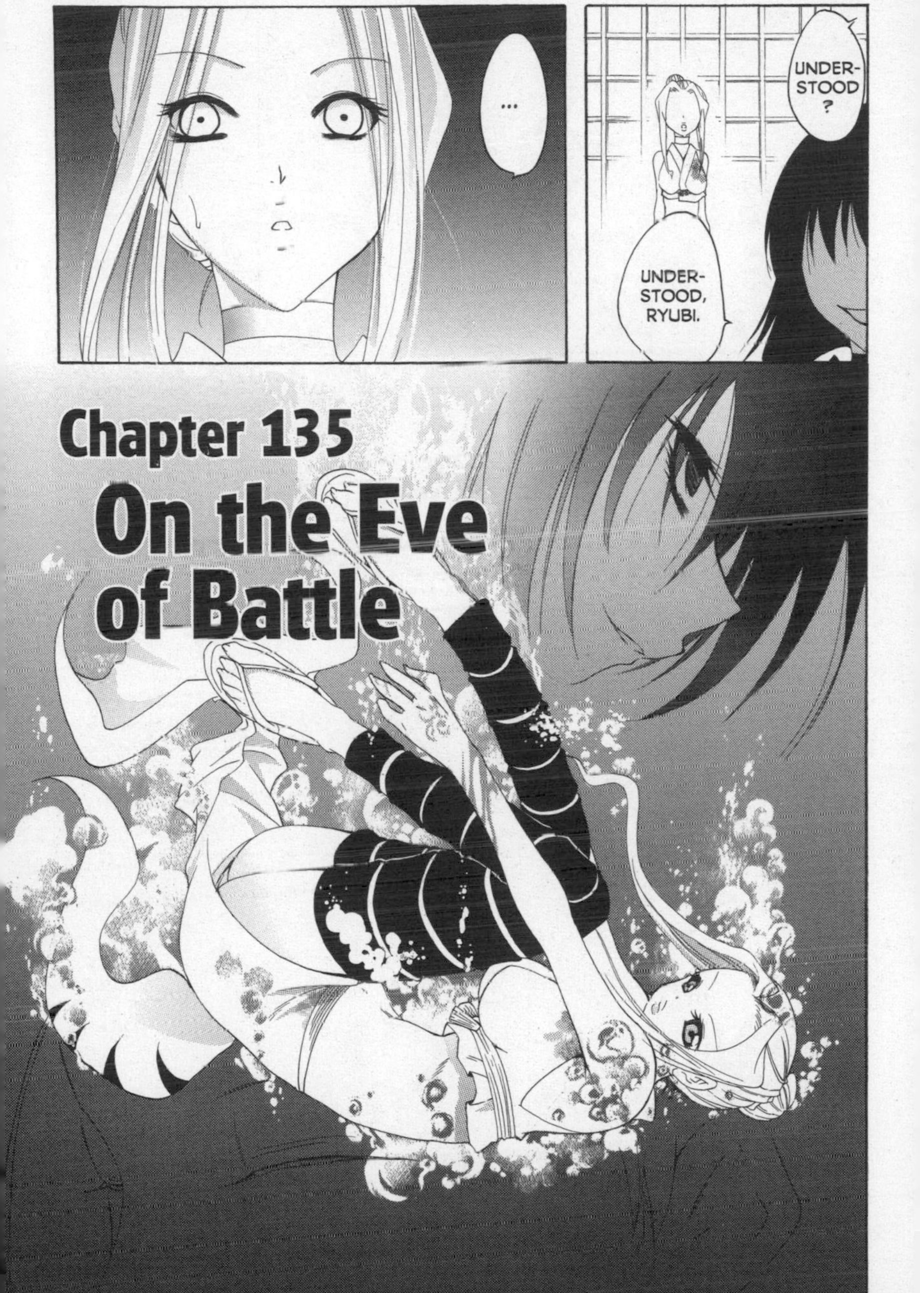
UNDER-STOOD?
UNDER-STOOD, RYUBI.
...
Chapter 135
On the Eve of Battle

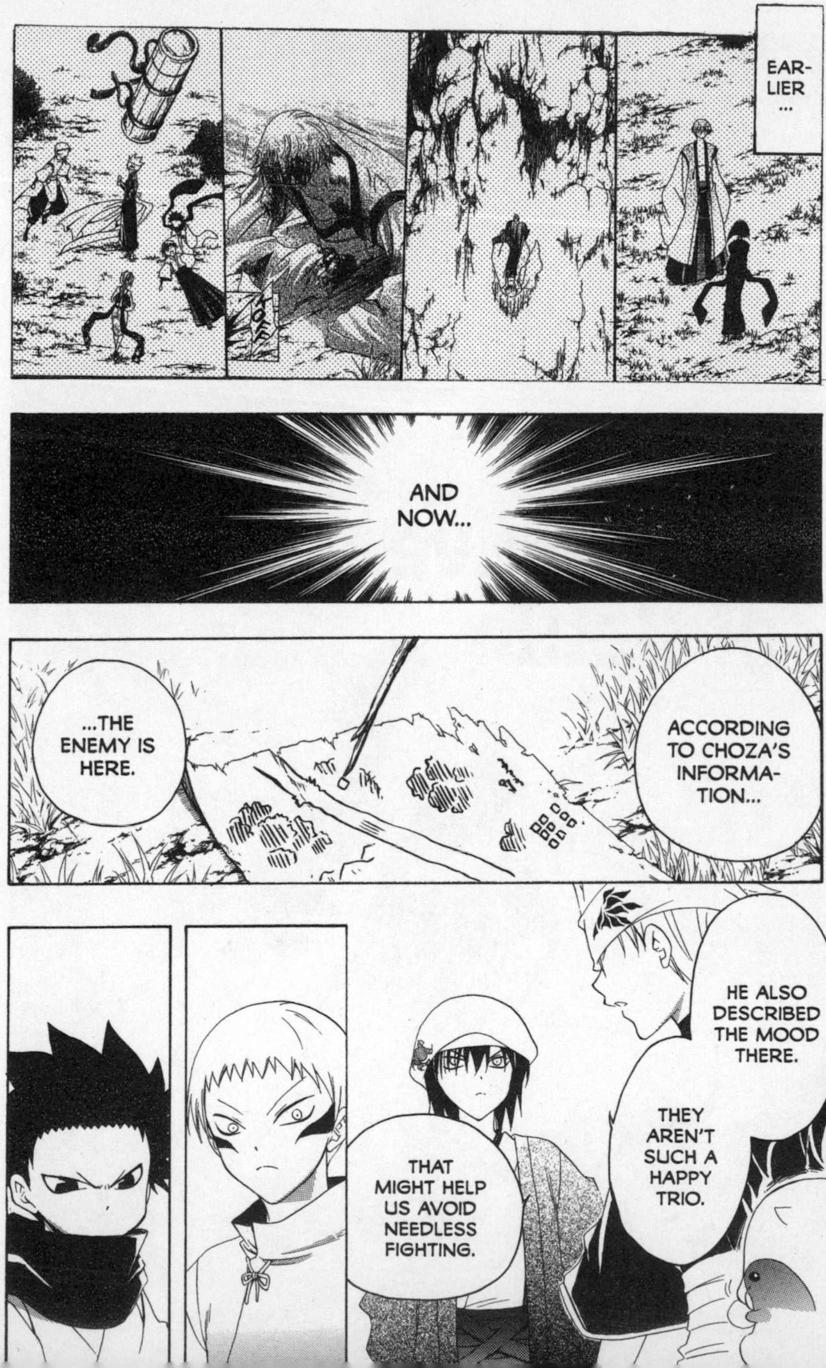
EAR-LIER ...
AND NOW...
ACCORDING TO CHOZA'S INFORMATION...
...THE ENEMY IS HERE.
HE ALSO DESCRIBED THE MOOD THERE.
THEY AREN'T SUCH A HAPPY TRIO.
THAT MIGHT HELP US AVOID NEEDLESS FIGHTING.

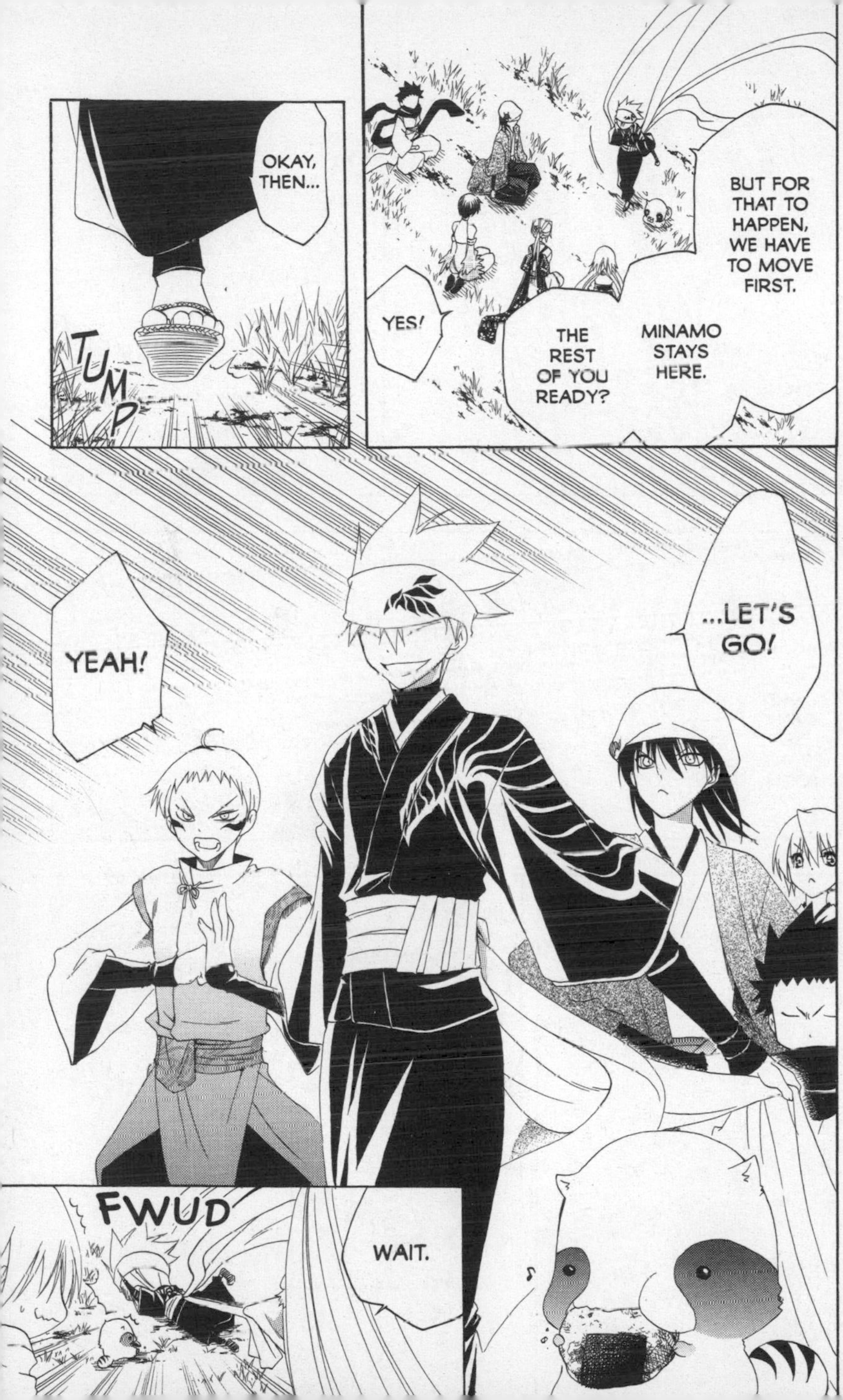
BUT FOR THAT TO HAPPEN, WE HAVE TO MOVE FIRST.
MINAMO STAYS HERE.
THE REST OF YOU READY?
YES!
OKAY, THEN...
TUMP
...LET'S GO!
YEAH!
WAIT.
FWUD

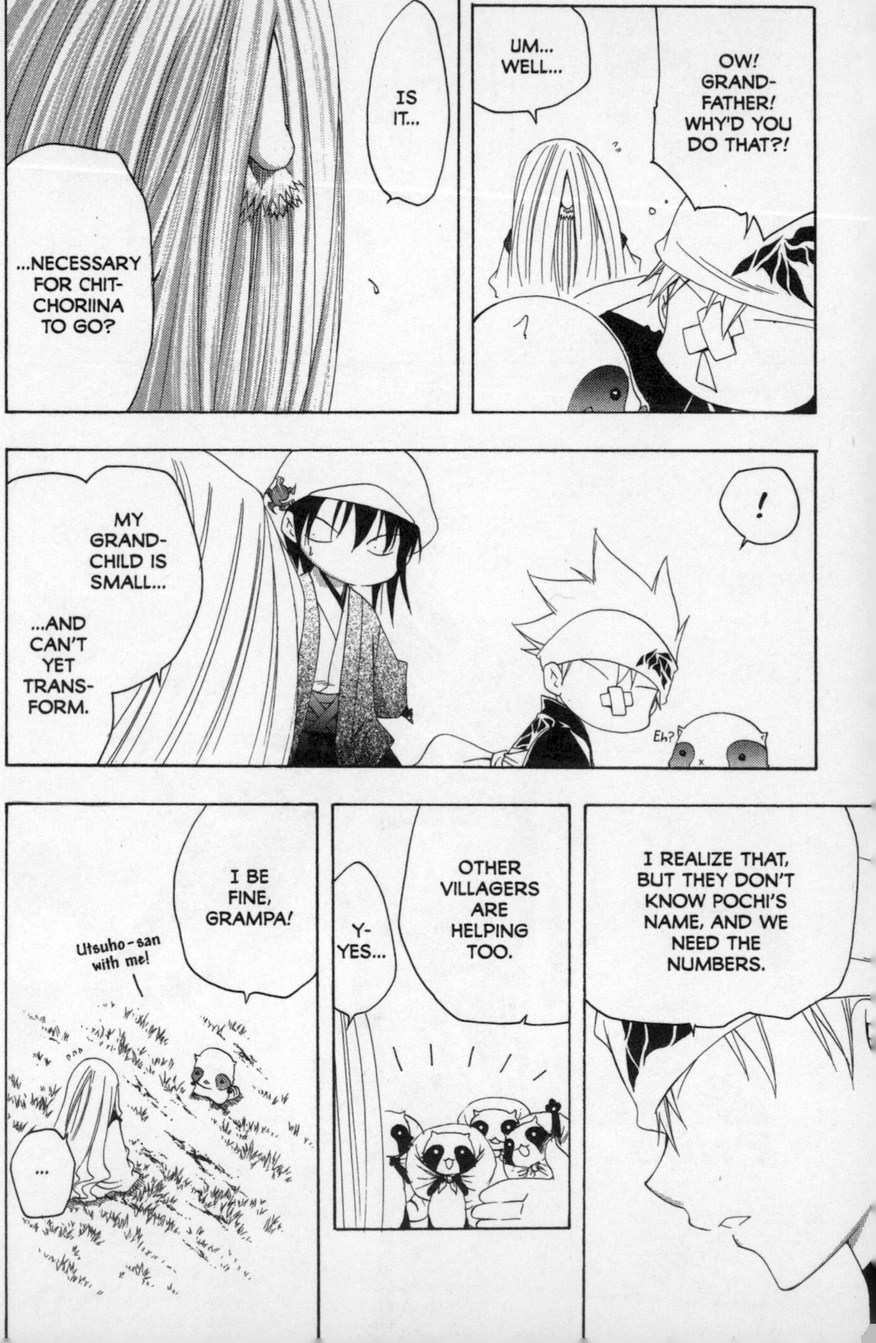
OW! GRAND-FATHER! WHY'D YOU DO THAT?!
UM... WELL...
IS IT...
...NECESSARY FOR CHIT-CHORIINA TO GO?
!
MY GRAND-CHILD IS SMALL...
...AND CAN'T YET TRANS-FORM.
Eh?
I REALIZE THAT, BUT THEY DON'T KNOW POCHI'S NAME, AND WE NEED THE NUMBERS.
OTHER VILLAGERS ARE HELPING TOO.
Y-YES...
I BE FINE, GRAMPA!
Utsuho-san with me!
...

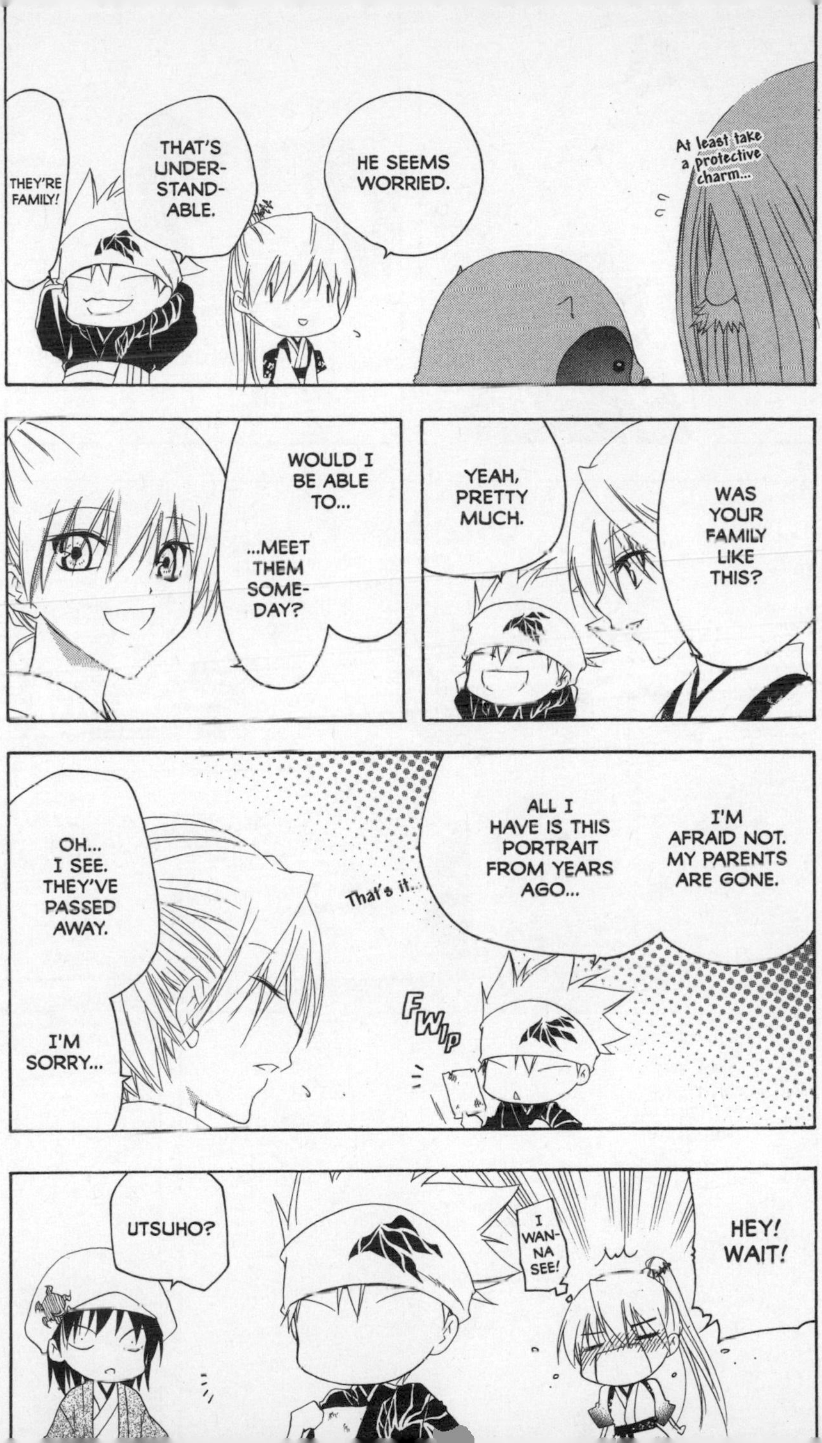
At least take a protective charm...
HE SEEMS WORRIED.
THAT'S UNDER-STAND-ABLE.
THEY'RE FAMILY!
WAS YOUR FAMILY LIKE THIS?
YEAH, PRETTY MUCH.
WOULD I BE ABLE TO...
...MEET THEM SOME-DAY?
I'M AFRAID NOT. MY PARENTS ARE GONE.
ALL I HAVE IS THIS PORTRAIT FROM YEARS AGO...
FWIP
That's it...
OH... I SEE. THEY'VE PASSED AWAY.
I'M SORRY...
HEY! WAIT!
I WAN-NA SEE!
UTSUHO?

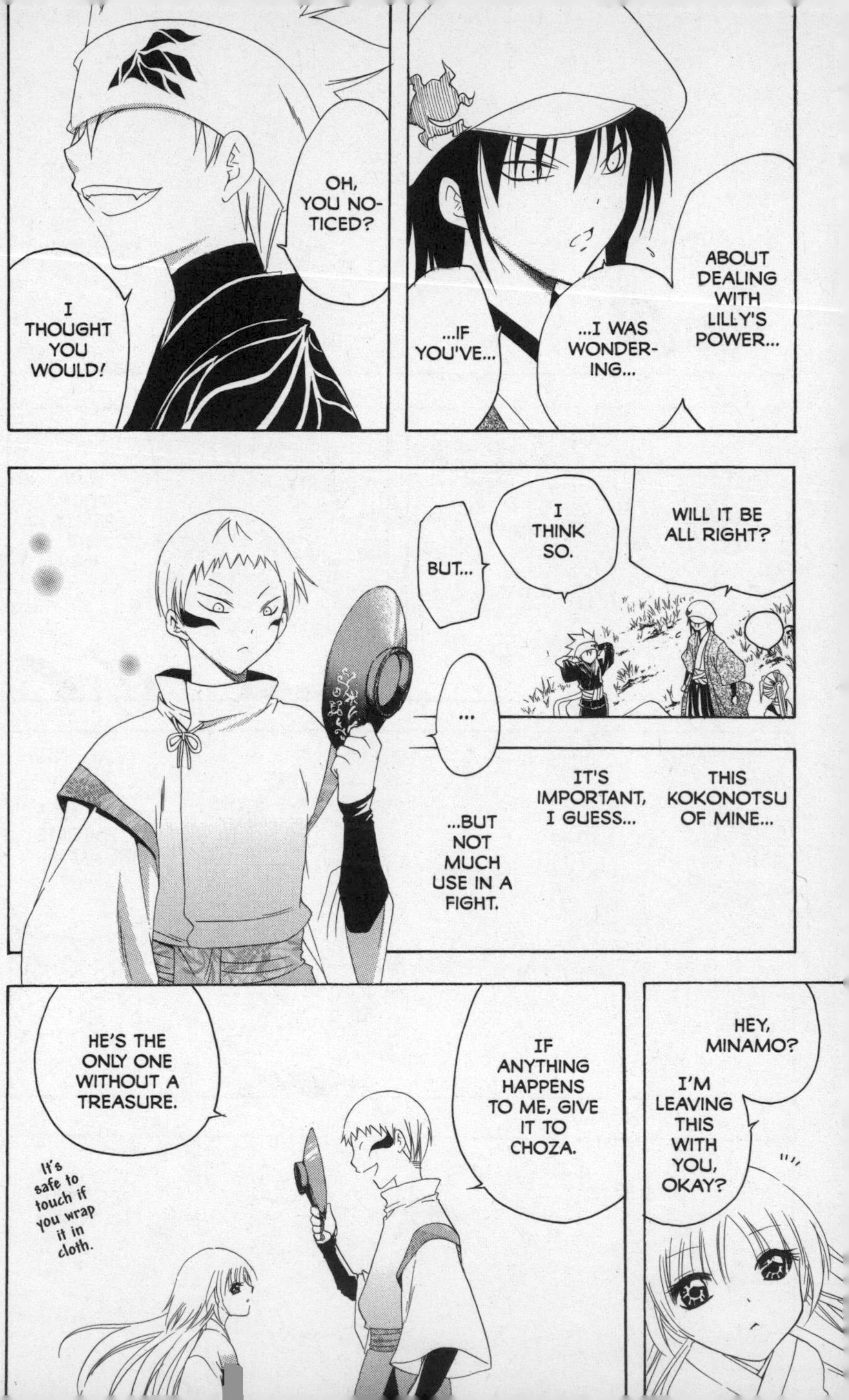
...I WAS WONDERING...
ABOUT DEALING WITH LILLY'S POWER...
...IF YOU'VE...
OH, YOU NOTICED?
I THOUGHT YOU WOULD!
WILL IT BE ALL RIGHT?
I THINK SO.
BUT...
...
THIS KOKONOTSU OF MINE...
IT'S IMPORTANT, I GUESS...
...BUT NOT MUCH USE IN A FIGHT.
HEY, MINAMO?
I'M LEAVING THIS WITH YOU, OKAY?
IF ANYTHING HAPPENS TO ME, GIVE IT TO CHOZA.
HE'S THE ONLY ONE WITHOUT A TREASURE.
It's safe to touch if you wrap it in cloth.

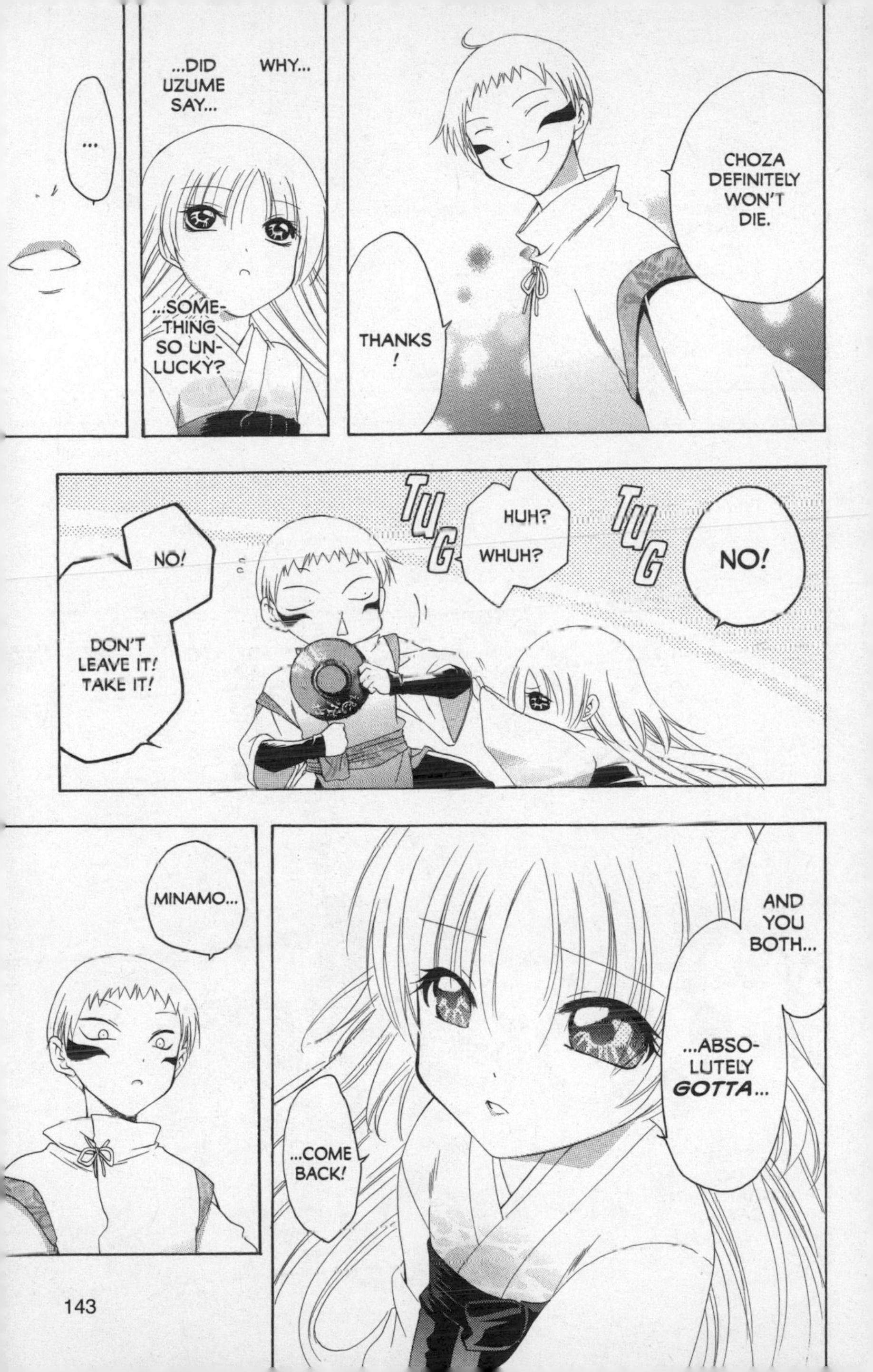
CHOZA DEFINITELY WON'T DIE.
THANKS!
WHY...
...DID UZUME SAY...
...SOME-THING SO UN-LUCKY?
...
NO!
TUG
HUH? WHUH?
TUG
NO!
DON'T LEAVE IT! TAKE IT!
AND YOU BOTH...
...ABSO-LUTELY GOTTA...
...COME BACK!
MINAMO...

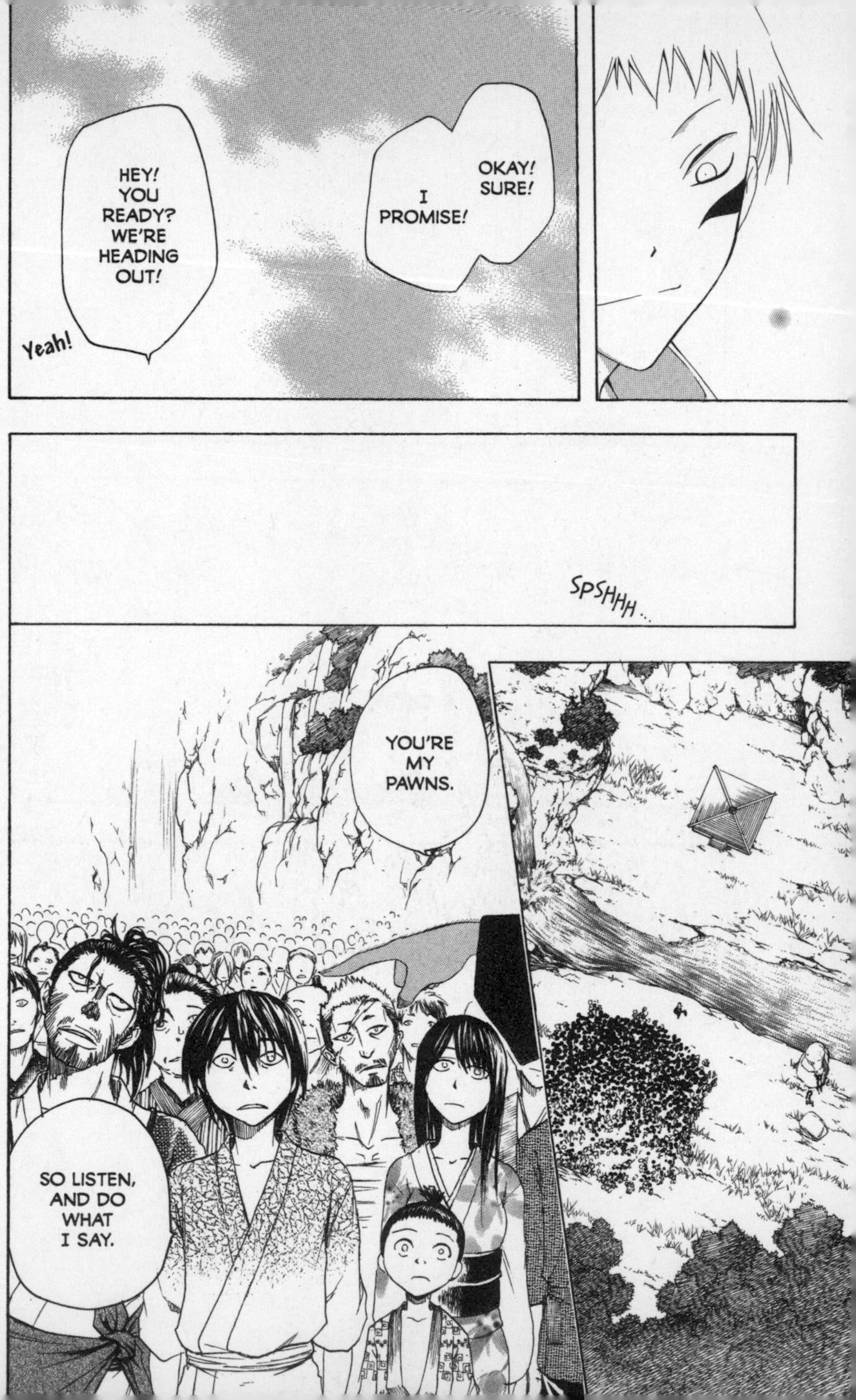
OKAY! SURE!
I PROMISE!
HEY! YOU READY? WE'RE HEADING OUT!
Yeah!
SPSHHH...
YOU'RE MY PAWNS.
SO LISTEN, AND DO WHAT I SAY.

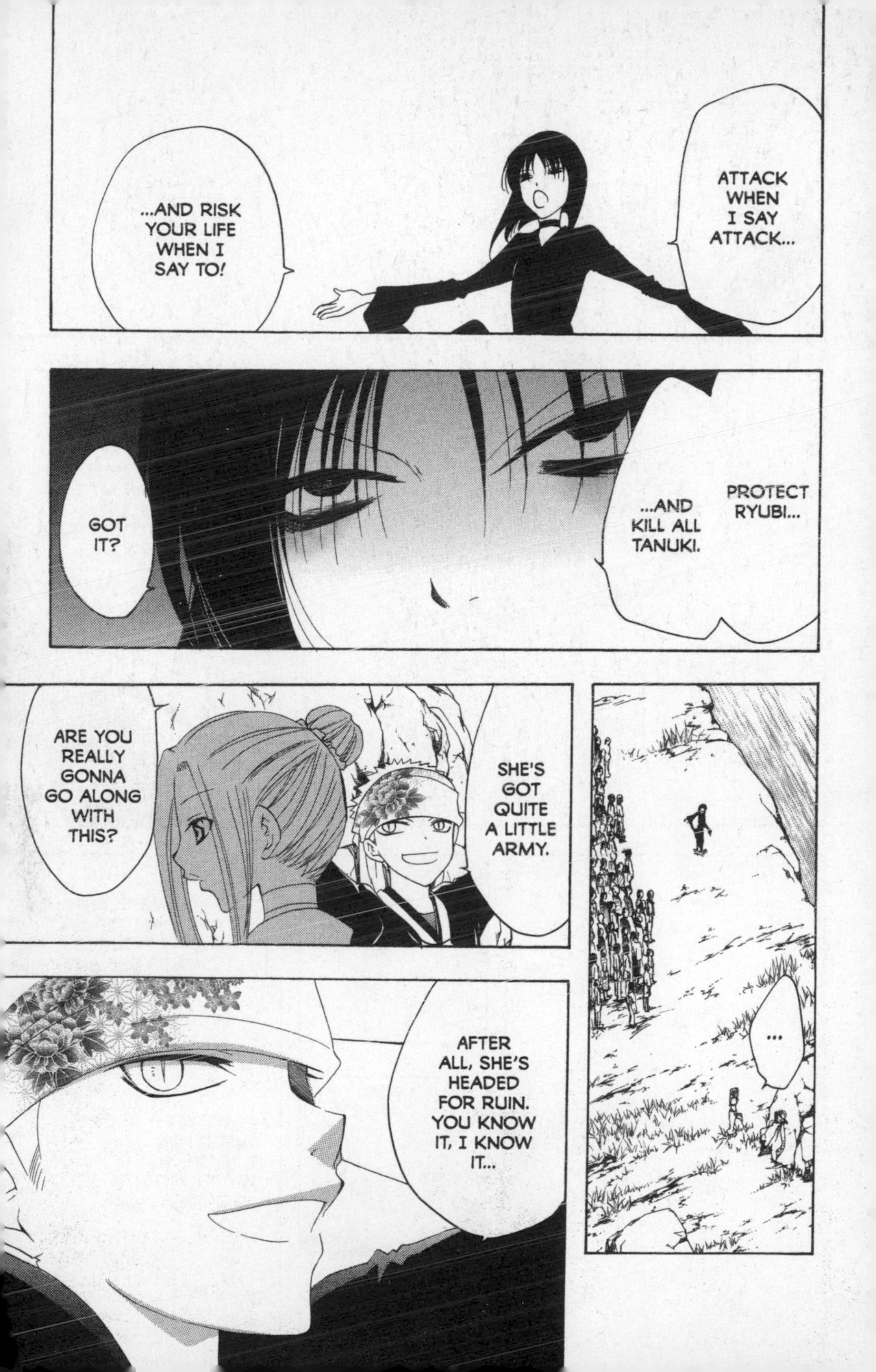

ATTACK WHEN I SAY ATTACK...
...AND RISK YOUR LIFE WHEN I SAY TO!
PROTECT RYUBI...
...AND KILL ALL TANUKI.
GOT IT?
...
SHE'S GOT QUITE A LITTLE ARMY.
ARE YOU REALLY GONNA GO ALONG WITH THIS?
AFTER ALL, SHE'S HEADED FOR RUIN. YOU KNOW IT, I KNOW IT...

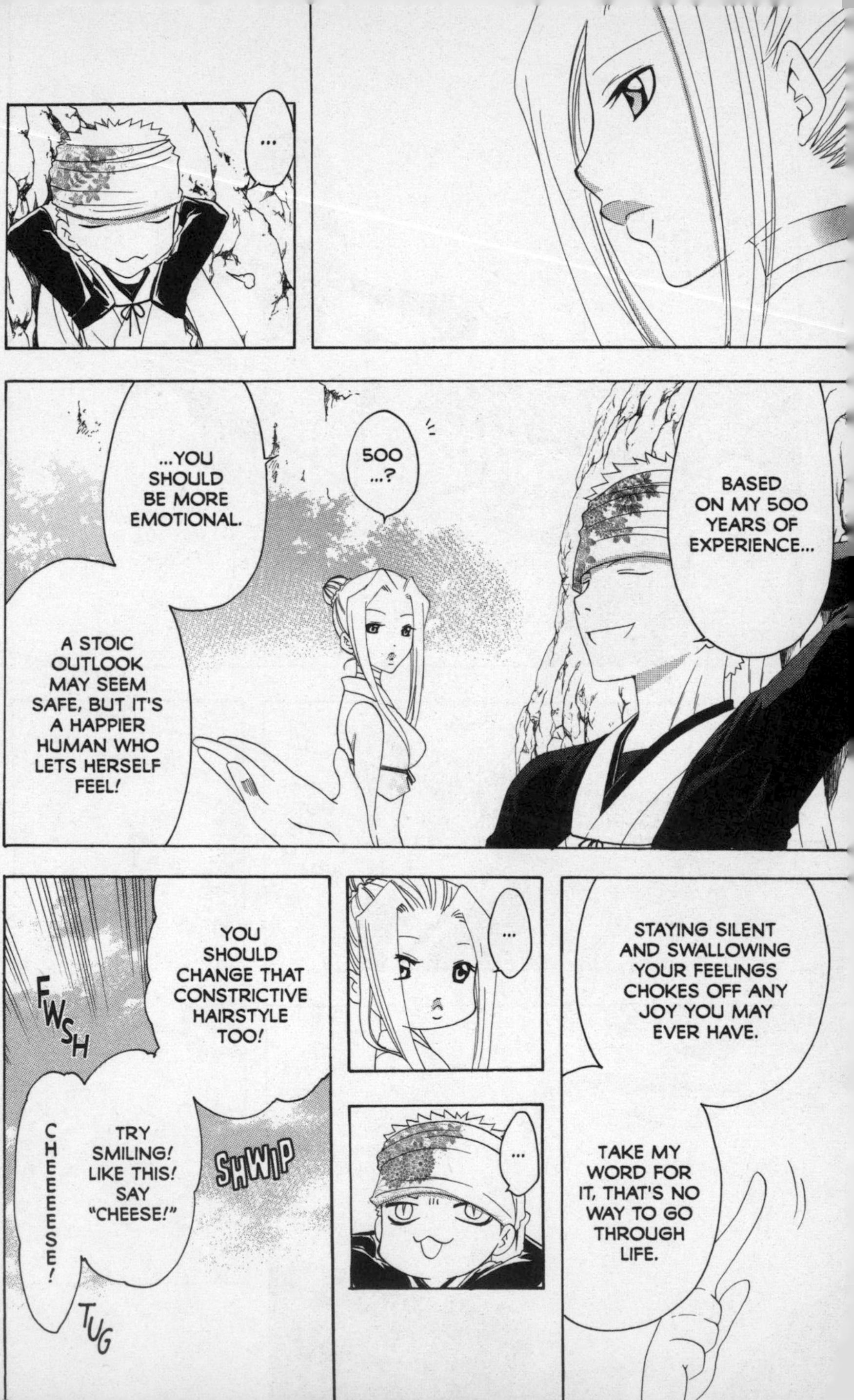
...
BASED ON MY 500 YEARS OF EXPERIENCE...
500 ...?
...YOU SHOULD BE MORE EMOTIONAL.
A STOIC OUTLOOK MAY SEEM SAFE, BUT IT'S A HAPPIER HUMAN WHO LETS HERSELF FEEL!
STAYING SILENT AND SWALLOWING YOUR FEELINGS CHOKES OFF ANY JOY YOU MAY EVER HAVE.
TAKE MY WORD FOR IT, THAT'S NO WAY TO GO THROUGH LIFE.
...
...
YOU SHOULD CHANGE THAT CONSTRICTIVE HAIRSTYLE TOO!
FWSH
TRY SMILING! LIKE THIS! SAY "CHEESE!"
SHWIP
CHEEEESE!
TUG

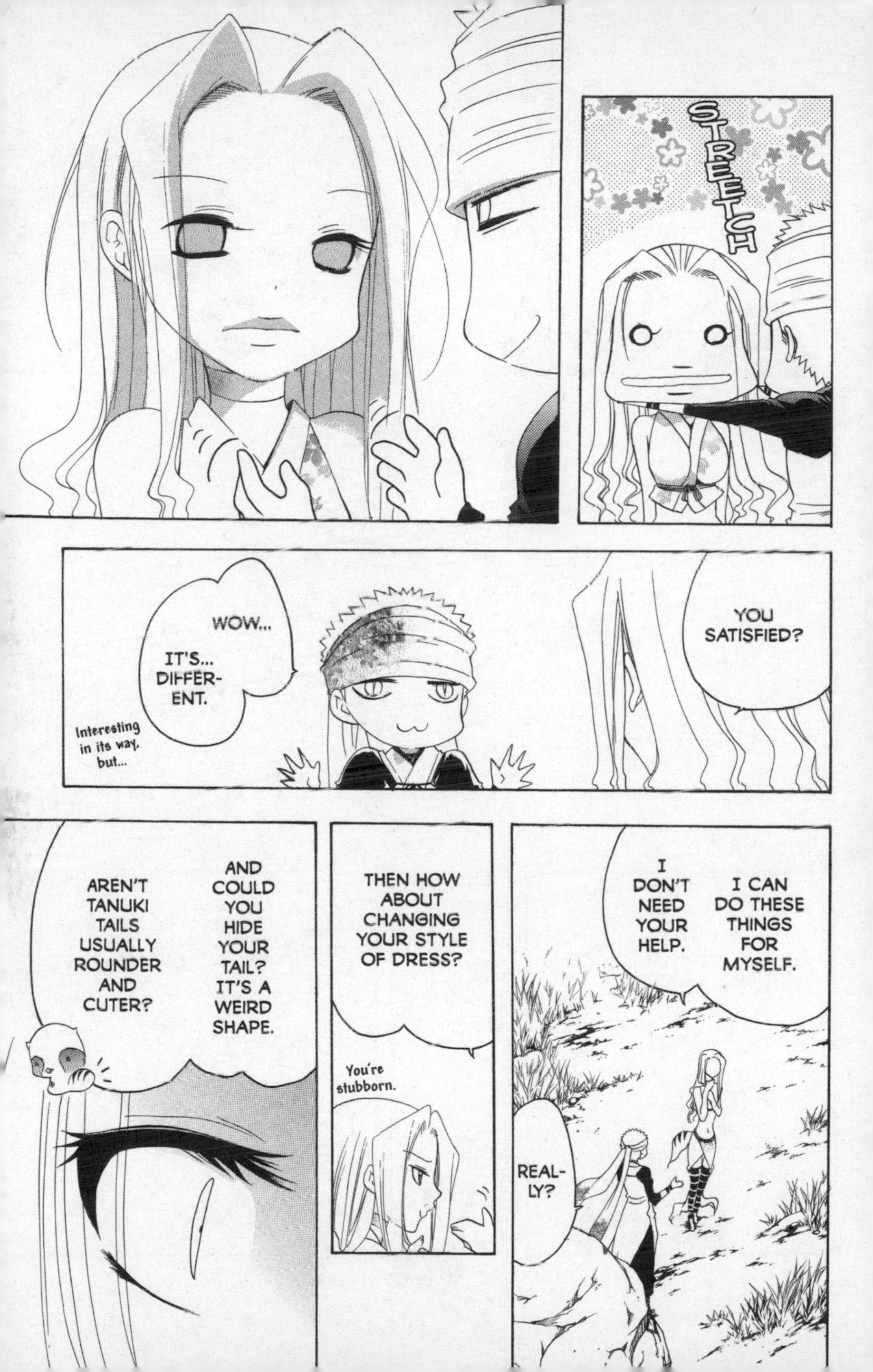
STRETCH
YOU SATISFIED?
WOW...
IT'S... DIFFER-ENT.
Interesting in its way, but...
I DON'T NEED YOUR HELP.
I CAN DO THESE THINGS FOR MYSELF.
REAL-LY?
THEN HOW ABOUT CHANGING YOUR STYLE OF DRESS?
You're stubborn.
AND COULD YOU HIDE YOUR TAIL? IT'S A WEIRD SHAPE.
AREN'T TANUKI TAILS USUALLY ROUNDER AND CUTER?

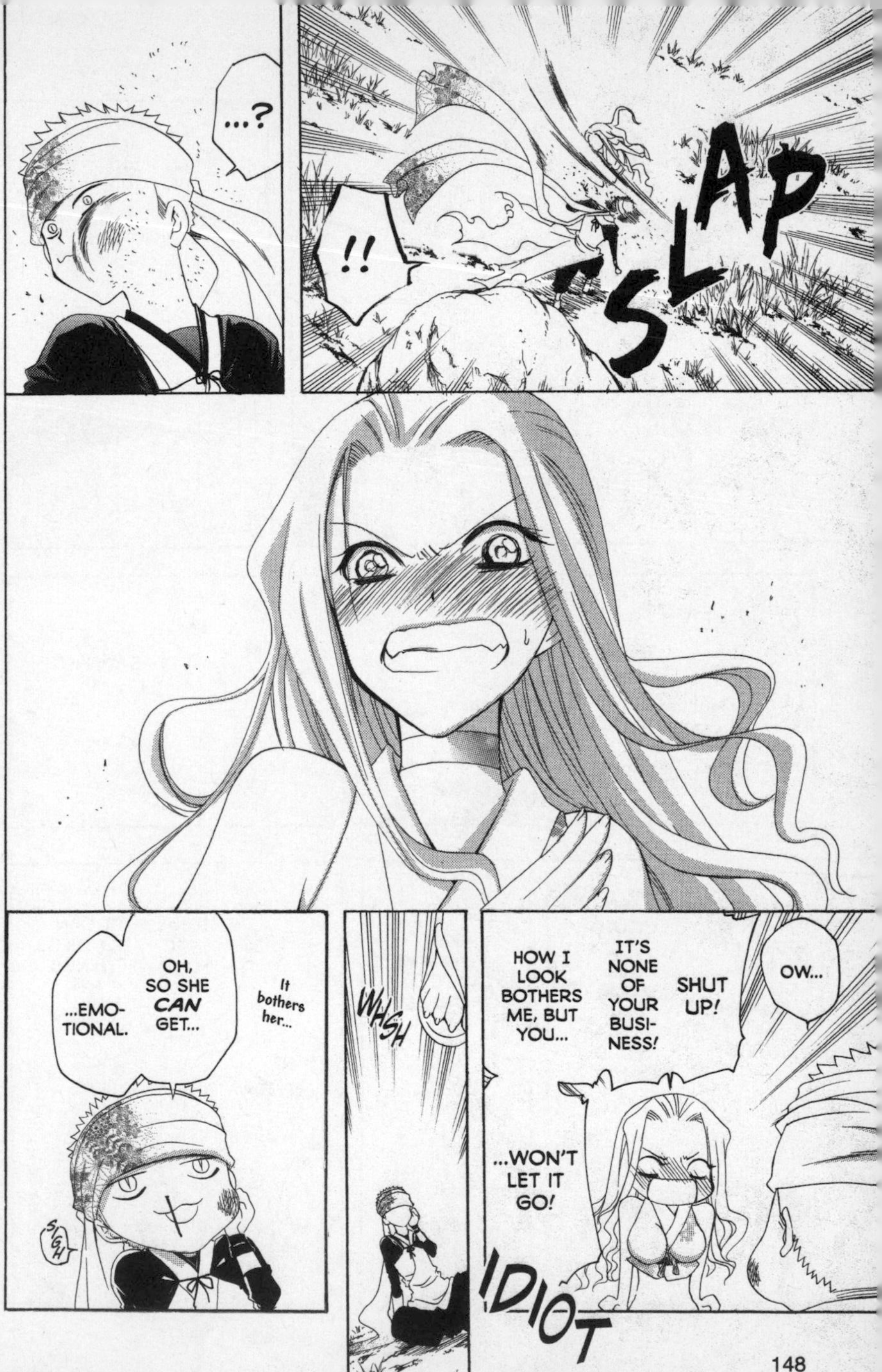
SLAP
!!
...?
OW...
SHUT UP!
IT'S NONE OF YOUR BUSI-NESS!
HOW I LOOK BOTHERS ME, BUT YOU...
...WON'T LET IT GO!
IDIOT
WHSH
It bothers her...
OH, SO SHE *CAN* GET...
...EMO-TIONAL.
SIGH

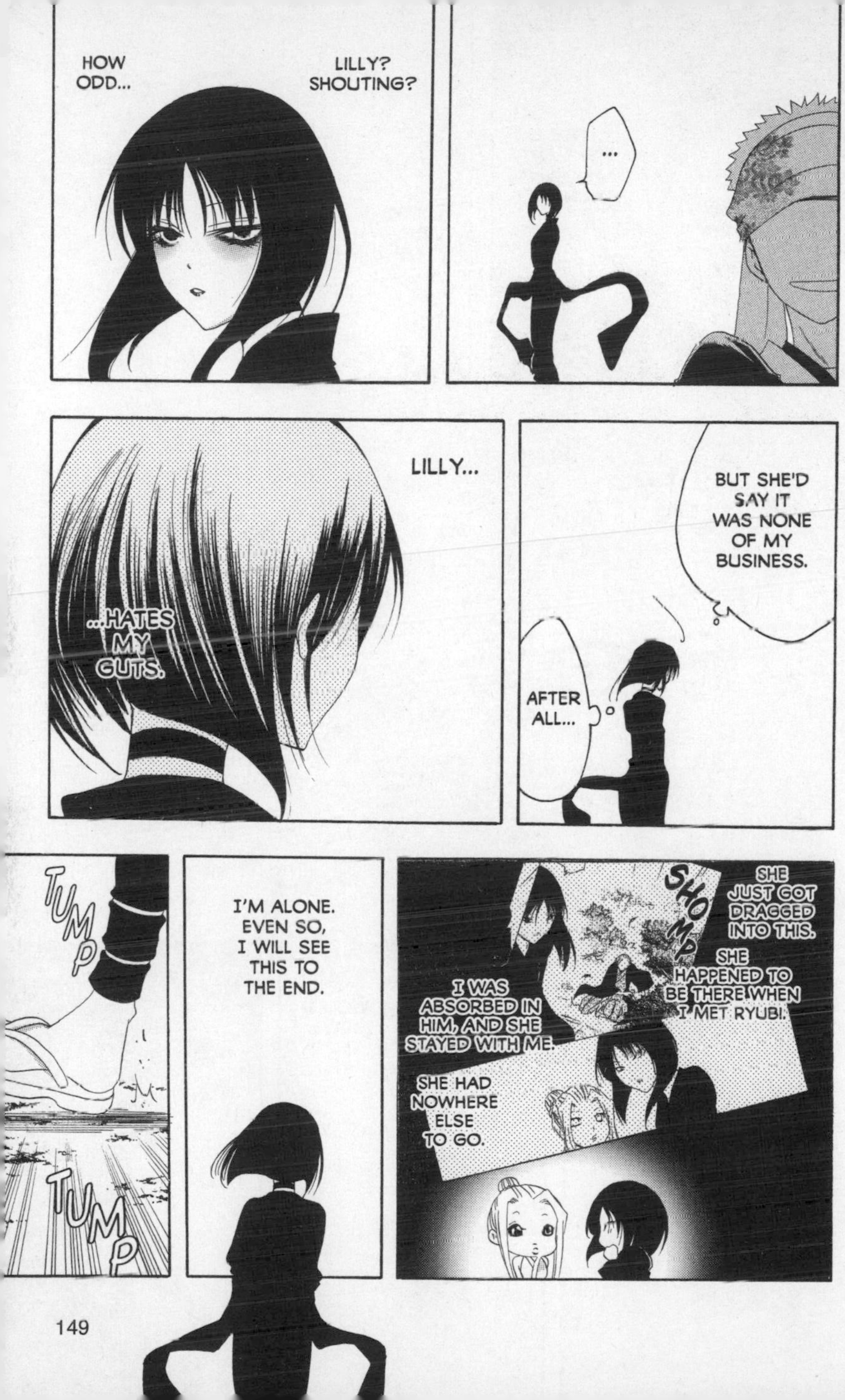
...
LILLY? SHOUTING?
HOW ODD...
BUT SHE'D SAY IT WAS NONE OF MY BUSINESS.
AFTER ALL...
LILLY...
...HATES MY GUTS.
SHE JUST GOT DRAGGED INTO THIS.
SHOMP
SHE HAPPENED TO BE THERE WHEN I MET RYUBI.
I WAS ABSORBED IN HIM, AND SHE STAYED WITH ME.
SHE HAD NOWHERE ELSE TO GO.
I'M ALONE. EVEN SO, I WILL SEE THIS TO THE END.
TUMP
TUMP

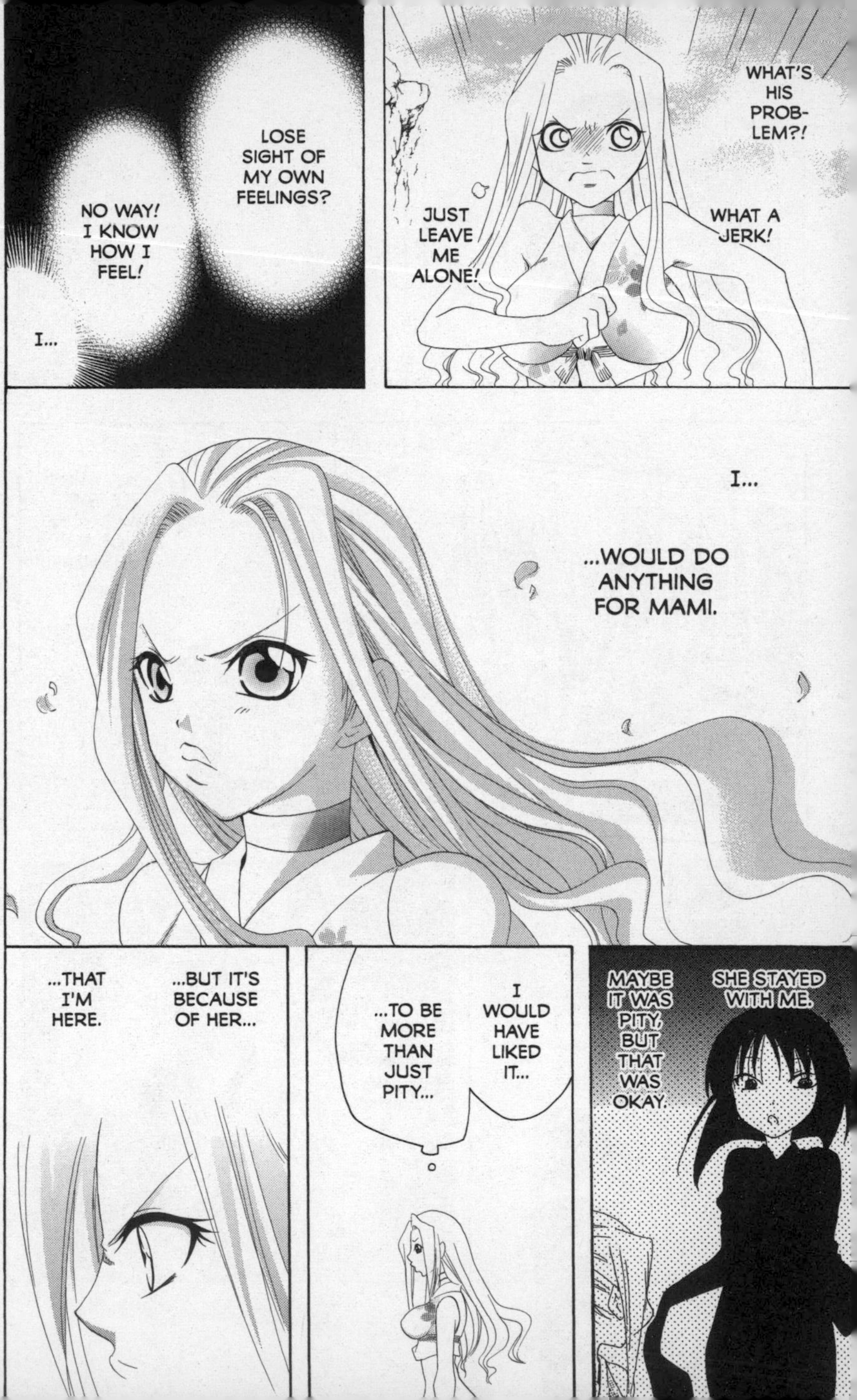
WHAT'S HIS PROB-LEM?!
WHAT A JERK!
JUST LEAVE ME ALONE!
LOSE SIGHT OF MY OWN FEELINGS?
NO WAY! I KNOW HOW I FEEL!
I...
I...
...WOULD DO ANYTHING FOR MAMI.
SHE STAYED WITH ME.
MAYBE IT WAS PITY, BUT THAT WAS OKAY.
I WOULD HAVE LIKED IT...
...TO BE MORE THAN JUST PITY...
...BUT IT'S BECAUSE OF HER...
...THAT I'M HERE.

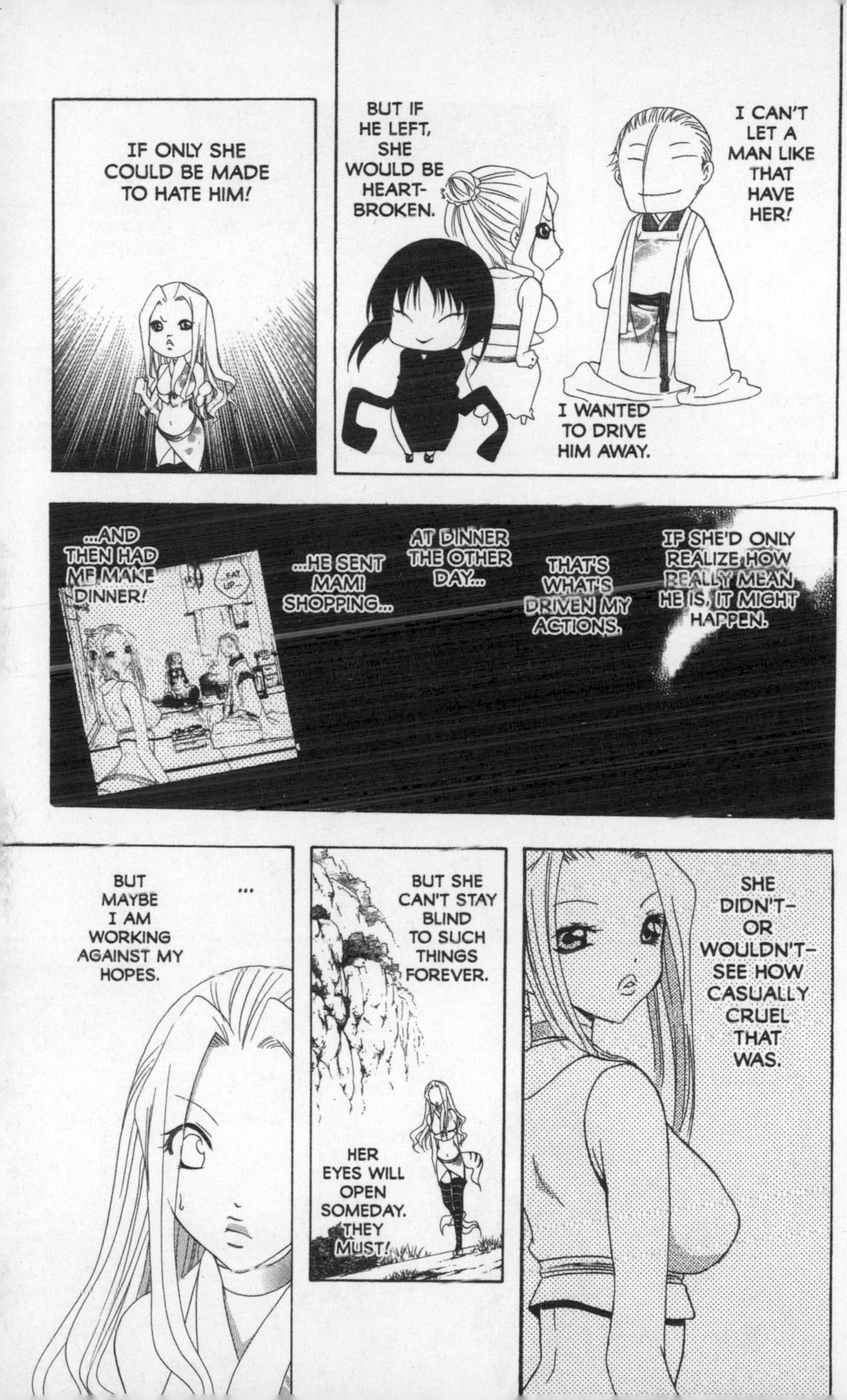
I CAN'T LET A MAN LIKE THAT HAVE HER!
BUT IF HE LEFT, SHE WOULD BE HEART-BROKEN.
I WANTED TO DRIVE HIM AWAY.
IF ONLY SHE COULD BE MADE TO HATE HIM!
IF SHE'D ONLY REALIZE HOW REALLY MEAN HE IS, IT MIGHT HAPPEN.
THAT'S WHAT'S DRIVEN MY ACTIONS.
AT DINNER THE OTHER DAY...
...HE SENT MAMI SHOPPING...
...AND THEN HAD ME MAKE DINNER!
EAT UP...
SHE DIDN'T— OR WOULDN'T— SEE HOW CASUALLY CRUEL THAT WAS.
BUT SHE CAN'T STAY BLIND TO SUCH THINGS FOREVER.
HER EYES WILL OPEN SOMEDAY. THEY MUST!
...
BUT MAYBE I AM WORKING AGAINST MY HOPES.

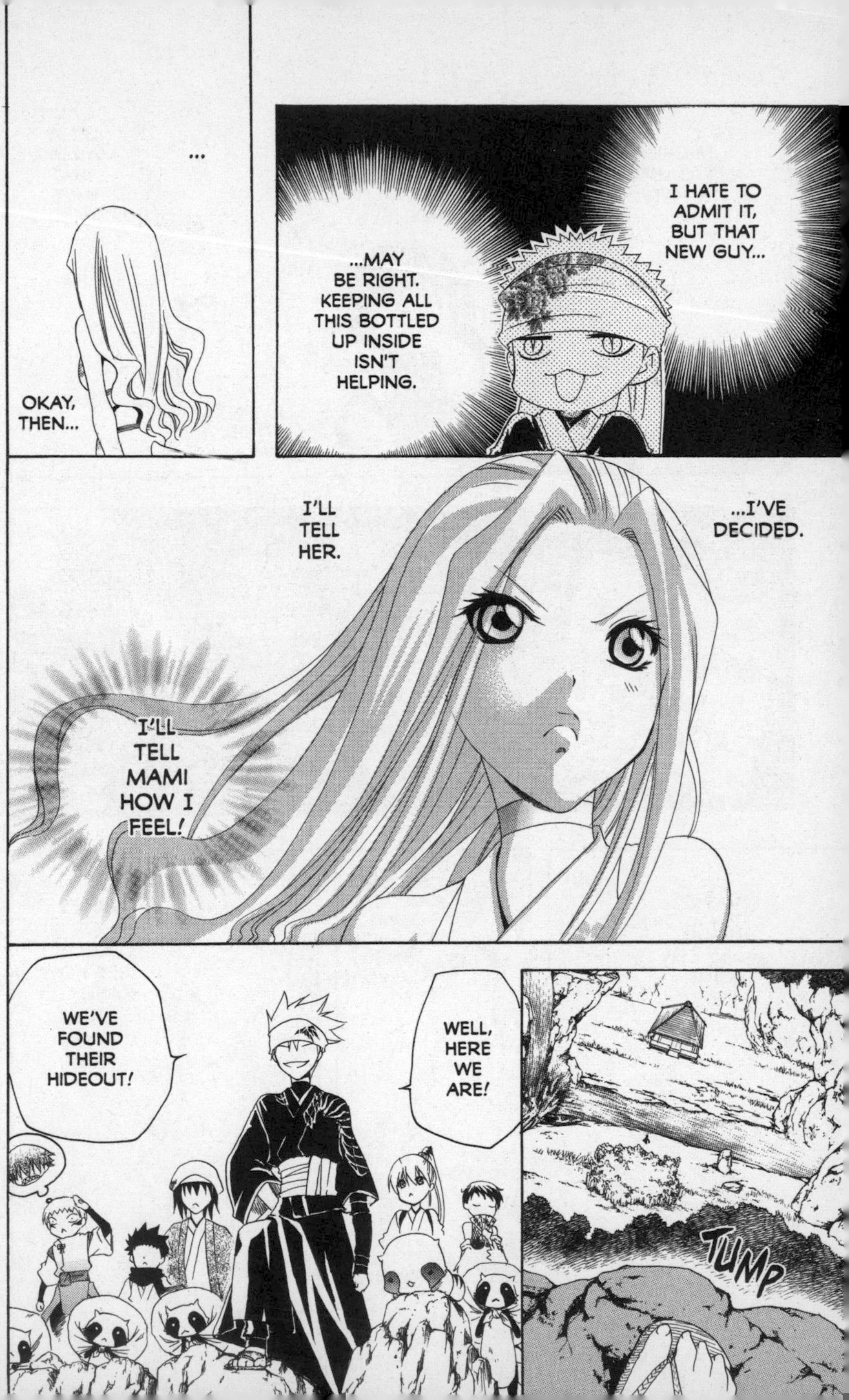
I HATE TO ADMIT IT, BUT THAT NEW GUY...
...MAY BE RIGHT. KEEPING ALL THIS BOTTLED UP INSIDE ISN'T HELPING.
...
OKAY, THEN...
...I'VE DECIDED.
I'LL TELL HER.
I'LL TELL MAMI HOW I FEEL!
TUMP
WELL, HERE WE ARE!
WE'VE FOUND THEIR HIDEOUT!

Chapter 136 Battle Begins

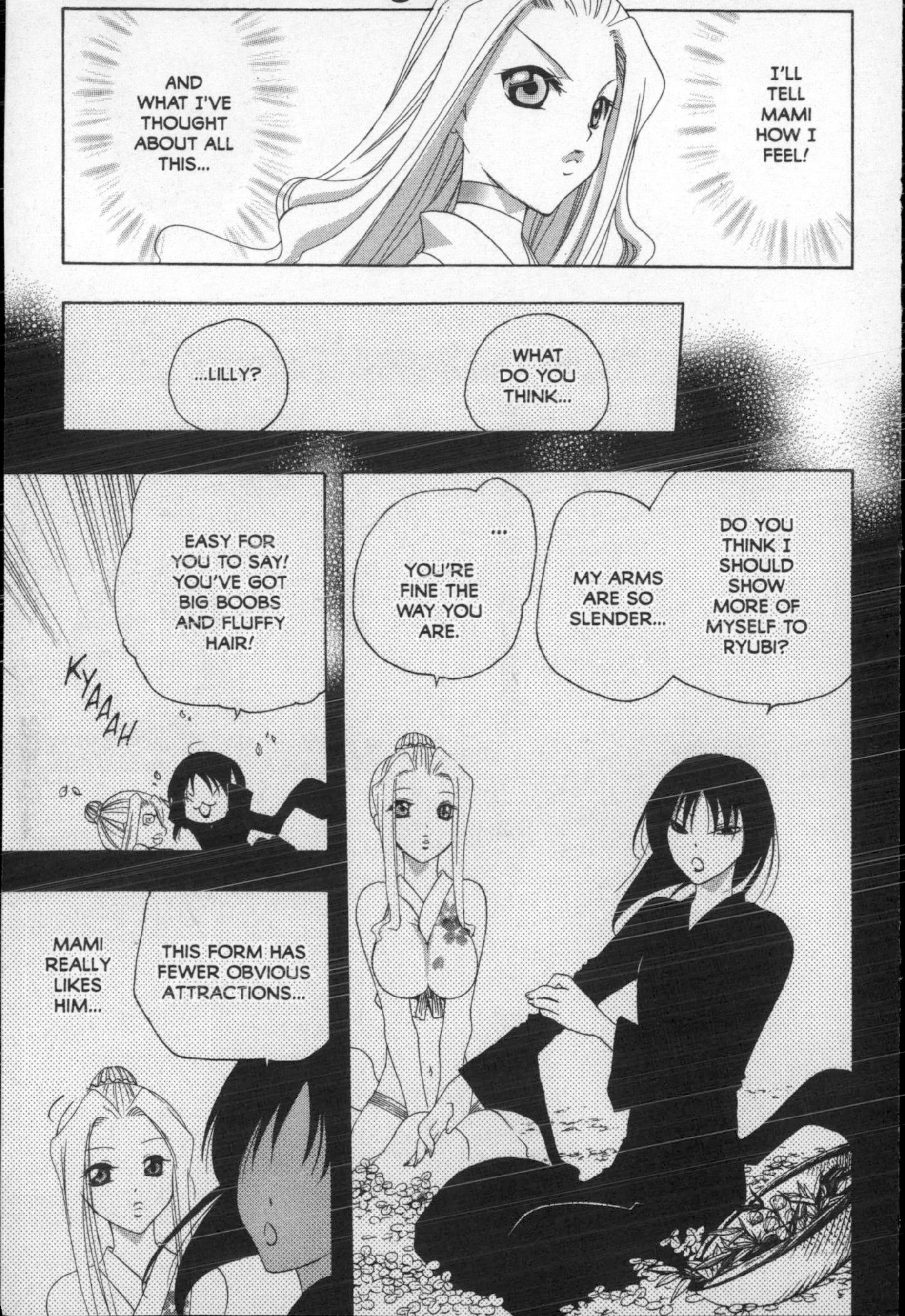
I'LL TELL MAMI HOW I FEEL!
AND WHAT I'VE THOUGHT ABOUT ALL THIS...
WHAT DO YOU THINK...
...LILLY?
DO YOU THINK I SHOULD SHOW MORE OF MYSELF TO RYUBI?
MY ARMS ARE SO SLENDER...
...
YOU'RE FINE THE WAY YOU ARE.
EASY FOR YOU TO SAY! YOU'VE GOT BIG BOOBS AND FLUFFY HAIR!
KYAAAH
THIS FORM HAS FEWER OBVIOUS ATTRACTIONS...
MAMI REALLY LIKES HIM...

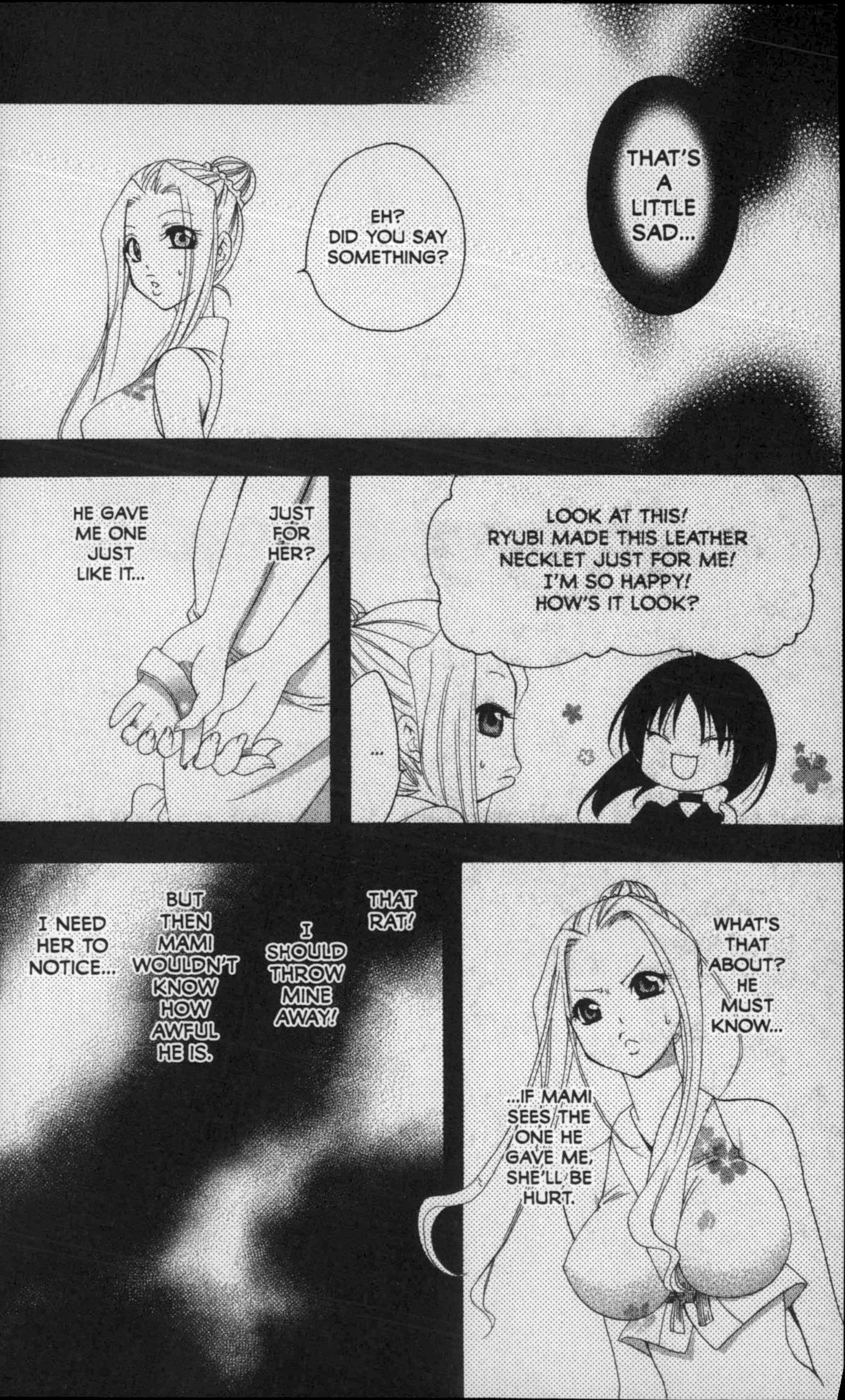
THAT'S A LITTLE SAD...
EH? DID YOU SAY SOMETHING?
LOOK AT THIS! RYUBI MADE THIS LEATHER NECKLET JUST FOR ME! I'M SO HAPPY! HOW'S IT LOOK?
...
JUST FOR HER?
HE GAVE ME ONE JUST LIKE IT...
WHAT'S THAT ABOUT? HE MUST KNOW...
...IF MAMI SEES THE ONE HE GAVE ME, SHE'LL BE HURT.
THAT RAT!
I SHOULD THROW MINE AWAY!
BUT THEN MAMI WOULDN'T KNOW HOW AWFUL HE IS.
I NEED HER TO NOTICE...

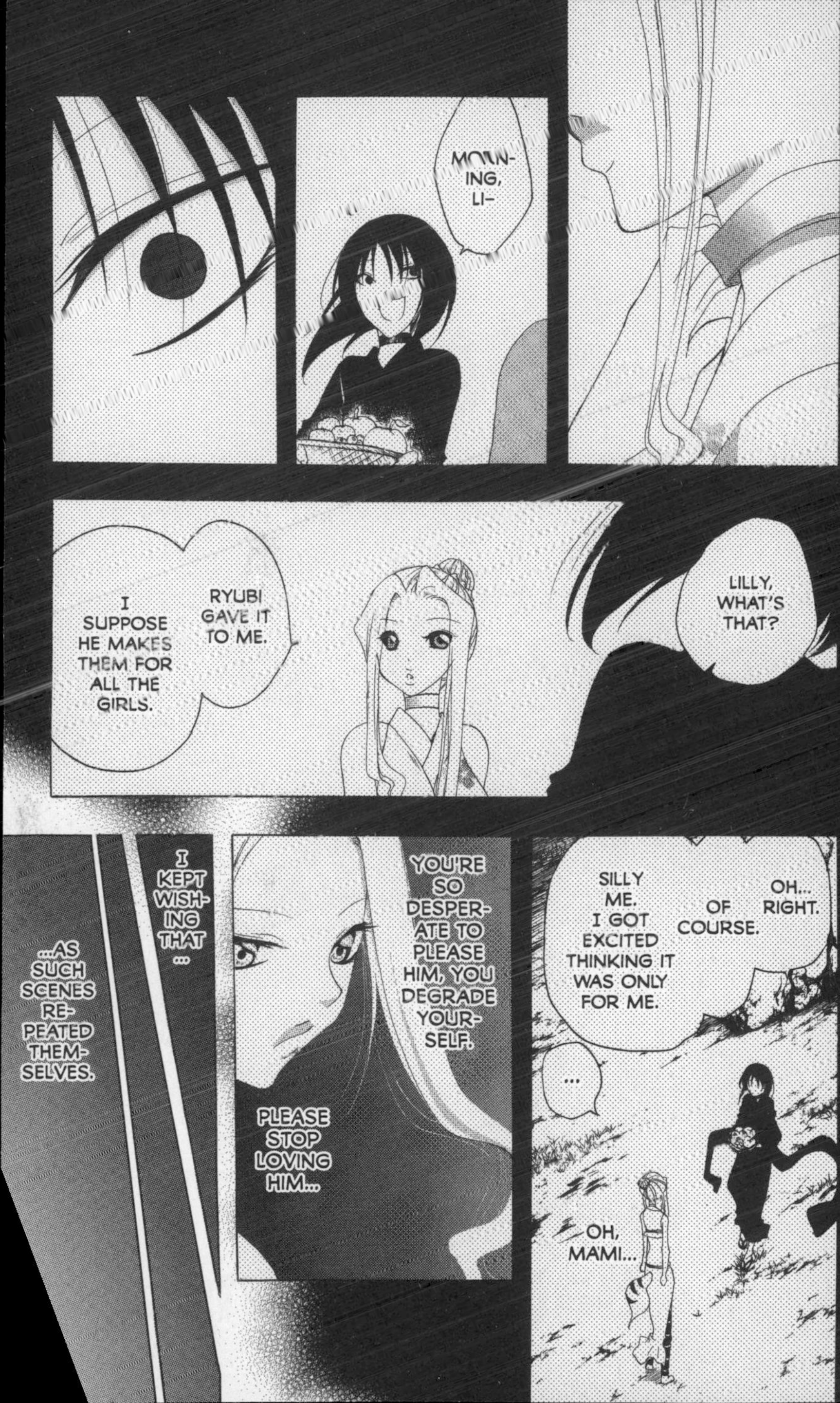
MORNING, LI-
LILLY, WHAT'S THAT?
RYUBI GAVE IT TO ME.
I SUPPOSE HE MAKES THEM FOR ALL THE GIRLS.
OH... RIGHT. OF COURSE.
SILLY ME. I GOT EXCITED THINKING IT WAS ONLY FOR ME.
...
OH, MAMI...
YOU'RE SO DESPERATE TO PLEASE HIM, YOU DEGRADE YOURSELF.
PLEASE STOP LOVING HIM...
I KEPT WISHING THAT...
...AS SUCH SCENES REPEATED THEMSELVES.

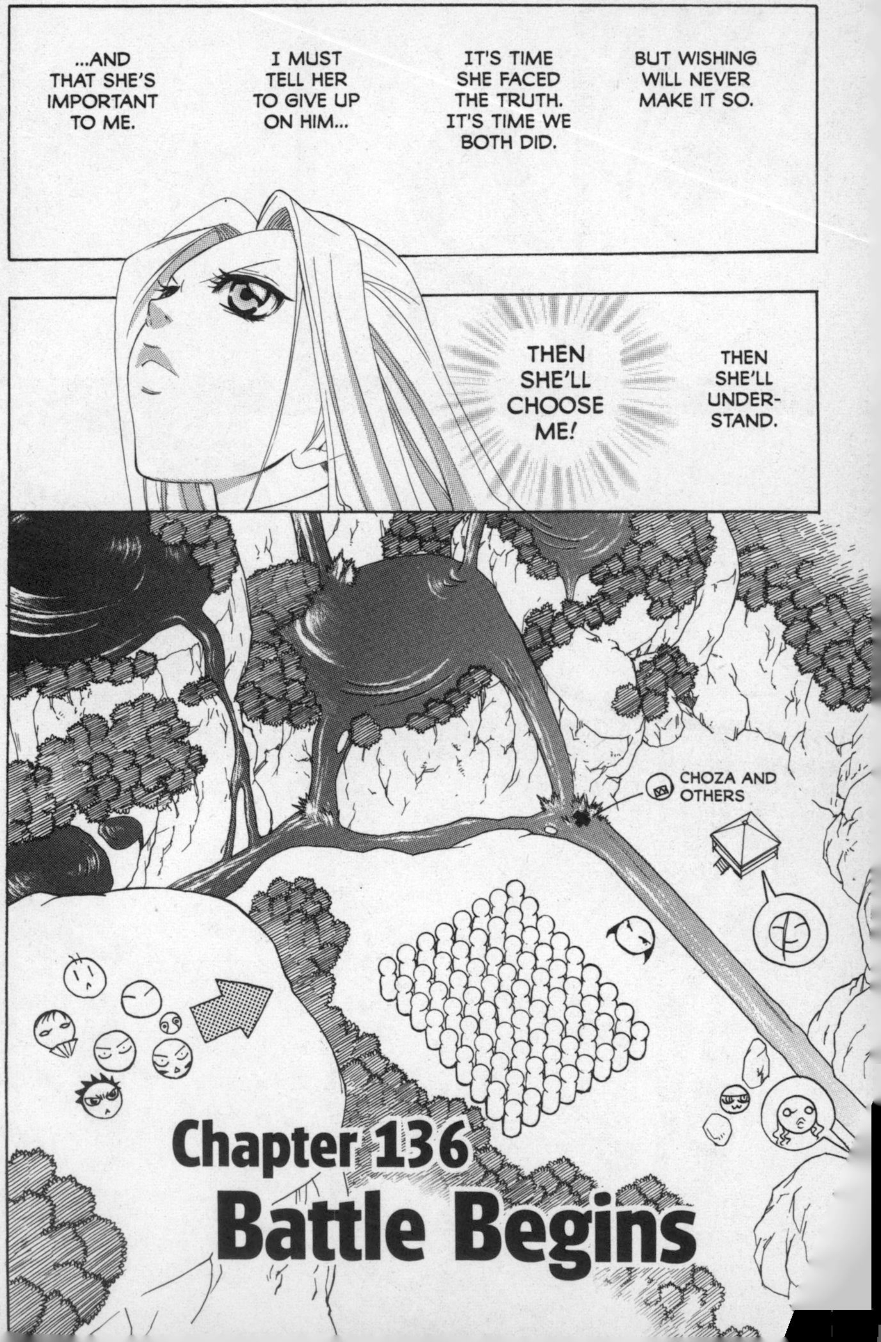
BUT WISHING WILL NEVER MAKE IT SO.
IT'S TIME SHE FACED THE TRUTH. IT'S TIME WE BOTH DID.
I MUST TELL HER TO GIVE UP ON HIM...
...AND THAT SHE'S IMPORTANT TO ME.
THEN SHE'LL UNDER-STAND.
THEN SHE'LL CHOOSE ME!
CHOZA AND OTHERS
Chapter 136
Battle Begins

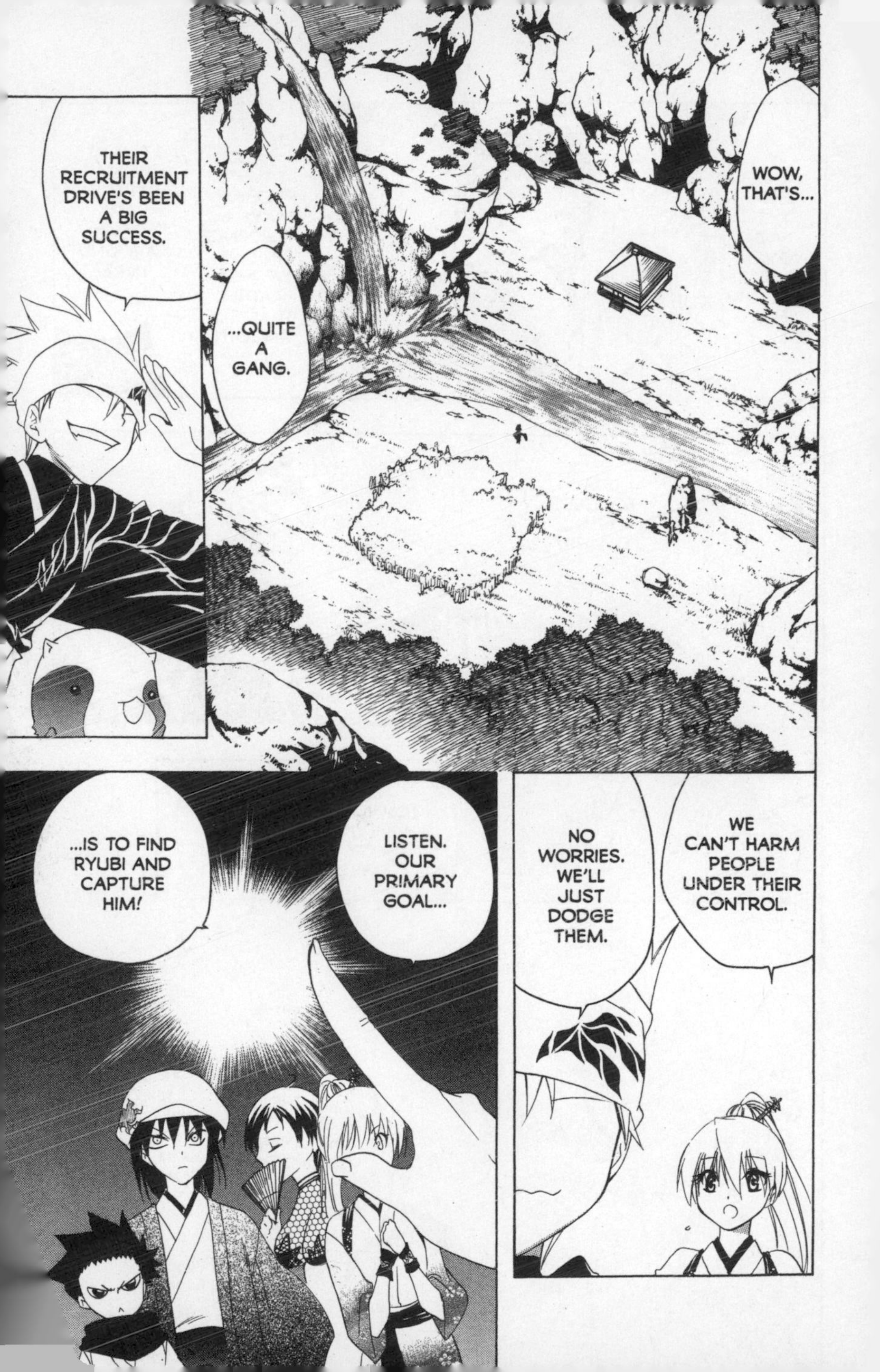
WOW, THAT'S...
...QUITE A GANG.
THEIR RECRUITMENT DRIVE'S BEEN A BIG SUCCESS.
WE CAN'T HARM PEOPLE UNDER THEIR CONTROL.
NO WORRIES. WE'LL JUST DODGE THEM.
LISTEN. OUR PRIMARY GOAL...
...IS TO FIND RYUBI AND CAPTURE HIM!

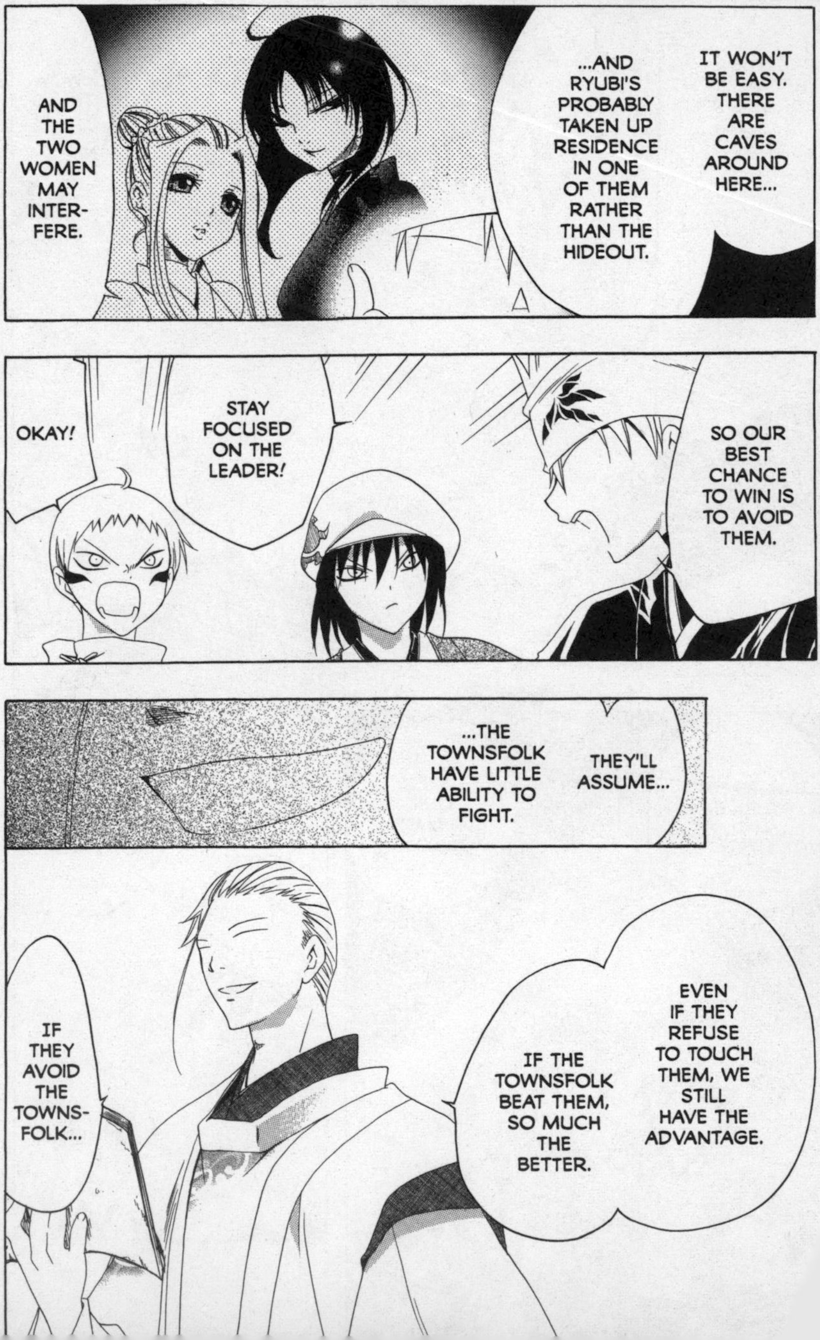
IT WON'T BE EASY. THERE ARE CAVES AROUND HERE...
...AND RYUBI'S PROBABLY TAKEN UP RESIDENCE IN ONE OF THEM RATHER THAN THE HIDEOUT.
AND THE TWO WOMEN MAY INTERFERE.
SO OUR BEST CHANCE TO WIN IS TO AVOID THEM.
STAY FOCUSED ON THE LEADER!
OKAY!
THEY'LL ASSUME...
...THE TOWNSFOLK HAVE LITTLE ABILITY TO FIGHT.
EVEN IF THEY REFUSE TO TOUCH THEM, WE STILL HAVE THE ADVANTAGE.
IF THE TOWNSFOLK BEAT THEM, SO MUCH THE BETTER.
IF THEY AVOID THE TOWNS-FOLK...

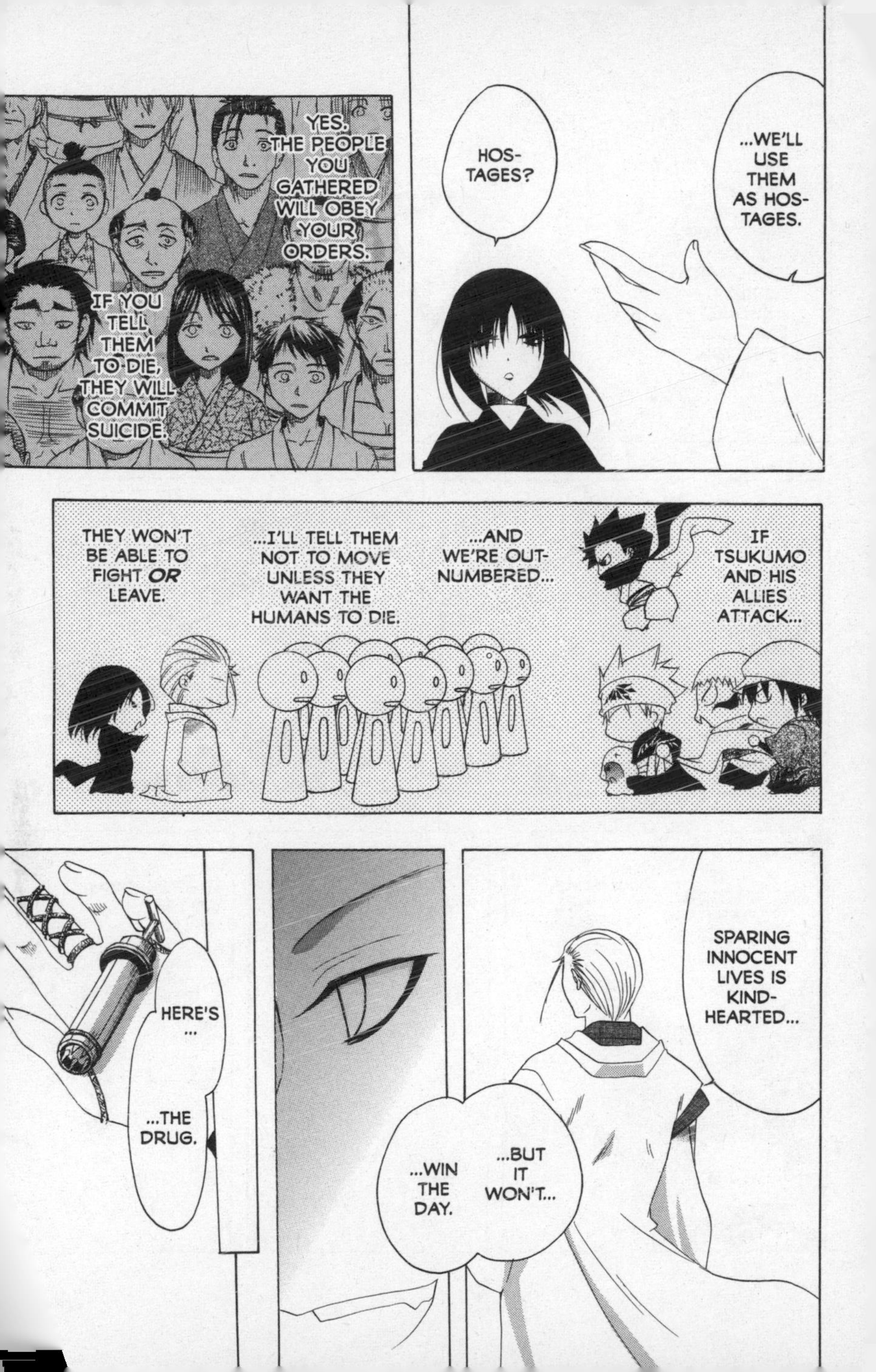
...WE'LL USE THEM AS HOS-TAGES.
HOS-TAGES?
YES. THE PEOPLE YOU GATHERED WILL OBEY YOUR ORDERS.
IF YOU TELL THEM TO DIE, THEY WILL COMMIT SUICIDE.
IF TSUKUMO AND HIS ALLIES ATTACK...
...AND WE'RE OUT-NUMBERED...
...I'LL TELL THEM NOT TO MOVE UNLESS THEY WANT THE HUMANS TO DIE.
THEY WON'T BE ABLE TO FIGHT *OR* LEAVE.
SPARING INNOCENT LIVES IS KIND-HEARTED...
...BUT IT WON'T...
...WIN THE DAY.
HERE'S ...
...THE DRUG.

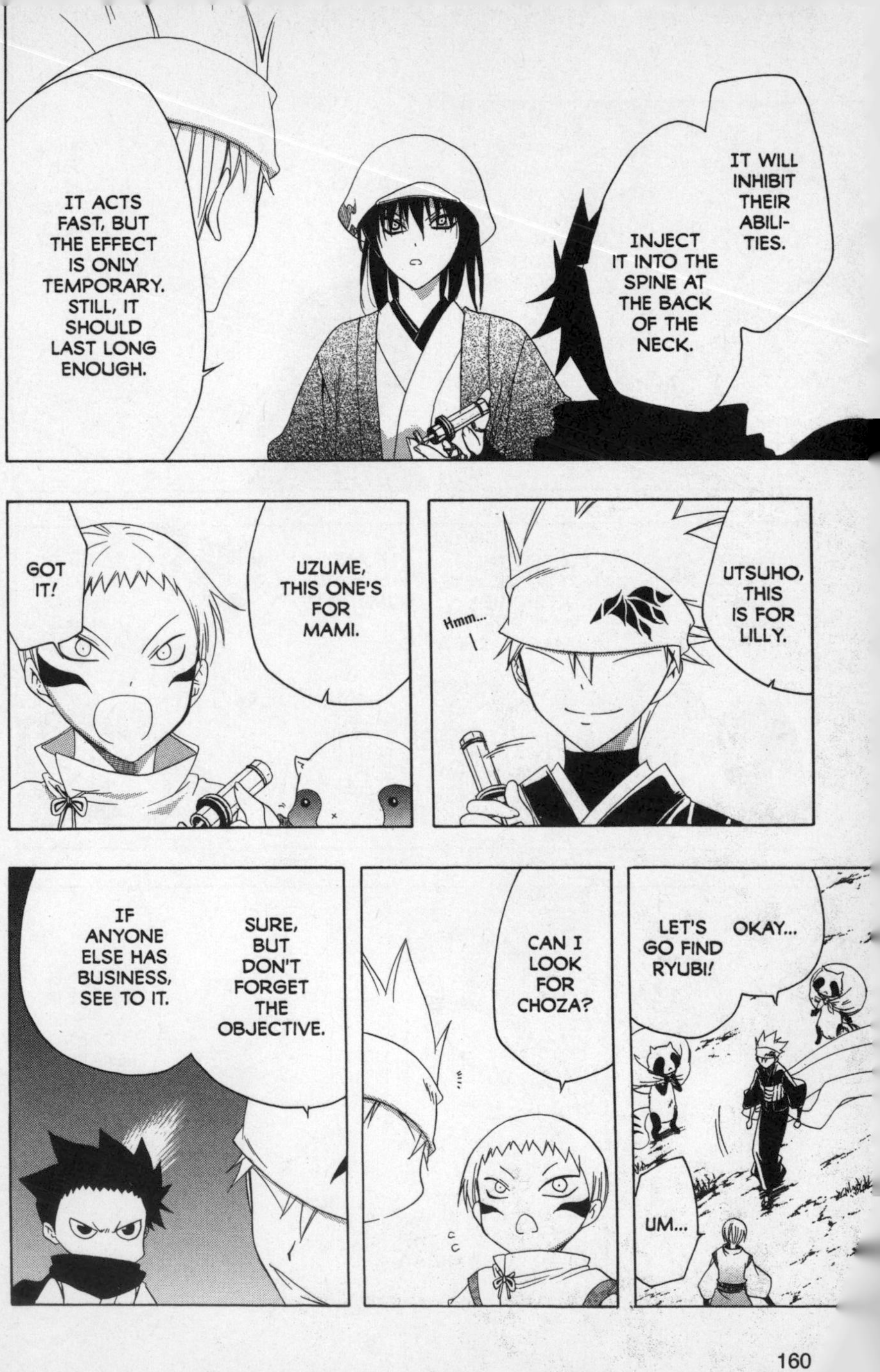
IT WILL INHIBIT THEIR ABILI- TIES.
INJECT IT INTO THE SPINE AT THE BACK OF THE NECK.
IT ACTS FAST, BUT THE EFFECT IS ONLY TEMPORARY. STILL, IT SHOULD LAST LONG ENOUGH.
UTSUHO, THIS IS FOR LILLY.
Hmm...
UZUME, THIS ONE'S FOR MAMI.
GOT IT!
OKAY...
LET'S GO FIND RYUBI!
UM...
CAN I LOOK FOR CHOZA?
SURE, BUT DON'T FORGET THE OBJECTIVE.
IF ANYONE ELSE HAS BUSINESS, SEE TO IT.

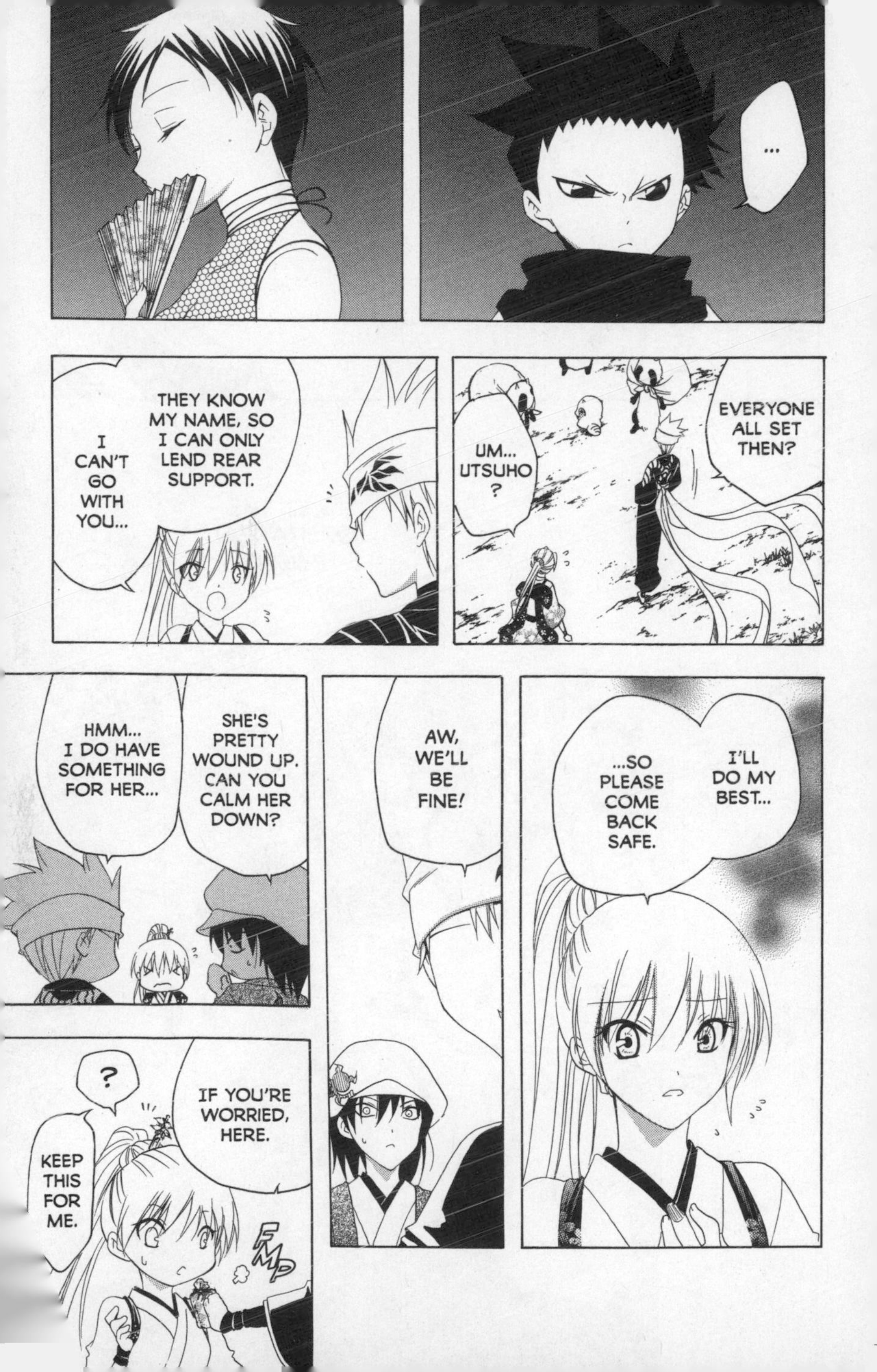
...
EVERYONE ALL SET THEN?
UM... UTSUHO?
THEY KNOW MY NAME, SO I CAN ONLY LEND REAR SUPPORT.
I CAN'T GO WITH YOU...
I'LL DO MY BEST...
...SO PLEASE COME BACK SAFE.
AW, WE'LL BE FINE!
SHE'S PRETTY WOUND UP. CAN YOU CALM HER DOWN?
HMM... I DO HAVE SOMETHING FOR HER...
IF YOU'RE WORRIED, HERE.
?
KEEP THIS FOR ME.
FMP

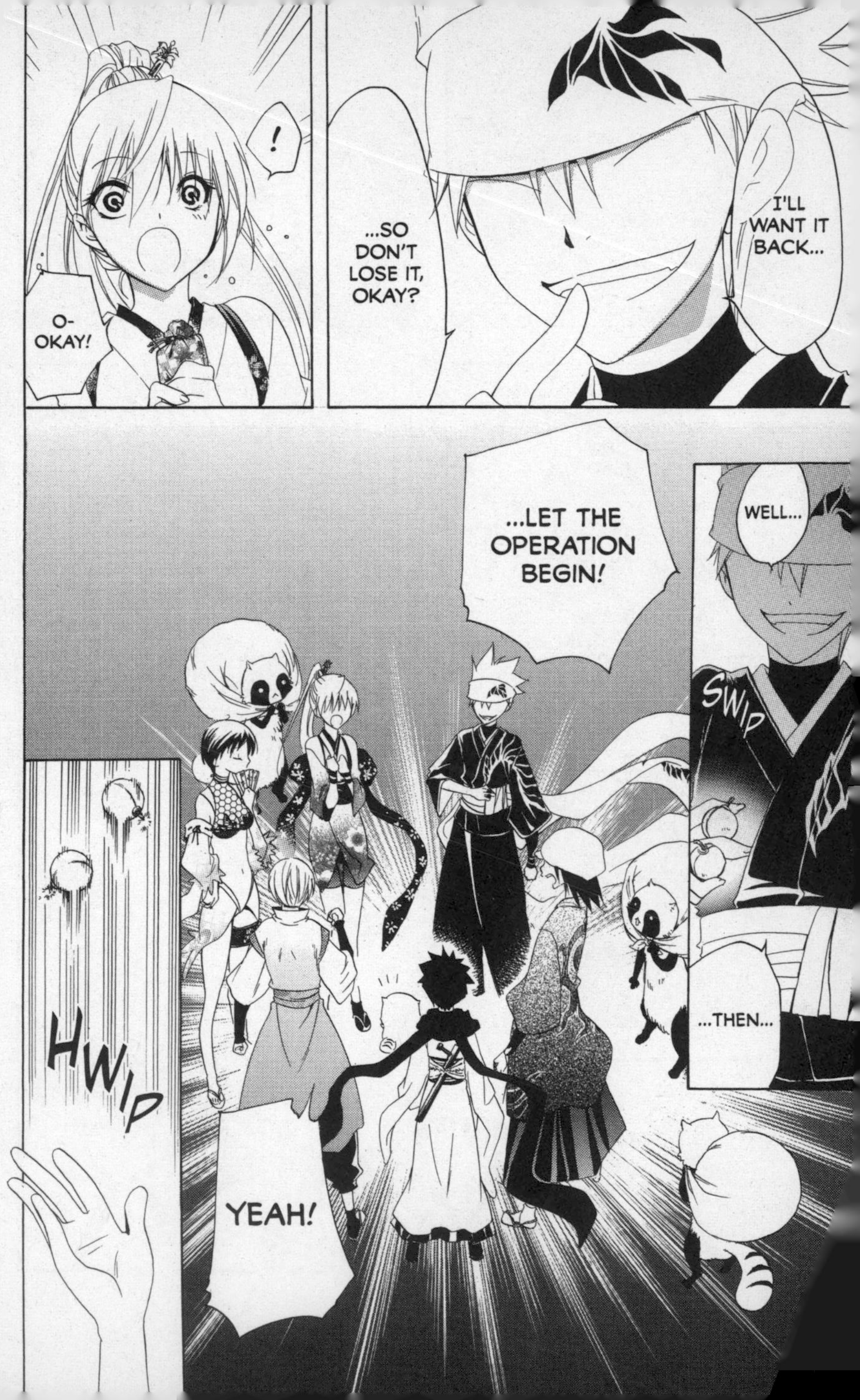
I'LL WANT IT BACK...
...SO DON'T LOSE IT, OKAY?
!
O-OKAY!
WELL...
SWIP
...THEN...
...LET THE OPERATION BEGIN!
YEAH!
HWIP

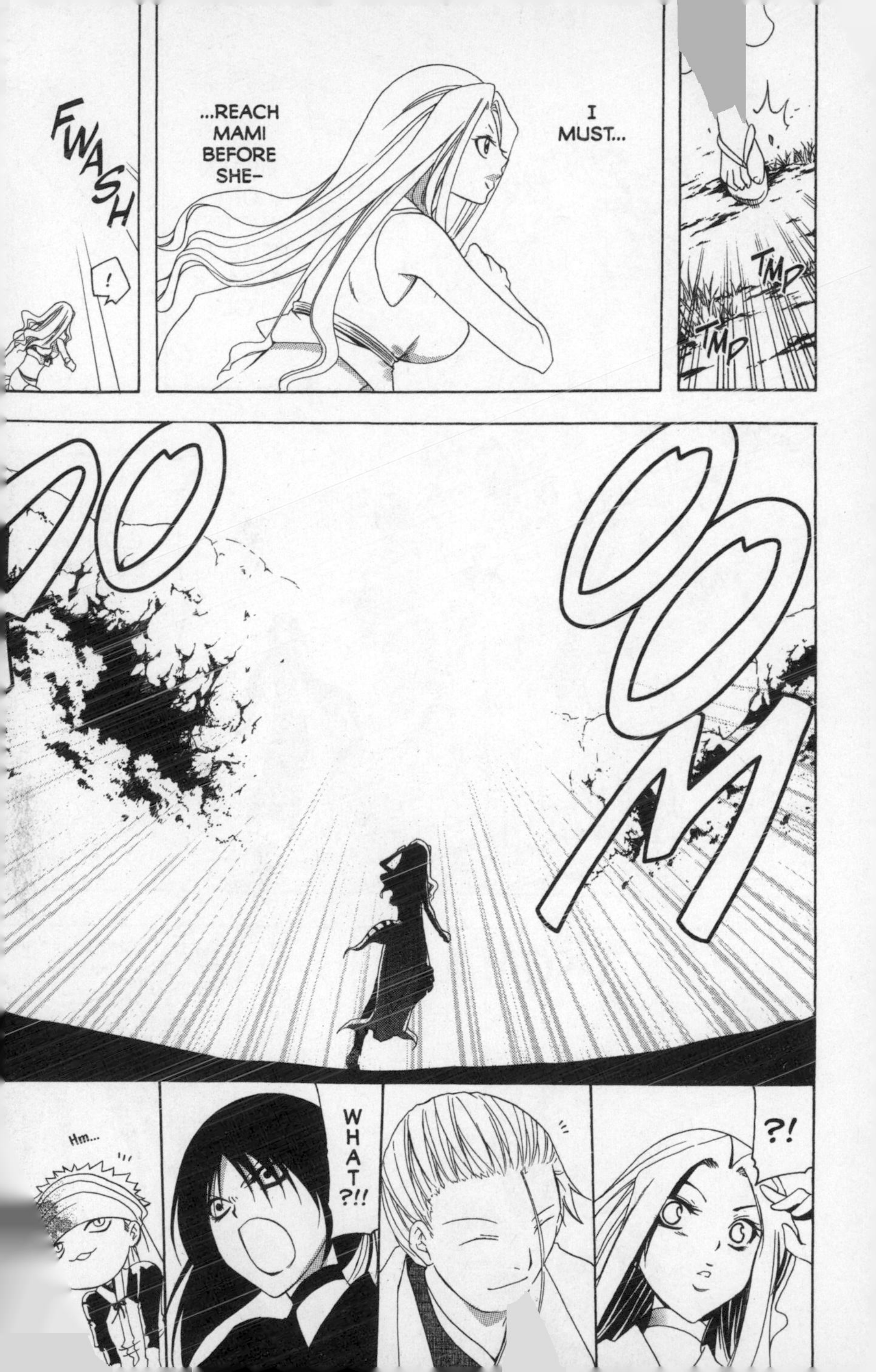
TMP
TMP
I
MUST...
...REACH
MAMI
BEFORE
SHE–
FWASH
!
DOOOOM
?!
!!
WHAT?!!
!!!
Hm...

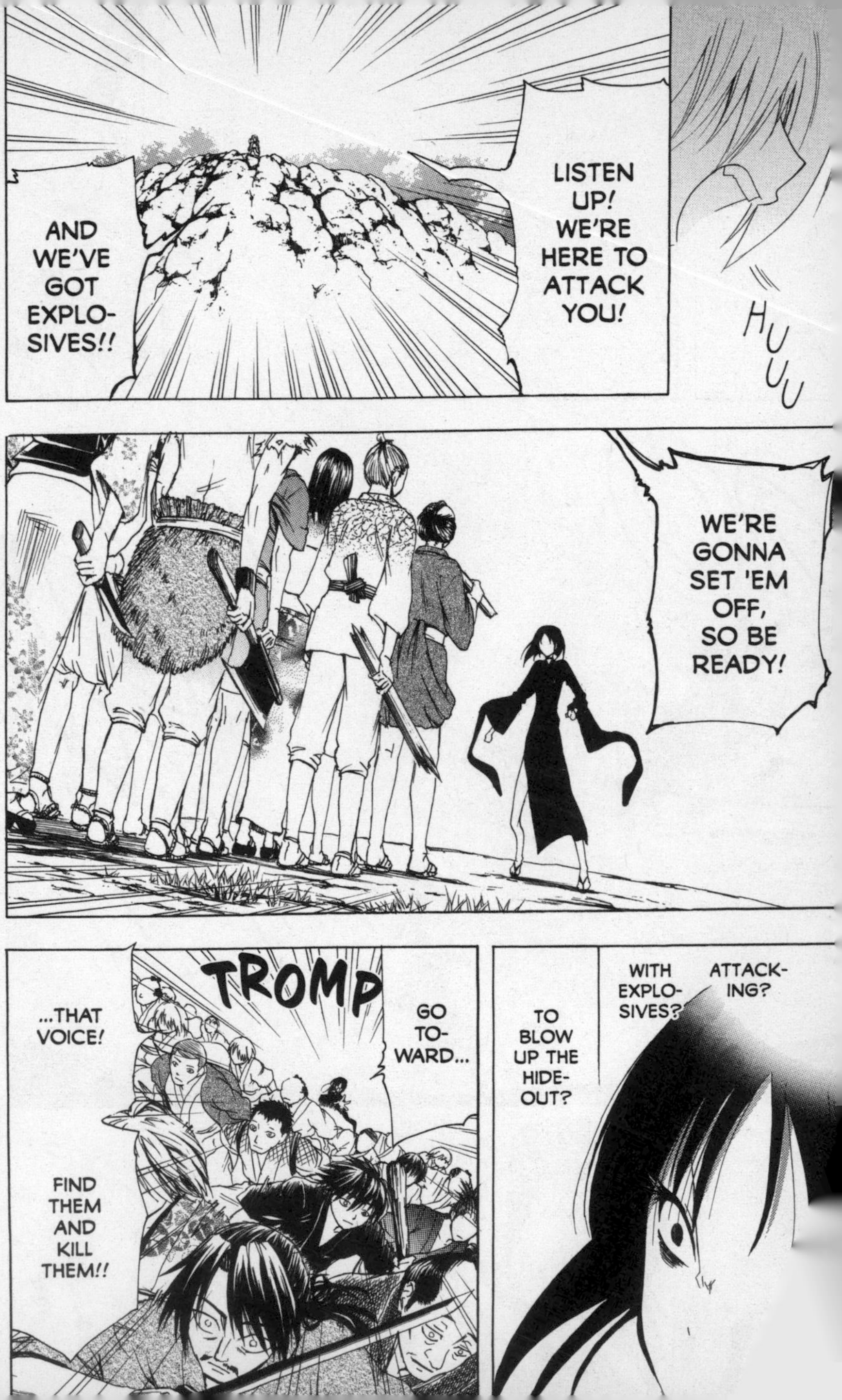
HUUU
LISTEN UP! WE'RE HERE TO ATTACK YOU!
AND WE'VE GOT EXPLOSIVES!!
WE'RE GONNA SET 'EM OFF, SO BE READY!
ATTACKING?
WITH EXPLOSIVES?
TO BLOW UP THE HIDEOUT?
GO TOWARD...
TROMP
...THAT VOICE!
FIND THEM AND KILL THEM!!

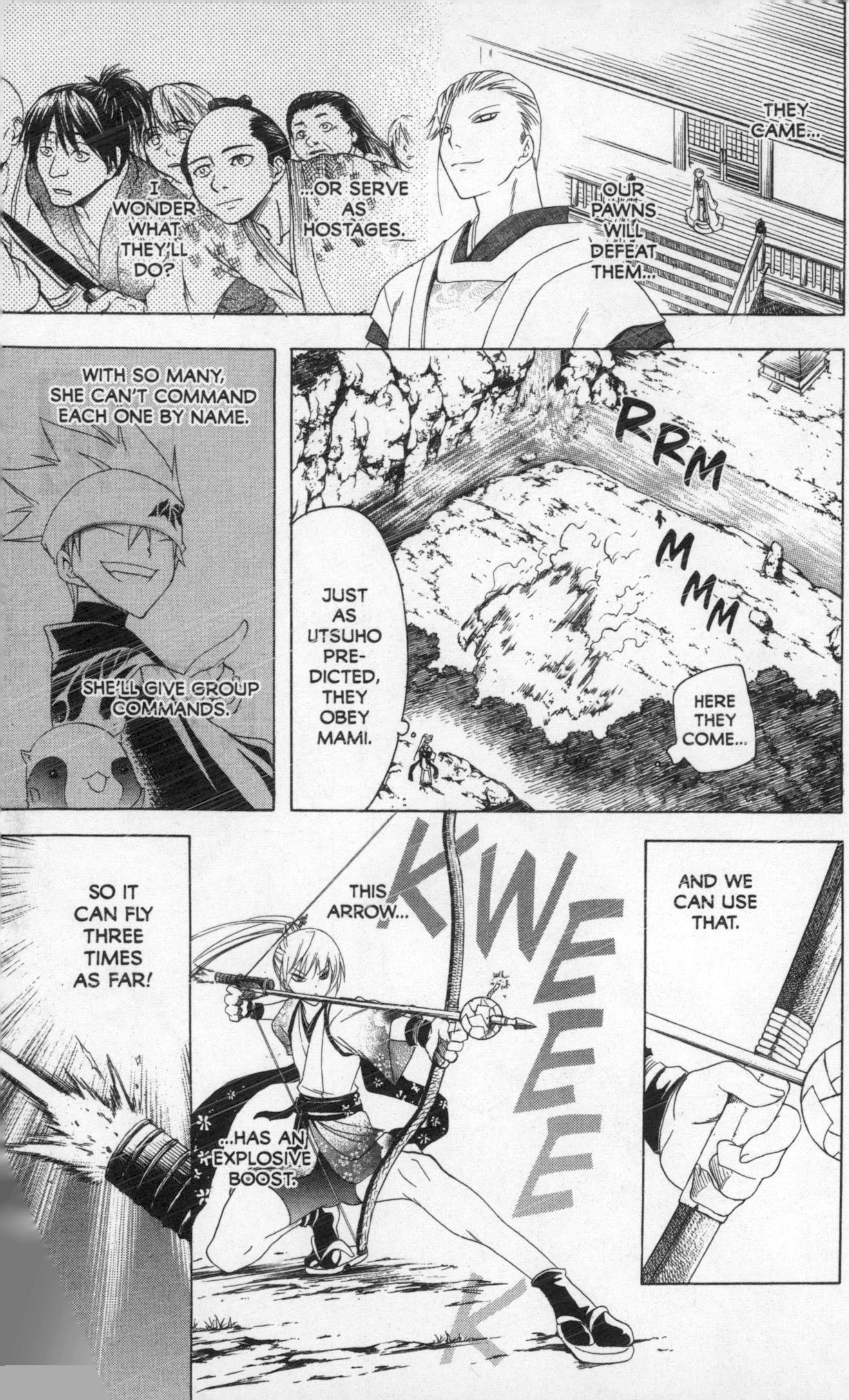
THEY CAME...
OUR PAWNS WILL DEFEAT THEM...
...OR SERVE AS HOSTAGES.
I WONDER WHAT THEY'LL DO?
RRM MMM
HERE THEY COME...
JUST AS UTSUHO PREDICTED, THEY OBEY MAMI.
WITH SO MANY, SHE CAN'T COMMAND EACH ONE BY NAME.
SHE'LL GIVE GROUP COMMANDS.
AND WE CAN USE THAT.
THIS ARROW...
KWEEEEEK
...HAS AN EXPLOSIVE BOOST.
SO IT CAN FLY THREE TIMES AS FAR!

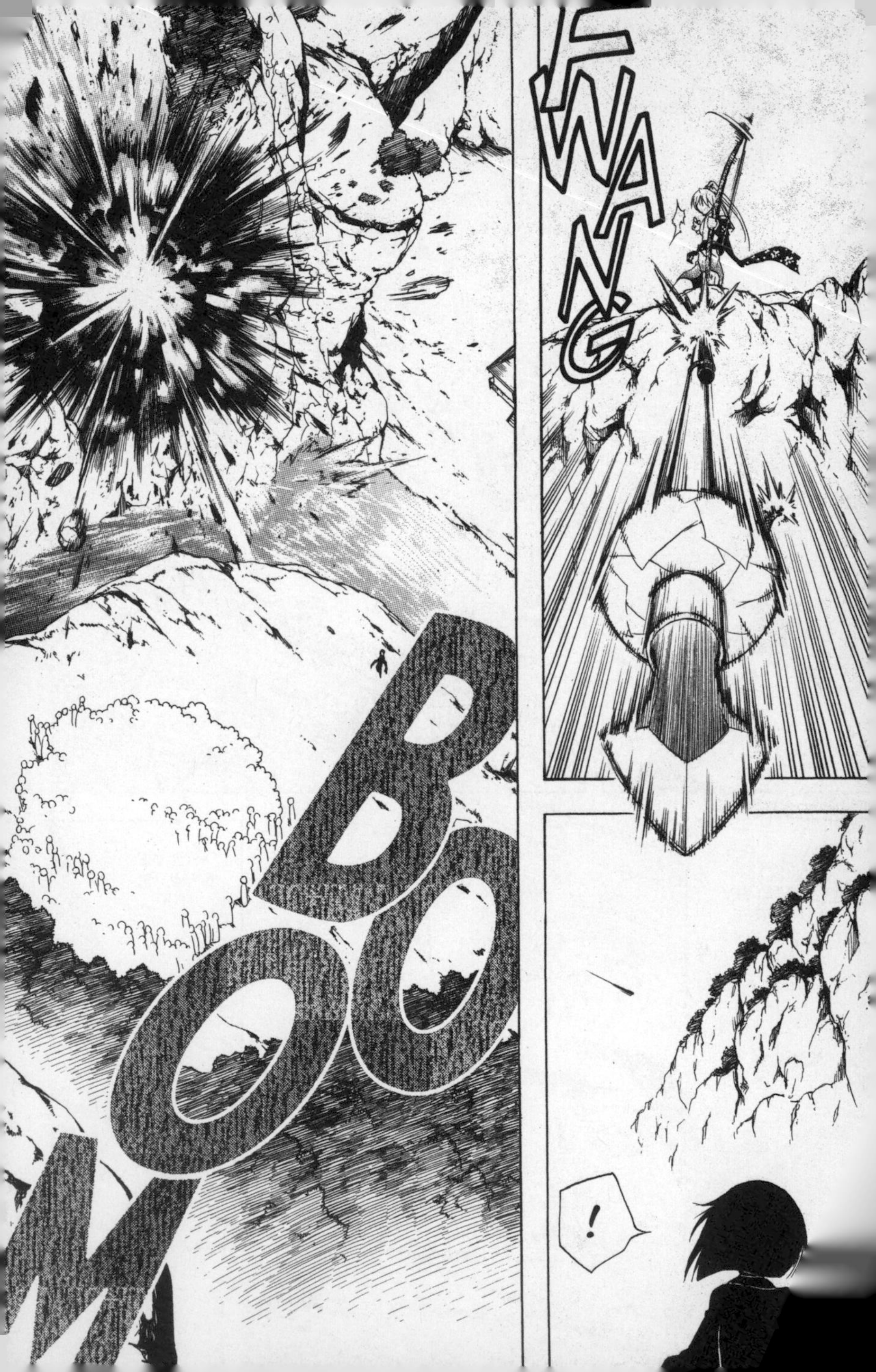
FWANG
!
BOOM

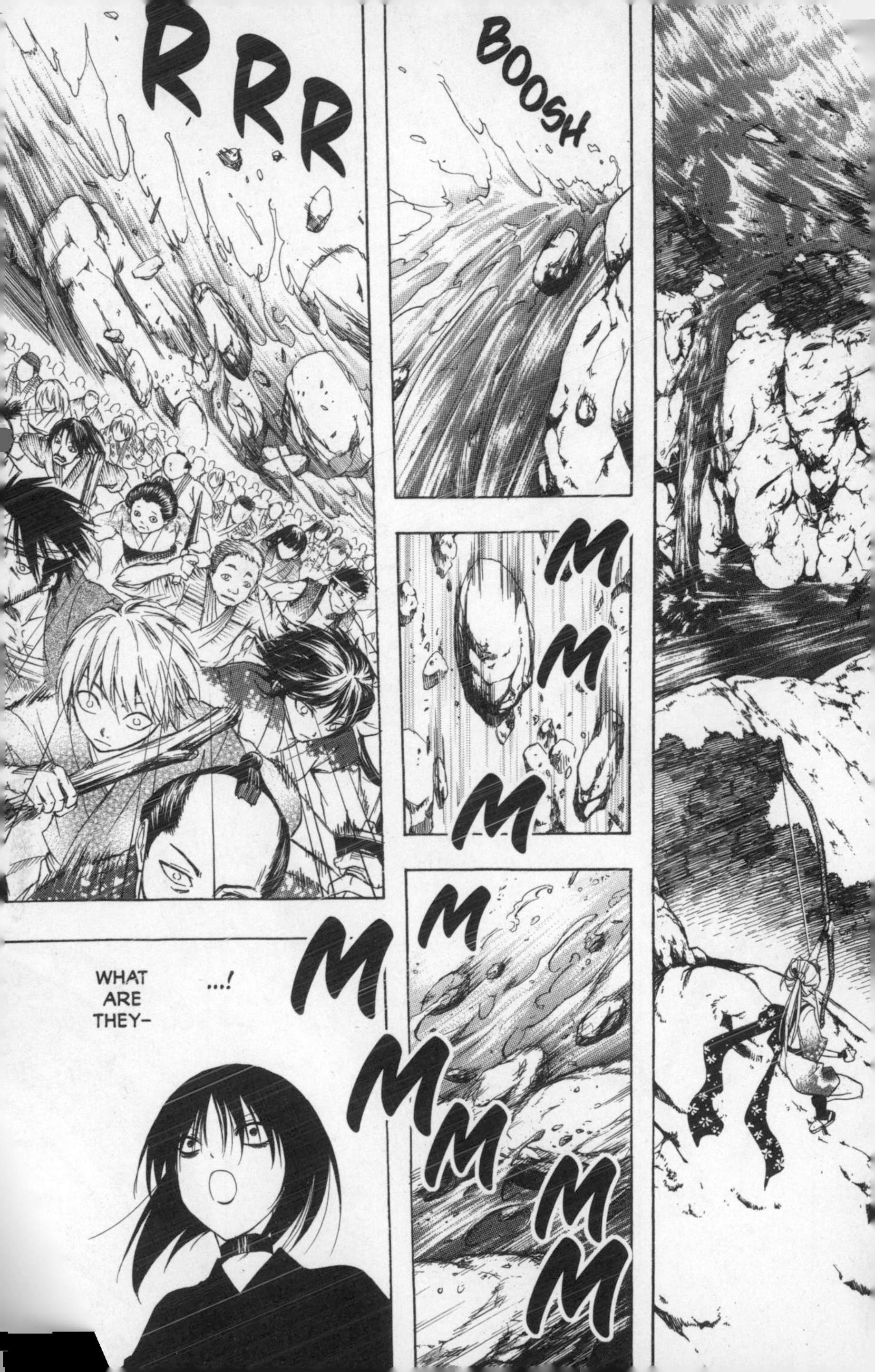
BOOSH
MMMMMMMMMMMMM
RRR
WHAT ARE THEY–
...!

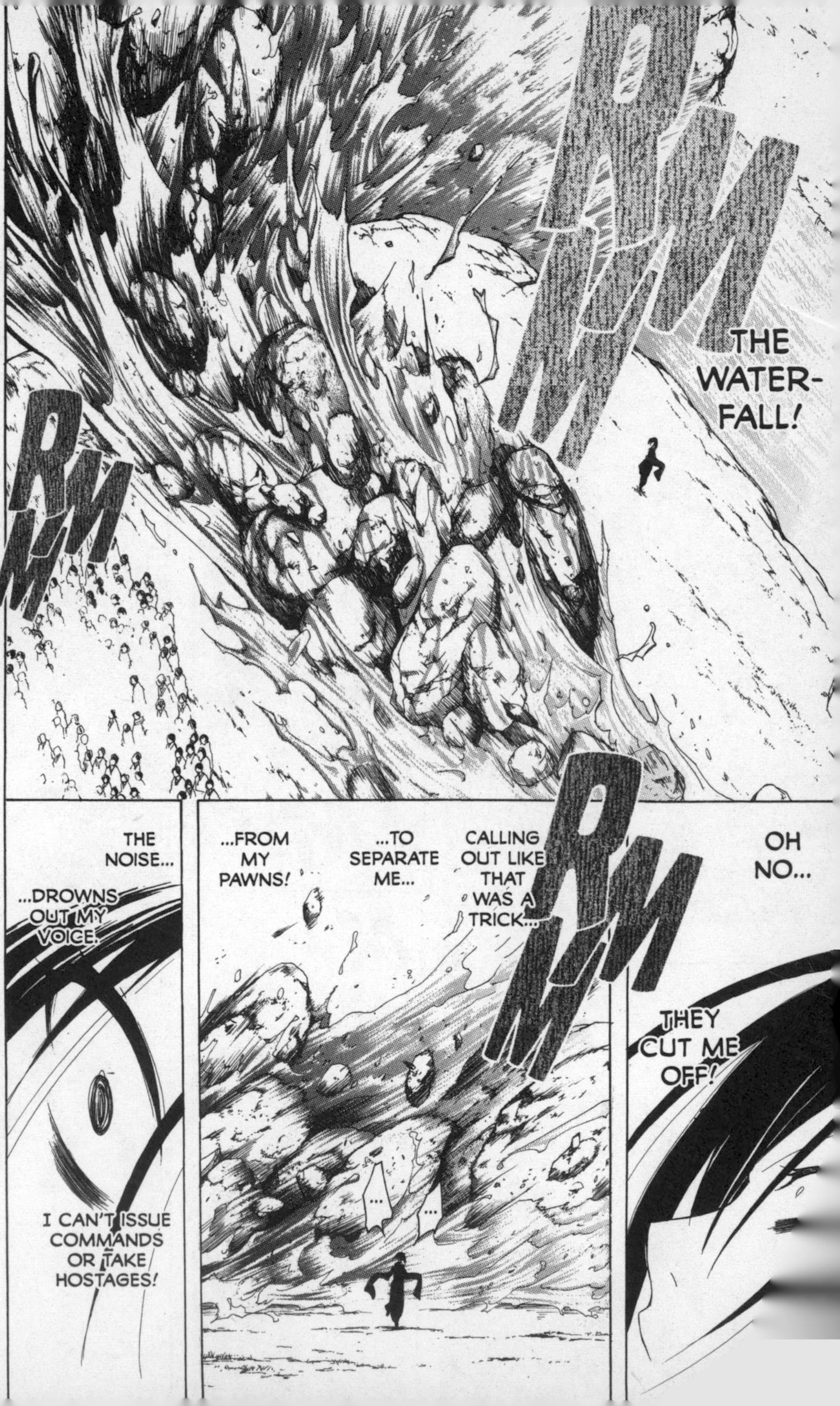
THE WATER-FALL!
RMM
RMM
OH NO...
THEY CUT ME OFF!
RMM
CALLING OUT LIKE THAT WAS A TRICK...
...TO SEPARATE ME...
...FROM MY PAWNS!
...
...
THE NOISE...
...DROWNS OUT MY VOICE.
I CAN'T ISSUE COMMANDS OR TAKE HOSTAGES!

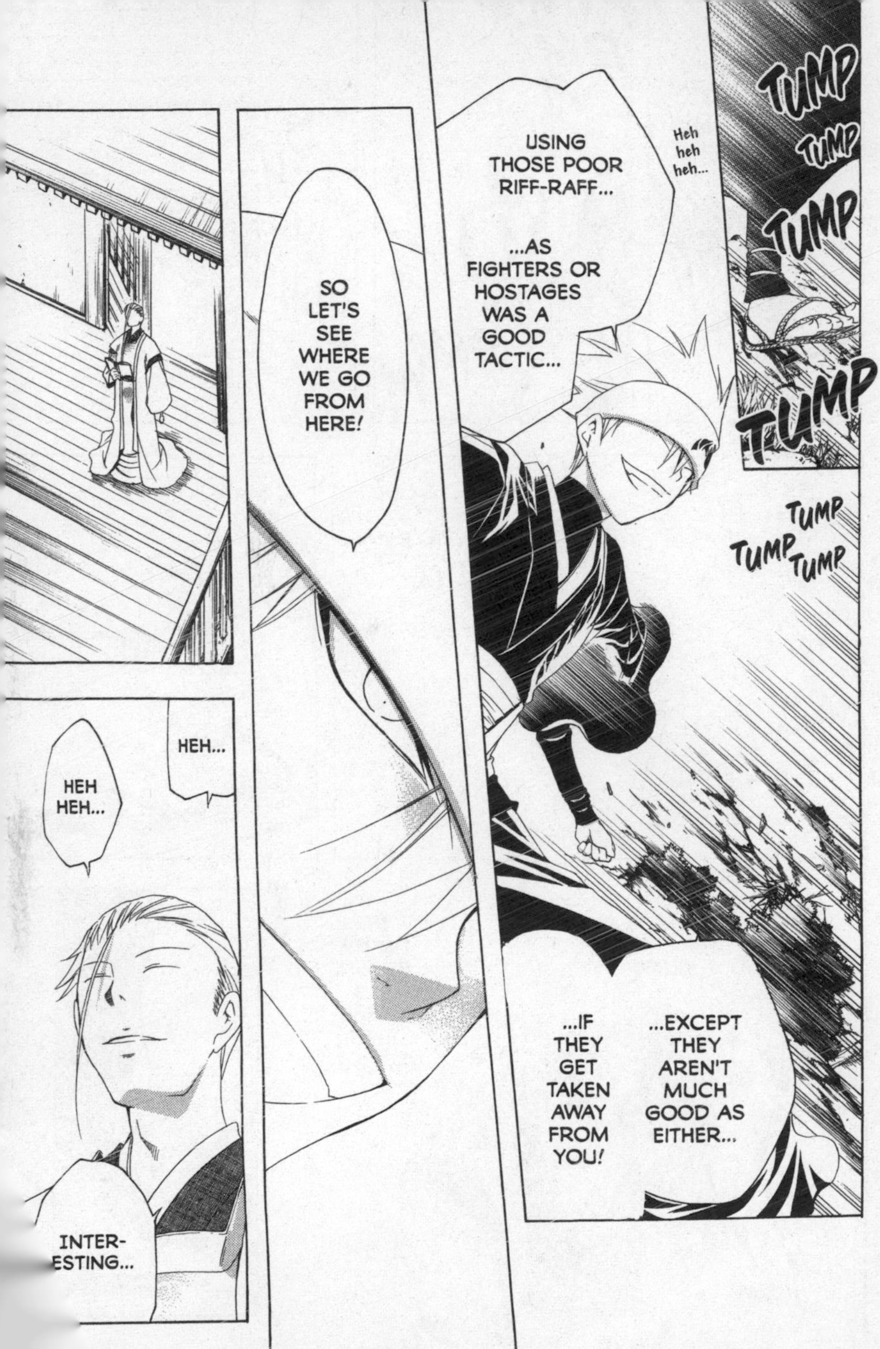
TUMP
TUMP
TUMP
TUMP
Heh heh heh...
USING THOSE POOR RIFF-RAFF...
...AS FIGHTERS OR HOSTAGES WAS A GOOD TACTIC...
TUMP TUMP TUMP
...EXCEPT THEY AREN'T MUCH GOOD AS EITHER...
...IF THEY GET TAKEN AWAY FROM YOU!
SO LET'S SEE WHERE WE GO FROM HERE!
HEH...
HEH HEH...
INTER-ESTING...

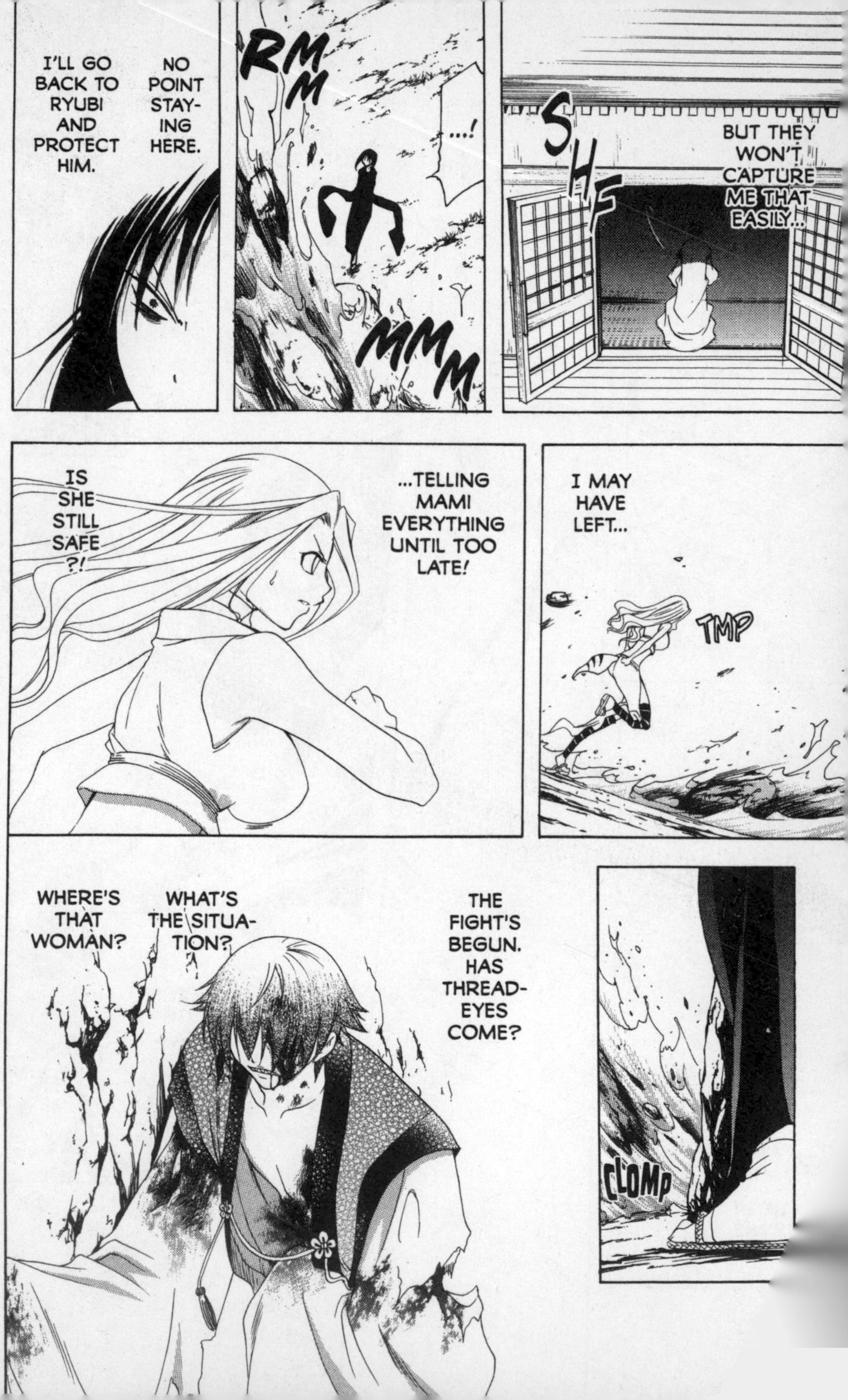
SHF
BUT THEY WON'T CAPTURE ME THAT EASILY...
RMMMMMM
...!
NO POINT STAYING HERE.
I'LL GO BACK TO RYUBI AND PROTECT HIM.
I MAY HAVE LEFT...
TMP
...TELLING MAMI EVERYTHING UNTIL TOO LATE!
IS SHE STILL SAFE?!
CLOMP
THE FIGHT'S BEGUN. HAS THREAD-EYES COME?
WHAT'S THE SITUATION?
WHERE'S THAT WOMAN?

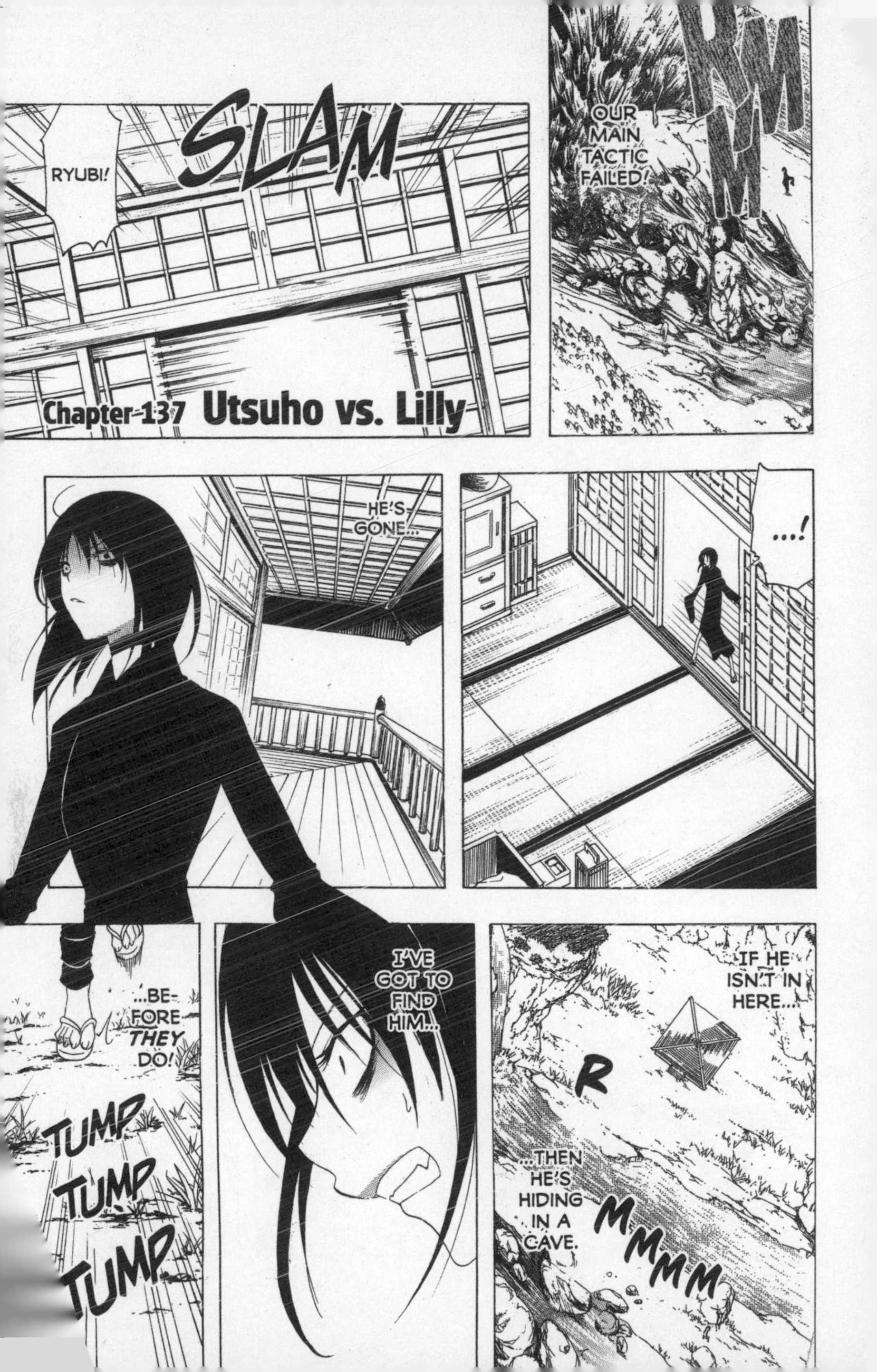
OUR MAIN TACTIC FAILED!
SLAM
RYUBI!
Chapter 137 Utsuho vs. Lilly
...!
HE'S GONE...
IF HE ISN'T IN HERE...
R
...THEN HE'S HIDING IN A CAVE.
MMMM
I'VE GOT TO FIND HIM...
...BE-FORE THEY DO!
TUMP
TUMP
TUMP

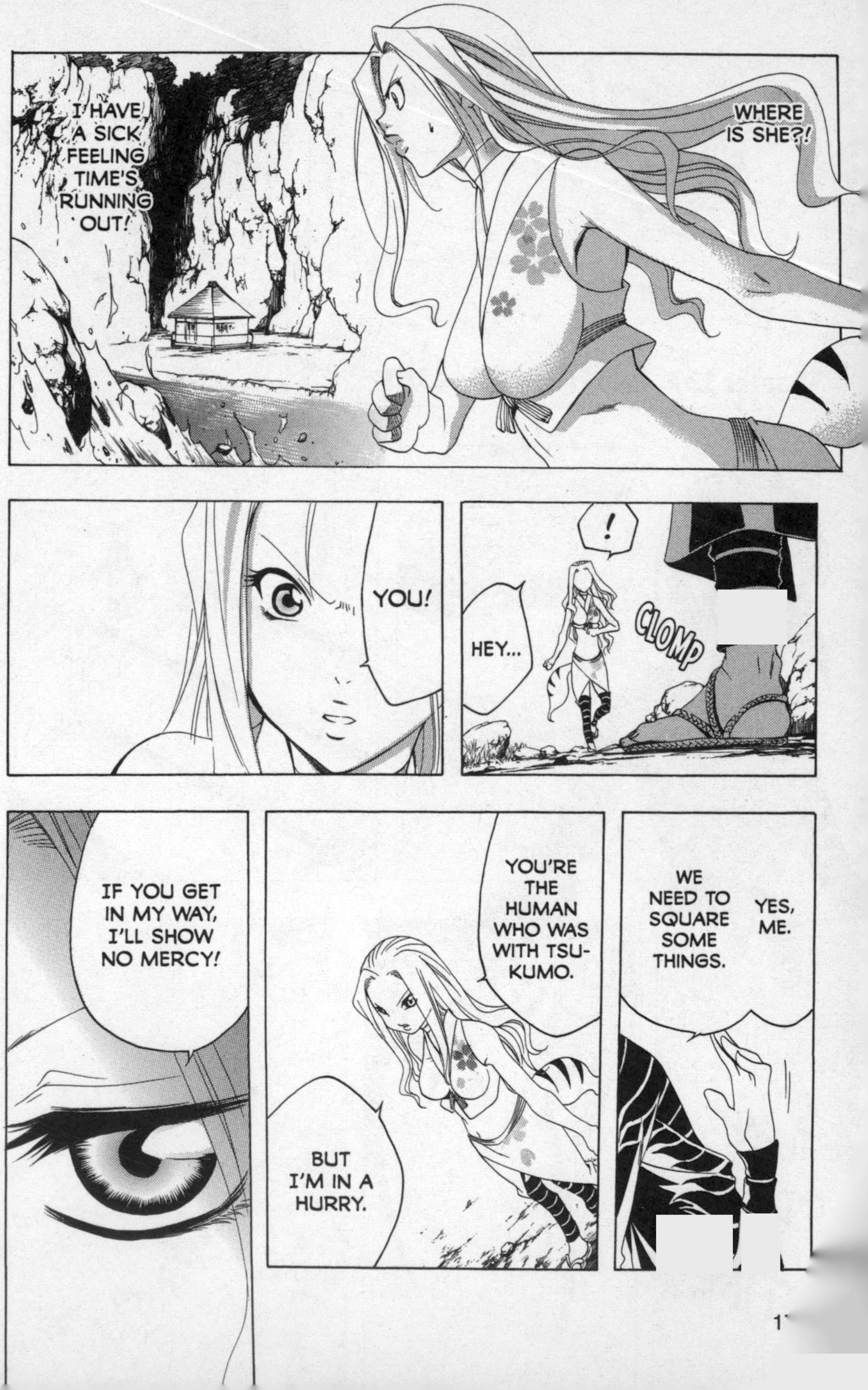
WHERE IS SHE?!
I HAVE A SICK FEELING TIME'S RUNNING OUT!
!
HEY...
CLOMP
YOU!
YES, ME.
WE NEED TO SQUARE SOME THINGS.
YOU'RE THE HUMAN WHO WAS WITH TSU-KUMO.
BUT I'M IN A HURRY.
IF YOU GET IN MY WAY, I'LL SHOW NO MERCY!

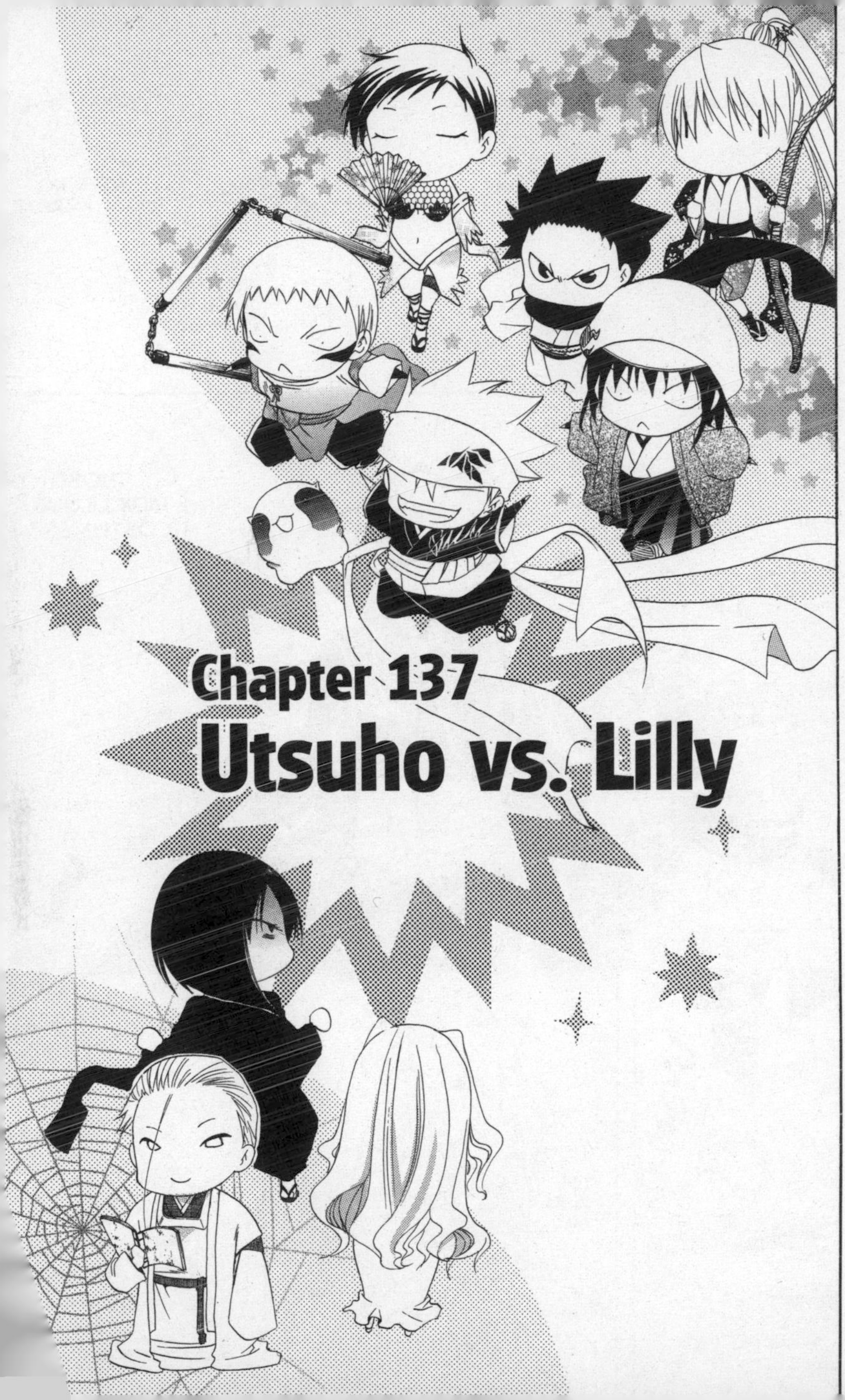
Chapter 137
Utsuho vs. Lilly

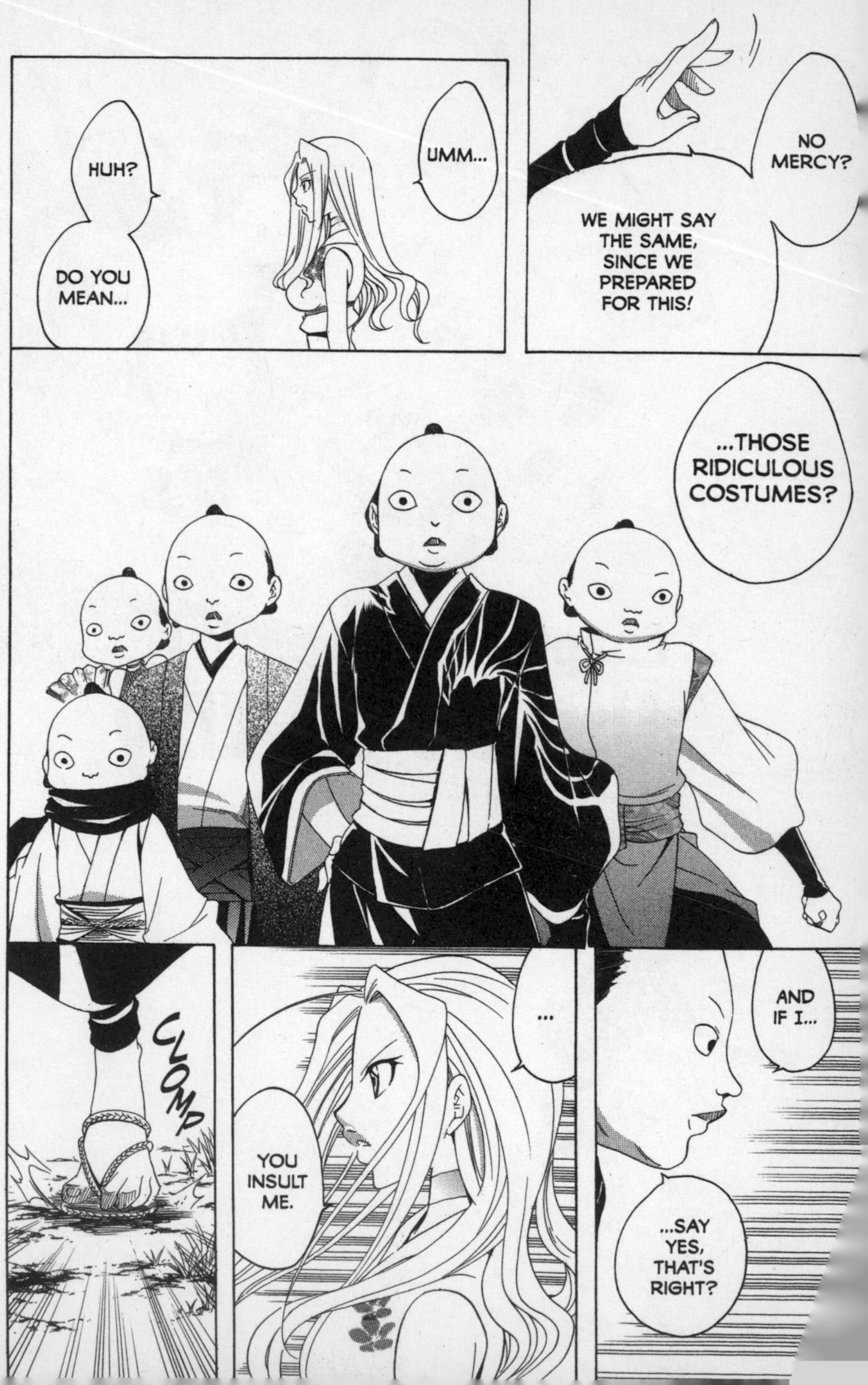
NO MERCY?
WE MIGHT SAY THE SAME, SINCE WE PREPARED FOR THIS!
UMM...
HUH?
DO YOU MEAN...
...THOSE RIDICULOUS COSTUMES?
AND IF I...
...SAY YES, THAT'S RIGHT?
...
YOU INSULT ME.
CLOMP

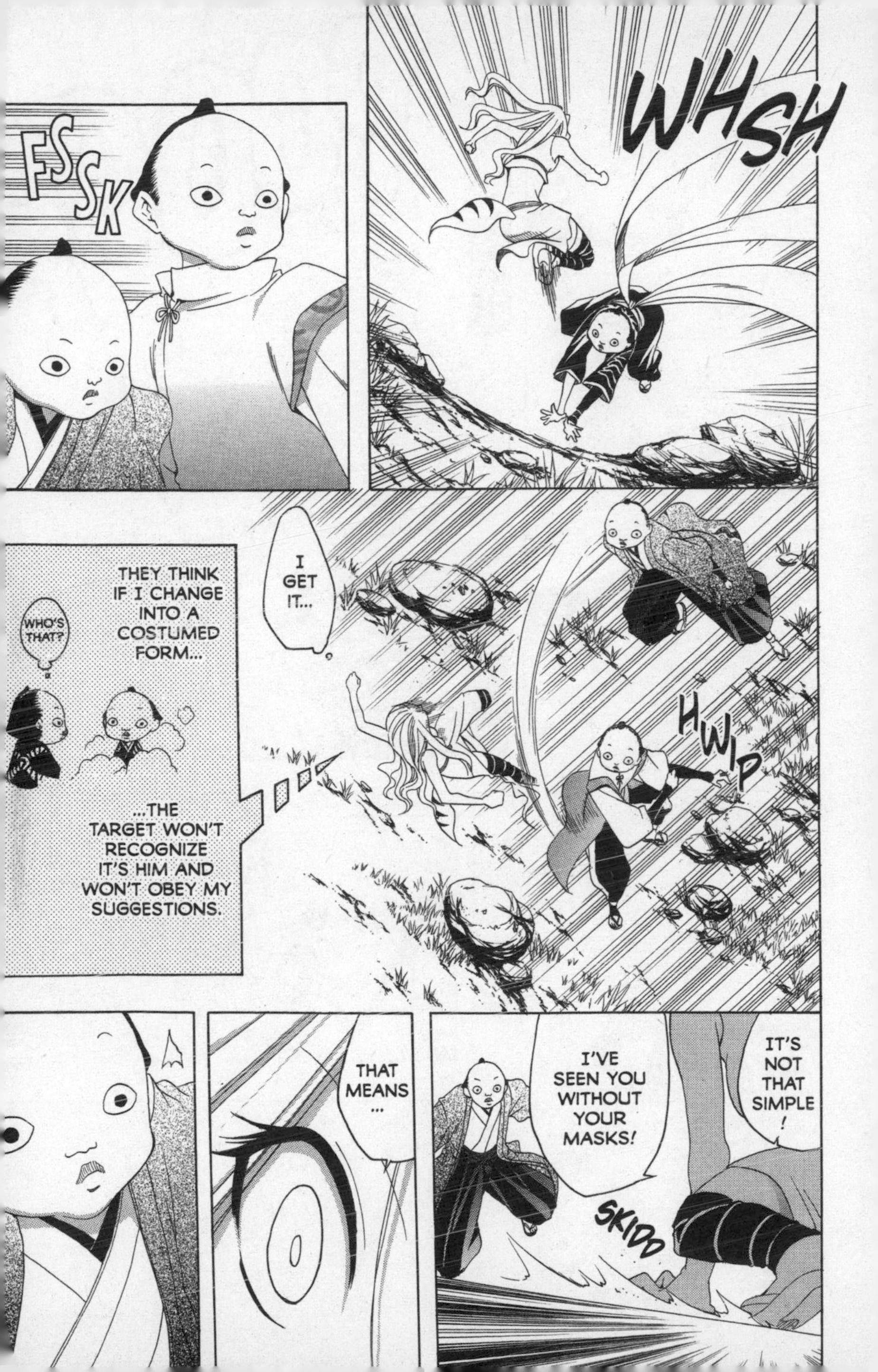
WHSH
FSSK
HWIP
I GET IT...
THEY THINK IF I CHANGE INTO A COSTUMED FORM...
WHO'S THAT?
...THE TARGET WON'T RECOGNIZE IT'S HIM AND WON'T OBEY MY SUGGESTIONS.
IT'S NOT THAT SIMPLE!
I'VE SEEN YOU WITHOUT YOUR MASKS!
SKIDD
THAT MEANS...

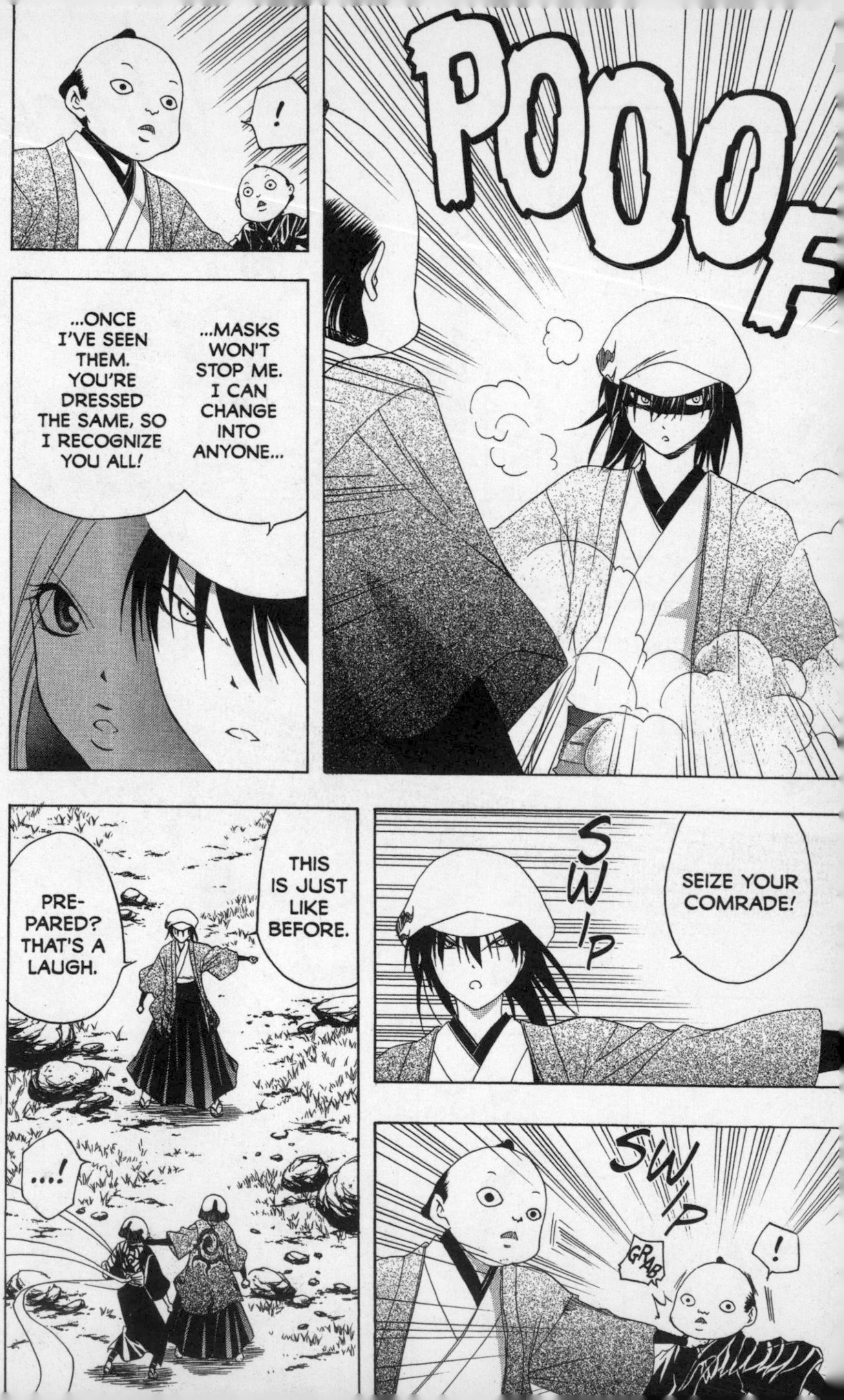
POOOF
!
...MASKS WON'T STOP ME. I CAN CHANGE INTO ANYONE...
...ONCE I'VE SEEN THEM. YOU'RE DRESSED THE SAME, SO I RECOGNIZE YOU ALL!
SEIZE YOUR COMRADE!
SWIP
SWIP
GRAB
!
THIS IS JUST LIKE BEFORE.
PRE-PARED? THAT'S A LAUGH.
...!

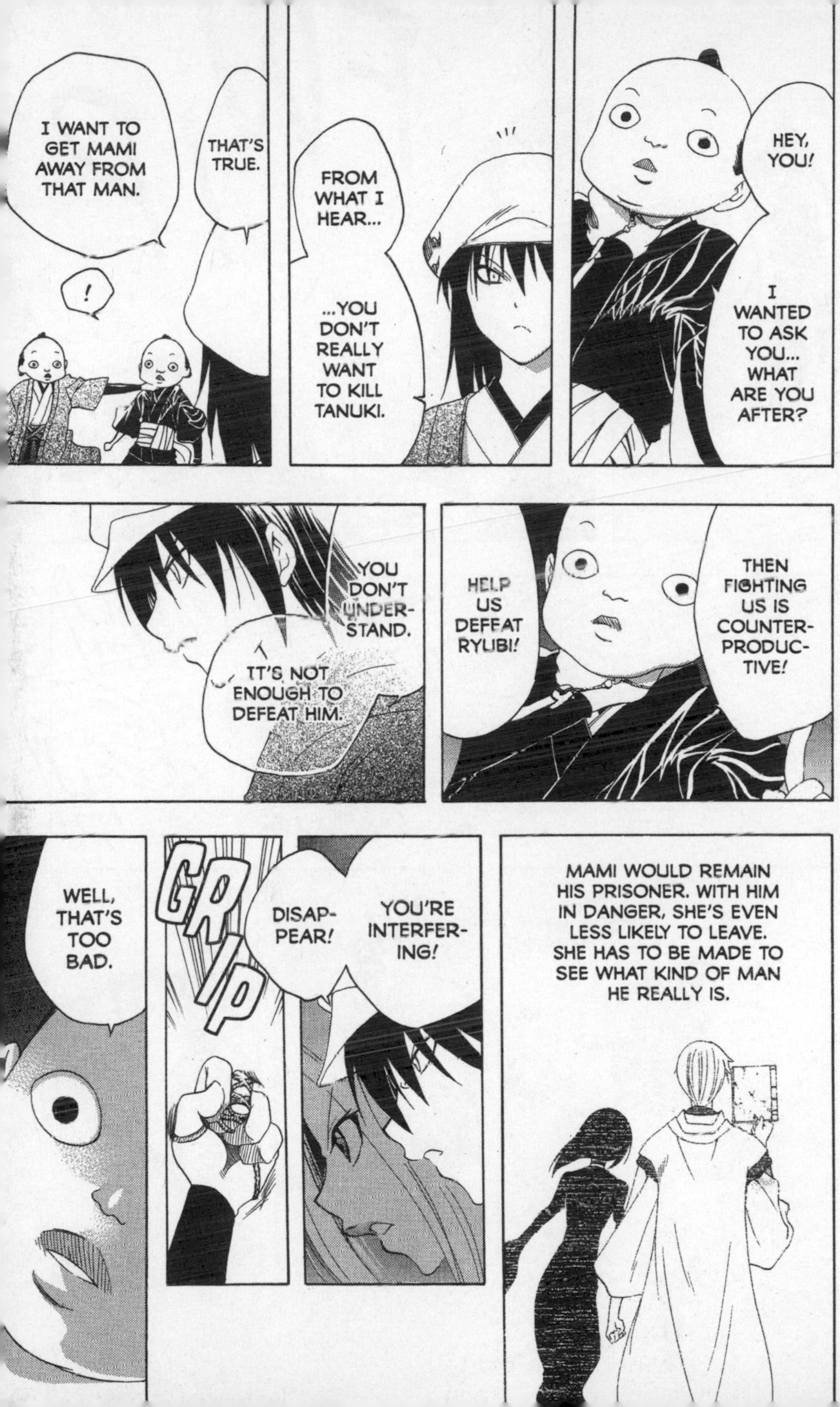
HEY, YOU!
I WANTED TO ASK YOU... WHAT ARE YOU AFTER?
FROM WHAT I HEAR...
...YOU DON'T REALLY WANT TO KILL TANUKI.
THAT'S TRUE.
I WANT TO GET MAMI AWAY FROM THAT MAN.
!
THEN FIGHTING US IS COUNTER-PRODUCTIVE!
HELP US DEFEAT RYUBI!
YOU DON'T UNDER-STAND.
IT'S NOT ENOUGH TO DEFEAT HIM.
MAMI WOULD REMAIN HIS PRISONER. WITH HIM IN DANGER, SHE'S EVEN LESS LIKELY TO LEAVE. SHE HAS TO BE MADE TO SEE WHAT KIND OF MAN HE REALLY IS.
YOU'RE INTERFERING!
DISAP-PEAR!
GRIP
WELL, THAT'S TOO BAD.

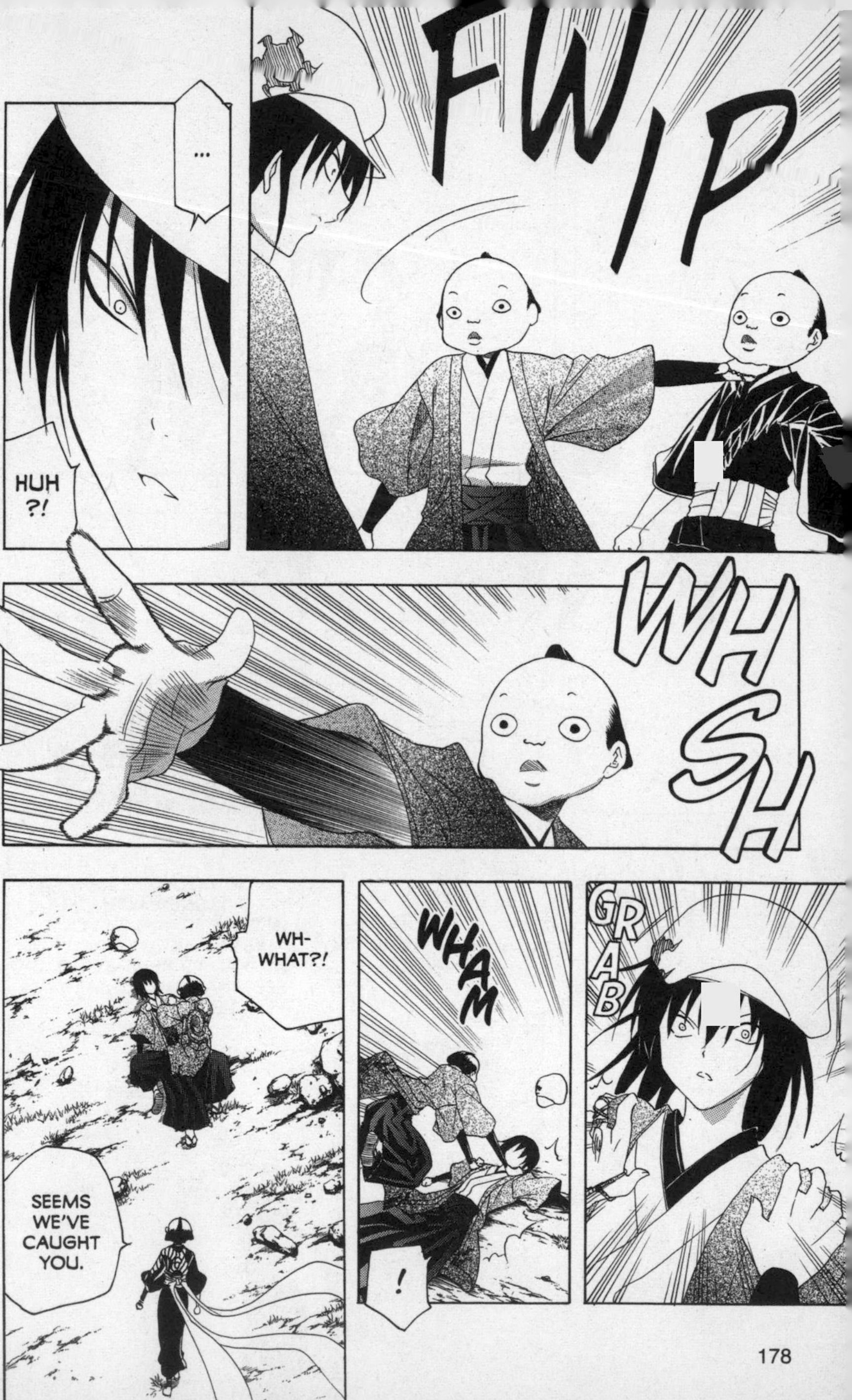
FWIP
...
HUH ?!
WHSH
GRAB
WHAM
!
WH- WHAT?!
SEEMS WE'VE CAUGHT YOU.

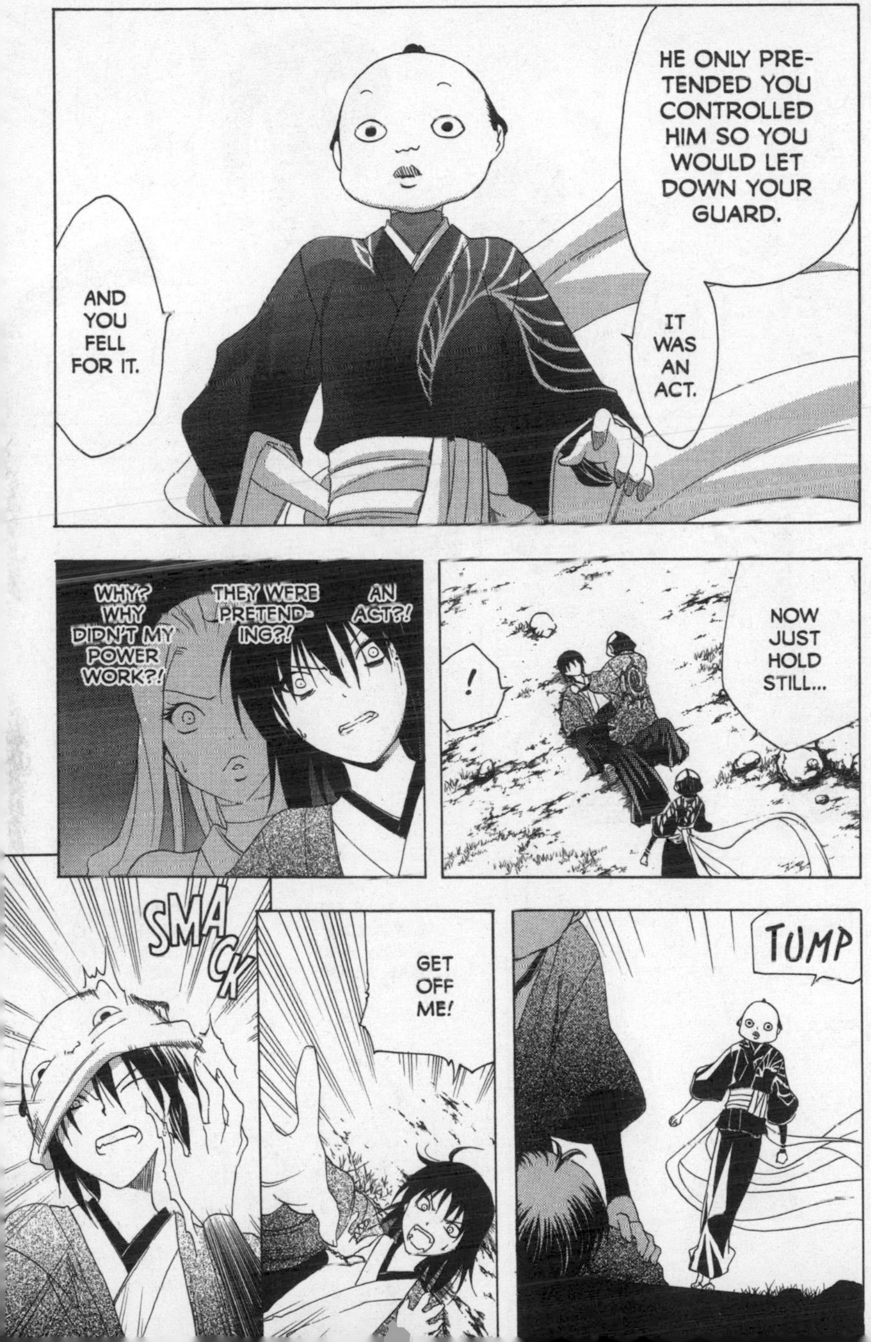
HE ONLY PRE-TENDED YOU CONTROLLED HIM SO YOU WOULD LET DOWN YOUR GUARD.
IT WAS AN ACT.
AND YOU FELL FOR IT.
NOW JUST HOLD STILL...
!
AN ACT?!
THEY WERE PRETEND-ING?!
WHY? WHY DIDN'T MY POWER WORK?!
TUMP
GET OFF ME!
SMACK

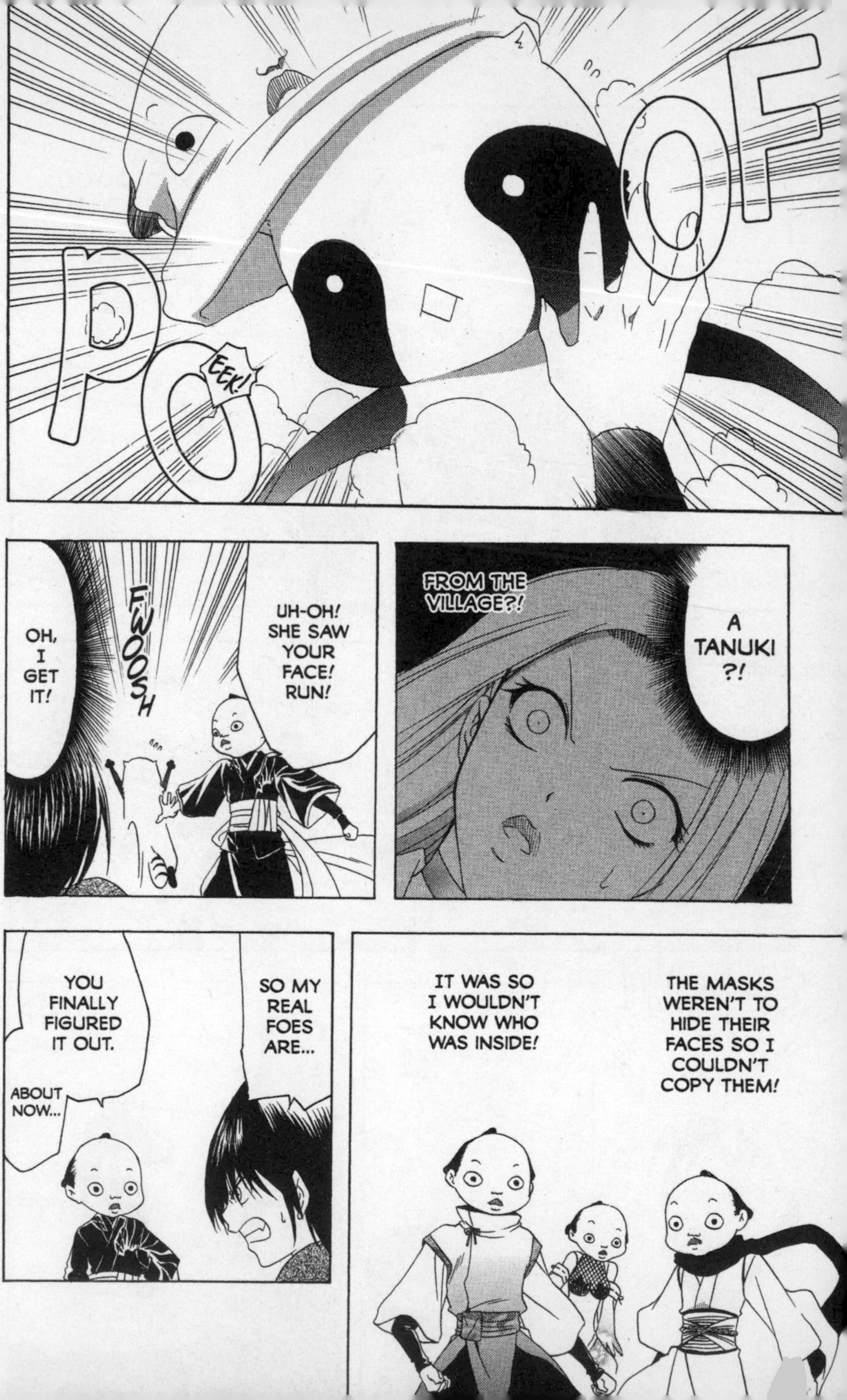
POOF
EEK!
A TANUKI ?!
FROM THE VILLAGE?!
UH-OH! SHE SAW YOUR FACE! RUN!
FWOOSH
OH, I GET IT!
THE MASKS WEREN'T TO HIDE THEIR FACES SO I COULDN'T COPY THEM!
IT WAS SO I WOULDN'T KNOW WHO WAS INSIDE!
SO MY REAL FOES ARE...
YOU FINALLY FIGURED IT OUT.
ABOUT NOW...

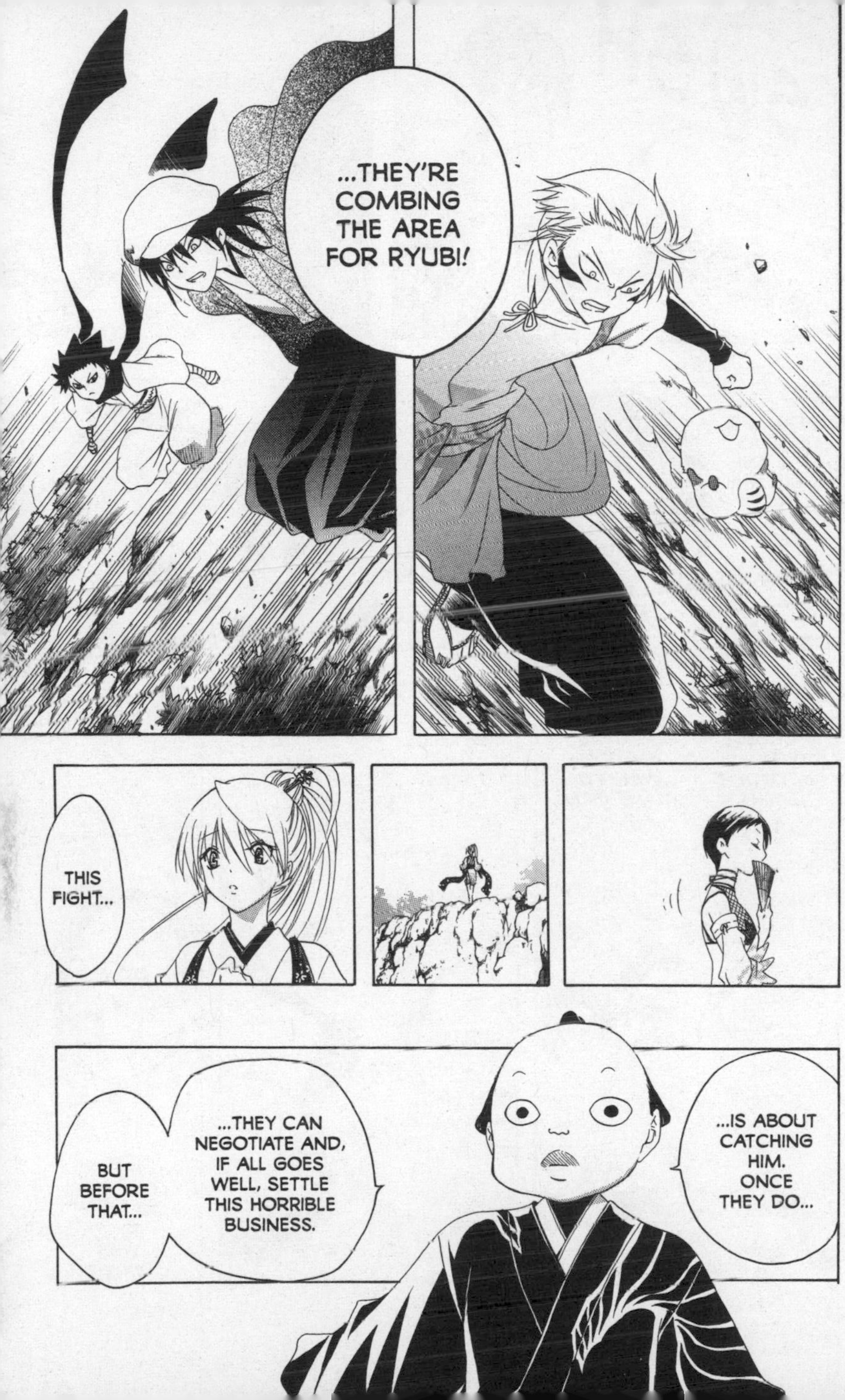
...THEY'RE COMBING THE AREA FOR RYUBI!
THIS FIGHT...
...IS ABOUT CATCHING HIM. ONCE THEY DO...
...THEY CAN NEGOTIATE AND, IF ALL GOES WELL, SETTLE THIS HORRIBLE BUSINESS.
BUT BEFORE THAT...

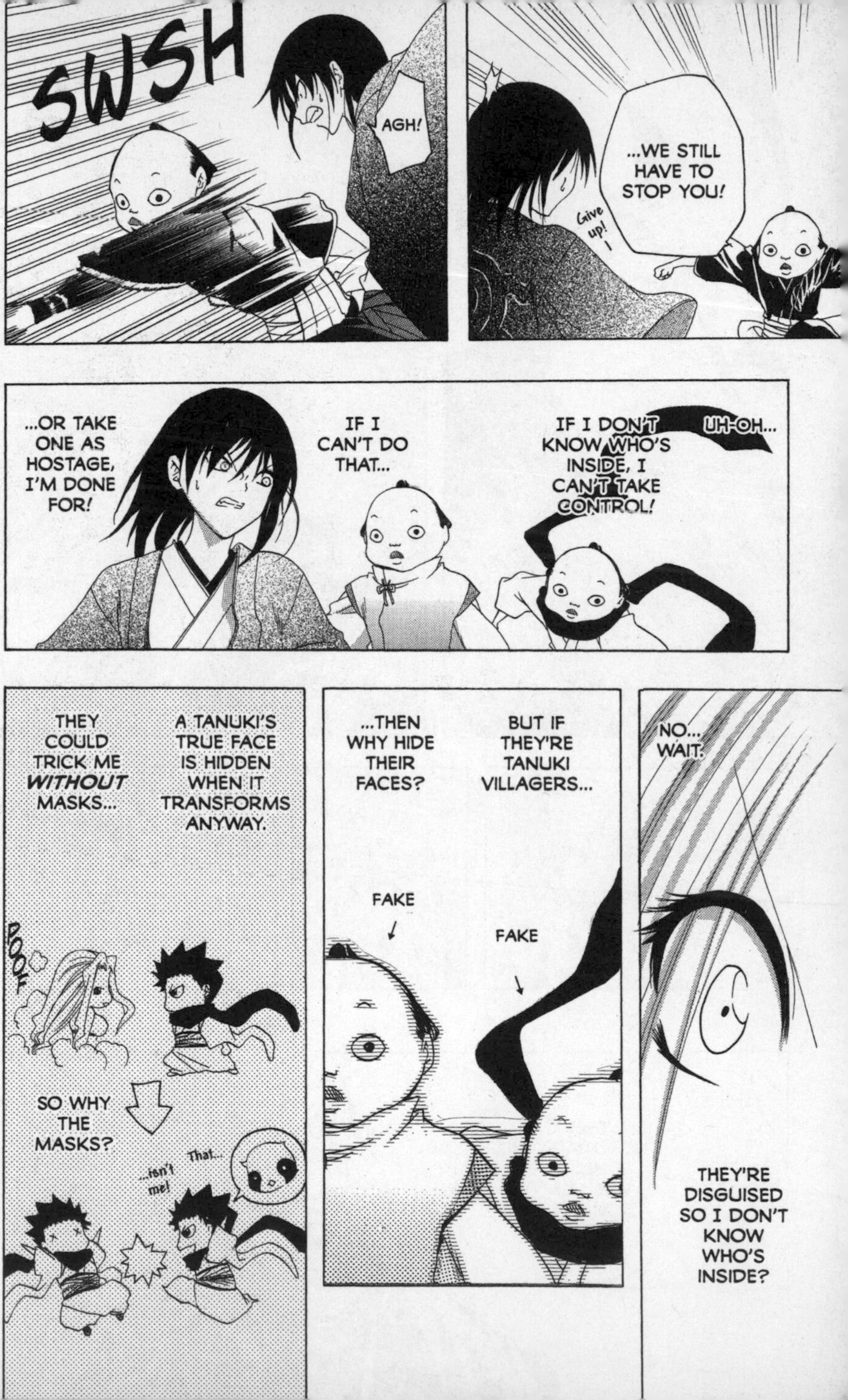
...WE STILL HAVE TO STOP YOU!
Give up!
SWSH
AGH!
UH-OH...
IF I DON'T KNOW WHO'S INSIDE, I CAN'T TAKE CONTROL!
IF I CAN'T DO THAT...
...OR TAKE ONE AS HOSTAGE, I'M DONE FOR!
NO... WAIT.
THEY'RE DISGUISED SO I DON'T KNOW WHO'S INSIDE?
BUT IF THEY'RE TANUKI VILLAGERS...
...THEN WHY HIDE THEIR FACES?
FAKE
FAKE
A TANUKI'S TRUE FACE IS HIDDEN WHEN IT TRANSFORMS ANYWAY.
THEY COULD TRICK ME *WITHOUT* MASKS...
POOF
SO WHY THE MASKS?
That...
...isn't me!

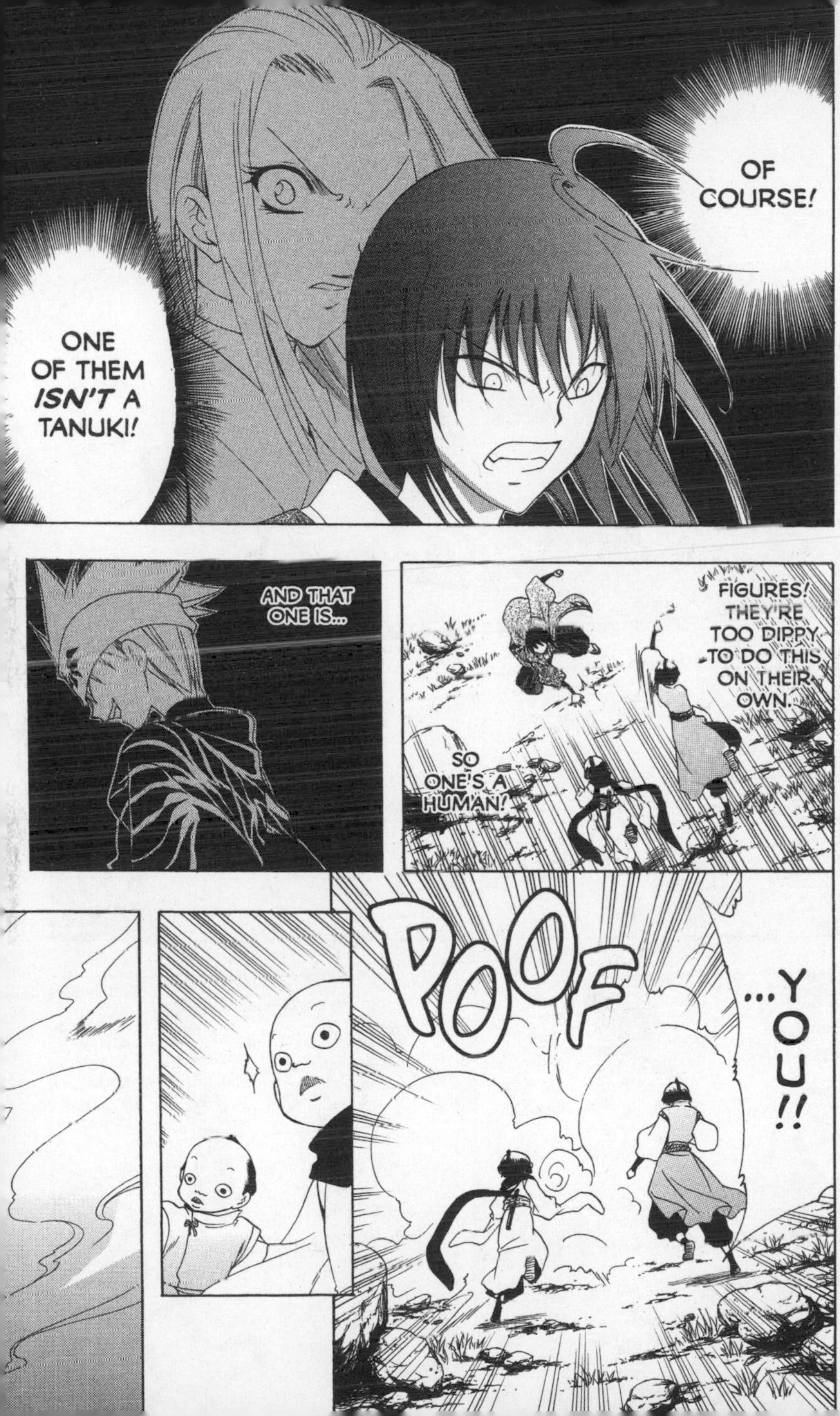
OF COURSE!
ONE OF THEM *ISN'T* A TANUKI!
FIGURES! THEY'RE TOO DIPPY TO DO THIS ON THEIR OWN.
SO ONE'S A HUMAN!
AND THAT ONE IS...
POOF
...YOU!!

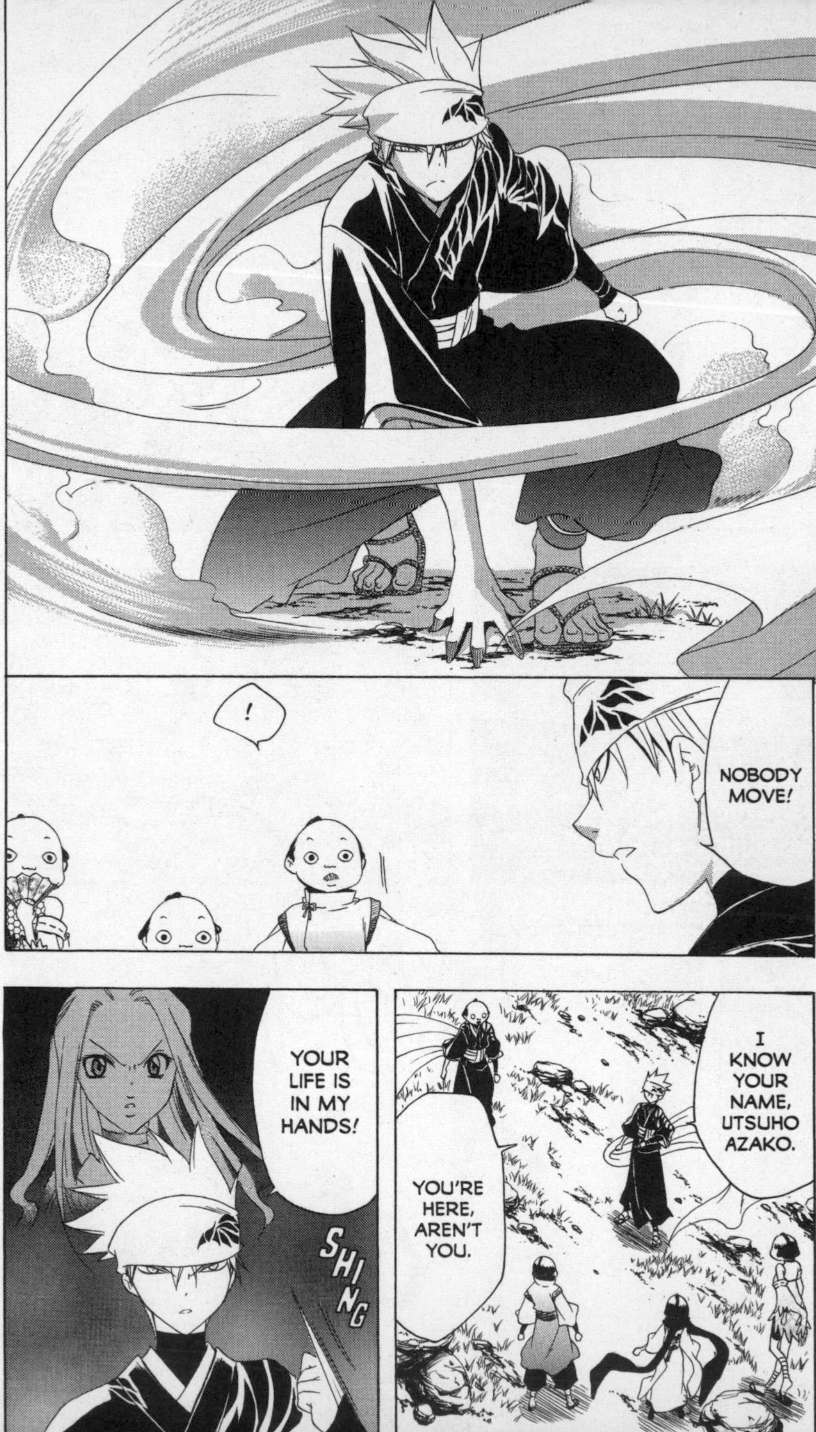
NOBODY MOVE!
!
I KNOW YOUR NAME, UTSUHO AZAKO.
YOU'RE HERE, AREN'T YOU.
YOUR LIFE IS IN MY HANDS!
SHING

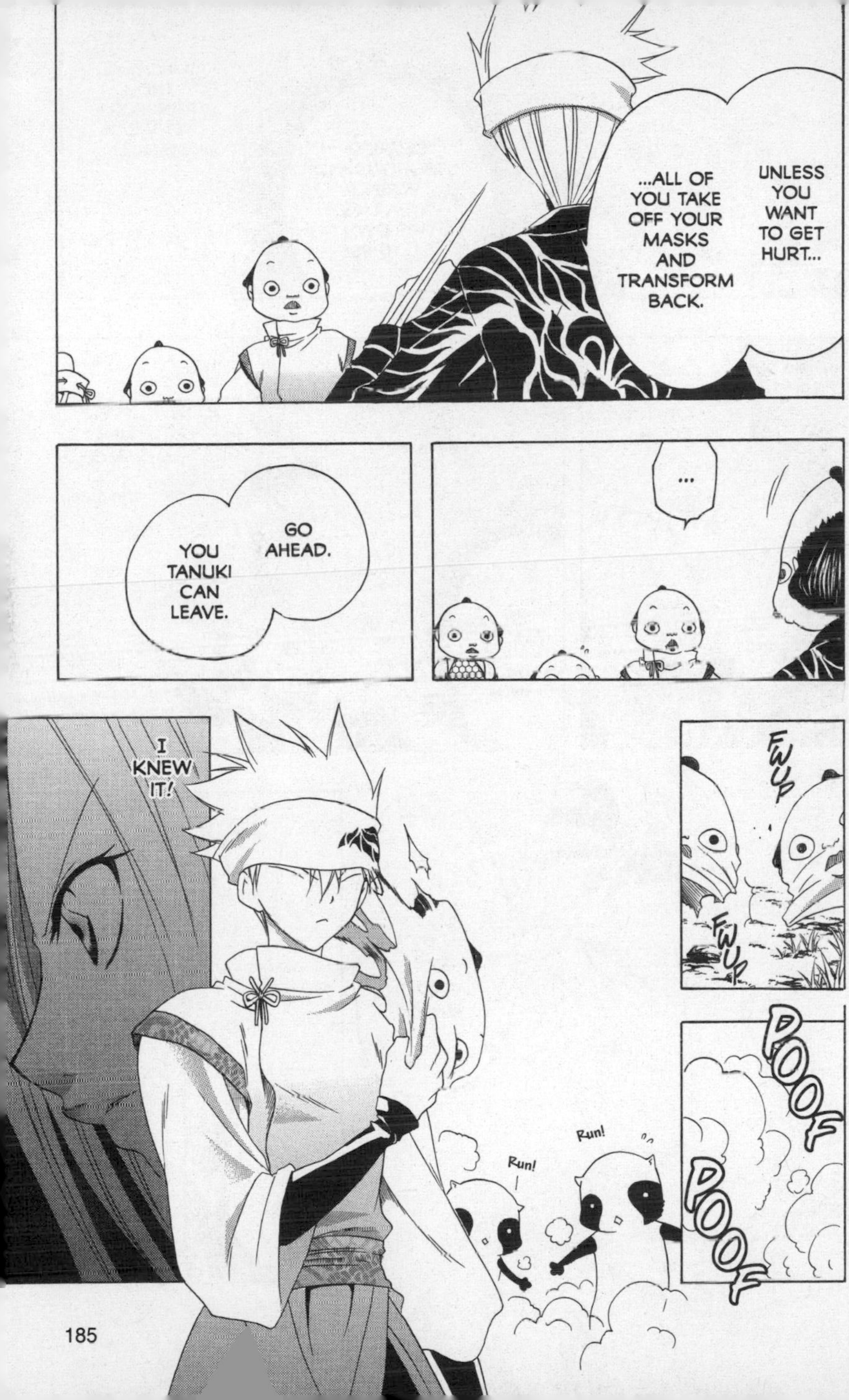
UNLESS YOU WANT TO GET HURT...
...ALL OF YOU TAKE OFF YOUR MASKS AND TRANSFORM BACK.
...
GO AHEAD.
YOU TANUKI CAN LEAVE.
FWUP
FWUP
POOF
POOF
Run!
Run!
I KNEW IT!

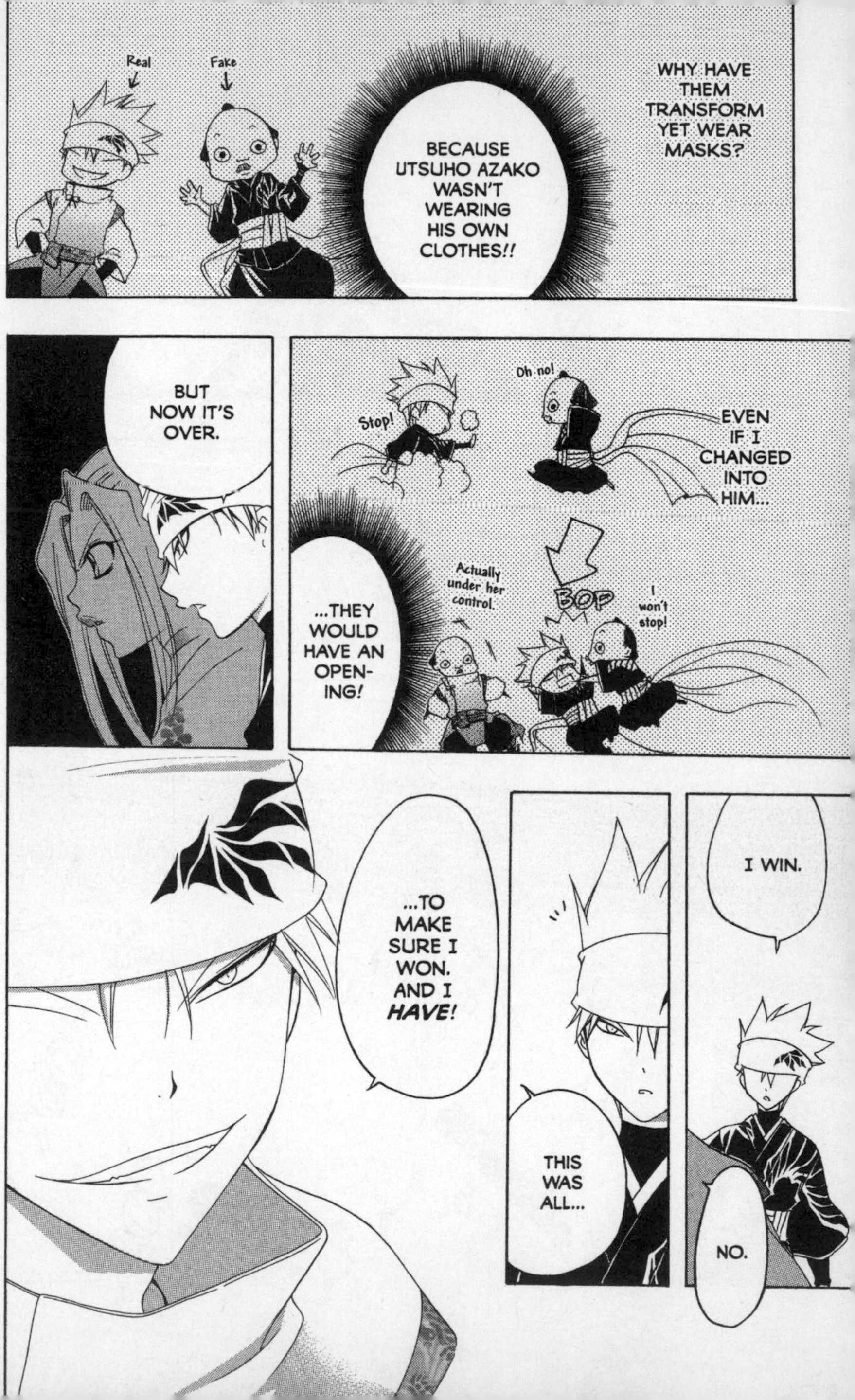
WHY HAVE THEM TRANSFORM YET WEAR MASKS?
BECAUSE UTSUHO AZAKO WASN'T WEARING HIS OWN CLOTHES!!
Fake
Real
EVEN IF I CHANGED INTO HIM...
Oh no!
Stop!
BOP
I won't stop!
Actually under her control.
...THEY WOULD HAVE AN OPEN-ING!
BUT NOW IT'S OVER.
I WIN.
NO.
THIS WAS ALL...
...TO MAKE SURE I WON. AND I *HAVE*!

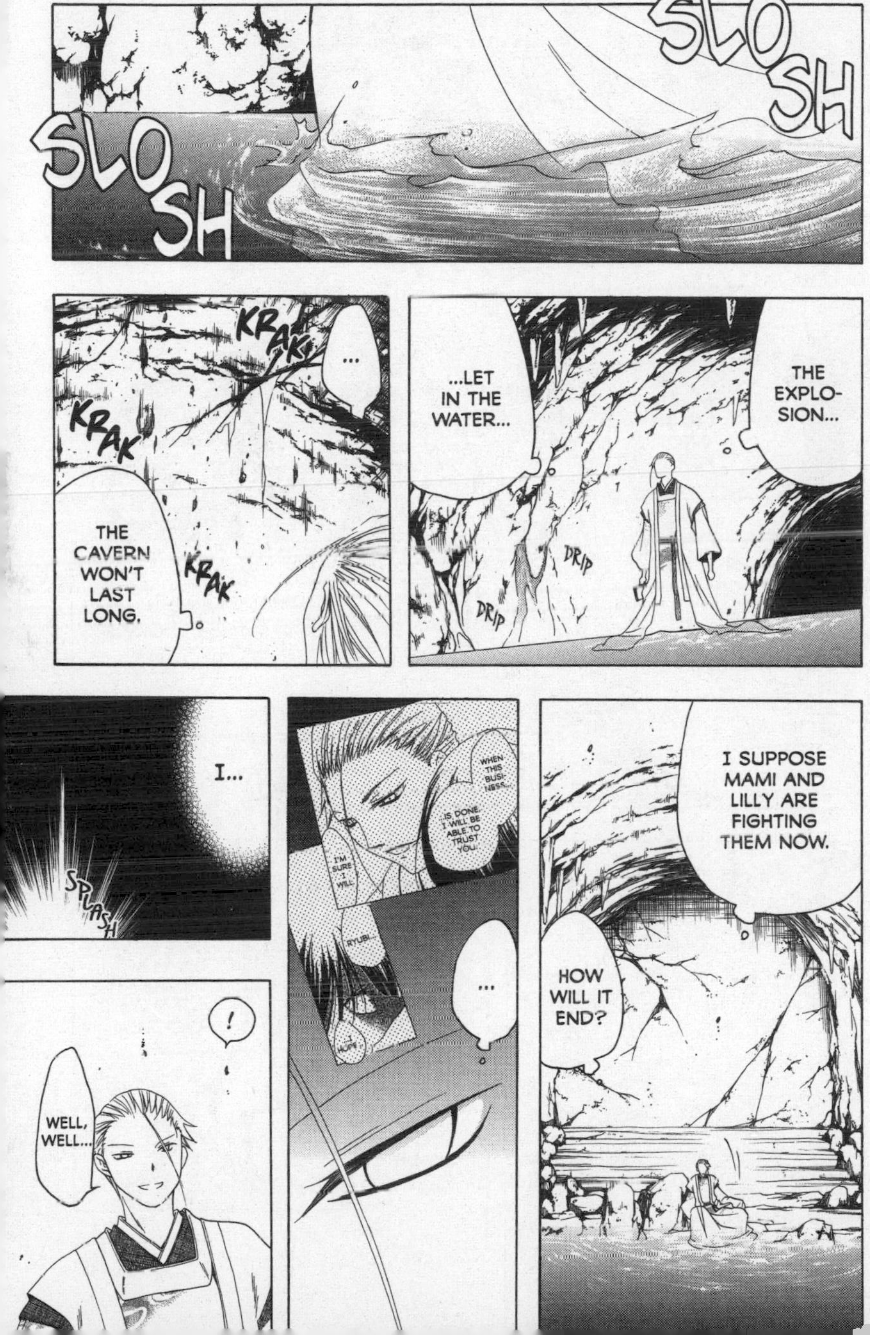
SLOSH
SLOSH
THE EXPLOSION...
...LET IN THE WATER...
DRIP
DRIP
KRAK
KRAK
KRAK
...
THE CAVERN WON'T LAST LONG.
I SUPPOSE MAMI AND LILLY ARE FIGHTING THEM NOW.
HOW WILL IT END?
WHEN THIS BUSINESS...
...IS DONE I WILL BE ABLE TO TRUST YOU.
I'M SURE I WILL.
RYUBI...
I HOPE.
...
I...
SPLASH
!
WELL, WELL...

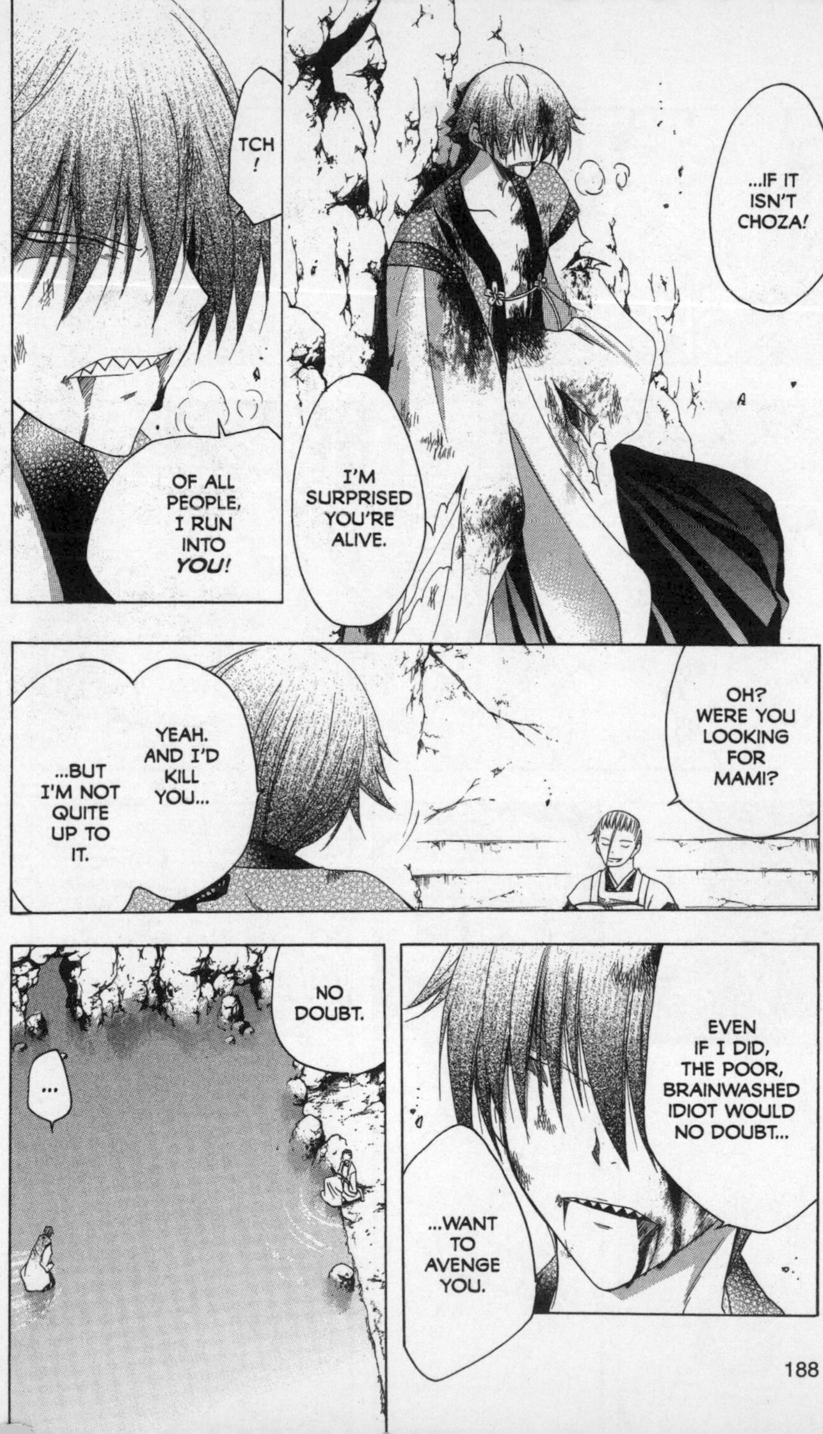
...IF IT ISN'T CHOZA!
I'M SURPRISED YOU'RE ALIVE.
TCH!
OF ALL PEOPLE, I RUN INTO *YOU*!
OH? WERE YOU LOOKING FOR MAMI?
YEAH. AND I'D KILL YOU...
...BUT I'M NOT QUITE UP TO IT.
EVEN IF I DID, THE POOR, BRAINWASHED IDIOT WOULD NO DOUBT...
...WANT TO AVENGE YOU.
NO DOUBT.
...

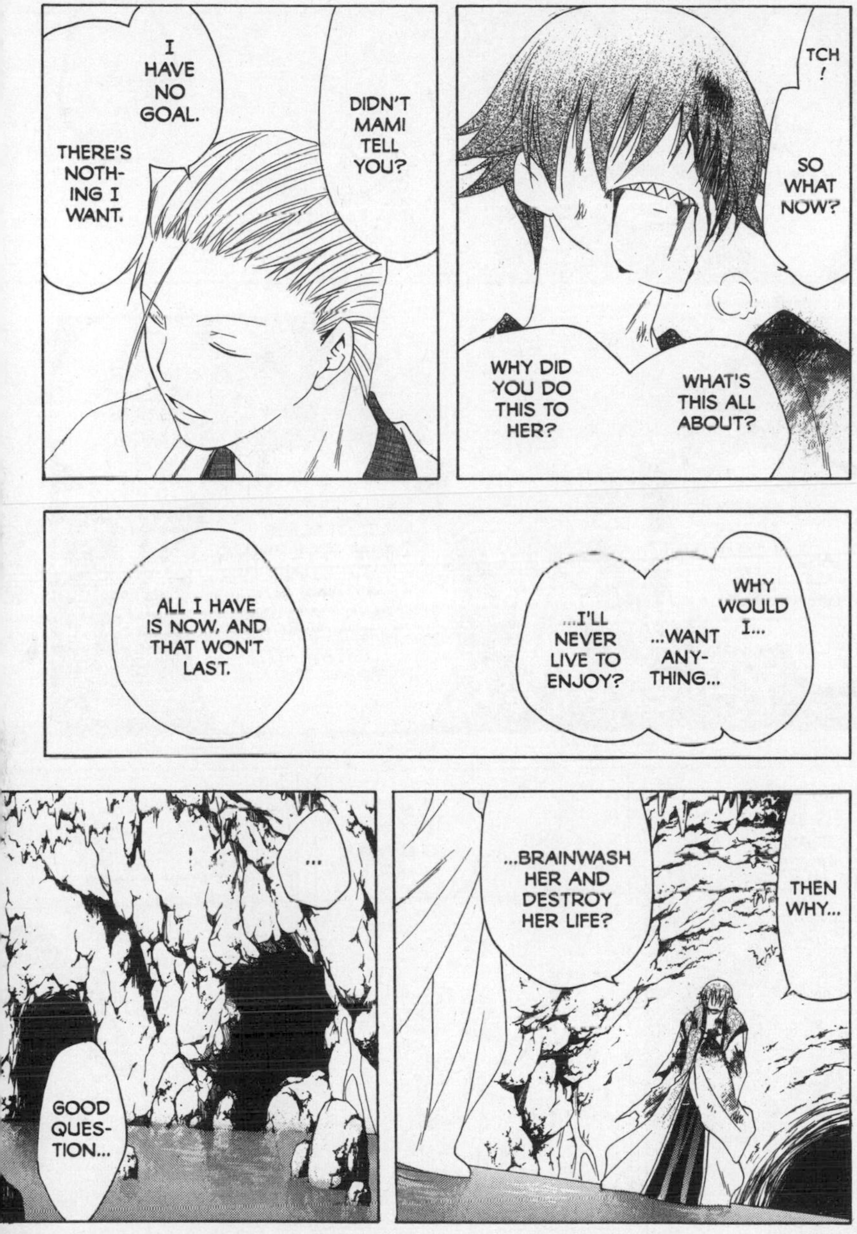
TCH!
SO WHAT NOW?
WHAT'S THIS ALL ABOUT?
WHY DID YOU DO THIS TO HER?
DIDN'T MAMI TELL YOU?
I HAVE NO GOAL.
THERE'S NOTHING I WANT.
WHY WOULD I...
...WANT ANYTHING...
...I'LL NEVER LIVE TO ENJOY?
ALL I HAVE IS NOW, AND THAT WON'T LAST.
THEN WHY...
...BRAINWASH HER AND DESTROY HER LIFE?
...
GOOD QUESTION...

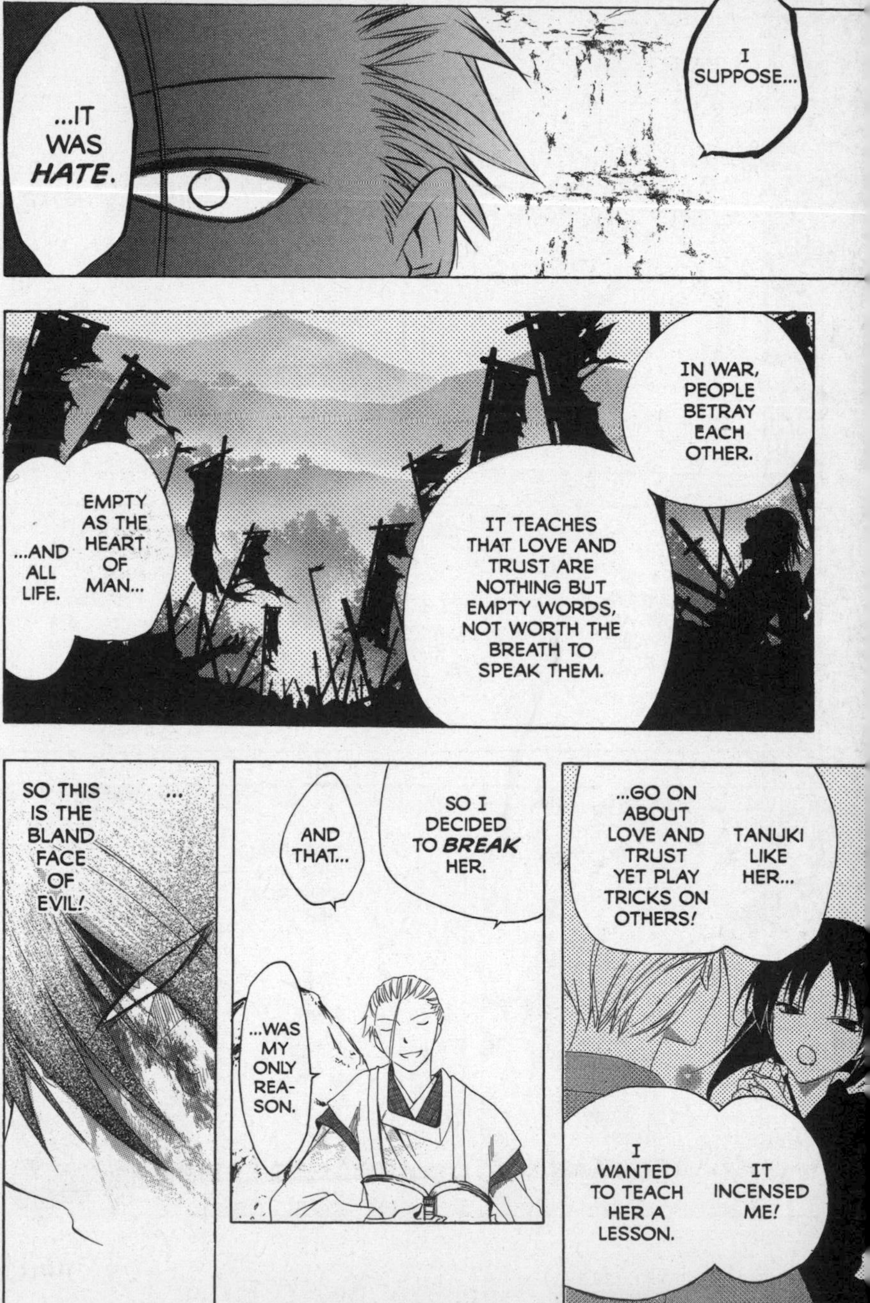
I SUPPOSE...
...IT WAS HATE.
IN WAR, PEOPLE BETRAY EACH OTHER.
IT TEACHES THAT LOVE AND TRUST ARE NOTHING BUT EMPTY WORDS, NOT WORTH THE BREATH TO SPEAK THEM.
EMPTY AS THE HEART OF MAN...
...AND ALL LIFE.
TANUKI LIKE HER...
...GO ON ABOUT LOVE AND TRUST YET PLAY TRICKS ON OTHERS!
IT INCENSED ME!
I WANTED TO TEACH HER A LESSON.
SO I DECIDED TO BREAK HER.
AND THAT...
...WAS MY ONLY REA-SON.
...
SO THIS IS THE BLAND FACE OF EVIL!